Greek Colonization in Local Contexts

Case studies in colonial interactions

Edited by
Jason Lucas
Carrie Ann Murray
Sara Owen

With a foreword by Martin Millett

University of Cambridge Museum of Classical Archaeology Monograph 4

OXBOW | books
Oxford & Philadelphia

Published in the United Kingdom in 2019 by
OXBOW BOOKS
The Old Music Hall, 106–108 Cowley Road, Oxford, OX4 1JE

and in the United States by
OXBOW BOOKS
1950 Lawrence Road, Havertown, PA 19083

Paperback Edition: ISBN 978-1-78925-132-6
Digital Edition: ISBN 978-1-78925-133-3

A CIP record for this book is available from the British Library

Library of Congress Cataloging-in-Publication Data: 2019935949

Printed in the United Kingdom by Short Run Press

Typeset in India for Casemate Publishing Services. www.casematepublishingservices.com

For a complete list of Oxbow titles, please contact:

UNITED KINGDOM
Oxbow Books
Telephone (01865) 241249
Email: oxbow@oxbowbooks.com
www.oxbowbooks.com

UNITED STATES OF AMERICA
Oxbow Books
Telephone (800) 791-9354, Fax (610) 853-9146
Email: queries@casemateacademic.com
www.casemateacademic.com/oxbow

Oxbow Books is part of the Casemate Group

Front cover: Detail from the François vase, c. 570 BCE. Museo Archeologico. Scala / Art Resource, NY.

Contents

Foreword vi
Martin Millett

1. Introduction 1
   Carrie Ann Murray and Jason Lucas

2. Constructing colonies: Physical manifestations of social action within Greek colonization 7
   Carrie Ann Murray

3. Locrian colonization in Magna Graecia: Cities and territories 25
   Adolfo J. Domínguez

4. Cultural and ethnic dynamics in Sicily during Greek colonization 43
   Sebastiano Tusa†

5. Marseilles: Greek settlement on the fringes of Iron Age Provence 59
   Jason Lucas

6. The Attic red-figure pottery of the Greek city of Emporion 77
   M. Teresa Miró i Alaix

7. Pistiros: A Thracian emporion in its cultural and natural environment 95
   Alexei Gotzev

8. The landscape in Aegean Thrace before and after Greek colonization 103
   Diamandis Triandaphyllos

9. Orgame necropolis in the Black Sea area 123
   Vasilica Lungu

10. Transformations of landscape use in the Lower Dnieper region 145
    Valeria Bylkova

11. Borysthenes and Olbia: Reflections on the character of contacts between Greeks and Natives during the initial stage of colonization 159
    Sergey Solovyov

12. *Polis, Chora* and the development of the colonial landscape in the Lower Bug region 183
Sergej Bujskikh and Alla Bujskikh

13. Colonial landscapes and colonial interactions in Skythia and the Euxeinos Pontos 193
Elias K. Petropoulos

14. Colonial location: Olbia on the Hypanis 215
David Braund

15. 'Greek' Colonization: The view from Ionia 231
Alan M. Greaves

In memoriam
Sebastiano Tusa

Foreword

Soon after I arrived in Cambridge in 2001, the idea emerged of a project to look at Greek colonization in the broader context of European development. The idea was to build on work that was re-thinking the concept of colonization, to explore through archaeology the relationship between colonized and colonizer, and to explore how different manifestations of colonization related to the development of Iron Age societies across Europe if one moved away from a discredited evolutionary model. The attraction of this to me was the prospect of exploring social connections on a broad canvas. We were fortunate to be granted funding for this project ('Greek colonization: its impact on Europe') from the Leverhulme Trust (ref F/09 798/C), with the research running from 2004 to 2007. Dr Jason Lucas, Dr Carrie Murray, and Dr Sara Owen were the research associates on the project, which explored aspects of Greek colonization through case studies in northeastern Spain, southern France, Italy, the northern Aegean and the Black Sea. Towards the end of the project in March 2007 we hosted a conference in Cambridge at which an international group of scholars presented papers and debated the ideas that had been explored in the project.

Through a combination of circumstances, the proceedings of this conference did not come to publication as we had planned, and the research team dispersed to develop their careers in different locations. The publication of a book resulting from the conference and the Leverhulme-funded project has nevertheless remained an objective, and I am very pleased to see it now come to fruition. Looking back at the questions raised in the original research it is clear that they remain pertinent today although some aspects of archaeological thinking have moved on. We are sure that the papers presented here will make a significant contribution to the continuing debates about Greek colonization, especially as they bring together evidence and thinking from across the whole Mediterranean/Black Sea World.

Martin Millett
Cambridge
November 2018

1

Introduction

Carrie Ann Murray and Jason Lucas

The Greek Colonization research project at the Faculty of Classics, University of Cambridge was borne out of the idea of shining light on corners of the ancient Mediterranean world that often fell into the shadows of research into Greek colonization. A central aim was to question the roles and agency behind the involved communities, both newcomer and local, and to question how these relationships may have changed over time. We sought to investigate the interplay between cultural and physical landscapes. Integral to these two areas: the Mediterranean Sea and the Black Sea were perceived of as connected and inseparable entities, and Phoenician/Punic involvement was considered as relevant as Greek involvement in colonization. The members of the project investigated different geographical and cultural areas, focusing on specific case studies. The specific site and regional foci contributed insights, illuminating case-specific developments. Rather than necessarily reflecting potential expectations of patterns, the case studies added points of colour in what sometimes appears to be broad brush overviews that dominate concepts behind Greek colonization.

The project was also the product of a burgeoning time of reconceptualizations of the Mediterranean world, addressing the multiplicity of voices, and an abundance of recent fieldwork. Of course, the *Corrupting Sea* (2000) caught the imagination of so many scholars of the ancient world, and here too, Peregrine Horden and Nicholas Purcell's creation of broad-ranging overviews with in-depth insights, questioning whether we should be dealing with the history *of* the Mediterranean or history *in* the Mediterranean, was inspirational. Research into areas, including Gocha Tsetskhladze's (1998) edited volume, *Greek Colonization of the Black Sea* and Tamar Hodos' work on cultural interaction in North Syria, Sicily, and North Africa (2006) were seen as important nodes of reference. In addition, Sara Owen, with Henry Hurst, had recently completed a volume on colonization before beginning this new project (2005).

What is there to say regarding the character of interaction amongst newcomers and locals in ancient Greek and Phoenician colonization? The nature and breadth of evidence is overwhelming from the monumental architecture of Posidonia to the incorporation of imported ceramics into local graves, and the insights provided by ancient texts. The development of colonial sites, trade relations, and material culture show us the dramatic changes that occurred in the contexts as frogs around a pond. Looking farther inland at the fascinating indigenous cultures that predated and co-existed with colonizers offers continued progress in this arena. The inscriptions from Pech Maho and Pistiros go some way to illustrating the varied and complex contexts of interaction, touching upon cultural identities, trade relations, and codes of conduct (for readings of the inscriptions Rodríguez Somolinos 1996; Chankowski and Domaradzka 1999, 247–256).

The symposium that forms the core of this volume was organized as part of the Greek Colonization project with the support of the Leverhulme Trust. In keeping with our aims for the project, the remit of the symposium was to explore evidence of cultural interactions amongst colonizers, primarily Greek, and local populations in a number of places across the Mediterranean. The selection of certain areas of study were meant to give keyhole views into a number of separate geographical and cultural areas with different historical contexts, and not act as a foundation for making generalized observations. Of particular note was our interest in bringing together scholars who were from and actively researching colonization in Mediterranean and Black Sea areas. For many of the participants, this was their first opportunity to publish for English language audiences. Additional speakers who contributed greatly to the event but do not appear in the volume are: Michael Dietler, Irad Malkin, Dieter Mertens, Marta Santos (jointly representing Xavier Aquilue, Pere Castanyer, Joaquim Tremoleda), and Gillian Shepherd.

The participants in the symposium drew upon work from across the ancient Greek world; however, the papers fell into different geographic areas, yielding the sections of the present volume. The first five chapters discuss different issues related to areas of the western and central Mediterranean.

In the first paper, Carrie Ann Murray discusses how despite the vast array of variability in the physical remains of Greek colonies, it is the less obvious social action present in the foundation and development of settlement and cemetery space that can reveal a finer picture of the relationship between colonizers and locals.

Adolfo J. Domínguez explores the connectivity of Epizephyrian Locri, that is, by questioning the foundation in terms of the possible 'mother-cities' of Eastern Locris and Western Locris, and also exploring the avenues of influence from Euboeans, Corinthians, and the indigenous people on the developing colony.

Sebastiano Tusa dissects the development of Sicily via the different colonial circumstances present in the regions of the island. He focuses particularly on the active role played by the Elymians in interactions with Greeks and Phoenicians.

Jason Lucas explores the patterns of interaction among Greek colonists and the indigenous peoples during the Early Iron Age in southern France. This interaction may be seen in the changing settlements patterns and distribution of ceramics, alongside other evidence of cultural change.

M. Teresa Miró i Alaix considers the complex dynamics of ceramic imports to Empúries, particularly the Attic red-figure material. This involves presenting updated data that includes a restudy of previously considered material, and moreover the importance of the ceramics in terms of the role of Empúries as a redistribution centre in western Iberia.

The next three chapters examine the interaction of Greeks and Thracians, drawing on work in Bulgaria and northern Greece.

Recent work in Bulgaria on several settlements provides the context for Alexei Gotzev's investigation of the ancient town of Pistiros, tracing the settlement's history as well as its links into trading networks across the region.

Diamandis Triandaphyllos discusses the cultural and economic landscape of north Aegean Thrace, summarizing studies of Abdera, Stryme, Maroneia, and Zone to understand the impacts between intensive exploitation of wealth-resources and to emphasize the importance of combining geological, geomorphological, archaeological, and historical studies.

Vasilica Lungu documents the Ionian colony of Orgame on the Black Sea coast of Romania, focusing on the necropolis and the changing nature of the burial rites as a reflection of colonial identity.

The final third grouping discusses Greek settlement in the Black Sea, focusing on the north coast.

Valeria Bylkova begins this section with a study of the changing patterns of landscape use in the Lower Dnieper region as a manifestation of the interaction among Greeks and natives, which become clearer when considering the differences between inland and coastal settlements.

Sergey Solovyov considers the contact between the Scythian and Greek populations in the northern Black Sea region, particularly as exemplified in the changing urban settlement patterns of Olbia and Berezan.

Sergej Bujskikh and Alla Bujskikh trace the development of the *chora* around the city of Olbia on the Black Sea coast in southern Ukraine during the archaic period.

Elias K. Petropoulos returns the interaction of Greeks and Scythians, exploring evidence for contact and trade hundreds of kilometres inland from the colonies, before discussing the larger-scale archaeological patterns from the whole of the Black Sea.

David Braund reviews the historical, archaeological, and epigraphic evidence for the colony of Olbia, its inhabitants, and the relation to the two key rivers, Dnieper and Bug. This leads to a discussion of the interplay between the siting of the colony, the interaction between Greeks and locals, and Greek knowledge of the landscape.

The final essay by Alan Greaves examines the idea of colonization from the perspective of the Ionian evidence, as a region of early colonization, which then founded many of the colonies discussed in the previous chapters.

A number of overlapping issues recur throughout this volume demonstrating how these scholars have pursued different facets of Greek colonization, a topic central to investigating the ancient world encapsulated in two words but representing an enormous breadth of possibilities. One common thread in many of the chapters is an emphasis on addressing the importance of agency on the part of the locals. There is an importance placed on recognizing the complex relationships at work in these contexts of colonization that can no longer be purposely or inadvertently characterized as simply Greek innovation paired with indigenous passivity.

Various aspects that are woven through the following works display the rich variety of questions at stake. Landscape acting as more than a mere setting is crucial to these works (see especially Braund). A temporal component in many of the chapters provides a crucial perspective for the importance of change over time (for instance Murray). Considerations of broader spatial settings across regions also comes to the fore, placing importance on understanding interactions beyond just one site to include issues such as coastal versus inland dynamics (Bylkova; Petropoulos). In this regard, trade networks are key to considering interactions over considerable distances of direct and indirect interactions (Gotzev; Lucas; Miró i Alaix; Triandaphyllos). Social practices are, of course, central to the discussions, in particular investigations related to settlement development, including urban and rural issues (Bujskikh and Bujskikh; Solovyov), and the significance of burial rites (Lungu). Acknowledging the complex situations of multiple colonizing and indigenous cultures broadens the discussion in many contexts (Tusa). The issues surrounding the relationships amongst colonizers and mother cities are explored too (Domínguez; Greaves). Throughout, a variety of different types of evidence are relied upon from historical sources and epigraphy to ceramics and settlement patterns.

We were delighted to have the opportunity to engage with all of the scholars at the symposium held in the Faculty of Classics, Cambridge in 2007, and we are pleased to collaborate with them on this volume. We thank the contributors for their patience in the delayed production of the volume; we extend our sincere apologies. The volume can provide those working on Greek colonization, or other areas of colonization, with views on distinct case studies, as well as broader regional perspectives. The relevance of local and newcomer groups within colonial contexts are considered on equal footing through material and historical evidence. The volume can also act as a teaching aid for undergraduate and graduate levels. Of course, no single work can be exhaustive; this volume can offer a variety of case studies to spark discussion and contribute to ongoing debates.

Acknowledgments

Sebastiano Tusa died tragically in a plane crash as this volume was going to print. His death has come as a shock to all who knew him. Sebastiano worked tirelessly throughout his long career for the promotion and preservation of archaeology in Sicily. While Sebastiano will be missed tremendously, his legacy will live on.

Abbreviations used in this volume

Str.: Strabo, *Geography*
Ps.-Scym.: Pseudo-Scymnus, *Periegesis ad Nicomedem regem*
Euseb. Chron.: Eusebius, *Chronicle*
Hdt.: Herodotus, *The Histories*
Dio Chrys.: Dio Chrysostom, *Orations*
Xen. Anab.: Xenophon, *Anabasis*

Bibliography

Chankowski, V. and Domaradzka, L. (1999) Réédition de l'inscription de Pistiros et problèmes d'interprétation. *Bulletin de Correspondance Hellénique* 123.1: 247–271.

Hodos, T. (2006) *Local Responses to Colonization in the Iron Age Mediterranean.* London, Routledge.

Horden, P. and Purcell, N. (2000) The *Corrupting Sea. A study of Mediterranean history.* London, Wiley-Blackwell.

Hurst, H. and Owen, S. (eds) (2005) *Ancient Colonisations. Analogy, Similarity and Difference.* London, Duckworth.

Rodríguez Somolino, H. (1996) The commercial transaction of the Pech Maho lead: A new interpretation. *Zeitschrift für Papyrologie und Epigraphik* 111: 74–78.

Tsetskhladze, G. R. (ed.) (1998) *Greek Colonization of the Black Sea Area.* Stuttgart, Franz Steiner Verlag.

2

Constructing colonies: Physical manifestations of social action within Greek colonization

Carrie Ann Murray

Fundamental to investigating Iron Age cultures of the Mediterranean is the recovery of settlement and cemetery remains. The location, dating of phases, construction techniques and burial practices are central to understanding the physical development of a site, or more broadly a culture. The physical remains are not just the tangible finds of stone and terracotta; they are also the result of social action. Decisions and actions made by individuals and groups lie behind the planning, design, and execution of the physical changes to a landscape during the development and lifetime of settlements and cemeteries. This work proposes how investigating the physical remains of settlements and cemeteries can shed light on the social action at work behind the construction and maintenance, and how this analysis may be applied, possibly even more pertinently, when examining the development of some of the Greek colonies in the Mediterranean. What follows here is a discussion of some elements related to the physical development of a number of Greek colonial settlements. The social acts of planning, construction, and maintenance of settlement and cemetery space will be discussed as a starting point for considering how the vast topics of the spatial organization, architecture, and funerary practices at Greek settlements in the West could help reveal changing social circumstances in a variety of ways. The activities of daily life, including archaeologically visible activities, provide insights into the choices made by individuals and groups that can help explain social change even when specific individuals cannot be identified (for a discussion, see Brumfiel 2000, 254; Hodder 2000, 22). Despite the variability in form and development of Greek colonial settlements, understanding the social contexts behind their construction and maintenance can reveal aspects of the nature of interactions between the newcomers and locals.

Interpreting the physical remains of settlements and cemeteries as direct insights into social actions and interactions could help create clearer understandings concerning the early stages and the long-term development of the related communities. How can we understand social interaction at sites just from archaeological evidence of architectural construction within settlement and cemetery space? In particular, examining details of the initial stages of settlement and cemetery creation (or at least the earliest phases of archaeologically visible remains) could reveal the social circumstances at work, including insights into social hierarchy, economic strategies, relationships with neighbouring communities, and ritual practices, including burial rites. These issues take on an added level of relevance when considering Greek colonial settlements, in order to investigate degrees of cooperation and integration, or animosity and isolation between indigenous and foreign inhabitants.

Social action and construction

Experimental archaeology can provide insights into the process of site construction. The social action involved in settlement construction, communication, and movement through the landscape was directly investigated by Sue Hamilton and Ruth Whitehouse as part of the Tavoliere-Gargano Prehistory Project (Hamilton *et al.* 2006). Individual and group participation in tasks was investigated at four Neolithic sites in Italy, in order to more systematically examine the experiential side of phenomenology that is not often discussed within a clear methodological framework. The tasks were set in contexts similar to those for establishing a settlement. They involved male and female participants engaging in communicating visually with gestures and verbally with sounds, whistling, speaking, and shouting. The findings, characterized by differing degrees of effectiveness in the means of communication and between the genders, open up the possibility of understanding the archaeologically invisible actions behind these physical processes. The varying levels of success in the tasks demonstrate how individual abilities and cooperation between individuals affect these processes (Hamilton *et al.* 2006, 47, 48).

Approaching issues of communication, such as in the Tavoliere-Gargano, leads to further questions to consider. Communication amongst people in a given landscape is crucial in the initial construction phases of a site, as well as during the continued existence at the site after structures are in place, potentially with more people present, and multiple activities occurring simultaneously (see Hamilton *et al.* 2006, 48). As the physical circumstances change at a site, the individuals present must cooperate with adoptive strategies in order to continue to communicate effectively as a group or groups. Communication is a part of continuous social action as an everyday part of life within a community. This perspective lends itself to consider if it is possible to understanding more about the social actions that resulted in the remains recovered in the archaeological record, which are so abundant from the Iron Age cultures of the Mediterranean, especially at many of the Greek colonies.

Creating and living at a site involves an organic structure of organized (and disorganized for that matter) activity with long- and short-term consequences. It involves the active participation amongst individuals in planning and construction;

the division of tasks along supervisory and labour roles are parts of the initial stages of creation, if not longer. The interactive process continues as the site is inhabited and used. Changes throughout the course of a site's existence illustrate the evolving social circumstances involved in continual planning and construction projects. As the saying goes 'no man is an island' and equally, no settlement is a static, solitary entity.

Settlements and cemeteries – physical and social remains

The discussion here will be bounded by general expectations of what might be present at settlements and cemeteries at Greek colonial sites. With such an enormous array of possibilities, it is difficult to generalize, but settlements can, for example, include structures and spaces for habitation, storage, religious activity, workshops, markets, transport, and defence. Cemeteries, on the other hand, can include – in addition to burials – monuments, walls, and structures for religious activity. These elements of both settlements and cemeteries can be found in a wide range of sizes and levels of monumentality from simple to grand. The archaeological remains of these items are physical manifestations of important social actions: planning, decision-making, communication, and the ability to control resources and labour. The physical remains and the involved social actions have tangible outcomes in terms of the use, visibility, and memory for the individuals living at the site.

Planning

Planning the location, form, and extent of a space, structure or larger construction project can involve any number of people. The greater the disparity between the number of planners and those involved in the construction implies a centralised hierarchy and a strong power relationship. These relationships of power could be in place specifically for the task at hand, or set more broadly across the community. Spatial planning for large-scale areas can show a well-executed, unified concept. Evidence of combinations of evenly spaced, rectilinear structures with parallel and perpendicular features, and grid- and orthogonal-plans are assumed in archaeological discussions to be the result of an organized central authority executing its control over the landscape. Alterations incongruent with earlier spatial plans can show a partial or total abandonment of previously accepted plans, and possibly the particular form of authority once present.

The planning and decision-making involved in choosing a settlement's location, the spatial extent, the internal organization of different areas of space could stem from individuals with powerful statuses enacting this power. There are potentially different types of social relationships involved in the construction of settlement areas. Communally used features like streets, suggest that there is some amount of centralized planning, regardless of the plan or regularity of the streets. These areas become zones for specific purposes, and so there must be some level of agreement that they remain as such. On the other hand, the planning and decision-making involved in choosing a cemetery's location, the spatial extent, the internal organization of different areas of space could, in some cases, result from a centralized authority, or could result from a more multifaceted, organic process, notwithstanding environmental factors that determine locations, *viz.* natural features in the landscape. The internal organization of cemetery space is potentially much more subject to gradual, non-systematic decisions.

Construction

Acts of physical construction recovered in the archaeological record have been regarded as important guides to symbolic social action. The ability to control labour and resources, particularly the consumption of other people's energy, can be directly associated with power. Monumental architecture is often seen as a visible example of this (Trigger 1990; Murray 2011), where control over construction labour is a physical demonstration of power, and the structure itself can be a long-term symbol of that harnessed power. Architecture also has the potential to 'consolidate new social, political, and economic formations', and a chosen emphasis for architecture in one area of social life, for instance, funerary over palatial or religious structures, can reveal much concerning the social circumstances in a specific context (Trigger 1990, 128). This power is assumed to be held by a relatively small number of elites, exerted over much of the rest of the community. The exercising of power is also evident in other aspects involved in monumental architecture.

Construction projects also include important networks of communication within a community enabling these ideas to come to fruition. The power of communication and persuasion is evident in controlling where, when, and exactly how something is constructed. The last of these particularly entails continual communication of information to be accepted and acted on. It is not just the acquisition, transportation and use of materials that reflect power; power is also implicitly involved in ensuring the execution of a design. In monumental examples, this is conducted through individuals for the commissioning, engineering, designing and decorating of a structure. Within an already established settlement, there must also be an added component of negotiating the exact location amongst other structures and defined spaces, or conversely ignoring and obliterating earlier structures.

The scale of a construction project is a visible means of projecting power. Small, minor scale projects can demonstrate the work of individuals who carried out the planning and construction themselves. Large, major scale projects can demonstrate a complex social hierarchy of planners and labourers, where individuals with specialized skills can be involved in specific aspects of the architectural design. The grandiose scale of a construction project can elevate or concretize the position of individuals within the social hierarchy through their associations with the architecture. Monumental architecture, by definition, is built on a scale that exceeds the basic requirements of the functions carried out there, often in terms of space, the durability of materials used, and decorative elaboration. The iconographic system chosen to decorate the structures can be used by those in control to communicate messages concerning how they would like their power to be perceived by the viewer (Marconi 2007; Sismondo Ridgway 1999; and for Roman contexts, see Zanker 1990). The ability to implement and control the construction of monumental architecture that visibly shows levels of excess through its scale demonstrates the power held by those individuals who are responsible for the structures. Continued maintenance of architecture demonstrates a level of respect and continued control for the structure and the powerful individuals who oversaw its construction. Repairs to substantial forms of architecture can necessitate a considerable amount of energy and labour, sometimes requiring the continued use of antiquated construction techniques. Destruction or disuse of monumental architecture can demonstrate a change in the powerful individuals controlling the use and design of space. In this case, the former presence of powerful individuals is eradicated by the destruction of any architectural legacy.

More particularly, in the cemetery context, consideration of the physical construction of burials, with expenditure of time and labour is also important. Expenditure of labour and cost of a burial is not necessarily directly proportional to the deceased individual's perceived level of social importance during life (Parker Pearson 1982, 112; Parker Pearson 2003, 32). The amount of labour, as well as the form, the shape, etc. of a burial represents choices made by the buriers, rather than the buried individual, in many cases (Parker Pearson 1982, 112; Parker Pearson 2003, 32). Monumentality in burial cannot then be necessarily assumed to reflect direct demonstrations of power in the social hierarchy of the attached community. Social action in the funerary sphere must be integrated with any understandings gleaned from the associated settlement. Because of the inevitability of death, the burial sphere could potentially involve all levels of the social hierarchy of a community (through funerary rites and burial construction), including individuals and small groups who usually do not hold powerful roles in the wider community.

Visibility and memory

There are group dynamics with long-term visibility implications at work in the creation and development of settlements and cemeteries. The importance of scale, monumentality, and maintenance within social action as mentioned above, also relates to the degree of visibility of the construction projects, so that these entities function as real and vivid symbols of the power behind them. Visibility, or even a lack of visibility, as an intended or unintended consequence after a structure is constructed, maintained, disused or destroyed lends itself then to the realm of memory. Memories of individuals and shared social memories of events, concerning the construction and the presence of structures, can be powerful elements in a society (Alcock 2002, 15–25; Middleton and Edwards 1997, 10–11).

In contrast with monumental architecture in settlements, much of the labour and structural elements involved in many burials are unsurprisingly not visible or evident after the closure of the burial, with the exception of a huge category of burials with prominent markers or superstructures. Deeper levels of significance in burial elements are often confined to the individuals directly involved in the funerary process, and to the limits of memory (for instance Jones 2007, especially 21, 39, 114).

Visibility and memory are important themes for understanding material culture and social action, which deserve more attention, but will not be discussed further here. It is worth noting that monumental examples of architecture, for the most part, demonstrate intentions of visibility and potentially long-term presence. Various levels of scale, visibility, and memory can affect how different social groups are represented in the archaeological record.

Colonial contexts of cultural interaction

Within this Greek Colonization project (see Introduction), investigating social interaction in colonial contexts is at the core of the study. It is not simply the archaeological remains and historical legacy left behind by the Greeks that is of interest here. The interactions of newcomers (Greek, Phoenician, and Etruscan), in areas away from their homelands, with the indigenous peoples around the Mediterranean are of equal importance. The individual circumstances found at each specific context have the potential of revealing new insights into the complex social relationships at work.

There is a question as to how much can be understood in terms of the social actions between these individuals and groups from the architectural and funerary remains. The construction of settlements and cemeteries in colonial contexts has been a natural focus for attempting to discern the relationships at work. Considering the decisions and actions involved in site development can take on further levels of complexity in colonial contexts where different cultural identities are present, along with different building techniques, uses of space, economic strategies, social activities, languages, and senses of belonging to a landscape.

There is an implicit notion that the colonists held powerful positions in deciding when, where and how to build a new settlement, without much input from local populations. This is partly based on ancient sources. According to Thucydides (6.2), colonization sometimes involved expelling local populations from pre-existing settlements in certain cases. Often 'the foundation process' is described with only scant reference to indigenous populations (Boardman 1964; Dunbabin 1948). Issues of equality and inequality amongst the colonists themselves have been a topic of discussion (see Graham 2006, 151). Much work has also countered these ideas by demonstrating impetus and action on the part of the indigenous groups (Dietler 2010; Dietler and López-Ruiz 2009; Hodos 2006; Hurst and Owen 2005; van Dommelen 2005).

The following sections will take a closer look at the creation and early development of some of the colonies in an effort to discern and describe social action on the part of the 'colonists' and 'indigenous'. Three themes of social practice involved in acts of creation in colonial contexts will be explored, including: the founding of settlements; changes in the use and organization of space; and the development of architectural styles and burial practices.

Palaiapolis-neapolis style settlement pattern

There are a number of examples of colonial settlements that were constructed in more than one phase with a palaiapolis-neapolis type of development, characterized by an older, often smaller original settlement co-existing, at least for a time, with a later, larger settlement located in the vicinity. Several colonies that were constructed in two separate phases begin with an initial colonial settlement located on an offshore island or isolated peninsula, followed by the construction of a later colonial settlement on the nearby mainland area.

This pattern of staged development could suggest changing relationships between the colonial and local communities over time. The construction of a second phase of settlement could reflect a longer-term vision of permanent residence on the part of the colonists, and it could potentially reflect acquiescence on the part of the local inhabitants. At many of the colonies across the Mediterranean, the precise location of indigenous settlements is often not known. Consequently, it is difficult to surmise if this process reflects the different communities coming together spatially to live in close(r) proximity. A few case studies are considered here.

The two separate, but interrelated settlements of Pithekoussai and Cyme illustrate an early example of this in southern Italy. Euboean colonists from Eretria and Chalcis settled first on the island of Pithekoussai in the Bay of Naples, evidenced by an acropolis at Monte di Vico and a cemetery at Valle di S. Montano (Ridgway 1992). There is evidence of Phoenician residents as well, indicated by the *enchystrismos* grave 575 from a family plot bearing three semitic inscriptions, one of which seems to relate to the re-use of an amphora for funerary purposes (Ridgway 1992, 111–118). Shortly afterwards, the Euboeans ventured onto the mainland in a more permanent way and created Cyme (Boardman 1999, 168; Graham 2006, 97–103).

The development of Syracuse, initially began on the island settlement of Ortygia facing natural harbour areas of what would become the expanded Syracusan complex. The local Sicels living in a pre-existing settlement on the island were apparently expelled by the newly arrived Corinthians (Thucydides 6.3.2). Its easily defensible position with harbours of its own made Ortygia an advantageous location for a settlement, not just as an initial phase, but for the long-term. Greek presence expanded quickly onto the nearby mainland. Eventually a causeway linking the island and mainland was constructed in the late sixth century BC. The large Sicel site, Pantalica, west of Syracuse was abandoned at approximately the same time as the appearance of the Corinthians (Boardman 1999, 172–173; Graham 2006, 105).

Emporion (at modern Empúries, Spain) also developed in two main phases. The first phase is created on the then island-like peninsula, of what Strabo (3.4.8) refers to as the 'Palaia Polis' (παλαιὰ πόλις) (see also Marzoli 2005, 69; Kaiser 2000). Here too local Iberians were already present, but the Phocaeans and Massalians seemed to have co-habited with the locals (Aquilue *et al.* 2000, 17–19). The earliest Greek burials from this period are found in El Portixol cemetery on the mainland (Aquilue *et al.* 2000, 20). After a short interval, a second, larger settlement was constructed on the adjacent mainland, now referred to as 'Neapolis'. Strabo mentions a main Iberian settlement, Indika, being separate but connected to the Greek city (3.4.8). Its location, however, has yet to be found.

This pattern of development could, in some cases, suggest that a close or peaceful relationship with the local inhabitants does not exist initially. In other cases, it seems that a cooperative relationship did exist between the local inhabitants and the colonists, indicated by instances of co-habitation in spatially restricted areas, such as at the Palaiapolis of Emporion. The development of the colonial settlements physically detached from the mainland suggests that even if the newcomers were living in very close proximity with the locals, the colonists chose not to move to the mainland from the outset. The reasons could include easy access to ships, a symbolic gesture to start their time there in a circumscribed way, or because of a sense of threat. Perhaps at Emporion, the creation of El Portixol cemetery on the mainland was a stepping stone towards gaining more ground, symbolically and physically. The acquisition of space at Syracuse seems to paint a very different picture, in terms of the relationship between the locals and colonists. These brief case studies help present the range of variety present at the colonial settlements.

This type of palaiapolis-neapolis progression suggests different social contexts at work, where the amount of space is not the defining factor in the initial location or extent of a settlement, and there is the opportunity to expand without disrupting the initial settlement area. Logistically, this type of change would require intense levels of communication, agreement and cooperation within the community of colonists and potentially with the locals. An expansion of settlement insinuates a certain degree of success, perhaps felt especially by a small number of elites, through the organization of labour, increased size of the settlement, and the seeming entitlement to the land. Expansion could also be rooted in the development of new social groups gaining power and the ability to strike out anew in a different location. Without more information, it is impossible to discern the reasons. Holding these questions in mind, however, could affect future research into these issues.

Changes in the spatial organization at colonies

The artistic skills and urban planning present at many Greek colonies have come to be synonymous with the idea of Greek cultural superiority (Holloway 1991, 52, 94; Boardman and Hammond 1982, xiv), in effect over local inhabitants (Dunbabin 1948, 136). This simplistic picture surrounding the development of Greek colonies is now thought to be much more complex (for instance Belarte 2009, 103; Dietler 2009, esp. 23; La Rosa 1996, and as noted above). The multiple construction phases and alterations in plan at many of the Greek colonies demonstrate dynamic circumstances at work in which each new settlement was subject to its own specific physical and social contexts. Changes visible on a monumental scale in the construction of particular structures or the plan of an entire settlement should be further explored.

Dieter Mertens and Emanuele Greco (1996, 257) note a few important constant features at many of these colonies, including: large spaces demarcated for urban areas with boundaries; broad separations between residential and public zones, further spatial organization of these separate zones, particularly with the use of roads; public areas with impressive public monuments 'symbolizing the cultural identity of the colonial community'; and new forms of architecture related to the specific contexts of each colony. All of these characteristics require a high degree of planning and construction to be carried out. Any changes to these features, once they have already been planned and the construction begun, show a powerful ability to dramatically re-use labour and resources to alter things for a new preference. Very few of the early Greek colonial settlements maintain the initial spatial organization and layout (or lack thereof) beyond their first stage of development. Minor and major changes in orientation, creation of grid plans, and monumentalization of structures often occurred at colonial settlements after an initial period of residence.

The initial layout of Megara Hyblaea is described as being agrarian-based characterised by some even and geometric spacing for the parcelling of previously unused land. This included a layout with regularly spaced *insulae* containing ground plots of equal area along parallel streets on a grip plan in two large areas. Between these two areas, space was left and demarcated for public use, which became the agora in the seventh century BC (Gras, Tréziny and Broise 2004, 456; Vallet, Villard and Auberson 1976, 404–428). Antonino Di Vita (1996, 268) asserts that the initial division of land from the foundation phase could not have been conceived as an '"urban" zoning scheme'. The remarkable spatial organization and street system at Megara Hyblaea does seem to show much forethought in planning, which is successfully maintained for some time. This is in part accomplished because of the vacant spaces included in the design, leaving room for growth of the community.

Casmenae, the subcolony of Syracuse, was constructed as a fortress-colony with all of the residential space confined within a city wall. This was planned and built from scratch in the mid-seventh century BC (Di Vita 1996, 274–278). The creation of Casmenae as a later offspring of the burgeoning settlement of Syracuse, and possibly for specific defensive purposes, gives many reasons why the form and plan of such a settlement would and could be constructed with a very regular plan of parallel streets. Circumstances such as these could reflect a centralized organisation based on a specific view of a small number of people with potentially limited objectives (compared to an average settlement).

The vast majority of Greek colonies, however, did not spring fully-formed into the landscape as urban settlements with grid plans. Many of the sites instead developed over time with more than one construction phase, the first of which was not laid out according to a grid. After all, the urban forms present in the Greek world in the mid-eighth century BC, at the time of departure of many of the Greek colonial groups, did not present a clear template for the colonists to imitate in southern Italy and Sicily (Di Vita 1996, 263). Di Vita identifies the first type of phase as the work of the initial colonists, with a largely egalitarian-based community, and the second type of phase as the result of territorial conquests, new shared wealth, and a newly emerged social structure (Di Vita 1996, 264).

Other settlements such as Naxos, Selinus and Himera do not show widespread, cohesive urban planning from their inception, but rather show significant changes in the use and organization of space. Initially, the sacred area at many of these sites is distinct and detached from the residential areas. These sacred areas were enlarged later in the course of the sixth century BC as temple buildings were constructed. The desire to enlarge sacred areas housing temples demonstrates the importance of the social role played by monumental architecture. Whereas an increased use of space for domestic, mercantile or industrial purposes might illustrate purely practical responses to increases in population size or economic growth in a community, the increased use of sacred space, which of course can also relate to many other social activities, could more broadly illustrate growing importance of the public sacred sphere and the elite power behind its maintenance.

At Naxos partial remains of two streets dating to the eighth century BC have been found. These run parallel to each other in a northeast–southwest direction, making them drastically different from the orientation of the remains of streets from the seventh and sixth centuries BC, and to the clear grid plan of the fifth century BC (Di Vita 1996, 279). Selinus was founded in the mid-seventh century BC, and was later redeveloped in the early sixth century BC with an impressive urban plan. The construction of additional structures on the acropolis in this second period forced the inhabitants to terrace the hillslopes in order to extend the acropolis area (Parisi-Presicce 1984, 118–121). Himera was also founded in the seventh century BC, but it was not until the second quarter of the sixth century BC that the area received a thorough overhaul with an urbanistic programme (Allegro and Bassallo 1992, 140–146).

Metapontum, for instance, which is sometimes discussed as an example of a colony where the regularized urban space and *chora* are defined from the outset of the foundation, is also characterised by changes in orientation and use of space more than once in the agora. The orientation of the first monumental sacred structures are not aligned with the street grid, but rather placed according to religious considerations. The construction of Temple AI was halted shortly after it began, in the second half of the sixth century BC, with a different orientation in order to be parallel with Temple B and in line with the street grid, referred to as Temple AII. This picture changes again in the fifth century BC, when the construction of new religious structures in the area do not conform to the grid system, but are instead placed and oriented possibly with religious considerations in mind. Mertens and Greco (1996, 253–254) suggest that the sudden decision to alter the orientation of Temple A, referred to as phase II, to be in line with the street grid demonstrates that the temples were the most prominent monuments of the town, and the change in orientation was needed to substantiate the sense of order imposed on the town. This might also powerfully demonstrate dissention and compromise or some other scenario within the decision-making process of the elites involved. The result was that some of the elites were able to impose their demands over the religious order in place, emphasizing the place of civic order and spatial organization over purely religious considerations.

Changes of this order of magnitude to alter the extent of public space or even reorient a temple during its construction must involve serious levels of communication, eventual agreement, and cooperation through the planning and disruption. In the sense that the term 'occupation phase' implies drastic, rather than gradual, change. Redevelopment of the settlement suggests success in the organization of labour, and the reconstruction of possibly bigger and better structures. The variability in the course of progress at these Greek settlements relates to the different social contexts through time in each case.

Expression through architectural styles and burial forms at Greek colonies

Architectural styles

The architectural styles and decorations of the structures can reveal much of the developing and changing social circumstances at these sites. Much scholarly attention has been paid to the architectural material found in the Greek settlements overseas, particularly in Sicily. The scale of the monumentality with innovation in construction and the portrayal of myth within architectural decoration demonstrate the importance placed on certain structures at these developing sites. Elements of variability and similarity in the forms of architecture at many of the sites suggest complex social relationships at work within and amongst the sites as well.

Mertens (especially 1996) has very ably elucidated us about much of the monumentality and construction at many of the Greek colonial settlements. He has noted a number of ideas that have strong resonance in the study of Greek colonization, including discussions on the independence and innovation of monumental architecture for the Greeks in the West from their homelands for reasons other than newfound space with which to experiment. There are also the issues of variability in architecture at many sites, partially related to the physical contexts and available materials, along with the development of the well-known architectural orders. The developing architecture at Posidonia, Metaponto, Sybaris, and Croton during the sixth century BC, just to name a few examples, demonstrates a variety in architectural characteristics, showing a progression towards Doric and Ionic canonical forms (Mertens 1996, 322). For Mertens, the 'ekklesiasterion' at Metaponto particularly illustrates the ingenuity of the colonists to create new, entirely original forms of architecture to meet their needs, where the central public space shares both sacred and secular functions in clear and monumental forms (Mertens 1996, 329; 2006, 163; Mertens and Greco 1996, 254; see also Carter 2006, 204–214). Many of the developments of monumental architecture are seen as relating heavily to the socio-political contexts at the Greek colonies. The early phases of monumental architecture are often ascribed to an assertion of independence from the 'mother-cities' and to claims of superiority and dominance over the landscapes and pre-existing, local populations (*e.g.* Mertens 1996, 318–319).

identity and a new set of values were formed in which local indigenous standards were matched to "colonial" objects and customs – which by that time had been around long enough to have become equally local' (2005, 136). This view appreciates the ingredients of time and long-term change, and it provides another option within the vocabulary to debate and consider.

Because local influence is often overlooked, another avenue for understanding the social circumstances at Greek colonial settlements is to look for the adoption, or possible adaption, of practices introduced to them by the local inhabitants of the area. One brief example of this could be the use of seashells as grave goods potentially in both local and Greek burials at Emporion (Spain) (*cf.* above).

The identity of the burials at Emporion has traditionally been defined as inhumation being the Greek burial custom, and cremation being the local Iberian burial custom (Almagro Basch 1955). It has been assumed that the presence of a number of separate cemeteries surrounding Emporion is evidence of two communities, colonizers and indigenous, existing separately during the sixth and fifth centuries BC (Aquiliué *et al.* 2000, 27). Drawing conclusions from the burial forms and grave goods remain difficult. On closer inspection, there seems to be a mixture of burial rites at most of the necropoleis. It is probably impossible to definitively identify cultural identity within burials in colonial contexts (for instance, see Shepherd 2005), such as at Emporion, and it is, of course, difficult to disentangle potential cultural interaction in the burial record, but potentially there is more that can be learned from the burial data.

The inclusion of unworked ecofacts as grave goods in many of the burials may be significant. Sea shells are found in a number of the cremations at Paralli and the North-East Wall necropoleis, as well as a number of cremations and inhumations at necropoleis such as Bonjoan, Martí, Mateu and Granada (as catalogued by Almagro Basch 1955). Shells were used as grave goods for burials of both funerary rites from the sixth century BC, and in necropoleis traditionally believed to be used separately by either group. It seems that both the burial rite and the cemetery used prove difficult in determining the Greek or indigenous identity of the deceased.

The cultural identity of individual burials cannot necessarily be determined, in order to definitively say whether or not the donation of sea shells was done exclusively for Greeks or locals, although a culturally exclusive practice does not appear to be the case. And after all, the choice of grave goods is determined by the individuals involved in the burial process; the choice of grave goods can have any number of reasons behind them, including the giver's own identity or the relationship with the deceased. There is no evidence that shells functioned as money or emblems of status in this region. Examples of this practice are known from the nearby region of Languedoc-Roussillon (Almagro Basch 1955). I believe that this practice of including unworked seashells in the burials at Emporion could prove to be a local or regional practice that is later adopted by the Greek colonists. Acceptance of the items as grave goods on the part of the Greeks within their burial sphere would show an intimate level of interaction. Evidence of other sorts of interaction such as this could be very revealing in understanding cultural interaction at Greek colonies. It is fortunate that the excavators recorded and published the inclusion of the seashells, which can now be brought into the discussion as possible evidence of cultural interaction.

The examination of cultural interaction within specific and well-detailed contexts, especially within ritual spheres of sacred and funereal activity, can potentially show an in-depth view into the relationship between individuals and groups at colonial settlements. The nomenclature used to describe these interactions – hybridization, adoption, adaption, etc. – can continue to be debated, but a premise still remains, that a level of importance should be placed on the actions of the locals.

Conclusions

With such an extensive amount of existing data and interpretations related to Greek colonization, it can be overwhelming to navigate through it. Two broad aspects for consideration are: the amount of variability at each colonial settlement, and the roles of the interacting individuals and groups within the colonial contexts. Many colonies share similarities with each other, but they are also each unique. It is no surprise with so many variables present in each case, including the participants, landscape, and timing that the developments would result in very different entities. There is also a need to see the complexity of the cultural interactions. In many cases, viewing contexts as a dichotomy between two groups (colonizers versus colonized, or even colonizers versus mother-city) can miss other crucial aspects. A group of Greek settlers cannot be assumed to be a homogenous collection, identical to another corresponding group of settlers in terms of motivations, social hierarchy, etc. The presence of others, including Etruscans and Phoenicians, in the same regions and even the very settlements in question should also be acknowledged. Above all, evidence of the extent of participation and interaction with locals should be sought after and recognized in an effort to understand the development of any colonial area.

Any and all of these elements are, of course, subject to change over time. Examining the archaeological evidence demonstrates that the creation of settlements and cemeteries is not a one-step or static process. Construction, deconstruction, alteration, and maintenance involve multiple levels of decision-making, communication, and action. The agency of individuals and communities plays an important role; even when individuals cannot be identified, acknowledging differential motivations at work and change over time allows for their stories to begin to be explored. The variety of forms at Greek colonies through location, use of space, architectural elements, and burial rites show complex processes at work. Consequently, there are no simple models that can explain the physical development of colonies or the cultural interaction at all or even at some Greek colonies. One means of tackling this situation is to examine each case study by bringing together the intricate details with the big picture in order to understand the short-term and long-term change and development in the material remains and socio-political relationships amongst the inhabitants.

Bibliography

Allegro, N. and Bassallo, S. (1992) Himera. Nuove ricerche nella città bassa (1989–92). *Kokalos* XXXVIII: 79–150.

Almagro Basch, M. (1953) *Las necrópolis de Ampurias*, vol. I. *Introducción y necrópolis griegas*, *Monografías Ampuritanas* III. Barcelona, Seix y Barral.

Almagro Basch, M. (1955) *Las necrópolis de Ampurias*, vol. II. *Necrópolis Romanas y Necrópolis Indîgenas*, *Monografías Ampuritanas* III. Barcelona, Seix y Barral.

Aquiliué, X., Castanyer, P., Santos, M. and Temoleda, J. (2000) *Empúries. Guidebooks to the Museu d'Arqueologia de Catalunya*. Barcelona, Museu d'Arqueologia de Catalunya.

Belarte, M. C. (2009) Colonial Contacts and Protohistoric Indigenous Urbanis on the Mediterranean Coast of the Iberian Peninsula. In *Colonial Encounters in Ancient Iberia. Phoenician, Greek, and Indigenous Relations*, 91–112. Chicago, Chicago University Press.

Boardman, J. (1999) *The Greeks Overseas. Their early colonies and trade*. London, Thames & Hudson.

Boardman, J. and Hammond, N. G. L. (1982) Preface. In *The Expansion of the Greek World, Eighth to Sixth Centuries BC The Cambridge Ancient History*, Second Edition, Vol. 3, xiii-xvi. Cambridge, Cambridge University Press.

Brumfiel, E. M. (2000) On the archaeology of choice. In M.-A. Dobres and J. Robb (eds) *Agency in Archaeology*, 249–255. London, Routledge.

Carter, J. C. (2006) *Discovering the Greek countryside at Metaponto*. Austin, University of Texas.

Dietler, M. (2009) Colonial Encounters in Iberia and the Western Mediterranean: An exploratory framework. In *Colonial Encounters in Ancient Iberia. Phoenician, Greek, and Indigenous Relations*, 3–48. Chicago, Chicago University Press.

Dietler, M. (2010) *Archaeologies of Colonialism. Consumption, entanglement, and violence in ancient Mediterranean France*. Berkeley, University of California Press.

Dietler, M. and López-Ruiz, C. (eds) (2009) *Colonial Encounters in Ancient Iberia. Phoenician, Greek, and Indigenous Relations*. Chicago, Chicago University Press.

Di Vita, A. (1996) Urban planning in ancient Sicily. In G. Pugliese Carratelli (ed.) *Western Greeks*, 263–308. Venice, Bompiani.

Dobres, M.-A. and J. Robb (eds) (2000) *Agency in Archaeology*. London, Routledge.

Dunbabin, T. J. (1948) *The Western Greeks*. Oxford, Clarendon.

Graham, A. J. (2006) (2nd ed) The colonial expansion of Greece. In J. Boardman and N. G. L. Hammond (eds) *Cambridge Ancient History*, III Part 3, *The Expansion of the Greek World, Eighth to Sixth Centuries BC*. Cambridge, Cambridge University Press.

Gras, M., Tréziny, H. and Broise, H. (eds) (2004) *Mégara Hyblaea. 5. La ville archaïque: l'espace urbain d'une cité grecque de Sicile orientale*, Paris, École Française de Rome.

Hamilton, S., Whitehouse, R., Brown, K., Combes, P., Herring, E. and Seager Thomas, M. (2006) Phenomenology in practice: towards a methodology for a 'subjective' approach. *European Journal of Archaeology* 9.1, 31–71.

Hodder, I. (2000) Agency and individuals in long term processes. In M.-A. Dobres and J. Robb (eds) *Agency in Archaeology*, 21–33. London, Routledge.

Holloway, R. R. (1991) *The Archaeology of Ancient Sicily*. London, Routledge.

Hurst, H. and Owen, S. (2005) *Ancient Colonizations: analogy, similarity and difference*. London, Duckworth.

Jones, A. (2007) *Memory and Material Culture. Topics in contemporary archaeology*. Cambridge, Cambridge University Press.

Kaiser, A. (2000) *The Urban Dialogue. An analysis of the use of space in the Roman city of Empúries, Spain*. British Archaeological Reports International Series 901. Oxford, Archaeopress.

La Rosa, V. (1996) The Impact of Greek Colonists on the non-Hellenic Inhabitants of Sicily. In Pugliese Carratelli, G. (ed.) *Western Greeks*, 523–532. Venice, Bompiani.

Marconi, C. (2007) Temple *Decoration and Cultural Identity in the Archaic Greek World: The metopes of Selinus*. Cambridge, Cambridge University Press.

Marzoli, D. (2005) *Die Besiedlungs- und Landschaftsgeschichte im Empordà, von der Endbronzezeit bis zum Beginn der Romanisierung. Iberia Archaeologica*. Band 5. Mainz Philipp von Zabern.

Martin, R. and Vallet, G. (1980) L'architettura monumentale religiosa e civile. In E. Gabba and G. Vallet (eds) *La Sicilia Antica* I, 271–314. Naples, Società editrice storia di Napoli e della Sicilia.

Mertens, D. (1990) Some principle features of West Greek colonial architecture. In J.-P. Descoeudres (ed.) *Greek Colonists and Native Populations*, 373–383. Oxford, Clarendon.

Mertens, D. (1996) Greek architecture in the West. In G. Pugliese Carratelli (ed.) *Western Greeks*, 315–346. Venice, Bompiani.

Mertens, D. and Greco, E. (1996) Urban planning in Magna Graecia. In G. Pugliese Carratelli (ed.) *Western Greeks*, 243–262. Venice, Bompiani.

Middleton, D. and Edwards, D. (1997) Introduction. In D. Middleton and D. Edwards (eds) *Collective Remembering*, 1–23. Sage, London.

Murray, C. (2011) Constructions of Authority through Ritual: Considering Transformations in Ritual Space as reflecting Society in Iron Age Etruria. In N. Terrenato and D. Haggis (eds) *State Formation in Italy and Greece: Questioning the neoevolutionist paradigm*, 199–216. University of North Carolina, Chapel Hill. Oxford, Oxbow.

Parisi-Presicce, C. (1984) La funzione delle aree sacre nell'organizzazione urbanistica delle colonie greche alla luce delle scoperte di un nuovo santuario periferico di Selinunte. *Archeologia Classica* XXXVI, 19–132.

Parker Pearson, M. (1982) Mortuary practices, society and ideology: An ethnoarchaeological study. In I. Hodder (ed.) *Symbolic and Structural Archaeology*, 99–114. Cambridge, Cambridge University Press.

Parker Pearson, M. (2003) *The Archaeology of Death and Burial*. Stroud, Sutton.

Polignac, F. de (1995) *Cults, Territory, and the Origins of the Greek City-State*. 2nd ed. Chicago, University of Chicago Press.

Pugliese Carratelli, G. (ed.) (1996) *Western Greeks*. Venice, Bompiani.

Ridgway, D. (1992) *The First Western Greeks*. Cambridge, Cambridge University Press.

Scully, V. (1979) *The Earth, the Temple, and the Gods*. New Haven, Yale University Press.

Shepherd, G. (1995) The *Pride of Most Colonials:* Burial and Religion in the Sicilian Colonies. In T. Fischer-Hansen (ed.) *Ancient Sicily, Acta Hyperborea*, 6, 51–82.

Sismondo Ridgway, B. (1999) *Prayers in Stone. Greek Architectural Sculpture (c. 600–100 B.C.E.)*. Berkeley, University of California Press.

Stein, G. (ed.) (2005) *The archaeology of colonial encounters. Comparative perspectives* (School of American research advanced seminars series). Santa Fe, School of American Research.

Trigger, B. G. (1990) Monumental architecture: a thermodynamic explanation of symbolic behaviour. *World Archaeology* 22.2, 119–132.

Vallet, G., Villard, F. and Auberson, P. (1976) *Megara Hyblaea. Le quartier de l'agora archaiche*. Paris, de Boccard.

van Dommelen, P. (1997) Colonial Constructs: Colonialism and Archaeology in the Mediterranean. *World Archaeology* 28.3, 305–323.

van Dommelen, P. (2002) Ambiguous Matters: Colonialism and Local Identities in Punic Sardinia. In C. Lyons and J. Papadopoulos (eds) *The Archaeology of Colonialism. Issues and Debates*, 122–147. Los Angeles, Getty Research Institute.

van Dommelen, P. (2005) Colonial interactions and hybrid practices. Phoenician and Carthaginian settlement in the ancient Mediterranean. In G. Stein (ed.) *The Archaeology of Colonial Encounters. Comparative Perspectives* (School of American research advanced seminars series), 109–141. Santa Fe, School of American Research.

Zanker, P. (1990) *The Power of Images in the Age of Augustus*. Ann Arbor, University of Michigan Press.

3

Locrian colonization in Magna Graecia: Cities and territories

Adolfo J. Domínguez

The sources on the foundation of Epizephyrian Locri are quite abundant and have been compiled and analyzed on various occasions (Niutta 1977, 255–235; Parra 1991, 191–201). In addition, we have an interesting historiographical debate about this colony carried on by important ancient authors: Timaeus versus Aristotle on the one hand, and Polybius versus Timaeus on the other. Unfortunately, the echoes of the controversy have come down to us only from Polybius' work, so we have lost much of the argument put forward by the two first authors in their accounts (Walbank 1962, 1–12). This is a very clear case in which the perceptions and realities of classical times have become forcefully involved in the reconstruction of Locri's colonial past. However, contrary to more negative interpretations, we should not reject that information completely, but we must try to recognise its inconsistencies and anachronisms in order to reconstruct what actually happened, focusing on the conditions that the settlers left behind in Greece and the new ones they found in Italy.

Debate concerning the foundation of Locri

One of the first questions associated with the foundation of this colony is discovering from which of the two Locris in Greece the settlers came. The ancient authors do not agree on this point. This divergence of opinions is probably due to the fact that there was no clear tradition amongst the Locrians of Greece concerning the origin of the colony, and no city considered itself the mother-city of the Italian colony. It is also, perhaps, a misleading debate, stirred up by later authors, such as Ephorus, who had an interest in establishing the origin of the colony in one of the two Locris as opposed to the lack of interest of the previous sources in giving more precise details (Luraghi 1991, 143–159).

In his analysis of the circumstances surrounding the foundation, Polybius provides some interesting, albeit indirect, information. According to him, Timaeus would have encountered written agreements between the Locrians of Greece and the colonists, and also decrees recognizing the mutual citizenship of the Locrians of both Greece and Italy (Polyb., 12.9.3–4). Naturally, although Polybius doubts that Timaeus saw these documents, there is no good reason to doubt that they existed. It is certainly possible that these treaties dated to a later period than the foundation, perhaps the time when *isopoliteia* between the Locrians of Greece and those of Italy was established; on this occasion perhaps those old agreements were reconstructed from oral traditions (Brown 1958, 48). As other cases show, such as the well-studied example of the foundation of Cyrene, traditions relating to the time of foundation could exist both in the mother-cities and, to a greater extent, in the colonies themselves (Graham 1960, 94–111).

It is possible, at least as a hypothesis, that there was no reference to individual cities of origin because neither the records of the Greek- nor the Italian-Locrians kept such information. A remarkable characteristic of the Locrian colonization, is that this was a unique case of a colony not being attributed to a particular mother-city but, on the contrary, to the whole of the Locrian *ethnos*. Another example of Locrian colonial activities, the reinforcement of Naupactus, may be a similar case (Musti 1977, 25). The colonization of Epizephyrian Locri, then, could have been an enterprise undertaken by all the Locrians, both Eastern and Western. Perhaps we can learn more if we observe the relationships between the two Locris and their respective neighbours.

Eastern Locris

Beginning with Eastern Locris, the archaeological finds dating to the eighth century BC are not very abundant (Fossey 1990, 129–132) and are limited to the well-excavated necropolis of Tragana, with several dozen tombs published (Onasoglou 1981, 1–57; Papakonsantinou-Katsouni 1986, 74; Pantos 1987, 235–238), and those of Phournos in Anavra (Theocharis 1964, 242; Kilian 1975b, 26–27; Kilian-Dirlmeier 1979, 151, 184; Dakoronia 1977; 1989), and one at Hagios Dimitrios close to Kainourgio (Theocharis 1964, 242; Kilian 1975a, 4–5, 112, 161; 1975b, 27; Kilian-Dirlmeier 1979, 151; Papakonstantinou and Sipsi 2009, 1029–1042), which is not very well-known, and some other tombs found in Proskyna, Atalanti and Megaplatano (Dakoronia 2002, 49–54). All of these necropoleis indicate a process of increasing wealth, with the presence of metal offerings, sometimes of excellent quality, including objects of gold and imports of Eastern origin (from Anatolia and Egypt). The pottery suggests relationships with the Euboean-Thessalian sphere of interaction, whereas the metals also suggest a Thessalian and Boeotian connection (Kilian 1975a, 4–5; Kilian-Dirlmeier 1979, 152–153). The existence of weapons, mainly in male tombs, and *phialai* in female ones (sometimes several in each tomb) suggests the existence of an aristocracy that was already consolidated and could obtain such wealth through the production of metals, trade, and navigation (Dakoronia 2002, 54; 2006, 483–504). The Locrians themselves probably made voyages, as some literary traditions suggest, such as those taking a maiden to the sanctuary of Athena Ilias in Troy each year. In addition, judging from the finds in Geometric cemeteries of Eastern Locris, they were probably in close contact with the Euboeans, who were the leading seafarers of the eastern and central Mediterranean (Morgan 2003, 118).

Western Locris

As for Western Locris, the archaeological knowledge is less complete, particularly for the earliest period. From as early as the eighth century BC, both the northern (Locrian) and the southern (Achaian) shores of the Gulf of Corinth formed a region of important cultural and economic exchange (Freitag 2005, 385–392). Communication between the two shores of the Gulf is well attested at different times during antiquity (Freitag 2005, 309–329), and it seems that from quite early on, Corinth was in maritime contact with those territories. This is demonstrated through the presence of Corinthian pottery at Delphi, site of the important sanctuary of Apollo, and also at Amphissa.

The little information concerning Amphissa in the Geometric Age, comes mainly from the necropoleis. One was located in an area northwest of the city, called Charmaina, and contains only one known tomb dating to the Late Geometric; this tomb contained metal items, including *fibulae*, pins, hair-pins (two of which were gold), and bracelets. The appearance of the whole set points clearly to northern and western Greece. Another tomb was located in a southern area, outside the walls of the classical city. The cemetery excavated here dates to the Late Geometric and continued to be used until Roman times; several items of Corinthian pottery were found, as well as metal objects, including pins of various types and *fibulae*. In later excavations, other tombs of the Middle and Late Geometric were discovered with grave goods that underline the importance of contact with Corinth, although some objects suggest other connections. The importance of Corinthian pottery until the end of the seventh century BC is clear (Kolonia 1989, 190–193; Tsaroucha 2006, 855–867). In the case of Amphissa, according to Morgan (1990, 116), the imports could have arrived through Delphi, because of their poorer quality compared with this centre.

Another site in this region, Galaxidi, has however yielded more information. A small necropolis here dated to the end of the eighth century BC reveals the existence of a number of individuals with a greater concentration of prestige objects, mainly metal, and pottery that is, to a large extent, inspired by Corinthian prototypes, as well as actual Corinthian pottery (Threpsiadis 1972, 201–205; Themelis 1983, 234–237). This cemetery is related to a fortified acropolis, also dating to the Geometric period, which has not yet been excavated (Baziotopoulou and Valavanis 2003, 189–209). The early occupation of this zone, located 2.5 km southwest of the modern town, is probably related to the development of Corinthian navigation westwards during the eighth century BC (Morgan 1990, 117–118, 254–256), although the Corinthians had other interests beyond contact with the local populations of this region (Morgan 1988, 313–338). Corinthian voyages during the eighth century BC, with increasing frequency from the second half of the century, could have acted as a stimulus for the populations of Western Locris to travel westwards.

Corinthian interest in the Delphi region has been associated with the possible supply of metals from the Thessalian area through the so-called 'Isthmus Corridor route' (Morgan 1990, 116; Kase *et al.* 1991). This route, and another that crossed Phocian territory through Thermopylae and Eastern Locris, would have also served to maintain contacts between the two parts of the Locrian *ethnos*. Perhaps Morgan (1990, 117–118; 1995, 334–335) is right when she suggests that the development of Corinthian travels in this region, from the eighth century BC onwards, potentially resulted in opening up these territories to wider perspectives.

Connections between the two Locri

There are interesting similarities between the Geometric tombs of Eastern Locris (Tragana, Anavra, Kainourgio) and Western Locris (Amphissa, Galaxidi) that are not restricted to the Locrian sphere. They clearly show the existence of contacts, mainly overland, between the coasts of the Maliac Gulf and the Gulf of Corinth, through Doris and Phocis and also further north with Thessaly. Perhaps the circulation of metal, especially as grave goods (dress fasteners, pins, diadems, weapons), indicates that those territories maintained relationships, mainly of an economic nature, during the second half of the eighth century BC. Traditionally the origin of the Locrian *ethnos* alluded to migratory processes from Eastern to Western Locris as a way of explaining the territorial discontinuity (*e.g.* Str. 9.4.9; Ps.-Scym. 480–482), but this cannot be corroborated. An interesting difference can be observed in the pottery repertoire present in the necropoleis, with a clearly Euboean hue seen in the imported pottery of Eastern Locris and the more clearly Corinthian shade visible in the necropoleis of Amphissa and Galaxidi. That is due, as suggested above, to the different relationships established by the two Locris with their respective neighbours, who in both cases were probably more involved in long-distance navigation than the Locrians themselves. Pottery of Euboean type is also present in Delphi, mainly pendent semicircle *skyphoi*, which could have reached the city via inland routes (Morgan 1998, 288–289). There are very few finds of Euboean origin in Corinth, perhaps arriving via Delphi, which confirms that the Euboean and Corinthian trading networks used different routes, and that the Euboeans were not present in the Gulf of Corinth (which, incidentally, seems quite logical) (Morgan 1998, 289, 293). If this was the case, then the two Locris were situated within different spheres of influence, one dominated by the Euboeans and the other by the Corinthians but, at the same time, the two Locris were connected by the inland routes linking the two territories, which were well attested by literary sources (for instance, Hdt. 8.31–35) (Kase and Szemler 1982, 353–366).

The data presented so far do not categorically prove the existence of contacts and close relationships between the two Locris, but they demonstrate that their existence was highly probable. Moreover, the two parts of the Locrian *ethnos* appear to have been involved in exchange with the leading Greek maritime territories, Corinth and Euboea, during the second half of the eighth century BC.

Greek trade and colonization

Euboeans and Corinthians thus developed their own maritime and terrestrial exchange networks, and when the colonizing process began, they settled their first cities (Naxos and Syracuse respectively) in neighbouring areas of Sicily almost simultaneously (Thuc. 6.3.1–2). The debate continues as to the possible precedence of the Euboeans of Eretria in Corcyra, as opposed to the Corinthians, mentioned by Plutarch (*Mor.* 293a) (*pro* Malkin 1998, 3–6; Antonelli 2000, 15–57; *contra* Morgan 1998, 293–295; mixed response Fauber 2002, 61–99). Perhaps the problem can be resolved by considering a possible Euboean establishment on the island not as a colony, an *apoikia* in the strict sense, but a port of call used for commercial purposes, in contact with the native population (D'Andria 1987, 36). The case of Corcyra has little to do at first sight with the Locrians, although it does show how the Corinthian and Euboean networks could have overlapped, not necessarily pacifically. The Locrian connection is established through an inscription found on a cenotaph in the Bay of Garitsa, the site of the main necropolis of Corcyra. The inscription, dated to the last quarter of the seventh century BC, states that it is for Menekrates of Oeanthea (a city in Ozolian Locris), *proxenos* of Corcyra. This is one of the oldest pieces of evidence for the institution of *proxenia*, and illustrates the great care taken by the Corcyrians in showing the special relationship between Corinthian colony of Corcyra and Ozolian Locris (*IG*, IX, 1, 867; Meiggs and Lewis 1988, 4–5; Van Effenterre, Ruzé 1994, 146–148; Fauber 2002, 159–161), although it is uncertain when these relationships originated.

The data presented so far suggest that the relationships between the Locrians, Corinthians and Euboeans were intense before Locrian colonization began, and that the literary traditions and epigraphy seem to reflect the extension of those contacts overseas. It is not unlikely that, when problems arose in Locris, the considerable information available to the Locrians about founding a new settlement in the West was taken into account when planning the expedition. So tentatively, on the basis of arguments that recognise the relationships between the two Locris and their neighbouring territories, it can be argued that colonists from both territories took part in founding Epizephyrian Locri.

The founding of Epizephyrian Locri

The impetus for colonization in this case will not be discussed here. It is important to consider, however, the implications of the account describing men from servile origin possibly marrying women of the Locrian nobility of the Hundred Houses. This set of circumstances could have instigated tensions throughout the whole Locrian *ethnos* related to social classes and land ownership rights (see Laws of Gortyn VII, 1–10), which could have led to the expulsion of this group from Locris, and resulted in the founding of a new colony (Domínguez 2007, 411–412).

The first place where the colonists settled, according to Strabo (6.1.7), was Cape Zephyrium (today Capo Bruzzano), where they stayed for no more than three or four years before settling the ultimate location of the Esopis hill. Strabo also states that the foundation of Locris occurred shortly after that of Croton and Syracuse (Str. 6.1.7). Cape Zephyrium was certainly a good port of call, refuge, or vantage point. It is also Strabo, although without giving much detail, who claims that the move from Cape Zephyrium to the city's final location was carried out with the cooperation of the Syracusans (Str. 6.1.7).

A relationship with the Syracusans does not appear in other sources that, on the contrary, consider the colony to be a Spartan foundation (Paus. 3.3.1) or, conversely, try to establish an association between the Locrian foundation and Sparta (Polyb. 12.6b). The differing accounts clearly reflect different traditions, but it is difficult to know if they relate to the time of colonization or the relations amongst the Epizephyrian Locrians with the Spartans and the Syracusans at a later date, or the relations between the Locrians of Greece and Sparta during classical times.

Archaeological evidence of the founding of Locri demonstrates that less than 2 km N-NW of the northern edge of Locri was a native settlement. The associated necropolis was excavated by Orsi between 1909 and 1912 and consists of the sites of Canale, Ianchina, Patariti and Scorciabove. Amongst the various grave goods, ceramic and metal, there were dozens of vases with shapes and decoration largely reminiscent of Greek prototypes (Orsi 1910, 155–168; 1926, 338–339; La Genière 1964, 23).

Mercuri's (2004, 9–137) recent study shows that the pottery of Canale-Ianchina was apparently produced by several indigenous potters, some more skilled than others, during the second half of the eighth century BC. No items made by Greek potters are so far known amongst the pottery found in those necropoleis, but its very existence suggests a strong and enduring link between these natives and the Greeks, who seem to have been Euboeans both from Euboea itself and from Pithecusae. Consequently, Mercuri (2004, 129) has suggested that there was an Euboean factory in the area, although this has not been found; it is possible that this was located in Cape Zephyrium (Sabbione 1982, 279–280). There is no doubt that there were native settlements in the vicinity of the colony; however, it is difficult to determine their nature and characteristics. Remains of indigenous tombs have appeared in some of the areas later occupied by the city; several of them are considerably older than the Greek foundation, but it seems that, in general, these cemeteries remained in use until the Greek city was established. Some native burials without well-defined contexts have also been discovered in the urban area (Sabbione 1982, 280–281; Lattanzi 1995, 742; Mercuri 2004, 132–133).

These data show that Locrian presence in this region of Italy was previously dominated by Euboean interests. The appearance of the Euboean pottery found in the cemeteries of Canale and Ianchina confirms that the Euboeans, on their way to the coasts of the Tyrrhenian Sea and Sicily, had established relationships with those native populations, perhaps at Cape Zephyrium, before the middle of the eighth century BC.

The Locrians may have come to this region thanks to their contacts with the Euboeans, unless it is assumed, that Syracusan assistance in the move to their ultimate location, and the Euboeans objecting to their presence in the Zephyrium, which would have led to their evacuation and later establishment in Locri. The establishment in the Zephyrium can, consequently, be explained from both an Euboean and Corinthian-Syracusan perspective; the Locrian choice would have made sense in either case. Nevertheless, it is unclear why the Locrians settled in an area where the Euboeans already had an interest, and why there was apparently Corinthian (or Syracusan) support given to the Locrians to help them occupy a larger territory more permanently. Perhaps the Locrians' relationship with the Corinthians and Euboeans in their native territories showed that the Euboeans would benefit from the Locrians occupying the Zephyrium. Using Greeks from other regions perhaps reinforced their colonizing policy (Domínguez 2014), whereas the transfer to the colony's final location was in the interests of the Corinthians who had founded Syracuse only a few years previously.

In their voyages westwards, ancient Greek ships needed protected harbours; thus, the foundation of Croton around 708 BC undoubtedly implied its control over Cape Lacinian (Diod. Sic. 8.17.1), which was one of the main points of reference for navigation on the coasts of the Ionian Sea (Osanna 1992, 192) and, possibly, of Caulonia very shortly afterwards. Caulonia was located on Cape Stilo, another point of interest for seafarers (Gargini 2001, 13–25; Facella 2001, 103–116). So perhaps the Corinthians wanted to control, through the Locrians, an easy access to the Cape Zephyrium area, until then under the Euboean influence (Fig. 3.1). At the same time, the foundation of Locri does not seem to have worried the Euboeans of Rhegium; the two cities seem to have maintained good relations judging by the assistance the Rhegians gave the Locrians during the battle of the River Sagra (Str. 6.1.10; Just. 20.3) in the first half of the sixth century BC (Giangiulio 1989, 249–251; La Genière 1991, 63; Cordiano 1995,

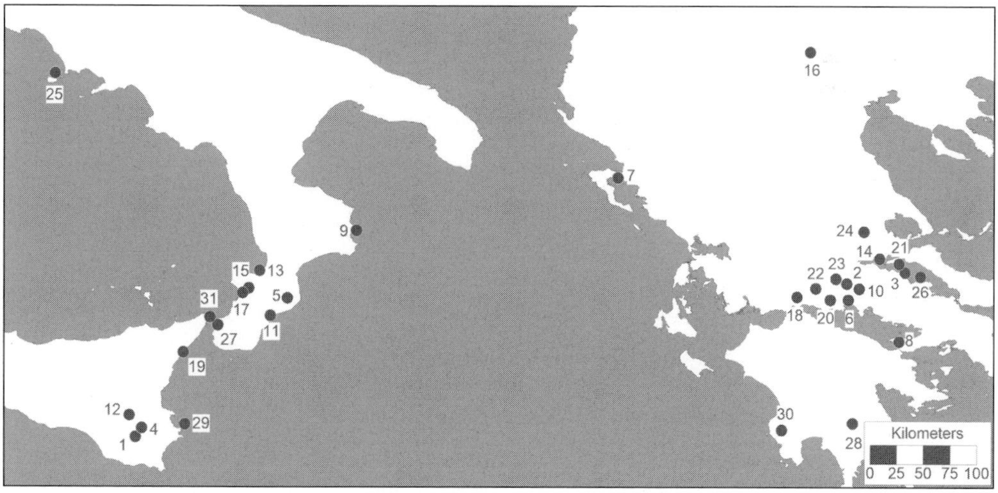

Fig. 3.1. Sites and regions mentioned in the text. 1. Acrai. 2. Amphissa. 3. Atalanti. 4. Casmenai. 5. Caulonia. 6. Chaleion. 7. Corcyra. 8. Corinth. 9. Croton. 10. Delphi. 11. Epizephyrian Locri. 12. Euboea. 13. Hipponion. 14. Kainourgio. 15. Medma. 16. Megaplatano. 17. Metaurus. 18. Naupactus. 19. Naxos. 20. Oeanthea. 21. Opuntian Locris. 22. Ozolian Locris. 23. Phocis. 24. Phournos. 25. Pithecusae. 26. Proskyna. 27. Rhegium. 28. Sparta. 29. Syracuse. 30. Tragana. 31. Zancle.

82–83, 89–90). Euboean overseas expansion was abruptly interrupted at the end of the eighth century BC, although Corinthian expansion continued during seventh century BC. It is possible that the interests of the Euboeans of Rhegium turned to the Tyrrhenian rather than the Ionian coast (as it had done previously). All of this suggests that the colonization of the Locrians cannot be divorced from their relationships with their former neighbours in Old Greece.

The Locrians took advantage of the enterprising Corinthians and Euboeans, mutual enemies and rivals, to find a place in the West where they could settle. The Euboeans showed the Locrians where to begin, and the Corinthians of Syracuse helped them to settle in their ultimate location. If there were people from both Locris in the Locrian colony, as seems almost certain, some would have taken advantage of their links with the Euboeans while others would have done the same with the Corinthians. That dual link would explain Locrian colonization in the area where the city was founded.

The finds from the initial period of Greek occupation date to the late eighth or early seventh century BC. Orsi excavated several enchytrismoi and cist tombs from an archaic cemetery in the Moschetta and Monaci areas; dating to the early seventh century BC (Orsi 1909, 323; La Genière 1972, 245). Although Orsi did not publish drawings of the tombs or materials, these tombs seem similar to those known in both Greek Locris. Later studies of materials excavated by Orsi and other later excavations at the site, discovered Proto-Corinthian pottery dated to the late eighth century BC and other Corinthian objects dating to the first and second half of the seventh century BC (Sabbione 1982, 281–287). All of the items were found in areas that were continuously used as cemeteries, which suggests that residential areas and burial grounds were defined by the late eighth century BC. This is several decades earlier than the dates transmitted by the literary tradition represented by Eusebius, who puts the foundation between 678 and 673 BC. However, the archaeological data fit well with the date given by Strabo (6.1.7), mentioned above, who places the foundation of Locri shortly after that of Syracuse and Croton. A small bronze horse, without context, could be related to those earlier finds; the figure displays Corinthian prototypes but it seems to have been made in Greece, perhaps in Locri itself, and has been interpreted as an object that one of the first colonists brought with him. It is dated to the late eighth century BC (Sabbione 2003, 185; Milanesio Macri 2003, 464).

Historical sources

The Locrian settlement on the Esopis hill placed the Locrians in direct contact with the natives who lived in the area. Both the ancient sources and archaeology provide some information, which is not always consistent in describing the relationships between the two groups. First to consider the literary tradition, Polybius (while rejecting Timaeus' testimony and the existence of treaties between the Locrians of Italy and Greece), states that they all knew by tradition of [a treaty] with the Sicels: of which they give the following account. When they first appeared, and found the Sicels occupying the place they now dwell in, and the Sicels being terror-struck at their arrival admitted them out of fear; and the newcomers swore an oath with them (Polyb. 12.6).

The Greeks broke the oath by duplicity, which resulted in the expulsion of the natives. Later authors, such as Polyaenus (6.22), mention the stratagem claiming that the expulsion of the natives took place the day after the oath. Deceptions of this kind, which involved playing with words, are quite frequent in colonial situations (Dunbabin 1948, 184).

However, in another passage where Polybius explains the Locrian custom of the cup-bearer priestess in the processions, he asserts that the Locrians expelled the Sicels who were occupying the place and that they adopted many Sicel rites, since they did not have any ancient rituals of their own (Polyb. 12.5). This information is contradictory, suggesting the Locrians simultaneously expel the natives, and yet adopt native rituals. The Locrians of Polybius' time seem to have believed in the authenticity of this tradition, judging by the expression he uses: 'again, the following account of the cup-bearing priestess had been received traditionally by them' (Polyb. 12.5.10).

In other cases, such as the foundation of Syracuse, the ancient authors emphasize that the natives were expelled when the colony was actually founded. Consequently, the references to treaties between Greeks and natives must be taken seriously because they belonged to the city's oldest traditions. This is why, even by classical times, the new 'corrected' versions try to show how the Greeks managed to break those treaties but without incurring the wrath of the gods, who guarantee treaties; that is, they used a subterfuge (Nenci and Cataldi 1983, 595–599). All of this suggests that pacts or treaties existed with the natives, which made it easier for the Locrians to establish their colony and that some native customs were adopted by the Greeks, including that of the cup-bearer, whatever its precise nature may have been. Dunbabin (1948, 184) himself even acknowledged that 'it is not *a priori* impossible that some customs in a Greek colony should be derived from the natives by way of intermarriage with their women', although he immediately rejects this possibility in the case of Locri.

Lastly, it would be strange for Locri to have accepted, even in Polybius' time, that there was a relationship between native customs and their own, unless this was generally believed, whether true or not. In the same way, it was also believed, despite the obvious contradiction, that the co-existence between Greeks and natives was short-lived – only one day, according to Polyaenus' witness. Why make a pact, which was to be broken immediately? If the Greeks were in the stronger position, an agreement would not have been necessary because Greek occupation would have meant the immediate expulsion of the natives; but if, on the other hand, Locrian tradition says that a pact existed (*cf.* Polyb. 12.9.3–4), and some indigenous customs were present, there is no reason to doubt it.

Therefore, when the Locrian *polis* re-works the traditions of its foundation, it cannot deny the existence of treaties and so must resort to the tradition of a

It is reasonable to assume, then, that the Locrian colonists may have included native communities in their territory, and that some of their members kept their existing land rights while others with a less favourable status were forced to work the land ceded to the colonists in a similar way to the communitarian servitude well known in other parts of the Greek world, including other colonies (Lotze 1959; Mossé 1979, 85–97; Garlan 1984, 99–121). The survival of native settlements in the vicinity of Locri, as well as the possible integration of some of the natives into the *polis* would explain the adoption of Sicel customs purported by the Locrian tradition.

The Locrian case, in spite of continued debate, seems to be especially suitable for 'the study of the ways in which Greek settlers integrated into existing landscapes', as recently suggested by Owen (2005, 20). The markedly aristocratic character of Locrian colonization, assured by feminine lineage, served as a link between the colonists and the Hundred Houses to which the Locrian women belonged (Polyb. 12.5.11), perhaps facilitated integration with local elites while reasserting the subordinate role of those who did not belong to that world. Even in small Locrian communities, such as Chaleion, in Ozolian Locris, inscriptions confirm that certain institutions, such as juries, had to be filled from amongst the ranks of aristocrats (*aristindan*) as late as the fifth century BC (Van Effenterre and Ruzé 1994, 217–221).

It is certainly interesting to note that the necropolis of Santo Stefano di Grotteria, in a place which overlooks the course of the Torbido river, was apparently still in use in the early sixth century BC, when it is clear that the Locrians were in the process of expanding towards the Tyrrhenian Sea (Sabbione 1982, 296–297). This necropolis displays continuous assimilation of Greek elements throughout this whole period, which suggests that it played a similar role to that of Gerace in the early days of Locrian territorial control, and it could have facilitated Locrian penetration towards the Tyrrhenian Sea. The territory of Epizephyrian Locri consisted of a coastal plain surrounded by an elevation area that limited its agricultural potential to some extent (Sabbione 1982, 297; Osanna 1992, 210–214). For this reason, most scholars agree that Locrian expansion towards the Tyrrhenian Sea was intended to provide new opportunities for colonists without agricultural resources in the territory, potentially due to a ruling that *palaioi kleroi* (the oldest lots) could not change hands under Locrian law (Arist., *Pol.* 1266b 18).

Locrian expansion in Italy

In practice, however, the expansionist model chosen by Locri implied extending its territory by creating subcolonies, whose independence or submission to Locri is not easy to determine. It is probable that the model chosen by Locri was similar to that used by Syracuse, whose subcolonies, especially Acrai and Casmenai, seem to have been simple extensions of their mother-city's territory. Even in the fifth century BC Casmenai seems to have remained under the control of Syracuse, because the Syracusan *gamoroi* expelled by the *demos* sought refuge there (Hdt., 7.155).

The two Locrian foundations, Medma and Hipponion (Ps. Scymn. 308; Str. 6.1.5), are thought to date to the late seventh or early sixth century BC (Givigliano 1989, 741–742; D'Andrea 1989, 765–786), and both have the same territorial design, imposed by the topographical circumstances of the routes between the two seas (Paoletti 1981, 147). Perhaps Metaurus, an old settlement that belonged to the Chalcidians of Zancle, was annexed some time later, around the mid-sixth century BC (Cordiano *et al.* 2006, 19–20). In all three cases, the material culture that has survived is mainly of a cultic nature, and the appearance of these cities is clearly Locrian (Paoletti 1996, 95–97; Parra 1996, 139–141; Cordiano *et al.* 2006, 26–39).

The Locrian expansion, then, carried out by overland routes, has to be considered as extending the mother-city's *chora*, the two subcolonies being her dependencies, although perhaps they acquired their own personalities in the course of the sixth century BC, as some dedications in Olympia suggest. Certainly, these dedications seem to show that Hipponiates, Medmaeans and Locrians defeated the Crotoniates (Lombardo 1989, 423–426; Maddoli 1996, 193–202). The main inscription on a shield, however, shows the combined action of the three Locrian cities, and the existence of common interests opposed to the aspirations of Croton, whose expansionism affected the regions bordering both the Ionian and the Tyrrhenian Seas (Domínguez 2006, 167–168). Naturally, the fact that these three cities shared borders, as Thucydides (5.5.3) indicates for 422 BC, would have contributed to their joining forces, at least in the Archaic period.

It is not known, although some dubious traditions have made suggestions (Lyc., *Alex.* 1083–1086), whether Locrians from Greece took part in this sub-colonization and, if so, under what conditions. A well-known inscription from Galaxidi (ancient Chaleion) shows the intervention of Eastern Locrians and some Western Locrians in the colonial reinforcement of Naupactus; this document establishes requirements and guarantees for the colonists that, in certain conditions, preserve their political rights and property in their mother cities, but also their obligations in Naupactus (Meiggs and Lewis 1988, 35–40; Van Effenterre and Ruzé 1994, 179–185). Perhaps the treaties with the Locrians from Greece, referred to by Timaeus (*ap.* Polyb. 12.9), which related to colonial rights and an acknowledgment of *isopoliteia*, date to this time, but unfortunately, this cannot be proved. Be that as it may, and at least during the Archaic period, it is not unlikely that the mother-city and the colonies had a very close relationship and, although it is not certain that they helped Locri in the battle of the Sagra River, they did fight together again against Croton not long afterwards.

Conclusions

To conclude, I would like to emphasize the main points that arise from this study. First, the Locrian colonization seems to have been a joint enterprise by the peoples of both Greek Locris, perhaps based on the interests of their neighbours, Euboeans and Corinthians, who were much more involved in navigation in the Mediterranean.

Second, this dual relationship with the Euboeans and the Corinthians may have played an important role in selecting the location, because the Locrians occupied a place previously frequented by the Euboeans, but received support for their final establishment from the Corinthians of Syracuse. I have suggested that the Locrians may have acted as mediators between the interests of the two groups, who would not have raised any serious objections or may even have encouraged the Locrian settlement. Third, Locrian foundation traditions refer to treaties with the natives at the time of the colony's foundation, and to the adoption of indigenous customs by the Locrians. It is not relevant here that at a later time, with the emergence of the Greek ethnic consciousness, those treaties were reinterpreted and appear to have been broken early on. At the same time, archaeological data that has on many occasions been interpreted as proof of the expulsion or massacre of the natives can be interpreted in a different way. During and after the rise of Locri, socially structured native groups seem to have continued to live in the city's area of direct economic interest. Fourth, Locrian sub-colonization takes the form of an extension of the *chora*, although two cities, Medma and Hipponion could very well have been 'dependent *poleis*' to use Hansen's terminology (2004, 87–94). The fact that in later times the two colonies fought against the mother-city to gain their independence does not concern us here. The three cities (mother-city and colonies) fought together in a war against Croton during the second half of the sixth century BC.

Lastly, an analysis such as the one I have attempted here, based on a specific colonizing process, as at Locri, can provide interesting keys and approaches to the peculiarities of each Greek colonial mechanism. As a point of discussion for the future, it is possible, that Locrian colonists had to adapt to many factors within this complex process, including the local contexts, affected by the traditions of the natives and Greeks from previous inhabitations, and the Locrian Greek contexts, affected by their own traditions and close relationships with both Euboeans and Corinthians (despite conflict between these two Greek groups). The attachment within particular groups or specific identities, in this case Locrian, could also explain the differences between the colonial behaviour of the different Greek groups that took part in Greek colonization.

Bibliography

Antonelli, L. (2000) *KERKYRAIKA. Ricerche su Corcira alto-arcaica tra Ionio e Adriatico.* Roma, L'Erma di Bretschneider.

Baziotopoulou, E. and Valavanis, P. (2003) Deux acropoles antiques sur les montagnes de Galaxidi. *Bulletin de Correpondance Hellenique* 117, 189–209.

Brown, T. S. (1958) *Timaeus of Tauromenium.* Berkeley, University of California Press.

Cordiano, G. (1995) Espansione territoriale e politica colonizzatrice a Reggio (ed a Locri Epizefiri) fra VI e V secolo a.C., *Kokalos* 41, 79–121.

Cordiano, G., Accardo, S., Isola, C. and Broggi, A. (2006) *Nuove ricerche storico-topografiche sulle aree confinarie dell'antica chora di Rhegion.* Pisa, Edizioni ETS.

D'Andrea, M. (1989) Recenti campagne di scavo alla necropoli occidentale di Hipponion. In *Giornate di Studio su Hipponion-Vibo Valentia, Annali della Scuola Normale Superiore di Pisa* 19, 765–786.

D'Andria, F. (1987) Problèmes du commerce archaïque entre la Mer Ionienne et l'Adriatique. In *L'Illyrie méridionale et l'Epire dans l'Antiquité*, 35–38. Clermont-Ferrand, Adosa.

Dakoronia, F. (1977) Anavra Lokridos. (In modern Greek). *Archaiologikon Deltion* 32-B-1, 104–105.

Dakoronia, F. (1989) Rings. Pre-numismatic items of Geometric Age. *Archaiologike Ephemeris* 128, 115–120. Δακορώνια, Φ. (1989) Κρίκοι. Προνομισματικές μορφές Γεωμετρικής Εποχής. *Archaiologike Ephemeris* 128, 115–120.

Dakoronia, F. (2002) Eastern Lokris. Its History from the Monuments and the Archaeological Research. In *Lokrida. History and Culture*, 17–95. Athens, Ktima Chatzimichalis. Δακορώνια, Φ. (2002) Ανατολική Λοκρίδα. Η ιστορία της μέσα από τα μνημεία και τις αρχαιολογικές έρευνες. In Λοκρίδα. Ιστορία & Πολιτισμός. Athens, Κτήμα Χατζημιχάλη, 17–95.

Dakoronia, F. (2006) Early Iron Age Elite Burials in East Lokris. In S. Deger-Jalkotzy and I. S. Lemos (eds) *Ancient Greece: From the Mycenaean Palaces to the Age of Homer*, 483–504. Edinburgh, Edinburgh University Press.

Domínguez, A. J. (2006) De la identidad étnica a la identidad política: los locrios de Grecia y de Italia. In D. Plácido, M. Valdés, F. Echeverría and M. Y. Montes (eds) *La construcción ideológica de la ciudadanía. Identidades culturales y sociedad en el mundo griego antiguo*, 147–170. Madrid, Editorial Complutense.

Domínguez, A. J. (2007) Fear of enslavement and sacred slavery as mechanisms of social control among the ancient Locrians. In A. Serghidou (ed.) *Fear of Slaves-Fear of Enslavement in the Ancient Mediterranean*, 405–422. Besançon, Presses universitaires de Franche-Comté.

Domínguez, A. J. (2014) Eubeos y locrios entre el Jónico y el Adriático. In L. Breglia, A. Moleti (eds) *Hespería. Tradizioni, rotte, paesaggi*, 189–210. Paestum, Pandemos.

Dunbabin, T. J. (1948) *The Western Greeks. The History of Sicily and South Italy from the foundation of the Greek colonies to 480 BC.* Oxford, Clarendon Press.

Facella, A. (2001) Capo Cocinto (Punta Stilo) nella geografia della Calabria antica. In M. C. Parra (ed.) *Kaulonía, Caulonia, Stilida (e oltre). Contributi storici, archeologici e topografici, I*, 103–116. Pisa, Scuola Normale Superiore di Pisa.

Fauber, C. M. (2002) *Archaic Kerkyra: An historiographical examination of the formation and formulation of an ancient Greek polis*. Unpublished thesis, University of Chicago.

Fossey, J. M. (1990) *The Ancient Topography of Opountian Lokris*. Amsterdam, Gieben.

Freitag, K. (2005) *Der Golf von Korinth. Historisch-topographische Untersuchungen von der Archaik bis in das 1. Jh. v. Chr.* Munich, Tuduv-Verlagsgesellschaft.

Gargini, M. (2001) Kaulonia nel contesto delle tipologie insediative arcaiche. In M. C. Parra (ed.) *Kaulonía, Caulonia, Stilida (e oltre). Contributi storici, archeologici e topografici*, I, 13–25. Pisa, Scuola Normale Superiore di Pisa.

Garlan, Y. (1984) *Les esclaves en Grèce Ancienne*. Paris, La Découverte.

Giangiulio, M. (1989) *Ricerche su Crotone arcaica*. Pisa, Scuola Normale Superiore di Pisa.

Givigliano, G. (1989) L'organizzazione del territorio. In *Giornate di Studio su Hipponion-Vibo Valentia, Annali della Scuola Normale Superiore di Pisa* 19, 737–764.

Graham, A. J. (1960) The authenticity of the HORKION TON OIKISTERON of Cyrene. *Journal of Hellenic Studies* 80, 94–111.

Hansen, M. H. (2004) A Typology of dependent poleis. In M. H. Hansen and T. H. Nielsen (eds) *An Inventory of Archaic and Classical Poleis*, 87–94. Oxford, Oxford University Press.

Kase, E. W. and Szemler, G. J. (1982) Xerxes' march through Phokis (Her. 8.31–35). *Klio* 64, 353–366.

Kase, E. W., Szemler, G. J., Wilkie, N. C. and Wallace, P. W. (1991) *The Great Isthmus Corridor Route. Exploration of the Phokis-Doris Expedition*, I. Dubuque, Kendall Hunt.

Kilian, K. (1975a) *Fibeln in Thessalien von der mykenischen bis zur archaischen Zeit*. Munich, Beck.

Kilian, K. (1975b) Trachtzubehör der Eisenzeit zwischen Ägäis und Adria. *Prähistorische Zeitschrift* 50, 9–140.

Kilian-Dirlmeier, I. (1979) *Anhänger in Griechenland von der mykenischen bis zur spätgeometrische Zeit. (Griechische Festland, Ionische Inseln, dazu Albanien und Jugoslawischen Mazedonien).* Munich, Beck.

Kolonia, R, (1989) Amphissa. Streets Bishop Philotheos and Athanasopoulos (plot P. Katsibra). *Archaiologikon Deltion* 44, *Chronika*, 190–193. Κολώνια, Ρ. (1989) Άμφισσα. Οδός Φιλοθέου Επισκόπου και Αθανασοπούλου (οικόπεδο Π. Κατσίμπρα). Αρχαιολογικόν Δελτίον 44, Χρονικά 190–193.

La Genière, J. De (1964) Note sur la chronologie des nécropoles de Torre Galli et Canale-Janchina. *Mélanges de l'École Française de Rome* 76, 7–23.

La Genière, J. De (1972) Aspetti e problemi dell'archeologia del mondo indigeno. In *Le genti non greche della Magna Grecia. Atti del XI Convegno di Studi sulla Magna Grecia*, 225–272. Taranto, Istituto di Studi sulla Magna Grecia.

La Genière, J. De (1991) L'identification de Lagaria et ses problèmes. In *Epéios et Philoctète en Italie. Données Archéologiques et traditions légendaires*, 55–66. Napoli, Centre Jean Bérard.

Lattanzi, E. (1995) Attività della Soprintendenza Archeologica della Calabria nel 1994. In *Corinto e l'Occidente. Atti del XXXIV Convegno di Studi sulla Magna Grecia.* Taranto, Istituto di Studi sulla Magna Grecia.

Lombardo, M. (1989) Fonti letterarie e problemi della storia di Ipponio. In *Giornate di Studio su Hipponion-Vibo Valentia. Annali della Scuola Normale Superiore di Pisa* 19, 419–462.

Lotze, D. (1959) *METAXY ELEYTHERON KAI DOYLON. Studien zur Rechtsstellung unfreier Landbevölkerungen in Griechenland bis zum 4. Jahrhundert v. Chr.* Berlin, Akademie Verlag.

Luraghi, N. (1991) In margine alla tradizione sulla metropoli dei Locresi Epizefiri. *Historia* 40, 143–159.

Maddoli, G. (1996) La dedica degli Ipponiati ad Olimpia (SEG XI 1211) e il suo contesto storico. In *L'incidenza dell'Antico. Studi in onore di Ettore Lepore, vol. II*, 193–202 Napoli, Edizioni Luciano.

Malkin, I. (1998) Ithaka, Odysseus and the Euboeans in the eighth century. In M. Bats and B. d'Agostino (eds) *Euboica. L'Eubea e la presenza euboica in Calcidica e in Occidente*, 1–10. Napoli, Centre Jean Bérard.

Meiggs, R., Lewis, D. (1988) *A selection of Greek historical inscriptions to the end of the fifth century BC (Revised Edition).* Oxford, Oxford University Press.

Mercuri, L. (2004) *Eubéens en Calabrie à l'époque archaïque. Formes de contacts et d'implantation.* Rome, École Française de Rome.

Milanesio Macri, M. (2003) Figurine of a horse. End of the 8th-beginning of the 7th *c.* BC. In N. C. Stampolidis (ed.) *Sea Routes... From Sidon to Huelva. Interconnections in the Mediterranean 16th-6th c. BC*, 464. Athens, Greek Ministry of Culture.

Morgan, C. (1988) Corinth, the Corinthian Gulf and Western Greece during the eighth century BC. *Annual of the British School at Athens* 83, 313–338.

Morgan, C. (1990) *Athletes and Oracles. The Transformation of Olympia and Delphi in the eighth century BC.* Cambridge, Cambridge University Press.

Morgan, C. (1995) Problems and prospects in the study of Corinthian Pottery Production. In *Corinto e l'Occidente. Atti del XXXIV Convegno di Studi sulla Magna Grecia*, 313–344. Taranto, Istituto di Studi sulla Magna Grecia.

Morgan, C. (1998) Euboians and Corinthians in the Area of the Corinthian Gulf. In M. Bats and B. d'Agostino (eds) *Euboica. L'Eubea e la presenza euboica in Calcidica e in Occidente*, 281–302. Napoli, Centre Jean Bérard.

Morgan, C. (2003) *Early Greek States beyond the Polis.* London, Routledge.

Mossé, C. (1979) Les dépendants paysans dans le monde grec á l'époque archaïque et classique. In *Terre et paysans dependants dans les sociétés antiques*, 85–97. Paris, CNRS.

Musti, D. (1977) Problemi della storia di Locri Epizefirii. In *Locri Epizefirii. Atti del XVI Convegno di Studi sulla Magna Grecia*, 23–146. Napoli, Istituto di Studi sulla Magna Grecia.

Nenci, G. and Cataldi, S. (1983) Strumenti e procedure nei rapporti tra greci ed indigeni. In *Forme di contatto e processi di trasformazione nelle società antiche*, 581–605. Pisa-Roma, Scuola Normale Superiore di Pisa.

Niutta, F. (1977) Le fonti letterarie ed epigrafiche. In *Locri Epizefiri, I*, 255–355. Firenze, Sansoni.

Onasoglou, A. (1981) The Geometric Tombs of Tragana in Eastern Lokris. *Archaiologikon Deltion* 36, A, 1–57. Ωνασογλου, Α (1981) Οι γεωμετρικοί τάφοι της Τραγάνας στην Ανατολική Λοκρίδα. Αρχαιολογικόν Δελτίον 36, Μελετές 1–57.

Orsi, P. (1909) Lokroi Epizehyrioi. Quarta campagna di scavi (1909). *Notizie degli Scavi*, 319–326.

Orsi, P. (1910) Appunti di protostoria e storia locrese. In *Saggi di storia antica e archeologia offerti a G. Beloch*, 155–168. Roma, Loescher.

Orsi, P. (1926) Le necropoli preelleniche calabresi di Torre Galli e di Canale, Ianchina, Patariti. *Monumenti Antichi dell'Accademia Nazionale dei Lincei* 31, 5–376.

Osanna, M. (1992) *Chorai coloniali da Taranto a Locri. Documentazione archeologica e ricostruzione storica.* Roma, Istituto Poligrafico e Zecca dello Stato.

Owen, S. (2005) Analogy, Archaeology and Archaic Greek Colonization. In H. Hurst and S. Owen (eds) *Ancient Colonizations. Analogy, Similarity and Difference*, 5–22. London, Duckworth.

Pantos, P. A. (1987) Tragana Lokridos. *Archaiologikon Deltion* 42, Chron., 235–238. Παντός, Π.Α. (1987) Τραγάνα Λοκρίδος. Αρχαιολογικόν Δελτίον 42, Χρονικά, 235–238.

Paoletti, M. (1981) Nota storica conclusiva. In *Medma e il suo territorio*, 145–150. Bari, De Donato.

Paoletti, M. (1996) I culti di Medma. In E. Lattanzi, M. T. Ianelli, S. Luppino, C. Sabbione and R. Spadea (eds) *Santuari della Magna Grecia in Calabria*, 95–97. Napoli, Electa Napoli.

Papakonstantinou, M. F. and Sipsi, M. (2009) Excavations in the cemetery of Geometric Age at Haghios Dimitrios, Kainourgio Fthiotidos. In *2nd Archaeological Meeting of Thessaly and Central Greece. From Prehistory to the Contemporary Period.* Volos, University of Thessaly, 1029–1042. Παπακωνστανίνου, Μ.Φ. and Σιψή, Μ. (2009) Το γεωμετρικό νεκροταφείο στη θέση Άγιος Δημήτριος Καινούργιο Νομού Φθιώτιδος. In Α. Μαζαράκης-Αινιάν (ed.) Αρχαιολογικό Εργό Θεσσαλίας και Στερεάς Ελλάδας 2, τόμος 2, 1029–1042. Volos, University of Thessaly.

Papakonstantinou-Katsouni, M. (1986) Tragana. *Archaiologikon Deltion* 41, Chron., 74. Παπακωνσταντίνου-Κατσούνη, Μ. (1986) Τραγάνα. Αρχαιολογικόν Δελτίον 41, Χρονικά, 74.

Parra, M. C. (1991) Locri. Fonti letterarie, epigrafiche e numismatiche. In G. Nenci, G. Vallet (dir.) *Bibliografia Topografica della Colonizzazione Grecia in Italia e nelle Isole Tirreniche, vol. IX*, 191–201. Pisa. Scuola Normale Superiore di Pisa.

Parra, M. C. (1996) I culti a Hipponion. In E. Lattanzi, M. T. Ianelli, S. Luppino, C. Sabbione and R. Spadea (eds) *Santuari della Magna Grecia in Calabria*, 139–141. Napoli, Electa Napoli.

Sabbione, C. (1977) Nota sul territorio di Locri. In *Locri Epizefirii. Atti del XVI Convegno di Studi sulla Magna Grecia*, 363–373. Taranto, Istituto di Studi sulla Magna Grecia.

Sabbione, C. (1982) Le aree di colonizzazione di Crotone e di Locri Epizefirii nell'VIII e VII sec. a.C. In *Grecia, Italia e Sicilia nell'VIII secolo a.C. Annuario della Scuola Archeologica di Atene* 60, 251–299.

Sabbione, C. (2003) South Calabria. The Aegean and Eastern-Mediterranean contribution and influence. In N. C. Stampolidis (ed.) *Sea Routes... From Sidon to Huelva. Interconnections in the Mediterranean 16th-6th c. BC*, 184–186. Athens, Greek Ministry of Culture.

Themelis, P. G. (1983) Delphi and its territory in the eighth and seventh centuries BC. In *Grecia, Italia e Sicilia nell'VIII e VII sec. a.C. Annuario della Scuola Archeologica di Atene* 61, 213–255. Θεμέλης, Π.Γ. (1983) Δελφοί και περιοχή τον 8ο και 7ο π.Χ. αιώνα. In *Grecia, Italia e Sicilia nell'VIII e VII sec. a.C. Annuario della Scuola Archeologica di Atene* 61, 213–255.

Theocharis, D. R. (1964) Antiquities and Monuments of Thessaly. *Archaiologikon Deltion* 19, 241–249. Θεοχάρης, Δ.Ρ. (1964) Αρχαιότητες και μνήμεια Θεσσαλίας. Αρχαιολογικόν Δελτίον 19, Χρονικά, 241–249.

Threpsiadis, I. (1972) Excavations at Galaxidi. *Archaiologike Ephemeris* 111, 184–207. Θρεψιάδης, Ι. (1972) Ανασκαφή Γαλαξιδίου. Αρχαιολογική Εφημερίς 111, 184–207.

Tsaroucha, A. (2006) The necropoleis of ancient Amphissa. In A. Mazarakis-Ainian (ed.) *1st Archaeological Meeting of Thessaly and Central Greece. From Prehistory to the Contemporary Period, II*, 855–867. Volos, University of Thessaly. Τσαρούχα, Α. (2006) Τα νεκροταφεία της αρχαίας Άμφισσας. In A. Μαζαράκης-Αινιάν (ed.) Αρχαιολογικό Εργό Θεσσαλίας και Στερεάς Ελλάδας 1, τόμος 2, 855–867. Volos, University of Thessaly.

Van Effenterre, H. and Ruzé, F. (1994) *Nomima. Recueil d'inscriptions politiques et juridiques de l'Archaïsme Grec. I.- Cités et institutions*. Rome, École Française de Rome.

Walbank, F. W. (1962) Polemic in Polybius. *Journal of Roman Studies* 52, 1–12.

4

Cultural and ethnic dynamics in Sicily during Greek colonization

Sebastiano Tusa[†]

Historical background

To begin, a discussion of Greek colonization in Sicily with the foundation of Greek colonies on the island, would miss the chance to understand the real interactions between the colonizers and indigenous, as well as, the real dynamics of a colony's particular circumstances. So, this story should begin much earlier, during the initial centuries of the first millennium BC.

The date of the foundation of Naxos, the first Sicilian colony, in 735 BC, is more than a century after Euboean traders regularly sailed to Ischia and south-east Sicily. In addition to Euboeans, there were other traders that regularly visited the 'island with three points', as it was known in the ancient world. During this period, the location of Sicily was viewed differently. It was believed that the western-most point of the island, Capo Boeo, was much closer to North Africa, and that the southeastern-most point, Capo Passero, was closer to Crete and Greece, than either point is in reality. Considering the ancient notions of geography can aid the investigations of Greek and Phoenician colonization in Sicily, and consequently, the different fates of the western and eastern parts of the island. The proximity of western Sicily to North Africa, strengthened by the exaggerated ancient imagination, was the main factor behind the earlier arrival and subsequent colonization and domination of this part of Sicily by the Phoenicians. In contrast, the eastern part of Sicily was deeply influenced and colonized by the Greeks. This clear partition gave rise to a third area in mid-western Sicily, where another ethnic, political and cultural group (originating from peninsular Italy), the Elymians, succeeded in maintaining autonomous control until

[†] Died March 10, 2019.

the Roman conquest. It is interesting to remember that this ethnic, political and cultural panorama has deep roots in the prehistory of Sicily.

Early cultural interaction

Even as early as the Bell Beaker 'colonization', a phenomenon limited to the western areas, and the Mycenaean commercial and cultural presence, limited to eastern and southern coasts, the history of Sicily was almost always divided into two or three territories. There is a period, however, during the middle and late Bronze Age, when all of Sicily was characterized by the same cultural horizon, that is the Thapsos and Pantalica Nord cultures. Despite the cultural unity in this period, Mycenaean trade involved only the eastern and southern coasts, whereas Cypriot, eastern Mediterranean and northern African imports were present in western and central Sicily. During the thirteenth and twelfth centuries BC, emporia developed on the eastern coasts, where different varieties of goods arrived from the Aegean, Cyprus and the Levant. At some sites, such as Thapsos, this intense presence gave rise also to an acculturation phenomena influencing urban planning and human behaviour, as witnessed in the adoption of courtyard model architecture and the abundance of imported Mycenaean and Cypriot pottery in the burials.

A brief discussion of the external contacts that Sicily had after the end of the first half of the second millennium BC is a helpful context with which to view the complex situation of colonization during the historical period, which had its roots in the Bronze Age. In western Sicily, the Mycenaean presence is almost totally absent. Only two sherds were found in the Belice valley at the Bronze Age site of Erbe Bianche along with a bronze hoard with Cypriot typological affinities (Tusa 1999a, 529–530). Pantelleria and south-central Sicily had, for some centuries, an intense connection with the eastern Mediterranean. The Bronze Age settlement of Monte Grande, near Agrigento, contained a substantial amount of Aegean and Cypriot pottery. The fortified settlement of Mursia in Pantelleria shows clear contacts with Malta, North Africa and the Levant.

The ethnic and cultural homogeneity lasts up to the Pantalica Nord (1250–1150 BC) and Pantalica II (1150–1050 BC) facies. Throughout all of Sicily there existed the same cultural aspect, with the emergence of a small number of large settlements, such as Pantalica (Tusa 1988; 1999a, 546–671), Caltagirone and Mokarta (Tusa, Nicoletti 2000). They were hierarchically superior centres of land control, following a typical Aegean model based on citadels that are settlements of power and wealth control. This cultural homogeneity should also be interpreted according to historical sources, particularly Thucydides (6, 2). According to Thucydides, the Athenian expedition against Syracuse identifies the last period of prehistory as the time of the Sicani. Thucydides states that the Sicani occupied the entire island until the arrival of the northern migrations of the Siculi, Ausoni, Morgeti and Elymians, who crossed the Straits of Messina and invaded Sicily and the Aeolian Islands *c.* 1000 BC (Fig. 4.1) (La Rosa 1989).

Siculi occupied the eastern part of the island; Ausoni – the Aeolian Islands; Morgeti – the central part of eastern Sicily; and Elymians – the mid-west. The

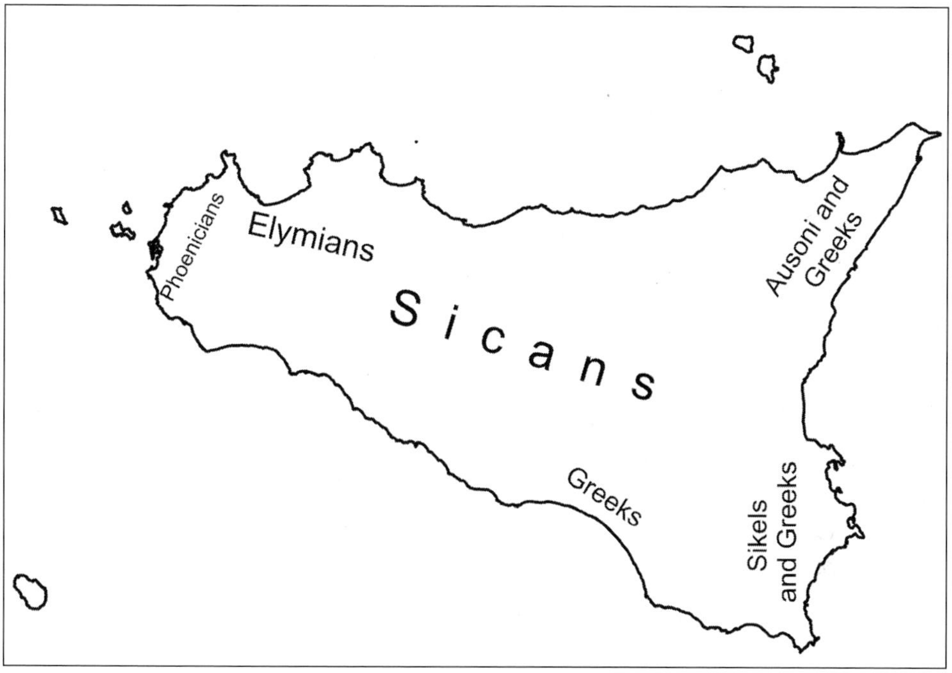

Fig. 4.1. Map of Sicily with the general locations of cultural groupings.

arrival of the newcomers pushed the Sicani towards central Sicily where they lived independently until the fifth century BC when the incoming Greeks from Akragas put an end to the last indigenous enclave in the central Platani Valley. The Sicani territory was continually reduced and shifted towards the centre of the island. In eastern Sicily, they were replaced by Siculi in Pantalica, during the transition to the Pantalica Sud phase (1050–850 BC). In western Sicily, the Sicani of Mokarta were destroyed by the Elymians at around the same period. Similarly, the Ausoni replaced the Sicani in the Aeolian Islands. This is the ethnic and cultural mosaic that characterized Sicily during the beginning of Phoenician and Greek colonization (Tusa 2005).

The ethnic and cultural panorama of the colonizers is similarly complex. There are not only two different civilisations such as Phoenician and Greek (Fig. 4.2), but also a differentiated composition of Greek colonizers. Moreover, there is a third entity – the Elymians – that maintained their autonomy until the Roman conquest. So, it is impossible to give a comprehensive interpretation of the entire Sicilian colonial phenomenon. In order to understand the real features of this period and of the dynamics, we must analyse Sicily on a case-by-case and a region-by-region basis.

Eastern Sicily

In eastern Sicily, the complexity of indigenous colonial dynamics did not rise when the first colony of Naxos was founded (735 BC), but rather shortly afterwards when other groups of Greek colonizers came to settle along the eastern Ionian coast of the island. Greek commercial presence in this part of Sicily started even earlier, evidenced

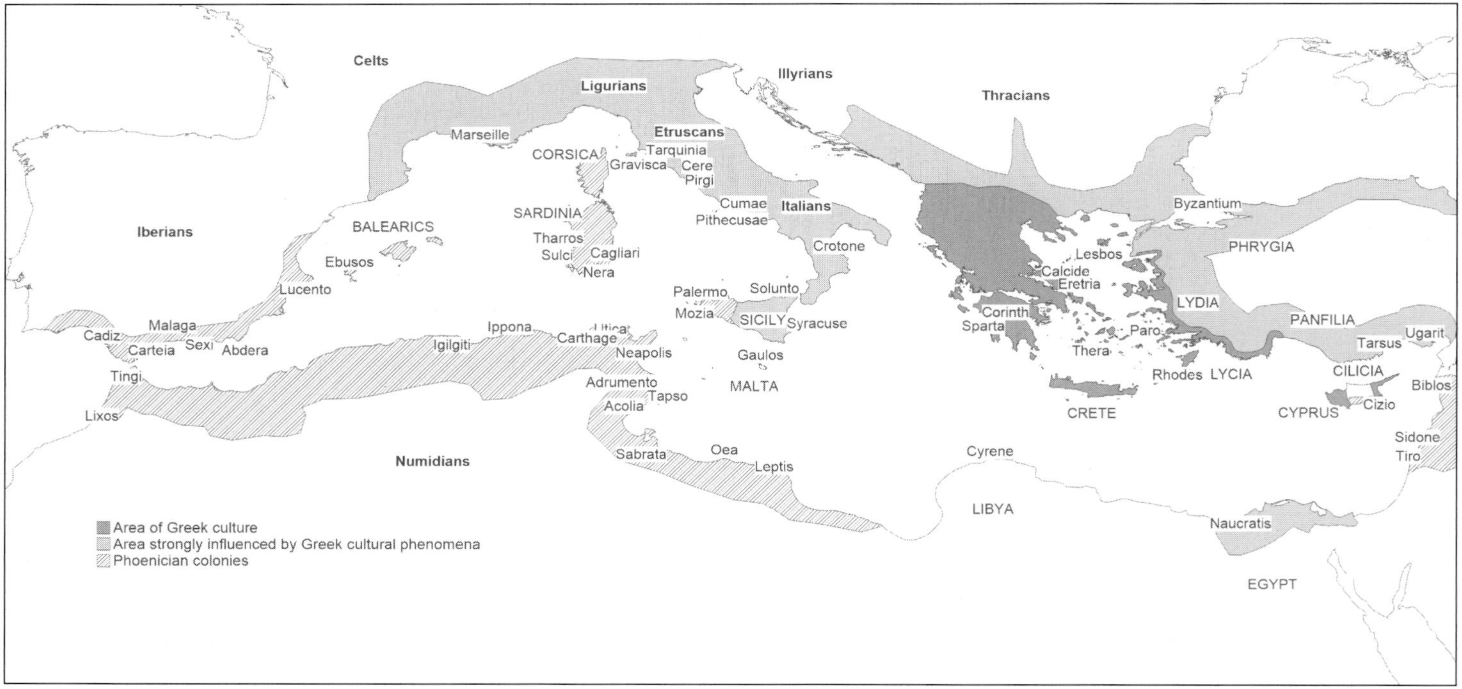

Fig. 4.2. Map of the Mediterranean depicting the areas of cultural influence by Greeks and Phoenicians.

by imported pottery and other items of the middle and late geometric periods found in indigenous archaeological contexts. Notable items include: the bronze fragment of a geometric tripod (first half of the eighth century BC) from Mendolito; the Euboean-Cycladic *skyphos* decorated with hanging festoons from grave 65 (type 6 Kearsley) and the Euboean-Cycladic chevron cup from grave 10 from Villasmundo; the middle and final geometric ware from Megara Hyblaea; late geometric pottery of Corinthian and Rhodian origins dating between the end of the eighth and beginning of the seventh century BC (Albanese Procelli 1997).

It seems reasonable that the Corinthian colonizers, shortly after the foundation of Naxos (734 BC) chose Ortigia and the two natural harbours nearby as the best place to settle and continue marine commercial activities along the eastern Ionian coast. Similarly, the Augusta Gulf was the logical choice for the Megarians in 727 BC, because it was the only remaining free area between Naxos, the Chalcidian colonies of Catane and Leontini, and Syracuse along the same coast.

It was not the result of a single event or creation of a new settlement, but rather the complex context of a slow and intense territorial occupation carried out by Greeks over a period of little more than ten years on the Ionian coast, which gave rise to a conflict with the indigenous living in the internal Iblaean highlands dominated by major settlements such as Pantalica and Finocchito. Eventually the hegemony of Syracuse developed and caused the disintegration of indigenous independence in eastern Sicily.

The first contact between the Greeks and indigenous was absolutely pacific and fruitful for both parties as is demonstrated by historical, as well as, archaeological sources (Tusa 2005). The legend of the indigenous king Hyblon, who kindly gave the Megarians the land in which they built their colony, is a clear example of such a good and pacific relationship (Tusa 1988). Archaeological evidence demonstrates that intense trade between colonizers and indigenous characterized this first phase of contact. But this good behaviour did not last for ever, and soon Syracuse showed her policy of land control not only along the coast but also inland through valleys, such as at Tellaro (Tusa 1988). It is possible that this peculiar behaviour of Syracuse towards the indigenous was continuous since the beginning of the colony's life, if the pre-existing protohistoric settlement on Ortigia was destroyed by Corinthian colonizers.

Syracusan policy towards inland control of southeastern Sicily came into conflict with two hegemonic indigenous settlements – Pantalica and Finocchito. The large and powerful Pantalica, one of the largest proto-urban settlements in Sicily, first occupied by the Sicani and later by Siculi, famous for the large cemetery with about five thousand rock-cut graves, dominated a large part of the Iblaean highland for centuries. The settlement of Pantalica lasted until the beginning of the seventh century BC, when Syracuse put Pantalica under its control. The archaeological evidence of such change was the abandonment of the town and the construction of a small military garrison near the strategic entrance of a wide plateau that had been previously inhabited (Tusa 1988).

Finocchito is located on an uphill position in the Tellaro valley; its first phase (end of the ninth to the first half of the eighth century BC) indicates a strong tradition of the Pantalica Nord and Cassibile cultures (Albanese Procelli and Tusa 1996). For instance, the pottery (shapes, incised decoration and marble painted decoration) shows geometric, as well as oriental affinities (such as the so-called Levantine *oinochoe*). The settlement is a hegemonic centre within the highlands, surrounded by small hamlets and multiple cemeteries. In the phase IIA, almost all of the pottery is imitation proto-Corinthian and Euboean-Cycladic wares. During this period, there is a wide diffusion of the typical three-handled 'scodellone' here and in the Greek colonies on the coast, showing an intense trade and cultural exchange between the two parties. During the last phase, IIB, Greek influence increases, but the construction of a considerable wall encircling the settlement suggests growing conflict.

The two phases of Finocchito demonstrate much in terms of cultural interaction (Albanese Procelli and Tusa 1996). The first shows an independent, indigenous settlement characterized by good relations with the first Greeks in the area. During second phase, the small hamlets were abandoned and the whole indigenous population occupied the newly fortified settlement. Although increasing wealth is indicated by the quantity of imported goods, such as pottery and ornaments during the second phase of Finocchito, resulting from intense trade between the indigenous and colonizers, the situation was not long-lasting. Change resulted from Syracusan policy of territorial expansion. A clear factor that underlines the beginning of Finocchito's demise at the end of the eighth century BC is the foundation of Syracuse's subcolony, Eloro, on the southern coast at the end of Tellaro valley between Finocchito and the sea. This demonstrates that Syracuse intended to gain direct control of the inland area. Finocchito was abandoned during the second quarter of seventh century BC, following the foundation of Akrai, another Syracusan subcolony, in the Iblaean highland.

Syracuse sought to acquire land to distribute to its subcolonies and did not hesitate to push and fight against the indigenous by taking their land and obtaining slaves (Frasca 1981). Syracusan strategy was clear when it founded Eloro, Akrai, Kasmene and Camarina. With the foundation of those towns during the seventh century BC, it completed the total occupation and control of southeastern Sicily with the disappearance of independent indigenous entities.

A similar destiny awaited another large and hegemonic settlement of inland Sicily: Morgantina, whose foundation is attributed to the Morgeti, another culture who came from peninsular Italy to Sicily *c.* 1000 BC. It was a large settlement near Enna, located on the hill of Serra Orlando, which could have been the centre of a wide chiefdom. The Morgeti of Serra Orlando maintained a strong peninsular tradition, visible in its pottery types and decoration, as well as in the bronze and iron objects. Architectural remains from the indigenous phase have been discovered below the later historical levels (Allen 1972–73). This settlement eventually fell into the hegemony of Syracuse.

Central Sicily

Moving farther west along the southern coast is the area of Rhodian-Cretan colonization based on the foundation of Gela in 698 BC and Akragas in 580 BC. Here the colonization model is completely different because it developed through gradual cultural influence with fruitful propaganda that used legends and myths to create the idea of a common destiny between this part of Sicily and Crete. The mythological presence of Minos and Dedalus in this region of the island in the past formed the idea of a common heritage that legitimated the presence of colonizers (Tusa 1999b). According to this policy, Greeks had a pacific co-existence with the indigenous. But the slow process of acculturation was irreversible and resulted in the total acquisition of south-central Sicily in the fifth century BC.

Some indigenous sites offer clear examples of their history, for example: Sant'Angelo Muxaro and Polizzello. It is possible that life in Polizzello was contemporary with Cassibile, but it was a powerful and autonomous settlement *c.* eighth century BC. Here the situation of indigenous sites was different in comparison to the eastern sites. There was much clearer continuity with previous cultural aspects of Thapsos and Pantalica Nord. There was a longer use of incised and impressed decoration lasting until the fifth century BC (Kolb, Tusa and Speakman 2006). This demonstrates the presence of the Sicani, particularly west of the Salso River.

During the seventh century BC at Polizzello, changes occurred in pottery production and the settlement itself, with the construction of a huge defence wall and a rectangular shrine. Imported items and terracotta temple models were abundant in Polizzello, Vassallaggi and Sabucina. The cultural changes during the seventh century BC could be interpreted as the fruitful exploitation of sea trade with Greeks after the foundation of Gela (698 BC). If other settlements were Hellenized during this period, this process did not occur at Polizzello (as stated by the Soprintendenza del Mare della Regione Siciliana).

The situation changed after the foundation of Akragas (580 BC) because it started the slow penetration of Greek cultural influence and materials along the Platani Valley. In about the middle of the sixth century BC, Polizzello obtained an increased amount of Greek pottery. It is possible that Polizzello fell into the sphere of Akragas during the conquests of Phalaris, the tyrant of Akragas (Palermo 1981).

Another large and hegemonic indigenous settlement of this area is Sant'Angelo Muxaro centrally located in the Platani Valley. The main settlement is located on a naturally fortified hill known as 'Monte Castello'. Around this centre were small hamlets, creating the sense of a chiefdom, that maintained its strong autonomy against the invading cultural and political influence of the Rhodians and Cretans of Akragas until the fifth century BC. Sant'Angelo Muxaro was frequently identified by many scholars with the town of Camicos, where Kokalos, king of Sicani hosted Minos (Tusa 1999b). Also well known are the famous gold rings and plates from Monte Castello, and the cemetery that shows strong geometric-orientalizing affinities (Tusa 1999b). The settlement was founded during the Pantalica Nord period and the following phase (thirteenth to tenth century BC). A strong centralization of power is clearly visible from the beginning. The following phase demonstrated affinities with Cassibile (tenth to ninth century BC). Between the ninth and seventh centuries BC, a large and rich pottery production showed strong geometric affinities, as at Pantalica Sud and Finocchito. But in contrast to the two eastern sites, Sant'Angelo Muxaro maintained its autonomy until the fifth century BC, as did Polizzello. There is only a visible change in pottery production during the sixth century BC when painted ware appears along with incised and impressed pottery (Palermo 2004). Imported Greek pottery remained marginal. Other sites in this central part of Sicily show the same process of slow and late acculturation, such as: Gibil Gabib, Sabucina and Vassallaggi.

Western Sicily

The historical events that occurred in western Sicily *c.* 1000 BC are, as mentioned above, totally different from other parts of the island. Due to its different geographical situation and position in the wider Mediterranean sphere, it was frequently a borderland between peoples and civilizations of various and distant origins (Kolb and Tusa 2001). In the colonial period, the main difference is the striking absence of a social hierarchy between colonizers and indigenous, as was the case in the rest of Sicily. The indigenous Elymians maintained their autonomy from the Greeks and Phoenicians/Carthaginians until the Roman conquest in the third to second century BC. There are two main factors that are fundamental to this peculiarity. First, there was the presence of two different and conflicting colonizing parties (Greeks and Phoenicians/Carthaginians) that reduced pressure on the indigenous. Second, there is the particular characteristic of the Elymians who exerted a clear hegemonic attitude in controlling the inland area of western Sicily.

Evident and long-lasting friction between the Greeks and Phoenicians/Carthaginians had two focal points: the conflict between Motya and Selinunte in the southwest, and the conflict between Panormus and Himera in the northwest. A clear boundary rose between those two 'worlds' weakening the inland penetration. In this way the Elymians were under less pressure in contrast with the powerful fight of Syracuse against the Siculi, and Akragas against the Sicani. Although the Elymians were frequently in conflict with the Greeks of Selinunte, they did not follow the tragic destiny of the Siculi (*i.e.* Pantalica and Finocchito) and the Sicani (*i.e.* Sant'Angelo Muxaro, Polizzello, Gibil Gabib) (Albanese Procelli 1997).

In recent decades there has been an increase in archaeological, as well as historical and linguistic research on the Elymians through many excavations, such as at: Segesta (Camerata Scovazzo 1997), Entella (Di Noto and Guglielmino 2001; Michelini and Parra 2001), Monte Finestrelle, Monte Bonifato, Erice, Maranfusa (Spatafora 2003), Pietra Colle and Verderame (Tusa 1992a; 1992b) and, mainly, Monte Polizzo (Morris and Tusa 2004). At Monte Polizzo, Vincenzo Tusa made a limited survey in the 1970s, and due to the stimulating results of these soundings, research resumed on this site in 1998 with an international team directed by the author, Kristian Kristiansen (University of Göteborg) and Christopher Prescott (University of Oslo). Prescott directed the excavations on the northern side of the settlement bringing to light a building (House 1) destroyed between 550 and 525 BC. Since 2002, Christian Mühlenbock and Kristian Kristiansen have been excavating parts of two buildings dating to the sixth century BC, south of House 1. In 1999, excavations began in the areas of: Portella Sant'Anna and near Vincenzo Tusa's trench, on the southern and eastern slopes of the acropolis. Buildings of sixth century BC were brought to light all over the large settlement showing the conspicuous size of this indigenous Elymian settlement. Between 1998 and 2000, Michael Kolb (Northern Illinois University) carried out a survey of the area around Monte Polizzo and excavated a Bronze Age grave at Pitrazzi on Montagna Grande (Kolb and Tusa 2001). Kolb started excavations in the town of Salemi in 2001, bringing to light classical and medieval ruins. In 2000, the University of Stanford, under the direction of Ian Morris, joined the project, digging on the acropolis. In 2003, Kristiansen started excavating in the westernmost part of the settlement, bringing to light large portions of sixth century BC buildings. Excavations in the cemetery were conducted from 1998 to 2004 under the direction of the author.

In addition to the above-mentioned sites, there is also the systematic research for 35 years, led by the University of Zürich, at Monte Jato, which demonstrated the importance of Elymian diffusion towards northwestern Sicily (Isler 2004). Other interesting settlements a few miles from Panormus must also be considered, such as Cozzo Paparina (Tusa, Lo Cascio and Mammina 1991).

Elymian development

Elymian emergence must be framed in the general context of Sicilian protohistory, and not only in terms of historical and philological studies as it has been in the past. The presence of clear typological affinities with Ausonian and Siculi elements within Elymian production shows that these people came to Sicily along with the other groups of peninsular origin such as the Siculi, Ausoni and Morgeti who invaded Sicily and the Aeolian Islands around 1000 BC (Tusa 1990; 1992a; 1998; 1999a, 546–671; 2000; 2002).

Like Pantalica, which was invaded by Siculi during the transition between the Cassibile and Pantalica Sud phases (around ninth to eighth centuries BC), Mokarta, the large Sicanian settlement that dominated western Sicily in the late Bronze Age, was destroyed at the end of the eleventh century BC by the Elymians. The excavations showed clear traces of destruction, such as the young woman killed at the entrance of a round house (Tusa and Nicoletti 2000). Survivors of Mokarta abandoned their home and were brought to Finestrelle and Polizzo, two settlements founded by Elymians. Finestrelle was a settlement that existed in the ninth century BC and showed clear indications of Phoenician trade such as scarabs, amber and faience beads, along with the typical Elymian pottery characterized by zoomorphic handles (Tusa 1999b).

Although it is difficult to differentiate Elyminian and Sicanian pottery production, between Elymian sites such as Segesta, Erice, Entella, Finestrelle and Polizzo from

Sicanian sites, such as Sant'Angelo Muxaro, Polizzello, Sabucina, some clear differences can be demonstrated. Elymian incised, impressed and painted pottery has many features, but the most typical is the anthro-zoomorphic handle. Although the Elymian handles have their typological roots in the Ausonian and Sicanian examples, these show a different attitude to exaggerate a sort of grotesque behaviour. Whereas the bronze and iron production show a strong peninsular affinity (such as in the spiral and snake-shaped *fibulae*) (Tusa 1990).

It seems evident that the Elymian products were a sort of mix between typological elements of peninsular Ausonian and Sicanian origin. The characteristics of the pottery and other goods are examples of the hegemonic behaviour of the Elymian settlements despite the Greek and Phoenician/Carthaginian towns on the coast. There were differences, however, in the relationships between the Elymians and these two groups. The Elymians chose to have a peaceful relationship with the Phoenicians/Carthaginians; this was clear since the arrival of Phoenician goods at Finestrelle (Tusa 1990).

The presence of Phoenician products during the ninth and eighth centuries BC in western Sicily illustrate a situation analogous with that in eastern Sicily, where similar products of Egyptian and Levantine origin appear at many indigenous sites (*e.g.* Finocchito, Realmese). This corroborates Thucydides' description of Phoenicians frequenting the entire shoreline of Sicily before the arrivals of the Greeks (Tusa 1990).

The Elymians resisted Greek attempts to expand towards western Sicily by strengthening their own position at the large settlements of Segesta, Entella and Erice, and leaving sites closer to the Greeks much weaker, like Finestrelle and Polizzo. It is important to consider that in addition to the Greek presence at the strong colony of Selinunte, founded in 627 BC by the Megarians, the Greeks attempted to establish other colonies, at least twice, in western Sicily with the expeditions led by Dorieus in 580 BC and by Pentathlus in 520 BC (Tusa 1990).

It is interesting to analyse the evidence of Selinunte in respect of her relations with the Elymians and indigenous. When Selinunte was founded at the end of the seventh century BC, some Elymian towns, such as Segesta, Erice and Bonifato, became fortified. The archaeological evidence of the earliest levels of Selinunte, however, suggest a pacific process of acculturation from the indigenous living at the site before the arrival of Megarian colonizers.

If the attitudes of the Megarian colonizers were amiable as suggested by their relationship with the Siculi and king Hyblon (Tusa 1990), their behaviour towards the Elymians was absolutely different. The small Elymian settlement, Montagnoli, not far from the mouth of the Belice, and a few miles east of Selinunte, was destroyed evidently by the people of Selinunte pushing the Elymians inland, during the eighth to the first half of the seventh century BC (Tusa 1990). Evidently the peaceful relationship between the indigenous and the inhabitants of Selinunte indicated by the findings from the earliest levels of that site suggest that the people living there before the Greeks were, not Elymian, but rather of Sicanian origin. The behaviour of

Fig. 4.3. Terracotta votive figure of seated female figure.

Fig. 4.4. Detail of extramural shrines in the Gaggera area of the Selinunte chora.

Selinunte towards the Sicanian indigenous seems to have always been pacific. The existence of a group of extramural shrines in the west part of the Selinunte *chora*, in the area of Gaggera, as it was wisely interpreted by Pugliese Carratelli (1988), shows that the Greeks found a means of connection with indigenous cultic places devoted to ecumenical deities of chthonian origin (Fig. 4.3), where the Greeks could also worship (Fig. 4.4). It is interesting to note that the impressive temples with *peristases* were placed on the other side of the *chora* towards the territories occupied by the Greeks of Akragas. It is not by chance that those three temples on the eastern hill were devoted to war deities such as Hera, Athena and Zeus in order to present a symbolic warning to other Greeks living to the east.

The continual conflict of Selinunte with Segesta and the Elymians was resolved by the Carthaginians who destroyed Selinunte in 409 BC. This was the end of one of the largest and most magnificent Greek towns in the Mediterranean with definite hegemonic urban planning since its beginning. By the end of the seventh century BC in western Sicily, there were clear partitions in three different areas of influence between the Phoenicians/Carthaginians, Greeks and Elymians. The latter two groups existed in continual conflict, evidenced by the frequent wars between Selinunte and inland settlements, such as: Polizzo, Finestrelle, Segesta, Entella, Bonifato, Monte Castellazzo and Erice (Tusa and Nicoletti 2003).

Polizzo existed from the end of the seventh century BC until the fifth century BC in a position of independence from its Greek and Carthaginian neighbours (Morris and

Tusa 2004; Muhlenbock 2004). During the sixth century BC, the settlement expanded to its largest extent (about 50 hectares) and was characterized by a strong presence of Greek imports such as Ionian cups B1 and B2, middle- and late-Corinthian vases, and black painted Attic ware (Morris and Tusa 2004). Almost all the *amphorae* were Punic and Etruscan showing the strong connections with Carthaginians of Motya and the other Punic Sicilian towns (Morris and Tusa 2004). Elymian peculiarities in Polizzo are also shown by the presence of a round sacred building in the highest place of the settlement, with several *pithoi* nearby. A cultic interpretation was proposed because of the deposition of deer horns, fine ware pottery, ashes, bone tools, and bronze and iron beads. Similar buildings are well known in other Elymian settlements such as Montagnoli, Polizzello (De Miro 1988) and Colle Madore, as well as Sicanian settlements such as Sabucina, Caltabellotta and Monte San Giuliano. The only other site containing deer horns is Colle Madore (Vassallo 1999).

The deer was an element peculiar to the Elymian culture, a notable example is the temple at Erice, dedicated to Artemis, a deity connected with deer. It is also noteworthy that the Romans returned to Segesta a statue of Diana that had previously been taken by the Carthaginians (Morris and Tusa 2004). Round shrines are a typical indigenous feature that is in contrast to the rational Greek architecture of Selinunte and other Greek towns. Religious considerations were critical to Polizzo and other Elymian and Sicanian settlements. The religious concerns, however, did not prevent progressive Greek acculturation that during the second half of the sixth century BC gave rise to rectangular buildings and an increase in Greek imported wares. Polizzo became a Punic garrison during the fifth century BC, but in other Elymian sites, such as Maranfusa and Entella, Greek imported wares dominated by the end of that century (Morris and Tusa 2004). A clear symbol of a strong Greek influence over the Elymians was the Doric temple of Segesta. It was a Greek temple only in the external shape; its lack of an *adyton* or any internal architecture, indicates that it was to be used for different ritual practices.

An important and determining factor that accelerated Greek influence over the Elymians, as well as the process of Elymians congregating in a few large settlements, such as at Segesta, Erice, Entella, Bonifato, could have been Carthaginian defeat in the battle of Himera (480 BC).

The Phoenicians and the succeeding Carthaginians or Punic culture were the third actors of the western Sicilian scenario. They played an important role in Mediterranean trade between the end of Mycenaean and Levantine trading activities (fourteenth to twelfth century BC) and the beginning of Euboean and Corinthian trading activities (tenth to ninth century BC). It is this period in which Eusebius places Phoenician thalassocracy between 837 and 784 BC. This short and precise time span indicates just part of the importance of Phoenician trade routes, which in reality date much further back in time, as is seen with the twelfth century BC foundation of Lixus, in Atlantic Morocco, Cadiz, on the Iberian Peninsula, and Utica in North Africa. In the first phase, the Phoenicians founded only emporia without any interest in territorial control, such as: Carthage, Tharros and Nora. This was also the situation in Sicily where they founded

Motya, Solunto and Panormus. It was during the sixth and fifth centuries BC that the leadership of Carthage over Sicilian Punic towns and territory became powerful.

The decline of such Carthaginian power began after the defeat at Himera in 480 BC, but it did not affect the presence of Carthaginian power over a large part of Sicily. The power struggle continued with the destruction of Selinunte in 409 BC, and the destruction of Motya in 397 BC. So both parties remained until the Roman conquest. Carthage lost Sicily after the significant defeat on March 10th in 241 BC with the Egadi naval battle. This was the beginning of the end of the tragedy that concluded with the destruction of Carthage in 146 BC.

The Carthaginians were also strongly influenced by the Greeks. An emblematic symbol of this is the famous marble statue of the charioteer found in Motya. It is a clear masterpiece from a fine sculpture workshop in Selinunte. The masked nudity ironically shown as if the body is covered by delicate drapery with the 'wet look' shows that it was made for a wealthy, Punic inhabitant of Motya with strong Hellenic influences.

After the foundations of Selinunte and Himera, the Carthaginians of Sicily were definitely confined to the westernmost part of Sicily, as stated by Thucydides. Here they could easily continue their main activity of sea trade because of the vicinity of Carthage, and with the help of the Elymians.

Panormus during the fifth century BC became very rich and powerful because of its excellent harbour. Greek imports were well appreciated as illustrated by some of the grave goods from as early as the seventh century BC. Solunto was the easternmost Punic settlement controlled by Panormus. The third town of Carthaginian dominion in Sicily was Motya, just off the coast of the westernmost point of the island. It was located in the middle of a lagoon, connected with the mainland through a sort of dam that later became a road or causeway. Motya was the most important Punic town in Sicily because it was well-connected with both Sicily and Carthage, making it the first harbour reached after departure from Africa. There are some traces of a pre-Phoenician occupation of the small island, but it is related to middle Bronze Age, much earlier than the colonial settlement. But the name of Motya shows a connection with the indigenous term 'Motyon'. Hecataeus mentions Motyon, an indigenous lady, who called on Heracles to tell him about a robbery. This name is attested in other places in Sicily. Phoenician occupation of Motya is attested mainly in the archaic graveyard that was later cut by the fortification wall. Phoenician archaic pottery was together with proto-Corinthian and late-geometric vases in small graves cut into the rock, where stone boxes were placed with grave goods and ashes of cremations.

Conclusion

I have tried to briefly explain that the colonization of Sicily was a complex phenomenon that is far from being completely understood. What should be emphasized is that there cannot be a clear idea of Sicilian colonization without knowing the proto-historic dynamics and the different features and histories of the multiple groups that participated in a fascinating game.

Bibliography

Albanese Procelli, R. M. (1997) Le etnie dell'età del ferro e le prime fondazioni coloniali. In S. Tusa (ed.) *Prima Sicilia*, 510–520. Palermo, Ediprint.

Albanese Procelli, R. M. and Tusa, S. (1996) L'età del ferro in Sicilia. In *XIII International Congress of Prehistoric and Protohistoric Sciences*, Italia 8/14 September 1996, Colloquia 12, *The Iron Age in Europe*, 113–125. Forlì, ABACO.

Allen, H. L. (1972–73) Per una definizione della facies preistorica di Morgantina: l'età del ferro. *Kokalos*, XVIII-XIX, 146–160.

Camerata Scovazzo, R. (1997) Note di topografia segestana. *Terze giornate internazionali di studi sull'area Elima, Atti*, 205–226. Pisa-Gibellina, Centro studi e documentazione sull'area Elima.

De Miro, E. (1988) Polizzello, centro della Sicania. *Quaderni dell'Istituto di Archeologia della Facoltà di Lettere e Filosofia della Università di Messina* 3, 25–40.

Di Noto, C. A. and Guglielmino R. (2001) Entella, le necropolis. In *Da una'antica città di Sicilia. I decreti di Entella e Nakona*, Catalogo della Mostra, 173–185. Pisa, Scuola Normale Superiore di Pisa.

Frasca, M. (1981) La necropoli di Monte Finocchito. In *Contributi alla conoscenza dell'età del ferro in Sicilia, Cronache di Archeologia* 20, 13–102.

Isler, H. P. (2004) Monte Iato: la trentatreesima campagna di scavo. *Sicilia Archeologica* 102, 5–34.

Kolb, M. J. and Tusa, S. (2001) The Late Bronze Age and Early Iron Age Landscape of Interior Western Sicily. *Antiquity* LXXV, 503–504.

Kolb, M. J., Tusa, S. and Speakman, R. J. (2006) La decorazione a "Denti di lupo". Identità sociale e interazione nell'Età del Ferro in Sicilia occidentale. *Sicilia Archeologica* 104, 33–46.

La Rosa, V. (1989) Le popolazioni della Sicilia. Sicani, Siculi, Elimi. In G. Pugliese Caratelli (ed.) *Italia omnium terrarum parens*, 1–110. Milano, Scheiwiller.

Michelini, C. and Parra, M. C. (2001) Entella: la città. In *Da una'antica città di Sicilia. I decreti di Entella e Nakona*, Catalogo della Mostra, 157–172. Pisa, Scuola Normale Superiore di Pisa.

Morris, J. and Tusa, S. (2004) Scavi sull'acropoli di Monte Polizzo, 2000–2003. *Sicilia Archeologica*, 102, 35–90.

Muhlenbock, C. (ed.) (2004) *The Sicilian-Scandinavian Archaeological Project, Field Reports* 2000–2003, Göteborg, Göteborg University.

Nenci, G., Tusa, S. and Tusa, V. (eds) (1990) *Gli Elimi e l'area elima*. Palermo, Società siciliana per la storia patria.

Palermo, D. (1981) Polizzello. In *Contributi alla conoscenza dell'età del ferro in Sicilia, Cronache di Archeologia* 20, 103–147.

Palermo, D. (2004) Caratteri e sviluppi della necropoli e del centro antico di Sant'Angelo Muxaro. In G. Rizza and D. Palermo (eds) *La necropoli di Sant'Angelo Muxaro*, 179–220. Catania, Università di Catania- Consiglio Nazionale delle Ricerche.

Pearce, M. and Tosi, M. (eds) (1998) *Papers from the EAA third annual meeting at Ravenna 1997*, Vol. I: *Pre- and Protohistory, BAR* Int. Ser.717.

Pugliese Carratelli, G. (1988) I santuari extramurani. In *Magna Grecia, III. Vita religiosa, culturale letteraria, filosofica e scientifica*, 149–158. Milan, Electa.

Pugliese Caratelli, G. (ed.) (1989) *Italia omnium terrarum parens*. Milano, Scheiwiller.

Rizza, G. and Palermo, D. (eds) (2004) *La necropoli di Sant'Angelo Muxaro*. Catania, Università di Catania- Consiglio Nazionale delle Ricerche.

Spatafora, F. (ed.) (2003) *Monte Maranfusa*. Palermo, Regione siciliana, Assessorato dei beni culturali, ambientali e della pubblica istruzione.

Tusa, S. (1988) *Pantalica e la valle dell'Anapo*. Palermo, Oida.

Tusa, S. (1990) Preistoria e protostoria nel territorio degli Elimi – La genesi di un ethnos e di una cultura. In G. Nenci, S. Tusa and V. Tusa (eds) *Gli Elimi e l'area elima*, 31–54. Palermo, Società siciliana per la storia patria.

Tusa, S. (1992a) Le fasi formative della cultura elima alla luce di recenti rinvenimenti. *Giornate Internazionali di Studi sull'Area Elima*, Atti, 603–615.

Tusa, S. (1992b) La "Problematica elima" e testimonianze archeologiche da Marsala, Paceco, Trapani e Buseto Palizzolo. *Sicilia Archeologica*, 78/79, 71–102.

Tusa, S. (ed.) (1997) *Prima Sicilia*. Palermo, Ediprint.

Tusa, S. (1998) Ethnic development and political formation in Sicily between II and I millennia a.C. In M. Pearce and M. Tosi (eds) *Papers from the EAA third annual meeting at Ravenna 1997*, Vol. I: *Pre- and Protohistory*, *BAR* Int.Ser.717, 284–289.

Tusa, S. (1999a) *La Sicilia nella preistoria*, Palermo, Sellerio.

Tusa, S. (1999b) Processi etnici e formazione politica in Sicilia tra il II e I millennio a.C. In *Natura, mito e storia nel regno sicano di Kokalos*, 175–189. Canicattì, Atti del Convengo.

Tusa, S. (2000) Ethnic dynamics during pre- and protohistory of Sicily. *Journal of Cultural Heritage* 1, sup. 17 – Sup. 28.

Tusa, S. (2002), Processi etnici e formazione politica. In *Sicilia tra il II e il I millennio a.C. Primi Popoli d'Europa*, 157–68. Firenze, All'Insegna del Giglio.

Tusa, S. (2005) Fenici, Indigeni ed Elimi alla luce delle nuove scoperte. In *Atti del V Congresso Internazionale di Studi Fenici e Punici*, 533–549. Palermo, Consiglio nazionale delle ricerche.

Tusa, S., Lo Cascio, G. and Mammina, G. (1991) Indagine topografica al Cozzo Paparina. *Sicilia Archeologica* 74, 29–61.

Tusa, S. and Nicoletti, F. (2000) L'epilogo sicano nella Sicilia occidentale: il caso Mokarta – capanna 1. In *Atti delle terze giornate internazionali di studi sull'area elima*, 963–977. Pisa- Gibellina, Scuola Normale Superiore Pisa.

Tusa, S. and Nicoletti, F. (2003) Saggi stratigrafici alle mura di Erice. *Quarte giornate internazionali di studi sull'area Elima, Atti* 1215–1238. Pisa-Gibellina, Scuola Normale Superiore Pisa.

Vassallo, S. (ed.) (1999) *Colle Madore: un caso di ellenizzazione in terra sicana*. Palermo, Assessorato peri Beni Culturali ed Ambientali, Regione Siciliana.

5

Marseilles: Greek settlement on the fringes of Iron Age Provence

Jason Lucas

In the Early Iron Age, the cultural landscape of southern France was a complex network of small-scale, heterarchical societies, engaged in the trade of ceramics (and presumably other goods) among local groups, with wares being distributed throughout the Rhone Basin via secondary connections. This trade in indigenous wares was supplemented by a carefully chosen and narrow range of goods from Etruscan and (later) Greek traders working along the coast of southern France, which accelerated greatly following the establishment of a permanent Greek settlement at Marseilles. As will be seen below, contact with the wider Mediterranean world, and especially wine, had profound and unintended consequences on Early Iron Age societies, reflected in both changing settlement patterns and the ceramic economy.

The cultural landscape arises from the interactions of the historical conditions (the social, political, and economic structures within which the colonists and indigenous peoples lived) and the material conditions (not only the landscape, but also artefacts, transportation networks, buildings, and sites). Because of this continuous interaction, the surviving material remains reflect the particular historical conditions in which they were created, at least to the extent that the archaeology has not been modified during intervening centuries. Although it may be almost impossible to exactly determine the historical conditions, study of the material culture, alongside other evidence such as inscriptions and textual sources, allows the development of interpretative models that can be tested against the data and modified as necessary in an iterative process.

The Marseilles region

Using this framework, the changing cultural landscape surrounding the Greek settlement at Marseilles is examined below, particularly with regard to the parallels between changes in the settlement pattern during the centuries before and after the foundation of Marseilles and the dramatic and enduring impact on the ceramic economy due to the introduction of Mediterranean imports. The Greek settlement of Massalia (modern Marseilles) was founded *c.* 600 BC by settlers from Phocaea on the Mediterranean coast of Turkey (Bouffier 2005, 218) within what was probably the territory of Segobriges (Boissinot 2005, 117–118), and certainly within a wider landscape already populated and controlled by several Iron Age peoples. The number and distribution of imported Mediterranean artefacts, particularly pottery, suggests a history of interaction and exchange between the indigenous populations and both Greek and Etruscan settlements prior to the foundation of Marseilles (Dietler 2005).

In order to evaluate the development and impact of Marseilles against this broader chronological and geographical context, the analysis below examines the period from 800 BC to 300 BC, roughly corresponding to the period from the Bronze Age to Iron Age transition through to the end of the Iron Age (see Dietler 2005, 25–38 for a detailed discussion of the local chronologies). The geographic bounds of the study area extend beyond the immediate vicinity of Marseilles to include much of the surrounding region, stretching from the River Rhone in the west to near the Italian border in the east, encompassing the later Greek foundations at Agde, Olbia, Antibes and Nice. This corresponds to the modern French *départements* of Bouches-du-Rhône, Var, Alpes-de-Haute-Provence, Vaucluse, Hérault and Gard (Fig. 5.1).

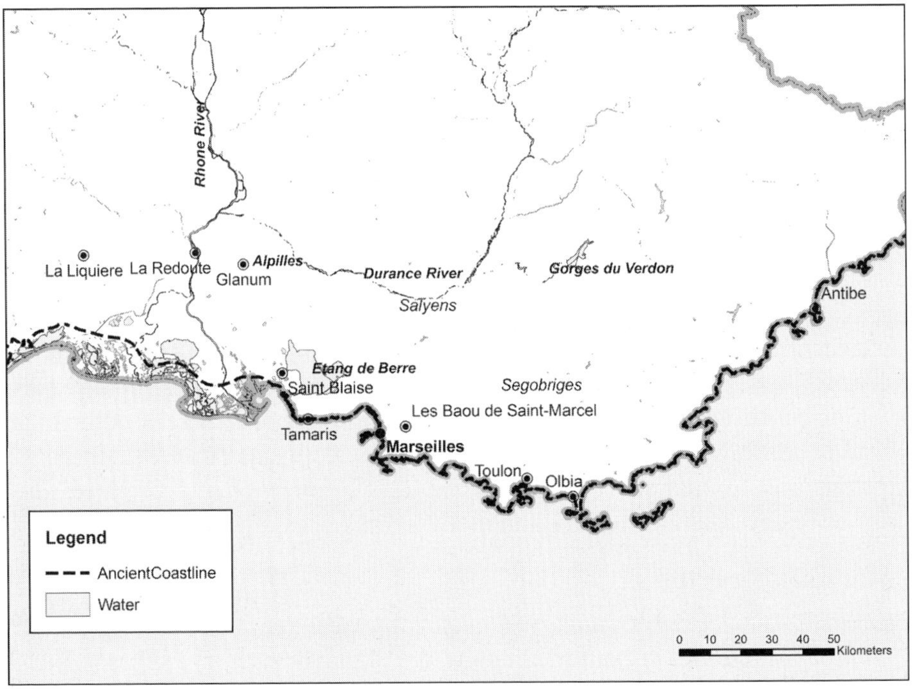

Fig. 5.1. The study region, showing the departmental boundaries, rivers and key sites.

Settlement patterns

The database of sites used to investigate these questions has been compiled from regional surveys. Due to the synthetic nature of this project, we cannot investigate each individual site in great detail, which means that for many sites we must rely on the brief summary of its characteristics from the relevant gazetteers and catalogues. Although this means that we may be adopting biases or omissions in the data, such as the decision of which sites to include or exclude from the catalogues, or with regard to the development of regional chronologies and gaps in archaeological knowledge, the results thus far indicate that significant cultural patterns can be deduced from this sometimes imperfect data.

The Iron Age within the Rhone basin and its interaction with other civilisations of the Mediterranean world has a long history of study, with more modern archaeological enquiries from the late nineteenth century and much of the published evidence is scattered across a range of local and regional French journals and reports. The main English summary and critique of this literature is found in Dietler's doctoral thesis (1990), which has been recently republished (Dietler 2005). The index of sites and their associated artefacts compiled by Dietler has formed the core of our data for the region, although this has been supplemented by the excellent and detailed catalogues of the *Carte archéologique de la Gaule* series for the Departments in the study area (Gateau *et al.* 1996; Schneider and Garcia 1998; Brun and Borréani 1999a; 1999b; Gateau 1999; Provost 1999a; 1999b; Dupraz and Fraisse 2001; Provost and Meffre 2003; Tallah 2004; Rothé and Tréziny 2005), which incorporate the results of numerous small- and large-scale archaeological surveys conducted over the last few decades, as well as other regional summaries (*e.g.* Delestre 2005).

The resulting database encodes detailed information for each site, including its location, relative size, the activities that occurred there (*e.g.* settlement, ritual, funerary, or industrial), the chronology of these various activities, and any changes in size over time. In turn, these data have formed the basis of the spatial analysis of site distribution patterns, which compares the density of settlement in a series of 'time-slices', each containing the site occupied at the moment of each 'slice'. To emphasise the changes from one slice to the next, the resulting density patterns were subtracted, *i.e.* the pattern of 700 BC was subtracted from that of 600 BC, highlighting areas where density increased or decreased (see Figs 5.2–5.7).

At the beginning of the Iron Age (the eighth century BC), settlement was concentrated in the upland areas on the margins of the Alpes-de-Provence and above the Rhone and Durance rivers (Figs 5.2, 5.3). A second zone of more dispersed settlement was located within approximately 20 kilometres of the coast. Of the 352 settlements in the study area, approximately half (173) were occupied during the eighth century. During the seventh century, a series of new settlements were established along the Mediterranean coast to the south of the Étang de Berre, as well as in the upper reaches of the Rhone valley (Fig. 5.4). Across the region, the number of settlements increased by nearly 20% (33 sites).

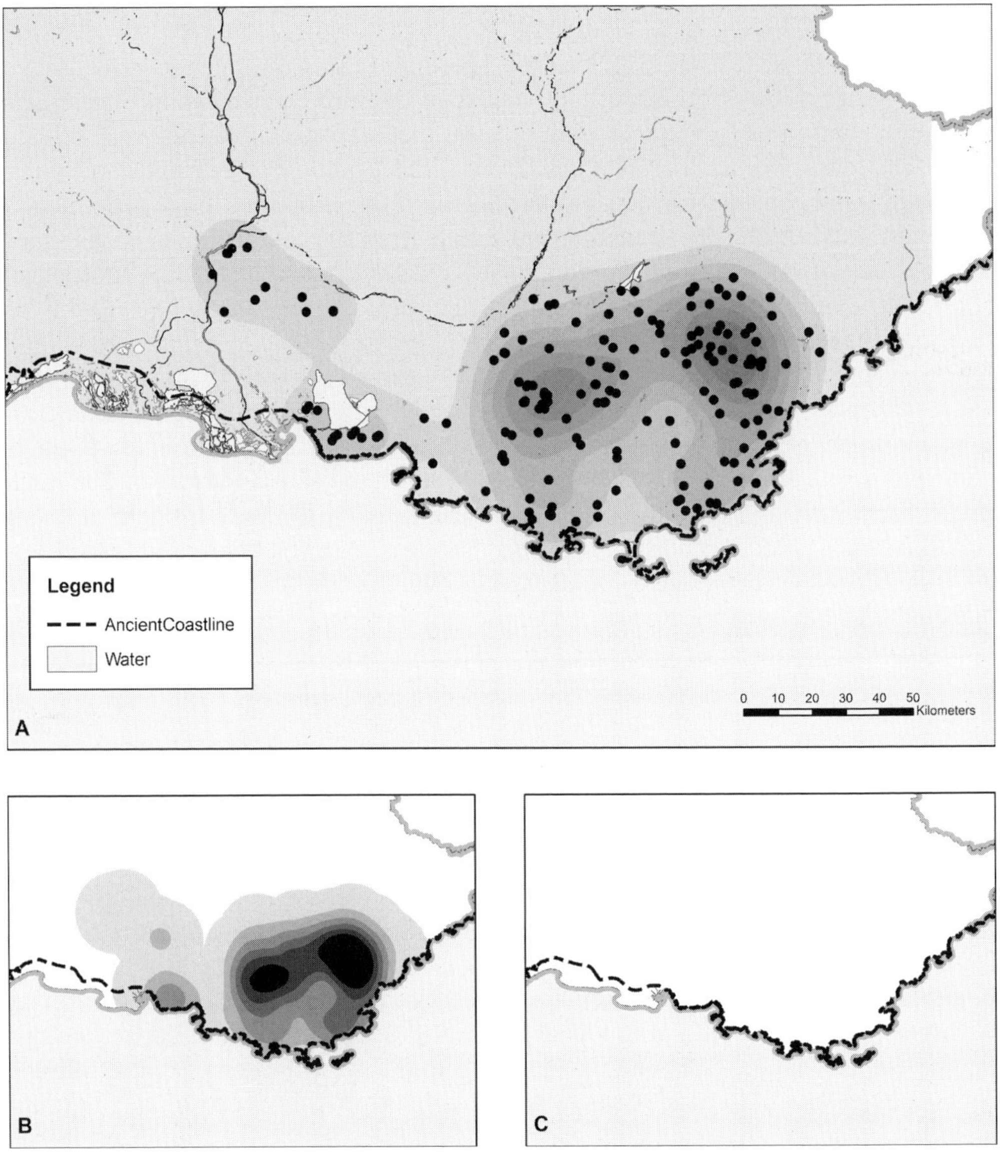

Fig. 5.2. Settlement patterns in the ninth century BC. A. The settlement pattern at 800 BC. B. Areas of increased settlement since 900 BC. C. Areas of decreased settlement since 900 BC.

In the century following the foundation of the Greek colony at Marseilles *c.* 600 BC, the number of settlements increased by a further 35% (75 sites), with continued intensification in the area surrounding the Étang de Berre and in the coastal zone, as well as expansion into the region between the Rhône and Durance rivers. Along the southern edges of the Alpes-de-Provence, settlement appears to have also shifted towards the coast (Fig. 5.5). The number of settlements continued to increase during the sixth century BC, with a noticeable intensification of occupation density to the

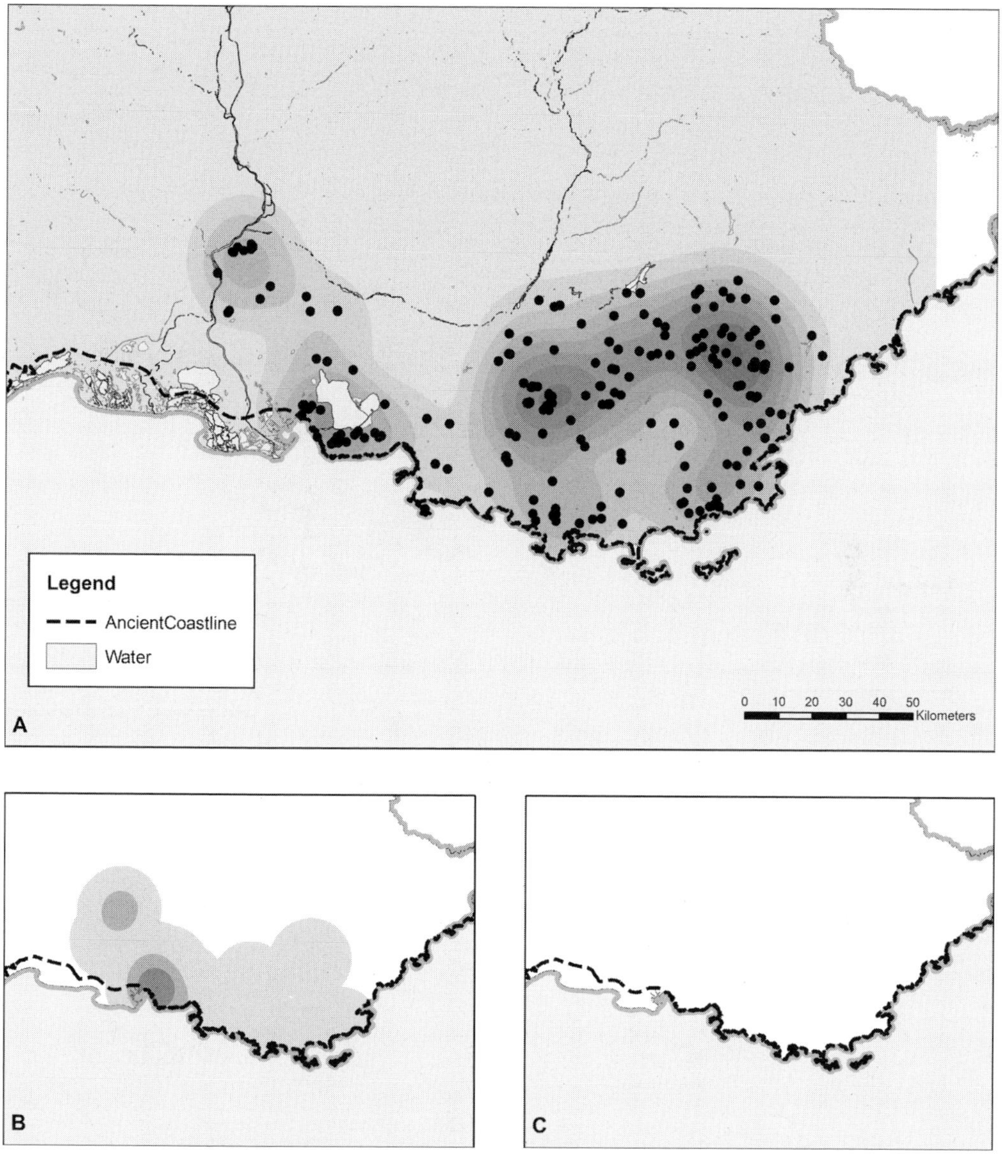

Fig. 5.3. Settlement patterns in the eighth century BC. A. The settlement pattern at 700 BC. B. Areas of increased settlement since 800 BC. C. Areas of decreased settlement since 800 BC.

northwest of the Étang de Berre and in the coastal area near Toulon. However, with 38 new sites and 5 abandoned sites the increase (*c.* 12%) is less than previous centuries. The small number of abandoned settlements may even indicate the beginnings of a period of abandonment that becomes apparent during the next 200 years.

The fifth century was a period of settlement change (Fig. 5.6). Although the overall number of sites varied little, this masked a shift in the settlement pattern, with the abandonment of numerous smaller sites in the area surrounding Marseilles and to the

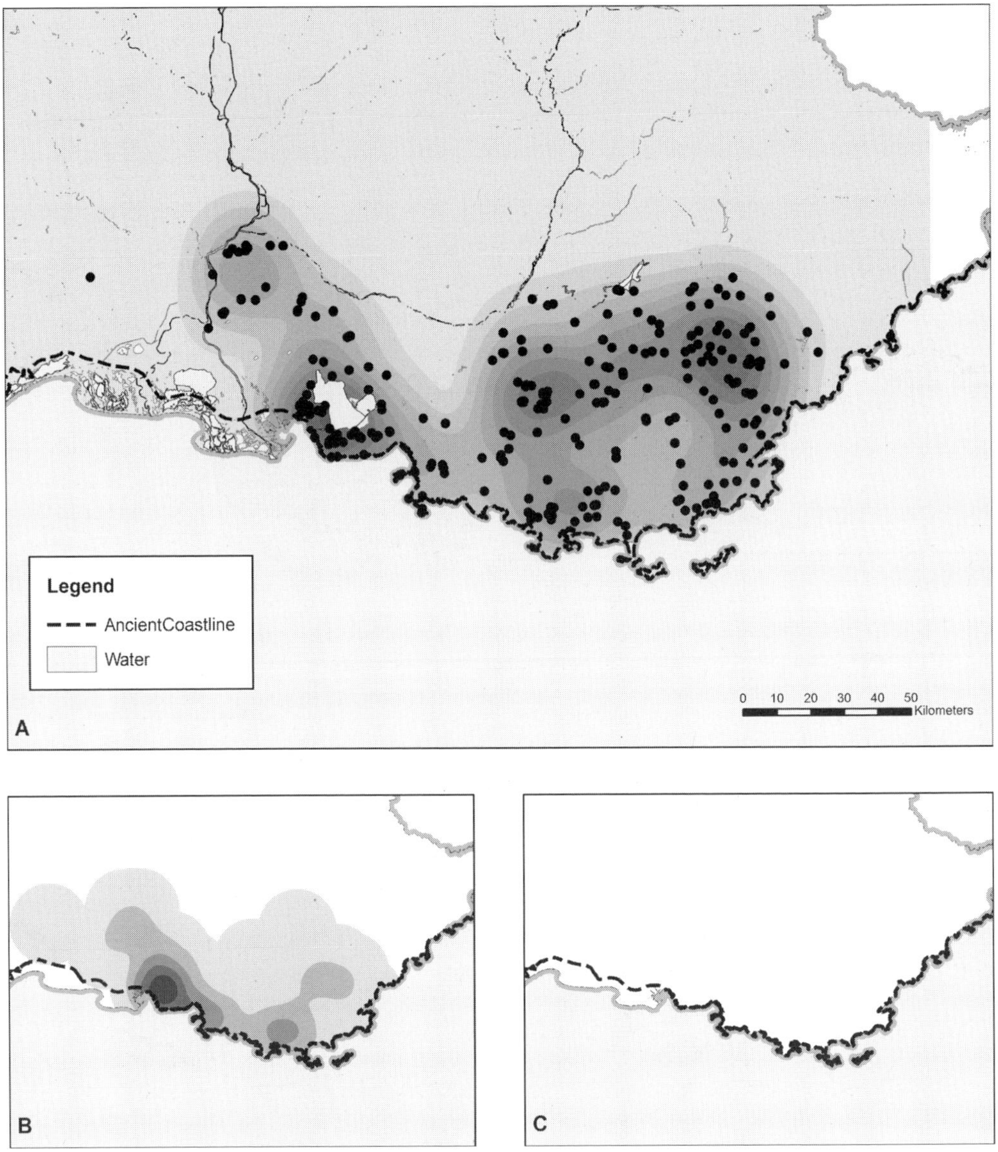

Fig. 5.4. Settlement patterns in the seventh century BC. A. The settlement pattern at 600 BC. B. Areas of increased settlement since 700 BC. C. Areas of decreased settlement since 700 BC.

north and west. Renewed expansion of settlement in the Martigues region between the coast and the Étang de Berre is an exception to this, reversing the small decline of the previous century. Furthermore, the foundation of a number of sites to the east of Marseilles also illustrates the continuing expansion of settlement within the region.

The abandonment of settlements to the north and west of Marseilles continues into the fourth century BC (Fig. 5.7), now complemented by a similar pattern to the

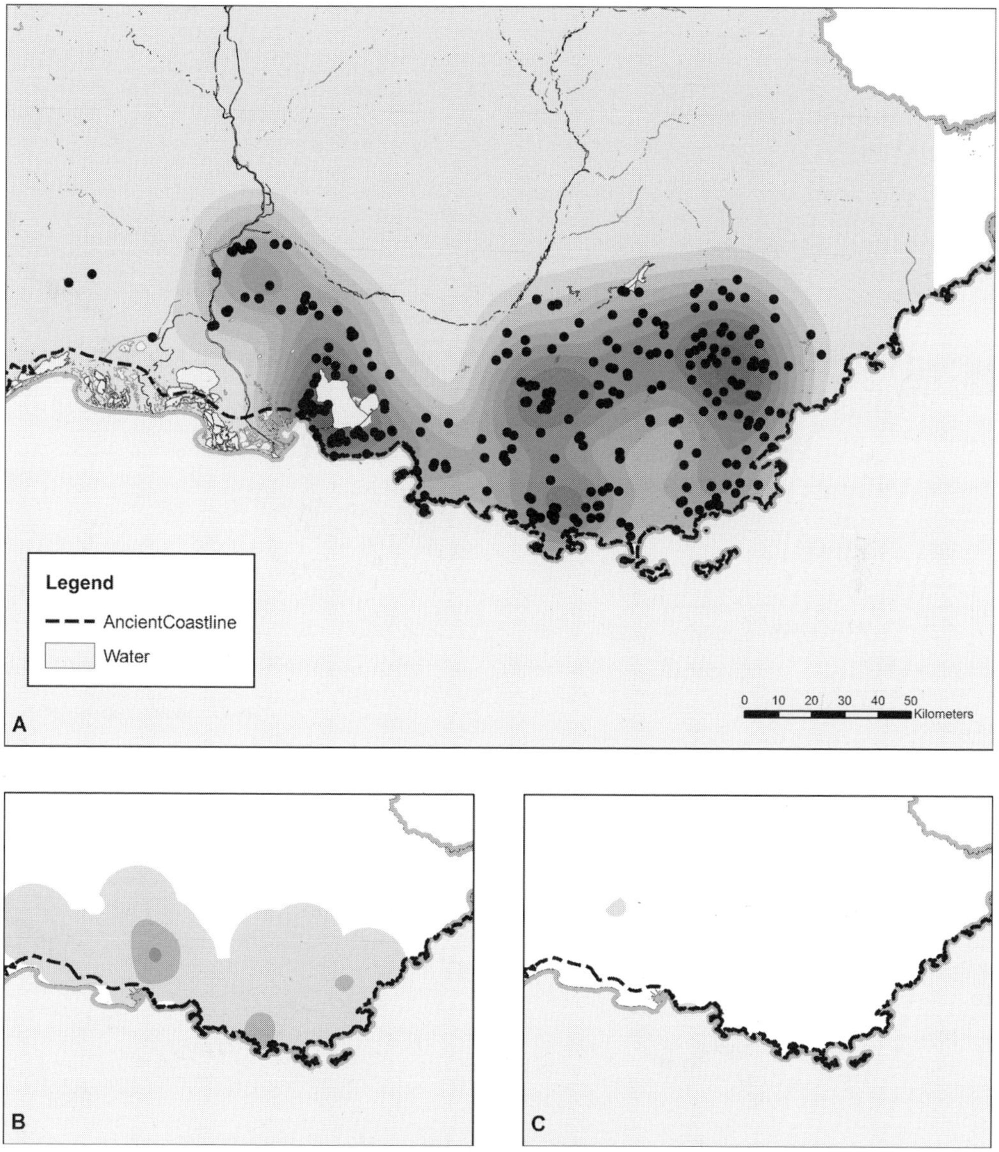

Fig. 5.5. Settlement patterns in the sixth century BC. A. The settlement pattern at 500 BC. B. Areas of increased settlement since 600 BC. C. Areas of decreased settlement since 600 BC.

east. Nearly one-fourth of sites were abandoned during this period (72 sites, 23%). The only area that contrasts with this sharp decline in settlement density is the peninsula to the south of Hyères, probably corresponding to the foundation of Olbia *c.* 300 BC (Brun and Borréani 1999a, 436–461). Furthermore, settlement density, measured as the average nearest-neighbour distance between settlements at any given period, mirrors these changes (Fig. 5.8) – it declined from approximately 3.1 to 2.4 kilometres

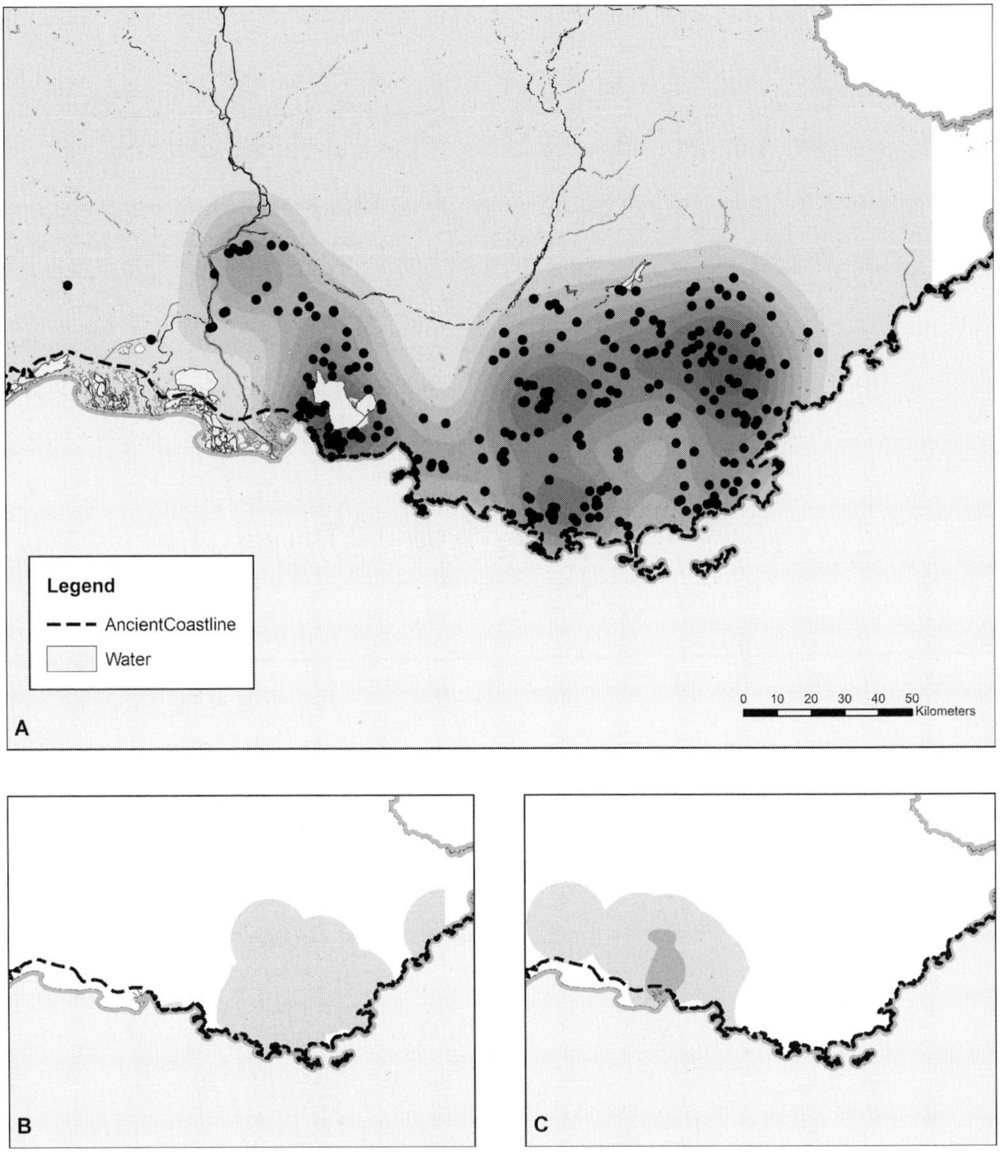

Fig 5.6. Settlement patterns in the fifth century BC. A. The settlement pattern at 400 BC. B. Areas of increased settlement since 500 BC. C. Areas of decreased settlement since 500 BC.

between 800 and 500 BC, reflecting the increasing concentration of settlement. During the fifth and fourth centuries, the distance increases again to almost 2.8 kilometres as settlements were abandoned during this period.

The general increase in settlement density of the first three centuries was accompanied by a marked shift in location towards the coast (Fig. 5.9). In the eighth century, 60% of settlements were more than 20 kilometres from the coast; by the end of the sixth century,

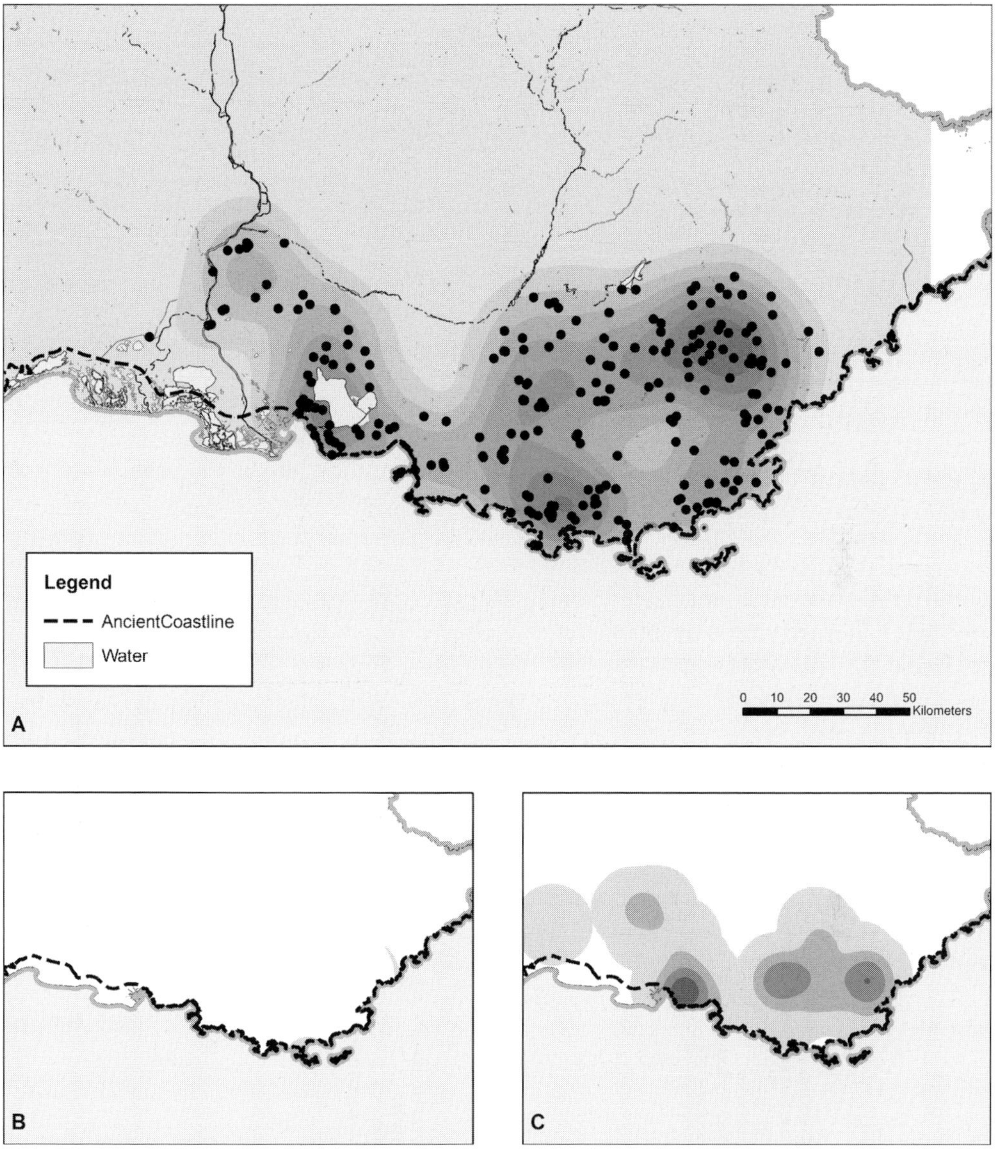

Fig. 5.7. Settlement patterns in the fourth century BC. A. The settlement pattern at 300 BC. B. Areas of increased settlement since 400 BC. C. Areas of decreased settlement since 400 BC.

this had fallen to 50%. The number of sites within 5 kilometres of the coast almost triples during this period, from 26 to 71 (from 15% to 24% of the total sites). Against this general migration of settlement towards the coastal zone, a consistent number of settlements greater than 50 kilometres from the coast remain occupied – between 11 and 15 settlements during each century, comprising between 4% and 7% of the total, including nine sites with evidence of occupation throughout the eighth to third centuries.

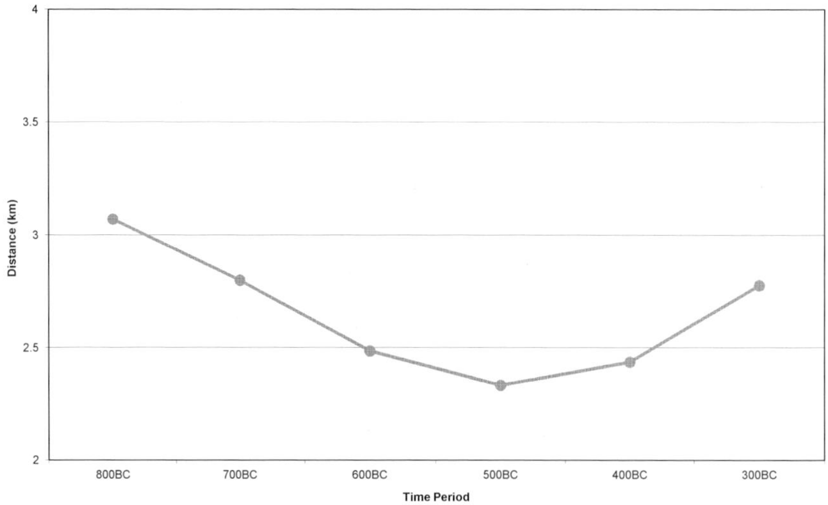

Fig. 5.8. Average distance between settlements from the eighth century BC until the third century BC.

Overall, the settlement pattern in the Marseilles region exhibits a general increase in site numbers from 800 to 500 BC, followed by a phase of slow decrease lasting until at least 300 BC. The relationship between the number of sites, site size, and population is complex, and as this analysis is based on the number and density of sites, it is currently unclear whether this decrease represents a decrease in population, a decrease in the number of sites accompanied by an increase in the degree of nucleation and site size,

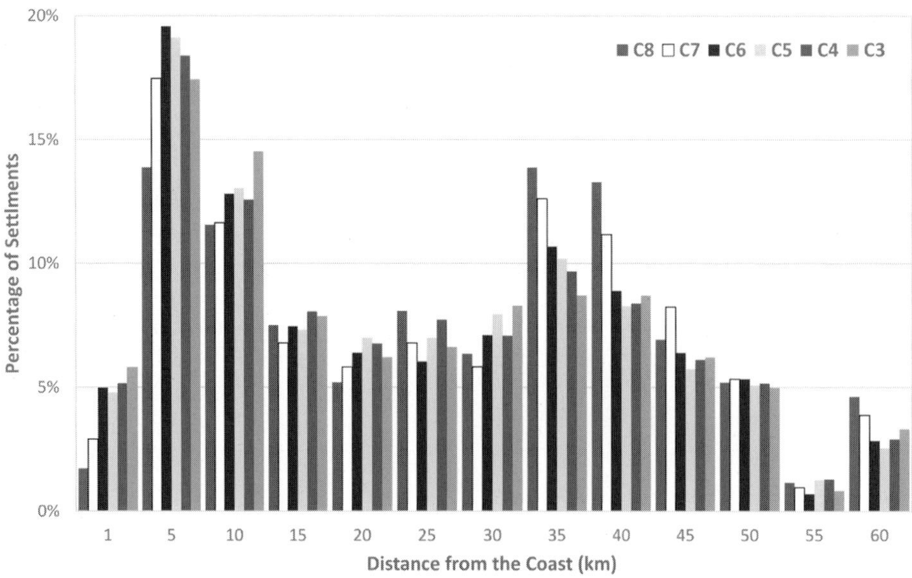

Fig. 5.9. The changing distance from the coast of settlements from the eighth century BC until the third century BC.

or a combination of the two. Some of the evidence, such as the territorial expansion and increasing complexity of sites such as Saint-Blaise (Gateau *et al.* 1996, 286–305; Garcia 2005, 87–92; Sourisseau 2005, 169), does suggest a general increase in the size of (at least some) sites over time.

From at least the eighth century BC (if not before), settlement within the region was undergoing a phase of expansion, which continued until the end of the sixth century. Occupation was concentrated in upland areas, particularly in the areas near the coast. The focus of settlement shifted increasingly toward the coast from shortly before the foundation of Marseilles, with the rate of change accelerating in the two centuries afterwards, extending into previously unoccupied lowland areas. This pattern may reflect an increasing involvement in developing exchange networks linked to the import of goods from other areas of the Mediterranean to Marseilles and other coastal sites.

Material evidence

Whilst the settlement pattern suggests a growing connection to the Mediterranean coast, it is the material evidence that provides detailed insight into the interaction of the indigenous people with Etruscans and Greeks trading, at first, along the coast and, later, from newly established settlements (although still probably making use of coastal trade networks (see Dietler 2005, 180–181)). The most archaeologically visible evidence is pottery, the majority of which is, as argued by Dietler, most likely related to the wine it contained (and the associated drinking paraphernalia), rather than any local desire for the vessels themselves (Dietler 2005, 40–41, 66). The second type of imported artefact is metalwork, although this is much less common, being known from only a handful of sites. This rarity and the recovery of most metalwork from funerary contexts, suggests ceramics and metalwork played different roles within indigenous societies (Dietler 2005, 61–63). As mentioned above, the research by Dietler (1990; 2005) has formed the core of our database; the following discussion, therefore, draws heavily on this, particularly in terms of the distribution of artefacts.

Imported Mediterranean ceramics fall into two distinct categories – transport amphorae and fine-wares. Those found within the Rhone basin originate from Etruria, mainland Greece (including Attic and Corinthian wares), Greek settlements in the eastern Mediterranean (including the so-called 'Ionian' and 'Rhodian' wares) and from the Punic areas of the western Mediterranean (Dietler 2005, 39). It should be noted that whilst there are sometimes significant quantities (at least in terms of sherd counts) of imported Mediterranean ceramics (or of those produced at either Marseilles or indigenous sites within the Rhone basin in similar styles – for simplicity, both categories are referred to as 'Mediterranean' below), these are almost always vastly outnumbered by the indigenous material (Arcelin 1971; 1986, 83). For example, at the key Early Iron Age site of Saint-Blaise, which has over 10,000 sherds of imported ceramics, Mediterranean wares only account for 10–15% of the total ceramic assemblage (see the useful site summary by Dietler 2005, 197–198).

The earliest imports are Etruscan. Amphorae (with finds dating from the final third of the seventh century BC onwards (Bouloumié 1987; Dietler 2005, 45–47; Py 1985)) are rapidly joined by fine-wares (*bucchero nero*) with forms, such as kantheroi, predominantly related to drinking wine (Py 1993, 134). These Etruscan imports are, from around 630 BC, also joined by Ionian fine-wares, some Corinthian and Etrusco-Corinthian vessels (Bouloumié 1978; Dietler 2005, 59) and by (from about 575 BC) Attic black figure and black gloss wares (Dietler 2005, 56–59). Drinking cups are again the most common form to be imported into indigenous sites. However, notable different patterns of use are present at Marseilles, where a large range of Ionian and Attic fine-ware forms are known, including bowls, plates, aryballoi, oinochoai, olpai, skyphoi, lamp and *kraters* (Dietler 2005, 54; Villard 1960).

In the earliest phase imported Etruscan, and Ionian fine- and coarse-wares and the Corinthian and Etrusco-Corinthian vessels seem to be mainly restricted to domestic contexts on the coast and its immediate hinterland, with the exception of occasional Ionian fine-ware finds from further inland (Dietler 2005, 46–59). Ionian amphorae are found in small quantities from the first half of the sixth century. Mixed cargoes of Etruscan and 'Ionian' amphorae have been recovered from shipwrecks at Dattier and Bon Porté (Liou 1974), so it is possible that at least some of the finds were imported by Etruscan traders (Bouloumié 1987). 'Ionian' amphorae become common at indigenous sites only from the second half of the sixth century, although these later finds may have been of Massaliot production. Overall, however, imported Greek amphorae constitute a very small proportion of the amphorae on indigenous sites (Dietler 2005, 48–53).

From the early sixth century (between *c.* 575 BC and 550 BC), imported coarse- and fine-wares constitute an increasingly smaller proportion of the Mediterranean ceramics, and are eventually dwarfed by regionally produced ceramics. This includes vessels produced at Marseilles itself, as well as the output of indigenous workshops, with both producing hybrid wares combining Greek technology and techniques (the wheel, open-draft kilns, comb-incised decoration) with a range of Greek- and indigenous-derived forms, in addition to the production of more traditional Greek forms at Marseilles. As Dietler suggests, these combine two parallel economic processes: the production of vessels at Marseilles in Greek and hybrid styles and intended for consumption at Marseilles and distributed to indigenous sites, and the production of Greek and hybrid styles in indigenous territory for consumption at indigenous sites. The former would be classed as 'imports' to indigenous sites, as they would have been supplied through Massaliot traders, therefore, from outside the traditional production and distribution networks, whilst the latter represents an indigenous response to cultural contact through the expansion of existing networks of ceramic production and exchange (Dietler 2005, 69–70). This is an important insight which will be discussed in more detail below.

By the end of the sixth century, Massaliot amphorae replaced Etruscan as the dominant type, although Etruscan amphorae continued to be imported until at least 450 BC, and possibly until the end of the fifth century (a small number of Punic amphorae are also known from coastal sites in this period). Massaliot amphorae are very common finds after approximately 550 BC, with over a dozen sites containing more than 100 sherds, and several sites with over 1,000 sherds. They are particularly well represented at coastal sites in a zone from Lattes to Antibes, but also known in substantial quantities from sites as far as 100 kilometres inland (Dietler 2005, 80). Interestingly, they are lacking from sites in the immediate vicinity of Marseilles; it may be that these sites acquired wine directly from the colony, obviating the need for amphorae, or that these sites were resistant to such imports. The overall pattern of amphora distribution suggests generally small scale, ship-based trading along the coast, which, although dominated by Marseilles, did not exclude other traders. Beyond the coast, amphorae probably moved through indigenous networks (Dietler 2005, 77–80).

Greek-derived fine-wares produced at Marseilles and indigenous sites consist of two types, Pseudo-Ionian and Monochrome Grey Ware. Pseudo-Ionian wares dated from about 575–475 BC and were (usually) painted with dark decorations on a light background, generally derived from eastern Greek prototypes. The earliest production was probably at Marseilles. From approximately 550 BC, this type is widely distributed and sherds have been recovered from most sites of this period. Forms fall into four general categories: imitations of Ionian vessels, imitations of Attic vessels, forms derived from a combination of Ionian and Attic forms, and those derived from indigenous forms (Dietler 2005, 80–87; Villard 1960, 59–62; Py 1979–80). Although a large range of general shapes are known, only the cups and pitchers (*e.g.* oinochoe/olpe forms) occur in significant quantities outside Marseilles. Indigenous-derived forms were also predominantly cups/bowls and urns. As with other fine-wares mentioned above, the most common forms are related to the serving and drinking of wine (Dietler 2005, 80–87; Villard 1960, 59–62; Py 1979–80).

The earliest finds of Grey-monochrome Ware date from the first half of the sixth century. Grey-monochrome Ware was a hybrid type, combining Greek production techniques, including the potters' wheel, reduction firing and comb-incised decoration to create monochrome grey to black (or occasionally brown) vessels, usually decorated with a horizontal band of straight or wavy lines. Ten major form groups have been identified (as well as a small number of forms only recovered in very small quantities) (Arcelin-Pradelle 1984). The most common form is a carinated bowl derived from indigenous forms, which constitutes just over 50% of the total Grey-monochrome Ware finds. Other indigenous forms include bowls, beakers or urns, which together comprise 15–20% of Grey-monochrome Ware finds, with the most common bowl making up 10%. Of the Greek-derived forms, only the oinochoe and drinking-cup forms are found in significant numbers outside of Marseilles (with each representing few percent of Grey-monochrome Ware finds) (Dietler 2005, 91–93; Arcelin-Pradelle 1984, 13–28). Again, the most common Greek-derived forms relate to the consumption of wine.

Between 550 BC and 450 BC, the distribution of Grey-monochrome Ware expanded to such a degree that it has been recovered from almost every Early Iron Age site, as well as many other sites of uncertain chronology and from surface collections throughout the region. At many sites this ceramic has been recovered in large quantities – at least 13 have more than 100 sherds. Grey-monochrome Ware was also the most significant (in terms of sherd counts) Mediterranean fine-ware from the majority of sites. Compared with Pseudo-Ionian, Grey-monochrome Ware is found in greater quantities on two thirds of sites, reflecting the more general preference fine-wares with indigenous forms, although this means that about one-third of sites have more Pseudo-Ionian pottery. Interestingly, the ratio of Grey-monochrome Ware to Pseudo-Ionian appears to remain roughly constant throughout the Early Iron Age at each particular site, even when nearby sites have noticeably different ratios (Dietler 2005, 97–98).

Grey-monochrome Ware finds from the interior of the Rhone basin seem to have been supplied mostly from Arcelin's Group 3 production centre(s), which appears to have been located in the region (Dietler 2005, 101; see also Arcelin-Pradelle *et al.* 1982; Arcelin-Pradelle 1984). Coastal sites demonstrate a more heterogeneous mix of production groups, often changing from one group to another over time. According to Dietler (2005, 101), the overall distributions suggest a few key points regarding the economy of Grey-monochrome Ware (and also relating fine-wares in general):

- At most of the sites in the interior of the Rhone Basin, Grey-monochrome Ware was locally produced and distributed through indigenous networks, even though these sites imported fine-wares and amphorae from Marseilles.
- Fine-wares flowed along exchange networks not only from the coast inland, but Grey-monochrome Ware simultaneous flowed south from indigenous workshops.
- At a number of coastal sites, wares produced at Marseilles were augmented, or in some cases replaced, by small scale indigenous manufacture.
- Indigenously produced Grey-monochrome Ware was also traded outside the region, notably into the Halstatt zone to the north.

In summary, the Early Iron Age population of the Rhone basin appears to have relatively rapidly (within as little as 25 years of the foundation of Marseilles) augmented the traditional domestic ceramic assemblage through the adoption and adaptation of a selected range of imported Greek wares and colonially-manufactured Greek and hybrid wares all related to the consumption of wine – specifically amphorae, cups and pitchers. A local fine-ware industry also developed to supply the ever-increasing demand for drinking vessels, with the manufacture of the Pseudo-Ionian and Grey-monochrome fine-wares at both Marseilles and a number of indigenous workshops. That the various Mediterranean wares were adopted so quickly implies that networks for the exchange of ceramics were already in existence, probably serving to distribute various locally-produced vessels across the region (Dietler 2005, 152). Furthermore, the continuing dominance of the traditional ceramic wares and forms illustrates that the production of Mediterranean wares in indigenous workshops did not compete with the traditional ceramic economy, but rather complemented (or possibly extended) it.

Conclusions

The discussions above demonstrate two complementary patterns in the archaeological evidence. First, my research on the settlement pattern shows a general shift in settlement focus from the interior towards the coast, alongside a tendency for lower settlement density, possibly reflecting increased nucleation. Secondly, Dietler's patterns from the ceramic evidence illustrate the extension of the native economy to include a specific range of Mediterranean ceramics, but only those objects which fit within existing indigenous cultural norms (the historical conditions).

Dietler (2005, 181) suggests that the availability of wine as a more durable form of alcohol (compared to the probably very short 'shelf-life' of prehistoric beer on the order of a few days) allowed both the escalation of the frequency of and expansion of the quantities associated with ritual feasting by making it possible to stockpile drink, rather than rely on the vagaries of harvest. The rapid and widespread uptake in drinking-related fine-wares certainly correlates with this. If this is the case, it also provides a possible explanation for the pattern I have noted of coastward shift of at least some proportion of the settlements, namely in order to be closer to the sources of wine. The possible tendency towards larger settlements might also be explained by the increase in indigenous ceramic industry at certain sites requiring an additional population of labourers, by the ability of increased feasting to support the more complex social relations corresponding to larger social groups, or a combination of these factors (although, of course, there may also be alternative hypotheses). This provides a clear example of how the material conditions (ceramics) simultaneously reflect the historical conditions (the necessity of alcoholic beverages for feasting rituals) and are shaped by them (the changing settlement pattern).

The long-term result of the foundation of Marseilles was the creation of a hybrid cultural landscape in the Rhone basin, built around indigenous cultural structures, but amplified through access to Greek material culture. These patterns also demonstrate that far from playing a dominant 'colonialist' role in the region, the Greek settlement at Marseilles seems to be operating from the fringes (both geographically and economically) of indigenous society. This is not to say that the impacts of Greek settlement and trade were minor; indeed, the above evidence suggests that they were certainly not. However, the influence of the Greek (and Etruscan) trade and contact was determined not by Greek political or economic structures, but negotiated by the indigenous population from within its own social frameworks, with the unintended consequences of wine introduction augmenting the indigenous social rituals and creating a spiral of cultural change.

Bibliography

Arcelin, P. (1971) *La céramique indigène modelée de Saint- Blaise* (Saint-Mitre-les-Remparts, Bouches-du-Rhône). Paris, Editions Ophrys.

Arcelin, P. (1986) Le territoire de Marseille grecque dans son contexte indigène. In M. Bats and H. Tréziny (eds) *Etudes Massaiètes I: Le territoire de Marseille grecque*. Actes de la Table-Ronde d'Aix-en-Provence, mars 1985, 43–104. Aix-en-Provence, Université de Provence.

Arcelin-Pradelle, C. (1984) *La céramique grise monochrome en Provence*. Revue Archéologique de Narbonnaise, Supplément 10. Paris, Boccard.

Arcelin-Pradelle, C., Dedet, B. and Py, M. (1982) La céramique grise monochrome en Languedoc oriental. *Revue Archéologique de Narbonnaise* 15, 19–67.

Boissinot, P. (2005) La Protohistoire du Bassin de Marseille. In M.-P. Rothé and H. Tréziny (eds) *Marseille et ses alentours*. Carte archéologique de la Gaule, 13/3, 117–140. Paris, Académie des inscriptions et belles-lettres.

Bouffier, S. C. (2005) Marseille pendant l'Antiquité grecque et romaine. In M.-P. Rothé and H. Tréziny (eds) *Marseille et ses alentours*. Carte archéologique de la Gaule, 13/3, 217–224. Paris, Académie des inscriptions et belles-lettres.

Bouloumié, B. (1978) La céramique étrusco-corinthienne de Saint-Blaise. *Revue d'Etudes Ligures* 44, 51–61.

Bouloumié, B. (1987) Le rôle des Etrusques dans la diffusion des produits étrusques et grecs en milieu préceltique et celtique, *Hallstatt-Studien*, Tübinger Kolloquium zur westeuropäischen Hallstatt-Zeit 1980, 20–43. Weinheim, VCH Acta humaniora.

Brun, J.-P. and Borréani, M. (eds) (1999a) *Le Var*. Carte archéologique de la Gaule, 83/1. Paris, Académie des inscriptions et belles-lettres.

Brun, J.-P. and Borréani, M. (eds) (1999b) *Le Var*. Carte archéologique de la Gaule, 83/2. Paris, Académie des inscriptions et belles-lettres.

Delestre, X. (ed.) (2005) *15 ans d'archéologie en Provence-Alpes-Côte d'Azur*. Aix-en-Provence, Edisud.

Dietler, M. D. (1990) *Exchange, Consumption, and Colonial Interaction in the Rhône Basin of France: A Study of Early Iron Age Political Economy*. Unpublished PhD thesis, Department of Anthropology, University of California at Berkeley.

Dietler, M. D. (2005) *Consumption and Colonial Encounters in the Rhône Basin of France: A Study of Early Iron Age Political Economy*. Monographies d'Archéologie Méditerranéenne. Lattes, UMR 5140 du CNRS.

Dupraz, J. and Fraisse, C. (eds) (2001) *L'Ardèche*. Carte archéologique de la Gaule, 7. Paris, Académie des inscriptions et belles-lettres.

Garcia, D. (2005) Villes et villages de la Provence protohistorique. In X. Delestre (ed.) *15 ans d'archéologie en Provence-Alpes-Côte d'Azur*, 82–97. Aix-en-Provence, Edisud.

Gateau, F. (ed.) (1999) *Les Alpilles et la Montagnette*. Carte archéologique de la Gaule, 13/2. Paris, Académie des inscriptions et belles-lettres.

Gateau, F., Trément, F. and Verdin, F. (eds) (1996) *L'Etang-de-Berre*. Carte archéologique de la Gaule, 13/1. Paris, Académie des inscriptions et belles-lettres.

Liou, B. (1974) Note provisoire sur deux gisements gréco-étrusques (Bon Porté A et Pointe du Dattier). *Cahiers d'Archéologie subaquatique* 3, 7–19.

Provost, M. (ed.) (1999a) *Le Gard*. Carte archéologique de la Gaule, 30/2. Paris, Académie des inscriptions et belles-lettres.

Provost, M. (ed.) (1999b) *Le Gard*. Carte archéologique de la Gaule, 30/3. Paris, Académie des inscriptions et belles-lettres.

Provost, M. and Meffre, J.-C. (eds) (2003) *Vaison-la-Romaine et ses campagnes*. Carte archéologique de la Gaule, 84/1. Paris, Académie des inscriptions et belles-lettres.

Py, M. (1979–80) Ensayo de clasificación de un estilo ceràmica de Occidente: los vasos pseudojonios pinta dos. *Ampurias* 41–42, 155–202.

Py, M. (1985) Les amphores étrusques de Gaule méridionale. In M. Cristofani, P. Moscati, G. Nardi and M. Pandolfini (eds) *Il commercio étrusco arcaico*. Atti dell'Incontro di studio, 5–7 dicembre 1983. Quaderni del Centro di Studio per l'Archeologia Etrusco-Italica 9, 73–94. Rome, Consiglio Nazionale delle Ricerche.

Py, M. (1993) Bucchero nero étrusque. In M. Py (ed.) *Dicocer: Dictionnaire des céramiques antiques (VIIe s. av. n. è.-VIIe s. de n. è.) en Méditerranée nord-occidentale (Provence, Languedoc, Ampurdan)*. Lattara 6, 134–140. Lattes, Association pour la recherche archéologique en Languedoc oriental.

Rothé, M.-P. and Tréziny, H. (eds) (2005) *Marseille et ses alentours*. Carte archéologique de la Gaule, 13/3. Paris, Académie des inscriptions et belles-lettres.

Schneider, L. and Garcia, D. (eds) (1998) *Le Lodévois*. Carte archéologique de la Gaule, 34/1. Paris, Académie des inscriptions et belles-lettres.

Sourisseau, J.-C. (2005) Les diversités culturelles en Provence à l'âge du fer. In X. Delestre (ed.) *15 ans d'archéologie en Provence-Alpes-Côte d'Azur*, 168–77. Aix-en-Provence, Edisud.

Tallah, L. (ed.) (2004) *Le Luberon et Pays d'Apt*. Carte archéologique de la Gaule, 84/2. Paris, Académie des inscriptions et belles-lettres.

Villard, F. (1960) *La céramique grecque de Marseille (VIe IVe siècle), essai d'histoire économique*. Bibliothèque des Ecoles Françaises d'Athènes et de Rome 195. Paris, Boccard.

6

The Attic red-figure pottery of the Greek city of Emporion

M. Teresa Miró i Alaix

The official excavations carried out in Empúries, ancient Emporion (L'Escala, Catalonia), without interruption for a century (from 1908 to present), together with a quantity of material recovered before this date, have demonstrated the importance of Attic red-figure pottery with overpainted decoration in the western Mediterranean. The study of the Attic red-figure pottery of Emporion can help us understand the trade relations in the Mediterranean during the fifth and fourth centuries BC, although the data provided by a single kind of material cannot be extrapolated to define all of the commercial activity; in which case, we would have to take into account the other Greek productions of table wares (East Greek, Western Greek, Corinthian, and Laconian), the rest of Attic pottery (particularly black glaze and black-figure from the end of the fifth and beginning of the fourth century BC), as well as Etruscan and Punic productions, especially *amphorae*. The flow of Attic imports, as the primary imported material during the fifth and fourth centuries BC, has always been used as one of the indices representative of the trade relations between the diverse peoples of the Mediterranean, and this data can be used as a basis for more overall studies.

Recovering the ceramics of Emporion

The material recovered from Emporion comes from three main areas: two inhabited areas (Neapolis and Palaiapolis) and the necropoleis, which enables us to see a differentiation between the kind of pottery found in each of them, with defined functions. The Neapolis is the area where more than 95.5% of the material has been recovered and where we find all the shapes documented and from all the periods, with the exceptions of the Panathenaic amphora, the *alabastron* and the *oinochoe* in the shape of a female head which only appear in funerary contexts (Fig. 6.1). In the Palaiapolis, which has been excavated to a lesser degree, fewer kinds, just drinking

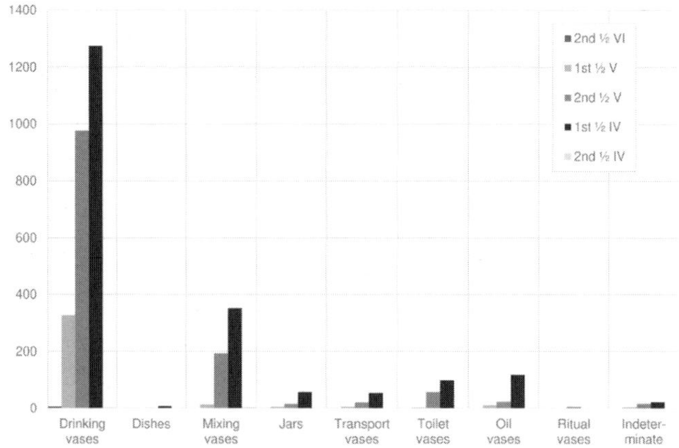

Fig. 6.1. Ceramics recovered from Neapolis, showing the functions of vases from the second half of the sixth to the second half of the fourth century BC.

vessels, mixing vessels, and toilette vessels, have been documented and correspond to 1.6% of the specimens found, which are mainly divided between the first half of the fifth and the first half of the fourth century BC (Fig. 6.2). Finally, it is interesting to consider material from the necropoleis (2.7%), although much of it is out of context, due to tomb robbing. In the necropoleis, perfume vessels are easily predominant, primarily *lekythoi*, and other shapes associated with the funerary sphere, like cups or *kraters*; the material from the necropoleis dates from the beginning of the fifth century to the mid-fourth century (Fig. 6.3).

In Emporion, almost all the shapes made in Attic red-figure pottery can be found. The overwhelming preference was for drinking vessels, particularly cups in the fifth century and *skyphoi* in the fourth century. There was also a heavy presence of mixing vessels, with all the varieties of *krater* represented except volute *kraters*; to a lesser

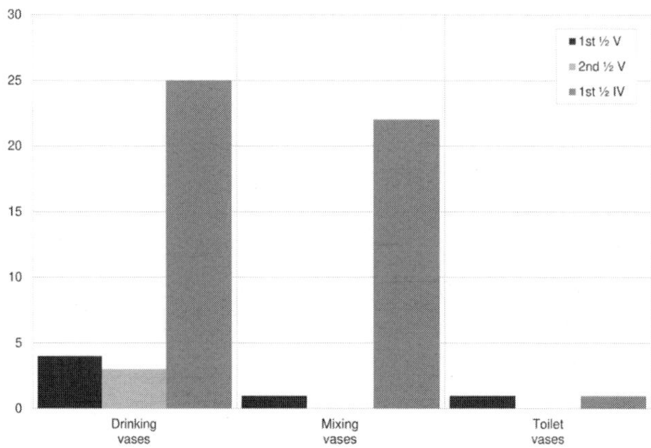

Fig. 6.2. Ceramics recovered from Palaiapolis, showing the functions of vases from the first half of the fifth to the first half of the fourth century BC.

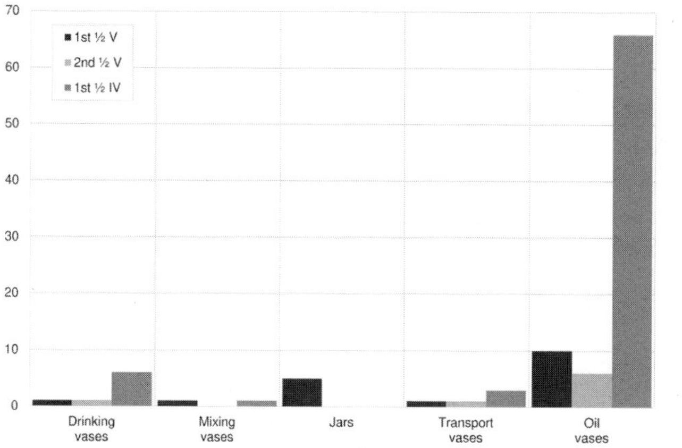

Fig. 6.3. Ceramics recovered from the necropoleis, showing the functions of vases from the first half of the fifth to the first half of the fourth century BC.

degree toilette vessels were present, *lekanides* more than than *pyxides*; perfumes vessels, in which the *lekythoi* were notable for their funeral character; an even smaller proportion of transport vessels, in which *pelikes* are more numerous than *amphorae* and *stamnoi*; as well as serving vessels and ritual vessels, like *loutrophoroi* or *lebetes gamikoi* (Fig. 6.4).

The first red-figure pottery arrived in Emporion at the end of the sixth century BC. Its presence is slight compared to that of Attic black-figure pottery, which is not all that abundant either. There are only six specimens of red-figure cups documented, found in the Neapolis (0.16% of the total), all from the old excavations and found in levels with later dating, which all correspond to the group of drinking vessels. This relative lack of Attic pottery contrasts with the number that Villard (1960) found for Marseilles during the same period, with a strong presence of Attic importations.

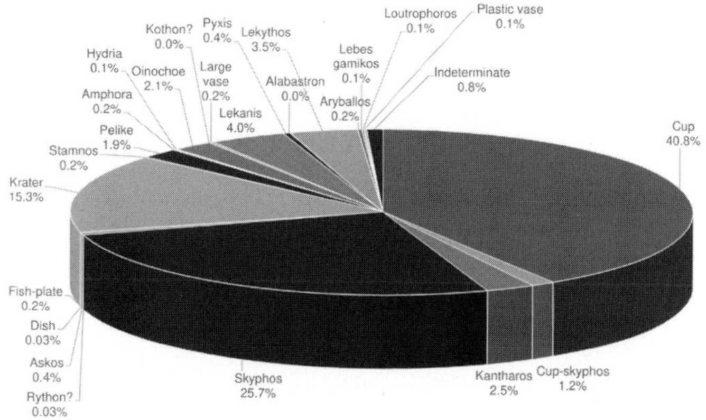

Fig. 6.4. Shapes of Attic red-figure pottery recovered in Emporion.

The fifth-century material

Throughout the fifth century BC, the number of arrivals gradually increased. During the first half of the century, they represented 10% of the total (if we take into account only the levels from the fifth and fourth centuries of the excavations carried out since 1985, they represent 10.73%), with a presence that was notably greater in the second quarter (49 specimens dating from the first quarter and 313 from the second) (Fig. 6.5). During this period, they continued to import the last productions of black-figure vases by the Haimon painter or from the Sappho and Diosphos Workshop, which were fairly widespread in Emporion. Almost all the black-figure vessels from the first half of the fifth century came from the necropolis, compared to the red-figure vessels, which primarily came from the Neapolis. The formal repertoire had broadened, despite the fact that the group of drinking vessels was still the majority, a constant that was maintained in all the periods. Examples from almost all the categories are documented; drinking vessels dominated (88.86%) followed by mixing vessels (3.80%), perfume vessels (2.99%), transport vessels (1.36%), serving vessels (1.36%) and toilette vessels (0.54%). Material was found from the first half of the fifth century in the Neapolis, the Palaiapolis, and the necropoleis. A few specimens from the Neapolis and all of the specimens from the Palaiapolis came from recent excavations, and therefore, come from securely dated contexts. The material from the necropoleis comes almost entirely from purchases made by the museums from clandestine diggers, and is therefore decontextualized. In the cases in which there was no direct information, their origin has been ascribed to the necropoleis as they are vessels with a markedly funerary character (*lekythoi*, *alabastra*). In the tombs from the beginning of the fifth century, excavated by Martín Almagro, such as those of the Bonjoan necropolis, almost all the Attic pottery found is black-figure and only the grave goods of Burial 19 of the Martí necropolis provided red-figure vessels (Almagro 1953). In view of the fact that at this time importations of red-figure exceeded that of black-figure pottery, we must seek an explanation as to why in the necropoleis they still preferred the older style. The vessels that have reached us are of rather good quality, although they cannot be

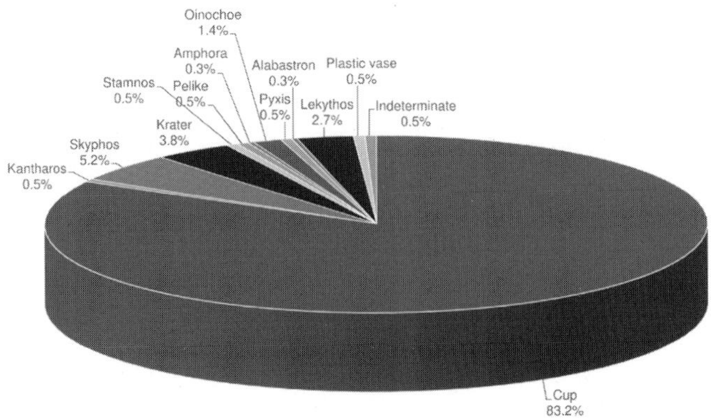

Fig. 6.5. Shapes of Attic red-figure pottery recovered in Emporion. first half of the fifth century.

Fig. 6.6. a. Cup of Makron. b. Krater of the Agrigento Painter.

considered to be deluxe specimens, the works of well-known painters can be found. From the first quarter are the Kleophrades Painter, Makron (Fig. 6.6a) or the Briseis Painter. From the second quarter are painters from the Makron and Douris school, the Painter of Louvre G456, Hermonax, the Providence Painter, the Agrigento Painter (Fig. 6.6b), the Villa Giulia Painter, the Alkimachos Painter, the Sabouroff Painter and the Pan Painter, when the massive arrival of the productions from the workshop of the Penthesilea Painter started.

In the second half of the fifth century BC, the importation of red-figure grew notably, and represented 35.63% (25.63% of the fifth and fourth century material excavated since 1985) (Fig. 6.7). In the third quarter of the fifth century, we can see a slight decrease compared to the previous period, with 247 specimens. Productions from the workshop of the Penthesilea Painter, among other painters like the Kleophon Painter or the Dinos Painter, continued to arrive, with those of the Eretria Painter being noteworthy (Fig. 6.8). In the final quarter of the fifth century, with 551 specimens, the arrivals almost doubled. At that time, the Meidias Painter was notable, together with the Sub-Meidian Cup-group and the Kadmos Painter (Fig. 6.8), and above all we should mention the heavy presence of the class of Saint-Valentin vases, including the *glaux* and the overpainted *skyphos* (Fig. 6.9). The material also comes from all of the areas, but with only a slight presence in the Palaiapolis and the necropoleis. In the Neapolis we have been able to excavate diverse levels from the end of the fifth century that have provided a great deal of material including: Attic black glaze, East Greek, painted and unpainted Iberian, painted Punic, Punic pottery of southern origin, turned and handmade cooking wares, Massalian mortar, indeterminate mortar, and *amphorae* (Corinthian, Samian, East Greek, Massaliote, Etruscan, Punic examples from the central Mediterranean, Punic-Ebusitan, and others from the Strait of Gibraltar area (Sanmartí *et al.* 1986)). The material from the Palaiapolis dating from this time

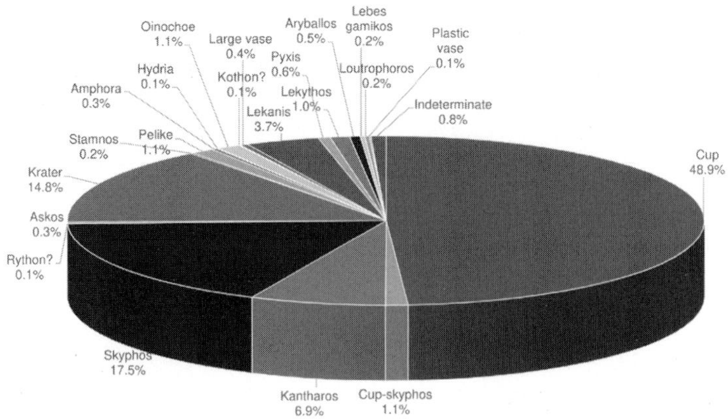

Fig. 6.7. Shapes of Attic red-figure pottery recovered in Emporion. second half of the fifth century.

Fig. 6.8. Kantharos of the Eretria Painter and krater of the Kadmos Painter.

Fig. 6.9. Glaux and skyphos of the class of Saint-Valentin.

corresponds to three sherds from the Almagro excavations. As far as the material from the necropolis is concerned, there is the same problem as for the material from the first half regarding its unknown origin (only 8 specimens from this period have been documented). In this period, a slight decline in the drinking vessels started (74.45%), and there was an increase in the mixing vessels (14.80%), transport vessels (1.60%), serving vessels (1.22%) and ritual vessels (0.46%).

The fourth-century material

During the first half of the fourth century BC imported ceramics were more numerous than in the fifth century, with 54.02% (63.64% of the fourth and fifth century levels of the excavations carried out since 1982), mainly during the first quarter with 568 specimens compared to 336 from the second quarter (Fig. 6.10). From these periods we find the same standardized productions that are found in the rest of the western Mediterranean: cups from the Jena Painter (Fig. 6.11a) and Meleager Painter in the first quarter, and vessels from the Telos Group, the YZ Group, the Group of Vienna 116 (Fig 6.11b), the Fat Boy Group (Fig. 6.11c) and from the Kerch Style (Fig. 6.11d) in the second quarter. As in the other periods, most of the material comes from the Neapolis, where several levels have been excavated, primarily dating from the first quarter of the fourth century, that have provided reliable contexts with the following types of ceramics: Attic black glaze, Massalian black glaze, Greek cooking wares, western Greek pottery, painted Iberian, rough-turned pottery, handmade pottery, Massalian pottery, Punic pottery from the central Mediterranean, pseudo-Ebusitan, Punic mortar, Phoenician *amphorae* from the Strait of Gibraltar area, and Corinthian *amphorae* (Sanmartí *et al.* 1986). Material from the Palaiapolis has also been recovered in recent excavations and dates to the first quarter of the fourth century, the phase which produced the most material from this location (Aquilué 1999; Entorn d'Empúries 2003). With regard to the material from the necropoleis, there are 77 specimens from this period, a good part of which comes from robbed tombs, mainly consisting of squat *lekythoi*, but we also have the excavations of Martín Almagro in which several tombs from these times were documented with red-figure vessels in the Martí necropolis and one in the Bonjoan necropolis, as well as the three tombs found in 1982 in the Parking Lot necropolis just south of the Neapolis (Almagro 1953; Sanmartí, Nolla and Aquilué 1985). In the analysis by functions, we can see how drinking vessels continue to dominate, but with a lower proportion (64.13%), followed by mixing vessels (17.71%), vessels for perfume (5.99%), toilette vessels (5.03%), serving vessels (2.92%), transport vessels (2.77%), and plates (0.35%).

The specimens dating from the second half of the fourth century BC and more specifically to the third quarter of the fourth century are very scarce, seven specimens that represent 0.19% (0.09% of the fourth and fifth century material from the excavations carried out since 1982) are all from the Neapolis showing a sharp drop in the importation of red-figure pottery. The black glaze pottery seems not to be so strongly affected, and ends *c.* 325 BC. Four *kraters* have been documented, two *skyphoi* and one *pelike*.

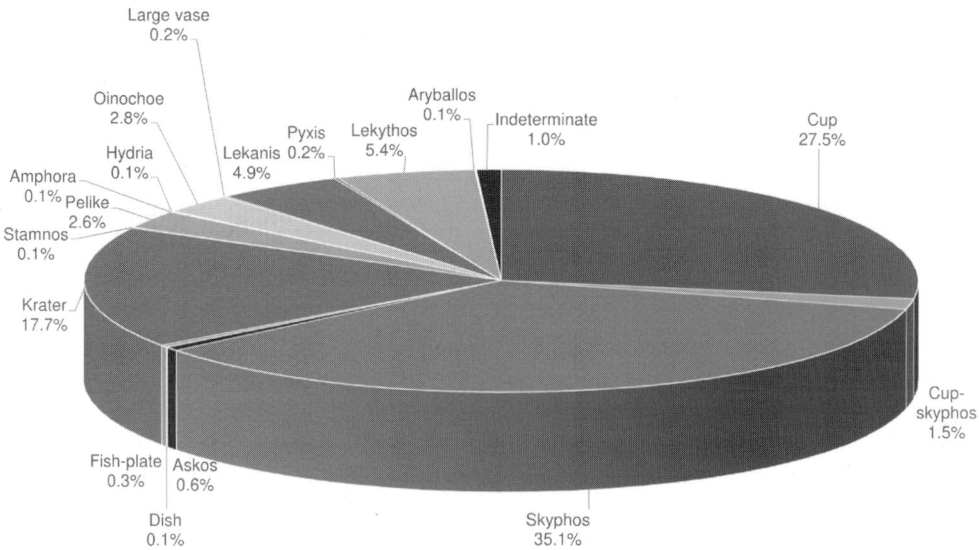

Fig. 6.10. Shapes of Attic red-figure pottery recovered in Emporion. first half of the fourth century.

Creating a new picture

Using the new data provided by this study, which compiles a quantity of material greater than that analyzed in previous studies, one can appreciate a difference in the percentages of Attic red-figure pottery that arrived in Emporion, and therefore, see a change in the trade activity that had been previously proposed for Emporion.

With a sample of 3,680 specimens, the percentages vary from the point of offering 45.90% of material corresponding to the sixth and fifth centuries BC (0.16% to the sixth and 45.62% to the fifth) and 54.1% to the fourth century BC, despite the percentages given by Trias (67.64% and 32.35% of 469 specimens) (Trias 1967), Jully (66.75% and 33.24% of 915 specimens) (Jully 1982–83) and Rouillard (59.9% and 40.1% of 834 specimens) (Rouillard 1991; 1992). In all these cases, we can observe a greater number of imports during the fifth century BC. As you can see, with my sample, the volume of importation of Attic red-figure pottery is very similar in both centuries, with an increase of eight points in the fourth century BC, which contrasts sharply with previously published studies that found differences of between 35 and 20 points for the same time period. If we only analyze the volume of material from the excavations carried out since 1982, which correspond to almost a third of all the material analyzed, this difference with regard to the greater volume of importation in the fourth century is accentuated, which could be as a result of more levels from the fourth century than from the fifth century being excavated. The data from the fifth century accounts for 31.99% and the data from the fourth century accounts for 68.01%; this corresponds to all of the material recovered in excavations since 1982 (1,169 specimens).

Fig. 6.11. a. Cup of the Jena Painter. b. Stemless cup of the Group of the Vienna 116. c. Skyphos of the Fat Boy Group. d. Chous of the Kerch Style.

Considering Emporion and the wider context

This data opens up a new perspective with regard to the importation of Attic pottery to Emporion during this period (fifth to fourth centuries BC) that should be completed with data provided by a study on Attic black glaze pottery, which I do not believe will significantly vary these results with regard to the overall arrivals in one or another century, despite the fact that the volume of importation of black glaze pottery is much more abundant, according to the data provided by the latest excavations, with an exhaustive collection of material, that offers a panorama in which red-figure pottery represents between 8% and 25% of the total of Attic pottery, and it seems unthinkable to believe in a totally different tendency for the material recovered in old excavations. The fact that red-figure table ware is only found in drinking vessels and not in dining vessels, apart from in the fourth century, where we find fish-plates and a dish, leads us to believe that the vessels in the table service for eating must be in black glaze pottery, if we wish to complete a full Attic service, or table wares from other productions, whether imported or locally made.

As far as the other kinds of fine, imported wares present in Emporion are concerned, if we look at just the material published from recent excavations (Sanmartí *et al.* 1986; Sanmartí 1988), we will see that Attic pottery, at the end of the fifth century and beginning of the fourth century BC represents the majority group with a considerable difference from the amount of Western Greek pottery. In fact, the other kinds of ceramics are not significant and correspond to Emporion productions such as Occidental grey pottery or local productions.

Despite the verification of a greater number of imports of Attic red-figure pottery in the fourth century BC, we should not neglect the significant number of specimens from the fifth century BC recovered, above all if we take into account that most of the old levels of the Neapolis have yet to be excavated. This leads us to believe that the volume of Attic material that arrived in Emporion had always been rather high, which confirms the city's constant trade contacts. This great number of arrivals is in sharp contrast to the very small amount of red-figure pottery recovered in the Iberian settlements in Catalonia, which leads us to believe that during the fifth century BC, Attic pottery received in Emporion was destined for domestic use, or at the very most, for trading with the centres that were directly under Emporion's influence, such as Ullastret or Pontós and the settlements in Languedoc. In this sense, we should take into account Padró and Sanmartí's (1987) hypothesis that, at this time, Emporion was too busy in its development as a *polis* to trade with the Iberian towns. This inland destination of most of the red-figure vessels that arrived in Emporion can also be seen in the wide repertoire of local shapes, only explicable in as much as they are commonly used vessels in a Greek city and that have no place in the Iberian settlements.

What seems to be true, however, is that the few red-figure pottery pieces distributed along the Catalan coast during the fifth century BC was due to Emporion acting as the distribution centre. This can be seen in a uniformity of shapes and painters, such as the cup of the Puig de Benicarló attributed to the Penthesilea Painter (Sanmartí and Gusi 1976), a workshop that was widely represented in Emporion, the cup of Vinya del Pau in Vilafranca del Penedès (Ros 2003), a *krater* of the Agrigento Painter of Turó de Ca n'Olivé of Cerdanyola (Asensio *et al.* 2000b), or a cup from Tarragona which should also be placed within the setting of similar productions (Asensio *et al.* 2000a). Nor would it have been unusual that the Attic pottery of Tarragona should have come straight from Massalia, given the large amount of Massalian productions documented (Adserias *et al.* 1993).

The role of Emporion as a re-distributor of Greek pottery during the fifth century BC has also been widely commented by Paloma Cabrera in her studies on Greek trade in Occidental Andalusia (Cabrera 1988–89; Fernández and Cabrera 1989; Cabrera 1994). Emporion acted as an intermediary between the Mediterranean cities with demand for mining, agricultural or fishing products and the areas in which these products were found. Cabrera talks of close relations between Emporion and Gadir from the mid-fifth century BC, as Gadir governed the trade to the southern area of the Iberian Peninsula. This could explain the presence of Attic material with a clear Emporion horizon (cups from the circle of the Marlay Painter, class of Saint-Valentin vases, *skyphoi* with overpainted decoration and *glauces*) in this area and other inland areas, for example, Zalamea. We should also bear in mind the role that the Iberians could have played in the redistribution of Attic material among the Iberian settlements, thanks to their relations with Emporion. The presence of Iberian traders can be verified in the lead letters found in Empúries (Sanmartí and Santiago 1987; 1988) and in Pech Maho (Lejeune, Pouilloux and Solier 1988), and from these texts, we can deduce that there was an active participation of local elements in the trade carried out by the people of Emporion.

Similarly, it is likely that some indigenous settlements would have acted as re-distributors of the Attic material that they received from Emporion among the inland populations such as the trading ports of Montjuïc in Barcelona, a significant site of silos directly related to trade and interchange, close to the Mediterranean Sea and to the estuary of the River Llobregat, a natural port and a centre for the concentration and distribution of goods inland using the Llobregat-Cardener and Llobregat-Anoia rivers, which were navigable in ancient times. Levels from the beginning of the fifth century are documented, with the presence of black-figure Attic pottery, although most of the silos are from the fourth century, the material documented includes Punic *amphorae* (from Ibiza and the Straits of Gibraltar), Massalia, Corinth, Samos, and Rhodes, with specimens that only have parallels close to Empúries (Miró 1998; 2001). Illeta dels Banyets, in Campello (Alacant), is considered a port of trade, where products were exchanged under the protection of a sanctuary, with a significant commercial and maritime activity, where the traders travelled through the valley of the River Sec to the regions of L'Alcoià and El Comtat, which received a repertoire of similar shapes (García Martín 2003). La Picola in Santa Pola (Alacant) was an Iberian settlement that depended on L'Alcúdia, with city walls, which was considered to be an emporium by its excavators and which had a clear commercial orientation (Badie *et al.* 2002).

We have already seen that in Catalonia, with the exception of the area closest to Emporion, the presence of Attic red-figure pottery during the fifth century was highly reduced until 425 BC when a steady increase began. This was also valid for the rest of the Iberian Peninsula in contrast to the south of France where, during the fifth century BC, there was plentiful red-figure Attic material, re-exported from Massalia and Emporion. There are no exceptional pieces, but a wide range of shapes (cups, *lekanides,* and *kraters*) is documented. This can be seen in a chain of settlements along the Mediterranean coast: Ensérune, Montlaurès, La Monediére, Pech Maho, Béziers, La Cayla de Mailhac, Lattes, Arles, and Ruscino. Jully highlighted the role played by Emporion in the trade of Attic pottery to some of those settlements, between which there is a considerable similarity with regard to the presence of the same painters (Jully 1976). Despite the possible activity of Emporion in the trade of Attic pottery in this area, especially in western Languedoc, we should take into account that a good part of the material must have been re-distributed from Massalia, although in the first half of the fifth century, it would seem that there was a collapse of the arrivals of Attic pottery in Massalia. The possible role of the Emporion traders in the distribution of Attic pottery to Languedoc and to Roussillon, apart from the presence of one or another painter, could be seen by the presence or absence of Massalian material as shown by Rouillard when he said

> le rôle de Marseille se dessine, disons plutôt s'esquisse, tout d'abord par rapport à celui d'Ampurias. Dans la région où le rôle d'Ampurias semble prépondérant, nous avons noté que du nord au sud le matériel marseillais se faisait de plus en plus rare (Rouillard 1992, 184).

During the fourth century BC, the role of Emporion as a re-distributor of Attic material in its areas of influence continued to be important, although we should not forget that the Punic traders were also now playing a determining role in the distribution of Attic pottery in the Iberian Peninsula. We need not insist on the importance of the finding of El Sec on the study of the distribution of the trading shipment in the fourth century BC with Greek material of various origins and on the Phoenician-Punic identity of the intermediaries (Trias 1989). Although it may seem that the Punic population and the people of Emporion might have shared some areas for distributing Greek products on the Iberian Peninsula, it is not clear if there was a single intermediary that delivered these goods to a specific place. For example, in Catalonia there is a greater presence of *skyphoi* than *kylikes* unlike in Andalusia, where there are plenty of low-foot *kylikes*, a highly important part of the shipment of El Sec vessels, which is within the Punic area, but on the other hand, the presence of Punic material, whether *amphorae* or not, in Catalonia is highly significant, both to Iberian settlements as well as to Emporion itself, which shows that in Catalonia, Punic trade was just as much or even more consistent than Emporitan trade. If we take the case of the squat *lekythos*, they are only found in large numbers in Emporion and in Ibiza and in both cases in funerary contexts, Greek ones in the case of Emporion, and Punic ones in the case of Ibiza, which could indicate relations between both cities as far as the trading of Attic vessels was concerned (Sánchez 1981). In fact, the amount of Attic material found on the Iberian Peninsula during the fourth century BC is very great, compared to that existing during the previous century, and the co-existence of Emporitan and Punic trading would not have been that unusual, although they would have had favourite distribution areas, at certain times these might have overlapped.

With regard to the distribution of material towards the settlements in the south of France, Emporion probably played a larger role in the fourth century BC when Attic imports to Massalia seem to have decreased (Gantès 2000), and those to Emporion increased. In addition, this city was probably more interested in distributing its own productions of clear paste than material from the other side of the Mediterranean among the nearby populations, as suggested by Ugolini (Ugolini and Olive 1995; Ugolini 2000). In any case, Py states that fourth-century Attic pottery from Lattes came from Massalia, even suggesting a monopoly (Py 1999). Campenon and Chaussery-Laprée (2000) talk about an evident role of Massalia in the redistribution for Martigues, however, they wonder if the Attic vessels were sold as a complement to the Massalian products or on their own. In Agde, the arrival of Attic pottery was much lower than that of Massalia and Emporion, despite the fact that it was also a Greek port (Ugolini 2000), and they would have redistributed Attic vessels to the settlements in their closest area; to Ensérune, where a great amount of Attic pottery arrived in the fourth century, it seems that the most intense influence was that of Emporion (Dubosse 2000). It is probable that there was a diversification in the distribution rather than being characterized by a single focus.

However, if we talk about re-distribution, we should also talk about the way in which Emporion was supplied with Attic pottery, both for its own consumption, as well as for making it the object of exchange in its commercial relations with nearby local populations. In this sense, we should bear in mind several forms. In the first place, there was the direct arrival of Attic pottery from Athens, probably through Emporitan traders. This method seems to have been used throughout the fifth century BC, when Emporion would have provided corn and other kinds of grain to the city of Athens, that desperately needed this product after the supply of grain from Sicily and the Magna Graecia dried up, when these colonies took the side of the Spartans during the Peloponnesian War. Emporion is found in an area where there was a plentiful production of grain, shown by the large number of fields of silos in the Empordà (particularly Mas Castellar of Pontòs as well as Creixell, Ermedàs, Peralada) and in Languedoc (Vallès and Penedès). In addition to the large field of silos in Montjuïc, which could have been for more commercial than agricultural purposes, this area contained numerous fields of silos at Can Xercavins in Cerdanyola del Vallès, Bellaterra, Can Fatjó in Rubí, Can Miano in Sant Feliu, Sitges, Mas Castellar and Vinya del Pau in Vilafranca, Turó de la Canya d'Avinyonet, L'Albornar in Santa Oliva.

The direct relation between Emporion and Athens can be seen in the adoption of the Athenian kind of coin with the head of Athena and the owl when, in the mid-fifth century BC, Emporion minted fractional coins of the drachma, which could be due to the need derived from fixed trade contacts. In addition to the grain, Emporion commercialized other products, such as wine, flax, salted products and minerals, from its immediate area as well as from the southeast of the Iberian Peninsula. During the final years of the sixth century and possibly at the beginning of the fifth century BC, we cannot completely rule out supply via Massalia, although later there was a clear differentiation in the lines of trade for the two cities.

Nor can we exclude the possibility that some loads of Attic pottery arrived in Emporion through Punic traders, particularly in the fourth century BC, when the commercialization of Attic red-figure pottery was more intense in the Iberian Peninsula, in the framework of coastal trading and the release of goods to diverse ports in the Mediterranean. We are aware of fluid economic relations between Emporion and the Punic centre of Gadir and Ebussus, shown by the plentiful presence of Punic material, especially *amphorae*, in the city. In the words of Sanmartí about *amphorae,*

> Con respecto a las ánforas, hay que decir que Ampurias parece estar lejos de haber orbitado alrededor del epicentro económico que representaba Massalia, pues la frecuencia de aparición de los envases de aquel origen, así como de otros productos – cerámicas, morteros, etc – que las acompañaban, se revela muy raquítico. Frente a eso, y a la escasez comprobable de ánforas de origen griego centro-mediterráneo u oriental, se alza la incuestionable superioridad del ánfora de forma púnico-ebusitana que se revela mayoritaria a lo largo de toda la secuencia, igual que ocurre en todos los estratos de los siglos V i IV excavados hasta ahora en la ciudad griega emporitana y junto a ella no faltan nunca – aunque minoritarias – las producciones púnicas del Mediterráneo Central o las fenicias del Círculo del Estrecho de Gibraltar, que vienen sin embargo a corroborar una probable llegada de las primeras desde la isla de Ibiza en donde ellas, a su vez, habrian encontrado la base de redistribución para acceder a las costas peninsulares. Da hecho, esta observación con respecto a las ánforas viene a corroborar las intensas relaciones económicas entre Ampurias e Ibiza puestas ya en evidencia hace algún tiempo a través del análisis de la cerámica ática que procedente de Ibiza se conserva en el Museo Arqueológico Nacional de Madrid (Sanmartí 1988, 118–119).

In any case, it would seem more logical that it would have been Emporion that distributed the Greek pottery to the Punic centres rather than the other way round.

The importations of Attic pottery to Emporion were initially destined to supply the needs of a Greek city. This can be seen by the wide formal repertoire, in which we find, in a certain quantity, diverse kinds of vessels which had functions characteristic of the Greek world: *lekythoi* destined for the funerary world, toilette vessels such as *lekanides* and *pyxides* which were an important feature in adornment, and ritual vessels such as *loutrophoroi* and the *lebetes gamikoi* that only had meaning within the setting of wedding ceremonies. Despite the fact that some of these shapes, such as *lekanides* and *lekythoi*, can be found in local settlements, they are nothing like the proportions that we find in Emporion. The heavy presence of drinking vessels, accompanied by others corresponding to the table service, such as mixing vessels and serving vessels, related to the banquet tradition and the consumption of wine in the Greek fashion: wine that would arrive in red-figure containers such as *stamnoi*, *amphorae*, and *pelikes*, apart from being imported in transport *amphorae*. Speaking of shapes, as mentioned previously almost all the shapes that exist in Attic red-figure pottery can be found in Emporion, apart from some rare ones. In the fifth century, many of the shapes that arrived, such as the cup, were difficult to package and transport, meaning that its considerable presence shows that there must have been a strong demand for these products that compensated the risk of transporting them from Athens.

The rest of the material was destined for re-distribution among the local settlements of the Iberian Peninsula and some sites in Languedoc, in exchange for obtaining the products that would serve the Emporitans to trade with Athens and other Mediterranean cities as well as covering their own needs. Emporion was a Greek city without a defined territory, despite the fact that sometimes the existence of an Emporitan chora has been talked about, that would perhaps have more commercial than political meaning. This lack of territory meant that it would have had to acquire the raw materials for its subsistence, as well as products manufactured as basic products. Emporion commercialized products from around the Mediterranean, among which Attic pottery would have played an important role, in exchange for grain and metals, which it re-exported to Athens, and Punic cities or other Greek cities in the western Mediterranean, such as Massalia.

Final considerations

To sum up, Attic red-figure pottery started to arrive in Emporion, although sparingly, from the beginning of its manufacture at the end of the sixth century. Over the fifth and fourth centuries, importation gradually increased until *c.* 350 when a decline began, and stopped arriving completely by *c.* 325 BC.

In Emporion, almost all the shapes of the Attic red-figure repertoire can be found. The overwhelming preference was for drinking vessels, particularly cups in the fifth century and *skyphoi* in the fourth century; there was also a heavy presence of mixing vessels, with all of the varieties of *krater* represented except volute ones; to a lesser degree toilette vessels arrived, *lekanides* rather than *pyxides*, and vessels for perfume, in which the *lekythoi* were notable for their funerary character, and an even smaller proportion of transport vessels, particularly *pelikes,* as well as *amphorae* and *stamnoi*, and also serving vessels and ritual vessels.

As far as the documented painters are concerned, in the fifth century there was quite a variety and an acceptable quality, although this did not include the deluxe vessels of the great masters. A notable amount came from the workshop of the Penthesilea Painter and the productions linked to the class of Saint-Valentin vases, the Marlay Painter, and reserved and overpainted *skyphoi*, possibly from the same Attic workshop. In the fourth century, the same kind of productions documented in the rest of the western

Mediterranean arrived: Telos Group, Group of the Vienna 116, and the Fat Boy Group. At an iconographic level, there were more real-life scenes than mythological ones. The most represented scenes are those that refer to the palaestra and the symposium.

Emporion played an important role in the re-distribution of Attic material in Catalonia, the Iberian Peninsula and Languedoc. During the fifth century it was the main, if not the only, distributor of Attic pottery to the Iberian towns and the Punic centres on the Peninsula, including for Cadiz and Ibiza, which simultaneously became centres of redistribution along with Massalia in its role for areas along the Gulf of Roses and the River Hérault. After the fourth century, redistribution to its areas of influence continued but seemingly lost markets in favour of the Punic traders.

Bibliography

Adserias, M., Burés, L., Miró, M. T. and Ramon, E (1993) L'assentament pre-romà de Tarragona, *Revista d'Arqueologia de Ponent* 3, 177–227, Lleida.

Almagro, M. (1949) Cerámica griega gris de los siglos VI y V a. de J. C. en Ampurias, *Rivista di Studi Liguri* 15, 62–122, Bordighera.

Almagro, M. (1953) *Las necrópolis de Ampurias, vol. I. Introducción y necrópolis griegas*, Monografías Ampuritanas III, Barcelona, Seix y Barral.

Almagro, M. (1964) *Excavaciones en la Palaiápolis de Ampurias*, Excavaciones arqueológicas en España 27, Madrid.

Aquilué, X. (dir.) (1999) *Intervencions arqueològiques a Sant Martí d'Empúries (1994–1996). De l'assentament precolonial a l'Empúries actual*, Monografies Emporitanes, 9, Girona, Museu d'Arqueologia de Catalunya-Empúries.

Asensio, D., Ciuraneta, M., Martorell, S. and Otiña, P. (2000a) L'assentament ibèric de Tarragona, L'excavació arqueològica al carrer dels Caputxins, núm. 24, l'any 1978, *Tàrraco 99. Arqueologia d'una capital provincial romana (Tarragona 15, 16 i 17 d'abril de 1999)*, 71–82, Tarragona, Universitat Rovira i Virgili.

Asensio, D., Francés, J., Ferrer, C., Guàrdia, M. and Sala, O. (2000b) La ceràmica àtica del Turó de Ca n'Olivé (Cerdanyola del Vallès, Barcelona). Comerç i distribució de vaixella fina importada a la Catalunya central (segles V i IV aC), *III Reunió sobre Economia en el Món Ibèric (València, 24–27 de novembre de 1999). Saguntum Papeles del Laboratorio de Arqueología de Valencia. Extra 3*, 369–380, València.

Badie, A., Gailledrat, E., Moret, P., Rouillard, P., Sánchez, M. J. and Sillières, P. (2002) *Le site antique de La Picola à Santa Pola (Alicante, Espagne)*, Paris-Madrid, Casa de Velázquez.

Cabrera, P. (1988–89) El comercio foceo en Huelva: cronología y fisionomía, *Tartessos y Huelva. Huelva arqueológica* X-XI, 41–100, 3, Huelva.

Cabrera, P. (1994) Cádiz y el comercio de productos griegos en Andalucía Occidental durante los siglos V y IV a.C., *Trabajos de Prehistoria, 51–2*, 89–102, Madrid.

Campenon, C. and Chausserie-Laprée, J. (2000) La céramique attique de Martigues au IVe siècle, *La céramique attique du IVe siècle en Méditerranée Occidentale. Actes du colloque international organisé par le Centre Camille Jullian, (Arles, 7–9 décembre 1995)*, 145–158, Napoli.

Dubosse, C. (2000) La céramique attique du IVe siècle d'Ensérune, *La céramique attique du IVe siècle en Méditerranée Occidentale. Actes du colloque international organisé par le Centre Camille Jullian, (Arles, 7–9 décembre 1995)*, 209–216, Napoli.

Entorn d'Empúries (2003) *10 anys d'arqueologia a l'entorn d'Empúries (1993–2002)*. Exposició Casa dels Forestals de Sant Martí d'Empúries (Del 6 de juliol al 30 de setembre de 2003), L'Escala, Ajuntament de l'Escala and Museu d'Arqueologia de Catalunya-Empúries.

Fernández, J. and Cabrera, P. (1989) Comercio griego en Huelva a fines del siglo V aC, *Grecs et ibères au IVe siècle avant Jésus-Christ. Commerce et iconographie. (Table Ronde Bordeaux 16–18 decembre 1986). Revue des Études Anciennes* LXXXIX 3–4, 149–159, Bordeaux.

Gantès, L-F. (2000) La place de la céramique attique dans une cité grecque de l'Extrême-Occident au IVe s.: l'exemple de Marseille, *La céramique attique du IVe siècle en Méditerranée Occidentale. Actes du colloque international organisé par le Centre Camille Jullian, (Arles, 7–9 décembre 1995)*, 131–144, Napoli.

García Martín, J. M. (2003) *La distribución de cerámica griega en la Contestania ibérica: el puerto comercial de La Illeta dels Banyets*, Alacant, Instituto Alicantino de Cultura "Juan Gil-Albert".

Jully, J-J. (1976) Les importacions attiques dans la Neapolis d'Ampurias du VIe s. au IVe s, *Revue Belge de Philologie et d'Histoire*, 25–51, Bruxelles.

Jully, J-J. (1982–83) *Céramiques grecques ou de type grec et autres céramiques en Languedoc Mediterranéen, Roussillon et Catalogne. VIIe-IVe s. avant notre ère et leur contexte socio-culturel*, Besançon, Centre de Recherches d'Histoire Ancienne, Université de Besançon.

Lejeune, M., Pouilloux, J. and Solier, Y. (1988) Étrusque et ionien archaïques sur un plomb de Pech Maho (Aude), *Revue Archéologique de la Narbonnaise* 21, 19–59, Montpellier.

Miró, C. (2001) Els ibers al Pla de Barcelona: el poblat ibèric de Montjuïc, *De* Barcino *a* Barcinona *(segles I-VII). Les restes arqueològiques de la plaça del Rei de Barcelona*, 112–139, Barcelona, Museu d'Història de la Ciutat.

Miró, M. T. (1998) La ceràmica àtica de figures roges d'Empúries. Una aproximació al seu estudi tipològic, *Empúries*, 51, 127–138, Barcelona.

Miró, M. T. (2006) *La ceràmica àtica de figures roges de la ciutat grega d'Emporion*, Monografies Emporitanes 14, Barcelona, Museu d'Arqueologia de Catalunya-Empúries.

Padró, J. and Sanmartí, J. (1987) L'ocupació del territori per la polis emporitana i la seva significació econòmica. Algunes hipòtesis, *Fonaments*, 6, 23–26, Barcelona.

Pons, E. (dir.) (2002) *Mas Castellar de Pontós (Alt Empordà). Un complex arqueològic d'època ibèrica (excavacions 1990–1998)*, Sèrie Monogràfica del Museu d'Arqueologia de Catalunya-Girona, 21, Girona, Museu d'Arqueologia de Catalunya-Girona.

Py, M. (1999) Le facies de la céramique lattoise du IVe siècle avant notre ère, *Recherches sur le quatriême siècle avant notre ère à Lattes*, Lattara 12, 287–438, Lattes.

Ros, A. (2003) El camp de sitges de Vinya d'en Pau (Vilafranca del Penedès), revalorització dels materials dipositats al Museu de Vilafranca, *Revista d'Arqueologia de Ponent, 13*, 191–209, Lleida.

Rouillard, P. (1991) *Les Grecs et la Peninsule Ibérique du VIIIe au IVe siècle avant Jésus-Christ*, Paris, Publications du Centre Pierre Paris.

Rouillard, P. (1992) La place de Marseille dans le commerce des vases attiques à figures rouges en Méditerranée occidentale (V^e^-IVe s. av.J.-C.), *Marseille grecque et la Gaule (Marseille, 18–23 novembre 1993)*, Études Massaliètes, 3, 179–187, Lattes/Aix-en-Provence.

Sánchez, C. (1981) La cerámica ática de Ibiza en el Museo Arqueológico Nacional, *Trabajos de Prehistoria* 38, 281–316, Madrid.

Sanmartí, E. (1988) Datación de la muralla griega meridional de Ampurias y caracterización de la facies cerámica de la ciudad en la primera mitad del siglo IV a. de J. C., *Colloque Grecs et Ibères, (Bordeaux 1986), Revue des Études Anciennes XC*, 99–137, Bordeaux.

Sanmartí, E., Castanyer, P., Tremoleda, J. and Barberà, J. (1986) Las estructuras griegas de los siglos V y IV a. de J. C., halladas en el sector sur de la Neápolis de Ampurias (campaña de excavaciones del año 1986), *Cuadernos de Prehistoria y Arqueología Castellonenses* 12, 141–184, Castelló.

Sanmartí, E. and Gusi, F. (1976) Un kylix del Pintor de Pentesilea procedente del poblado ilercavón de El Puig (Benicarló, Castellón), *Cuadernos de Prehistoria y Arqueología Castellonenses 3*, 205–218, Castelló.

Sanmartí, E., Nolla, J. M. and Aquilué, X. (1985) Les excavacions a l'àrea del pàrking al sud de la Neàpolis d'Empúries (informe preliminar), *Empúries* 45, 110–150, Barcelona.

Sanmartí, E. and Santiago, R. (1987) Une lettre sur plomb trouvée à Emporion (fouilles 1985), *Zeitschrift für Papyrologie und Epigraphik* 68, 119–127.

Sanmartí, E. and Santiago, R. (1988) La lettre grecque d'Emporion et son contexte archéologique, *Revue Archéologique de la Narbonnaisse* 21, 3–17, Montpellier.

Trias, G. (1967) *Cerámicas griegas de la Península Ibérica*, València, The William L. Bryant Foundation.

Trias, G. (1989) El Sec: la cerámica ática de figuras rojas, *Grecs et ibères au IVe siècle avant Jésus-Christ. Commerce et iconographie, (Table Ronde Bordeaux 16-18 decembre 1986,) Revue des Études Anciennes* LXXXIX 3–4, 21–49, Bordeaux.

Ugolini, D. and Olive, C. (1995) La céramique attique de Béziers (VIe-IVe s.). Approche de la diffusion et de l'utilisation de la vaisselle attique en Languedoc Occidental, *Sur les pas des Grecs en Occident, Hommage a André Nickels, Études massaliétes* 4, 237–260, Lattes.

Ugolini, D. (2000) La céramique attique d'Agde dans le cadre du Languedoc central et occidental. *La céramique attique du IVe siècle en Méditerranée Occidentale. Actes du colloque international organisé par le Centre Camille Jullian, (Arles, 7-9 décembre 1995)*, 201–208, Napoli.

Villard, F. (1960) *La céramique grecque de Marseille (VIe-IVe siècles). Essai d'histoire économique*, Paris.

7

Pistiros: A Thracian emporion in its cultural and natural environment

Alexei Gotzev

The study of Thracian settlement archaeology has really developed in the last 15–20 years. This has been achieved despite the constant struggle against the temptation of researching only extraordinary monuments, and despite the difficulties posed by the lack of a complete strategy for investigation of settlements from the first millennium BC. Despite this, archaeological investigations of settlements grow rapidly and the results are evident. Investigations are conducted on important settlement sites from different regions of Ancient Thrace. The immediate publication of results, the holding of symposia, and routine scientific discussions have become good practice. There is a tendency to reconsider and revise the results from earlier investigations of settlements of all types in order to achieve a more complete analysis of all the available data seen through the prism of contemporary archaeological methodologies. This paper features data from several main settlement sites which illustrate the problems of this kind of archaeological research, permit comparison between the separate monuments and draw a pattern of the development of the settlement structure in Thrace during the first millennium BC.

The archaeological site at Adzijska Vodenica in the area of Vetren town is distinctive among settlement sites south of the Balkans. The site, discovered by the late Prof. M. Domaradzki, and identified with ancient Pistiros, has been researched extensively and without interruption for 20 years, and for four to five months annually.

What makes Pistiros different? First of all, a unique combination of four international expeditions are researching Pistiros and its environs. Representatives from four different European archaeological institutions are present, each with their own methodical and organizational characteristics. Colleagues from the Charles University in Prague (Czech Republic), from the Liverpool University (Great Britain), and from the French School of Archaeology in Athens concentrated their efforts in different parts of the site as well as its surroundings. On the Bulgarian side, the National Archaeological Institute with Museum, the Bulgarian Academy of Sciences, the Archaeological Museum 'Professor M. Domaradzki' in the town of Septemvri, the National Historical Museum in Sofia, and the Regional Historical Museum in the town of Pazardzik are involved in the archaeological research. The aim is to compare the results achieved from each team at the end of the project and to draw some common conclusions regarding the evolution of the emporion during the second half of the first millennium BC.

The main research topics that were under investigation for the first ten years of archaeological research of the site were:

- tracking archaeologically the main three periods of development of this site.
- identifying the chronology, characteristics and dimension of cult practices in the site and as well their connection to the trace of metalworking documented within the frames of the emporion.
- analyzing the particular dynamics of the architectural evolution of the site owing to the periodical floods of the terrain caused by the Maritza river as well as the documented consecutive destruction levels caused by fires.
- investigating possible interactions between Thracians, Greeks, and eventually Celts on the base of a precise dating of the registered situations during the investigation of Pistiros and via a proper cultural and historical analysis.
- defining its location and its role in the settlement structure in the region of Upper Maritza river and parts of the West Rhodopi mountain in the middle of the first millennium BC.
- researching and explaining the development of the settlement structure before the foundation of the emporion in the region and also the changes that had occurred during its existence and afterwards.

The results from the research are published promptly and thus the scientific information for the development of the settlement structure in Ancient Thrace is constantly renewed. Apart from the three volumes on Pistiros (Bouzek *et al.* 1996; 2002; 2007), some major aspects of the research of the emporion were published in a Prague series (Bouzek *et al.* 2003).

Experts from other spheres also contributed to the explanation of the characteristics of the site. Palaeobiologists, osteologists, geomorphologists, and experts in making and working with metals, for example, contribute to the interpretation of the interaction between the archaeological site and its environment (Popova 1996; Baltakov *et al.* 2002; Salibras 2007; Sarafov 2007).

The famous inscription found in the environs of the site, which outlines the protection given to Greek traders at the site, points to the character of the site and even determines its name – an emporion in the heart of Thrace (Velkov and Domaradzka 1996).

When examining the characteristics of Pistiros we cannot neglect the wealth of archaeological materials and the diversity of structures and contexts. The reasons for this are complex. The frequent floods from the river and the repeated devastations caused by fires have given favourable circumstances for archaeological explorations (Domaradzki 2002, 18–24).

The numerous epigraphic and numismatic materials are useful for discussing the ethnic peculiarities of the inhabitants of the emporion, its leading characteristics, direction and intensity of its economical contacts (Taneva 1996; 2002; Bouzek *et al.* 2007; Domaradzka 2002; 2007). On the basis of past research, combined with the attained results from the recent expeditions, we can present a tentative scheme which defines the evolution of Pistiros (Bouzek *et al.* 2007, 11).

The natural environment of Pistiros

Research into the natural environment is at an early stage. We know little about the flora, fauna, and climate in this part of Ancient Thrace in the first millennium BC. This circumstance forces us to select carefully the natural factors which may be analyzed – *i.e.* those elements which have not changed dramatically for the last 2,500 years. Examples of these are, for instance, the relief of the area, water sources, and ore deposits (as far as there is information for their exploitation).

The location of Pistiros is exceptionally favourable. There, in the valley of Upper Maritza, the plain meets the mountain, and therefore the inhabitants were capable of utilizing the advantages of both. Surrounded by mountain massifs from 3 sides, Pistiros had abundant raw materials at its disposal – a fact which undoubtedly contributed to its prosperity. On the other hand, the closeness of the river Maritza and the plain situated to the East provided the habitants of the emporion with excellent communications. However, there are some peculiarities in this location of the site in one flat area. Such a location is a relatively uncommon practice in the Early Iron Age Thracian settlement system until this time. Usually settlements were located at the foot of the mountain or at isolated heights, which could be seen along the valley of the river Maritza. This location meant that both the growth of agriculture (in the flat area) and stock-rising and/or metallurgic activity (in the uplands) could be combined (Gotzev 1997, 409–412). Undoubtedly proximity to the river was essential as an opportunity for establishing contacts in the east and southeast directions and because of this other favourable possibilities for the location of Pistiros were neglected.

Assuming that the climate did not change dramatically during the past centuries, climate is also a factor conducive to settlement in the region of the Upper Maritza. Recent research indicates that this is the second sunniest region in Bulgaria (Sarafov 2007, 281–282).

Pistiros and its cultural environment

Communications

The emporion of Pistiros had an important role in defining communications in the region of the Upper Maritza. I will examine two (out of the many) important, communication routes in which the emporion of Pistiros takes part. The first is the Diagonal Road which in ancient times crossed the Balkans and connected the region around Belgrade with Byzantium. The other route is the so called Trans-Rhodopian roads which made possible communication between the people of the Aegean region with those from the inner part of Ancient Thrace. There are different opinions about the exact location of the latter but undoubtedly from the middle of the first millennium BC different contacts and interactions between the areas of Middle Mesta and Upper Maritza were established. At each end of this road the settlement centres at Koprivlen (see Koprivlen 2002) and Pistiros were located.

Situated on the point where both routes crossed, Pistiros undoubtedly took advantage of the opportunities to make contacts of all types and from any direction. The matter of whether and to where the river Maritza was navigable is still unknown, but the discovery of a large number of amphorae at Pistiros indicates that it was used for transporting goods at least this far. At the same time there is an indication that the Trans-Rhodopian road was used as well. Its route can be outlined by the mountain sanctuaries in West Rhodopi, which have been located in recent years. There are several reasons for the origin of these (in most cases they appear in the middle of the first millennium or a little earlier) but the main one is the advantage for establishing contact given by the natural route through the steep terrain.

The distance between the town of Koprivlen and the emporion of Pistiros is about 80–100 km and could be traversed on foot in 3–5 days. If horses were used (without carts because of the mountain terrain) this time could be shortened. Calculations show that the time needed to transport a load from Pistiros to Thasos using the river (river Maritza) and the sea (from the outflow of the river near Ainos) would have been about a month or a little less (Bouzek 1996, 221–222).

It should not be assumed that one or other type of route (river or road) was chosen in antiquity. Rather they were combined. It is likely that seasonally both routes were used. A good comparison with this situation is the (much later) one in Klondike, as described by Jack London in *Burning Daylight*. In this example supplies were delivered mainly through river Yukon when weather conditions allowed but mountain passes were also used for communications of other types.

Undoubtedly the emporion at Pistiros was a major node through which the Greeks established trade with the local Thracian tribes. The main raw material which attracted the attention of the ancient Greeks was metal. The remains of metallurgy and metalworking activity from the territory of the emporion were numerous. However, the preliminary dating of the metallurgy of the site, along with its character and extent, are still matters of controversy (Katincarova 1996, 103–108; 2005, 189).

Settlement structure

The programme of 'Surface Investigations and Sondages' commenced in 1995 and contributed a lot of information about the archaeological situation during the first millennium in the region of the Upper Maritza and the Western Rhodopi. This territory is one of the best archaeologically researched areas in Bulgaria, though most information is of a preliminary nature, and there is a lot of evidence for the existence of sites (and for human presence of different types) from the period which concerns us (Domaradzki 1996, 31–34; Chankowski and Gotzev 2002, 279–282).

There is a strange configuration of the settlement system in the environs of Pistiros. First of all, there are no Thracian settlements from the time immediately before the foundation of the emporion. The total terrain excavations in the period 1998–2002 resulted in nothing (Gotzev 2007, 111–112). Moreover, the human traces from Late Iron Age, *i.e.* the time after the foundation of the emporion, are individual and the surface observation gave no certain evidence for the existence of any settlement that could be dominated by, or even connected to Pistiros. Even the sondage excavations did not reveal anything about the settlement structure (Chankowski *et al.* 2004–2005, 1246–1253).

This anomaly in the settlement system could be explained in several ways. It may be that this pattern of settlement in the valley of Upper Maritza during the first millennium is due to secondary factors – alluviums which cover the valley of the river and were accumulated basically in the end of the millennium (Domaradzki 1996, 32). However, if these natural factors are not the cause, then it could be appropriate to accept that we are faced with a particular region which was not inhabited – due to the natural environment or perhaps some kind of religious taboo, or even perhaps because this region was assigned to the Greek colonials by the Thracian ruler as the inscription from Vetren perhaps implies (Velkov and Domaradzka 1996, 209–211).

Burial evidence

Regarding the necropoleis situated near Pisteros there are also many open questions. First of all, the necropolis of Pistiros itself has not yet been localized. This fact may lead us to speculate on its characteristics. First of all, we should consider whether this necropolis used mounds (a sustainable Thracian tradition) or was a flat one (closer to the Greek funeral practices from the middle of the millennium BC). Whilst more difficult to locate, a flat necropolis could be discovered by a consistent research with different geophysical methods or by chance. However, there are some funeral mounds outside the emporion at Pistiros. In one of them a stone tomb with a double burial was excavated which dates from the fourth century BC (Venedikov 1946, 194–196; Bouzek *et al.* 2006, 68–69).

Another funerary structure (this time entirely demolished) is the tomb with a circular central chamber found about three kilometers south of Pisteros in Malko Belovo (Velkov 1942, 37–44; Rousseva 2000, 124). In addition, excavated, but still not published entirely, is a mound necropolis, three kilometers west of Pistiros, which contains materials that coincide with the flourishing period of the site as well as some common elements from Thracian and Greek funerary practices. (Gizdova 2005, 115–121).

Evidence for cult activity

Another very interesting debate concerns the famous cult places in this area and the reasons for their appearance and connection to the site. First I should mention a famous cult monument near the village of Dolna Veselitza which was partially researched by sondage excavations in 2002 (Chankowski *et al.* 2004–2005, 1242–1245).

This is a cult monument that dates centuries earlier than the foundation of Pistiros, *i.e.* to the very beginning of the Early Iron Age (the end of the second to the beginning of the first millennium BC). It was most probably included in the system of Thracian cult centres which arose during this period, some of which existed even earlier. The rest of the famous cult places which coincide with the existence of Pistiros present an interesting pattern. It is possible that every cult centre along the north and south or southwest periphery of the Rhodope Mountains is an indicator of the existence of roads that cross the mountain (Gotzev 2005, 160–161).

Specific rituals may have been practised there which were thought to favour the safe passing through the inhospitable territory of the mountains. Equally, it is impossible to exclude the role of the mineral springs which were used by the local tribes and were respectfully honoured. Such an explanation regarding the location of cult places has grounding near the sites around the village Varvara where there are warm mineral springs (Gotzev 2007, 114). There is probably a cult centre situated east of Malko Belovo next to a destroyed beehive tomb (Chankowski *et al.* 2004–2005). The cult character of this site is as yet doubted, and it has not yet been researched in detail, but the cult hypothesis seems more probable in comparison with the idea that it was a settlement. The lack of settlement remains and the character of the cult layer and the finds support this hypothesis (Chankowski *et al.* 2004–2005, 1241–1242).

When we discuss a system of Thracian cult places in the West Rhodopi mountain from the second half of the first millennium, we should not neglect the idea that metallurgically-rich areas were a factor in defining the hierarchical pattern of Thracian 'holy places'. Because of the now well-known density of such cult places in these regions it cannot be merely accepted that these were cult centres for separate tribes but rather sanctuaries with significance and a role as meeting places and centres of integration between the tribes. It is very probable that the communications orientated north–south through the mountains, and metallurgic centres were the basic factors which formed the system of Thracian sanctuaries after the sixth century BC in the Western Rhodopi. The distinct traces of identical cult activities (registered by archaeological methods) also connect the existence of Pistiros with this system of religious centres in the area south of its territory.

Conclusion

The location of Pistiros is therefore very useful to us in determining the cultural interactions in this area and the trading links which we now know to have penetrated into the very heart of Ancient Thrace. Pistiros did not just happen to be on the crossroads – it was located there in order to exploit the trade routes which came north from the Aegean, by river and road, and across the Thracian territory which lay between Asia Minor and Central Europe.

Bibliography

Baltakov, G., Kenderova, R. and Fitova, E. (1996) Composing the geomorphological map of the Pistiros region for archaeological purposes. In J. Bouzek, L. Domaradzka and Z. Archibald (eds) *Pistiros* II. Excavations and Studies, 303–306. Prague, Charles University.

Bouzek J. (1996) Pistiros like a river Harbour: Sea and River transport in Antiquity and its Costs. In J. Bouzek, M. Domaradzki and Z. Archibald (eds) *Pistiros I. Excavations and Studies*, 221–222. Prague, Charles University.

Bouzek J., Domaradzki M. and Archibald Z. (eds) (1996) *Pistiros I. Excavations and Studies*. Prague, Charles University.

Bouzek J., Domaradzka L. and Archibald Z. (eds) (2002) *Pistiros* II. Excavations and Studies. Prague, Charles University.

Bouzek J., Domaradzka L. and Archibald Z. (eds) (2007) *Pistiros III. Excavations and Studies*. Prague, Charles University.

Bouzek, J., Musil, J. and Ondrejova, I. (2003) *Studia Hercyna VII*. Prague, Redactional Board.

Bouzek, J., Archibald, Z., Domaradska L., Gotzev, A., Katincharova D., Lazov G., Taneva V., Kolarova V., Yurikova Y., Ivanova, E. and Angelov, N. (2006) Емпорион Пистирос в Тракия. Проучвания и резултати (1998–2005). В – Поселищен животв Тракия. IV Международен симпозиум. 9–11 ноември 2005, 41–70. Издателство „Я." Ямбол.

Bouzek, J., Ruckl, S., Titz, P. and Tsotzev C. (2007) Trade amphorae. In J. Bouzek, L. Domaradzka and Z. Archibald (eds) *Pistiros III. Excavations and Studies*, 133–138. Prague, Charles University.

Domaradzka, L. (2002) Catalogue of graffiti discovered during the excavations at Pistiros – Vetren (1988–1998). Part one: Graffiti on imported fine pottery. In J. Bouzek, L. Domaradzka and Z. Archibald (eds) *Pistiros* II. Excavations and Studies, 209–228. Prague, Charles University.

Chankowski, V., Gotzev, A. and Nehrizov, G. (2004–2005). Pistiros: Etudes et Rapports. *Bulletin de Correspondance Hellenique* 128–129, 2. 1. 1225–1253.

Chankowski, V. and Gotzev, A. (2002) Pistiros et son environnement: Les premiers resultats de la prospection Franco-Bulgare. In J. Bouzek, L. Domaradzka and Z. Archibald (eds) *Pistiros II. Excavation and studies*, 271–282. Prague, Charles University.

Domaradzka, L. (2007) Catalogue of graffiti discovered at Pistiros – Vetren (1988–2004). Part two: Graffiti on pottery, used in the household. In J. Bouzek, L. Domaradzka and Z. Archibald (eds) *Pistiros III. Excavations and Studies*, 221–235. Prague, Charles University.

Domaradzki, M. (2002) An interim report on investigations at Vetren-Pistiros 1995–1998. In J. Bouzek, L. Domaradzka and Z. Archibald (eds) *Pistiros* II. Excavations and Studies, 11–29. Prague, Charles University.

Gotzev, A. (1997) Characteristics of the settlement system during the Early Iron Age in Ancient Thrace. In H. Andersen, H. Horsnaes, S. Houby-Nielsen and S. Rathje (eds) *Urbanization in the Mediterranean in the 9th to 6th Centuries BC, Acta Hyperborea* 7, 407–421. Copenhagen, Museum Tusculanum Press.

Gotzev, A. (2005) Contribution to the study of the Thracian cult practices of the 1st millenium BC in the Western Rhodopes. In J. Bouzek and L. Domaradzka (eds) *The Culture of Thracians and their Neighbours. Proceedings of the International Symposium in Memory of Prof. Mieczyslav Domaradzki, with a Round Table "Archaeological Map of Bulgaria"*, British Archaeological Reports International Series 1350, 156–162. Oxford, Archaeopress.

Gotzev A. (2007) Field Survey in the Environs of Vetren – Pistiros (1998–2004). In J. Bouzek, L. Domaradzka and Z. Archibald (eds) *Pistiros III. Excavations and Studies*, 111–16. Prague, Charles University.

Gotzev A. (2010). Thracian Cult Places in West Rhodopa Mountain, 1st. Millenium BC. In I. Candea, (ed.) *The Thracians and their Neighbors in Antiquity. Studia in Honorem Valeriu Sirbu*, 227–256. Braila, Muzeul Brăilei, Editura Istros.

Katincarova, D. (2005) Находища на метални руди със следи от металургична дейност от късножелязната епоха в района на емпорион „Пистирос." In Земите на България - люлка на тракийската цивилизацияр II том. Ред. Г. Китов, Д. Димитрова, 188–93. Университетско издателство „Св. Климент Охридски", София.

Katincarova-Bogdanova, D. (1996) Traces of metallurgical activity in the emporion. In J. Bouzek, M. Domaradzki and Z. Archibald (eds) *Pistiros I. Excavations and Studies.* 103–108. Prague, Charles University.

Koprivlen I: Bozkova, A. and Detev, P. (eds) *Koprivlen vol. 1. Rescue archaeological excavations on the road Gotze Delchev - Drama 1998-1999.* Sofia, NOUS Publishers.

Popova, T. (1996): The archaeobotanic samples from the clay altars. In J. Bouzek, M. Domaradzki and Z. Archibald (eds) *Pistiros I. Excavations and Studies,* 173–174. Prague, Charles University.

Rousseva, M. (2000) *Thracian Cult Architecture in Bulgaria.* Yambol, NOUS Publishers.

Salibras, S. (2007) Research questions and some preliminary results for the animal bones from excavations in Adjiska vodenitsa, Vetren, Bulgaria. In J. Bouzek, L. Domaradzka and Z. Archibald (eds) *Pistiros III. Excavations and Studies,* 264–271. Prague, Charles University.

Sarafov, A. (2007) Contemporary environment in the ancient emporion Pistiros in Thrace. In J. Bouzek, L. Domaradzka and Z. Archibald (eds) *Pistiros III. Excavations and Studies,* 280–282. Prague, Charles University.

Taneva, V. (1996) Seuthes III coins from Pistiros. In J. Bouzek, M. Domaradzki and Z. Archibald (eds) *Pistiros I. Excavations and Studies,* 115–116. Prague, Charles University.

Taneva, V. (2002) Coins of Macedonian rulers found in Pistiros. In J. Bouzek, L. Domaradzka and Z. Archibald (eds) *Pistiros* II. Excavations and Studies, 255–270. Prague, Charles University.

Тонкова М., Гоцев А. (ред. 2008) Тракийското светилище при Бабяк и неговата археологическа среда. София.

Velkov, I. (1942) Новооткрита куполна гробница при с. Малко Белово. Годишник на Народния археологически музей VII, 37–44.

Velkov, V. and Domaradzka L. (1996) Kotys I (383/359 BC) and emporion Pistiros. In J. Bouzek, M. Domaradzki and Z. Archibald (eds) *Pistiros I. Excavations and Studies,* 205–216. Prague, Charles University.

Venedikov, I. (1946) Тракийска гробница при с. Ветрен, Пазарджишко. Известия на българския археологически институт XV, 194–196.

8

The landscape in Aegean Thrace before and after Greek colonization

Diamandis Triandaphyllos

The settling of Greek colonists on the shores of the north Aegean was a momentous event which radically transformed the economic, geopolitical, and cultural landscape of Aegean Thrace. Literary sources have preserved very little information about the changes brought about by the colonists' activities. Archaeological research has added some important data, though certainly not enough to cover every aspect of the issue.

The testimonies from the sources concerning the Thracian tribes of the area are fragmentary. It is impossible, therefore, to define precisely the geographical boundaries of each tribe, in any given historical period, although general areas inhabited by each can be suggested. The Nestos region was home to the Sintoi or Saioi, who were identified with the Sapaioi in the days of Strabo (12. 3. 20, C549–550). The Lake Bistonis region may have been inhabited by the Bistonians. This is however believed by some researchers to have been a mythological rather than a historical tribe. The wider Ismarus region, which according to Herodotus (7.108) was known as Briantike, and formerly as Gallaïke, belonged to the Kikones, whom we know from Homer (Odyssey 9. 39–55). The name seems to have a geographical-mythological character and is not mentioned after the Persian Wars and the founding of the kingdom of the Odrysians. On the western bank of Hebros lived the Paitoi, who are mentioned by Herodotus as the easternmost tribe.

Surface investigations in the highlands of Rhodope and Ismarus, and in the plains and coastal regions, over the last three decades, have led to the discovery of archaeological sites dating from the end of the Late Bronze Age to the seventh century BC. In addition to the well-known acropolises of Ergane (or Asar Tepe) (Tsimbidis-Pentazos 1971, 90–93), Aghios Georgios of Maroneia (Tsimbidis-Pentazos 1971, 97–101; 1972, 90–93; Triandaphyllos 1987–90, 302) and Aghios Georgios of Petrota (Tsimbidis-Pentazos 1971, 93–94), other settlements, fortified enclosures and animal husbandry facilities have also been discovered on hilltops and slopes (Triandaphyllos 1990, 683–691). These sites have yielded handmade polished or unpolished vases with ribbing and grooves or with incised and impressed geometric designs.

Cemeteries of the Early Iron Age (ninth to eighth centuries BC) have been discovered in the villages of Roussa, Kotronia, and Koila (Triandaphyllos 1980, 145–163). These are large cist graves (dolmens), built of slabs of schist in the megalithic tradition of the southeastern Rhodope, although they are not as large as the monuments of Bulgaria and Turkey. The pottery includes *krater*-shaped vases and amphoras used as funerary urns, as well as cups and kantharoi offered to the deceased as funeral gifts. Many are decorated with characteristic horn-shaped protrusions (Buckelkeramik), grooves, and incised or impressed geometric designs. The rock-cut tombs of Askites and Petrota, which have a semicircular or rectangular floor plan and alcoves for offerings, date to the same period (Fig. 8.1). Sections of enclosures, rock-hewn altars (Fig. 8.2), niches and offering basins, discs of the sun, and cup-marks (Fig. 8.3) have all been discovered in the open-air sanctuaries on hilltops (Triandaphyllos 1985, 129–134). The sanctuaries are also associated with the rock engravings (Fig. 8.4) with incised or hammered designs, usually interpreted as having magical or apotropaic significance. Many hills with early Iron Age settlements became shrines to the Thracian Horseman Hero in the years of the Roman Empire (Triandaphyllos 1985, 134–140).

Fig. 8.1. Rock-cut tomb in Askites.

Fig. 8.2. Altar in the sanctuary of Monastiri Lofos.

Fig. 8.3. Cup-marks in Pandrossos.

Fig. 8.4. Rock-engravings in Roussa.

Abdera

Abdera was founded by the Clazomenians, led by Timesius, in 654 BC, in the bay of a large gulf near the mouth of the Nestos River (Fig. 8.5). The residents of Teos settled in the same spot in 545 BC. Excavations have brought to light sections of enclosures belonging to two building phases in the archaic period (Koukouli-Chryssanthaki 1997, 715–734; 2004, 235–248). The finds also indicate that the archaic cemeteries were in use throughout the sixth century BC, discrediting the testimony of sources that claim the Clazomenian settlers were immediately killed off by the Thracian tribes (Fig. 8.6) (Skarlatidou 1987, 421–429; 2004, 258). The inhabitants also suffered from malaria, as confirmed by a bone matter study (Agelarakis 2004, 339–341); this seems to have been the chief reason for the first settlement's gradual deterioration.

The founding myth of Abdera, which involves the eighth labour of Hercules, Diomedes, king of the Bistonians, and Abderus, eponymous hero of the city, provides a mythological link between the settlers and the Bistonians. But in the period when the settlement was founded, the inhabitants of the region are described as the Sapaioi. Pindar refers to the attacks of the Paionians against the Abderites, who defeated them in the battle of Melamphyllon (Pindar 59–70). Another battle followed against unidentified Thracians near the Strymon or Nestos River (Pindar 73–79). The Paionians were not immediate neighbours of the Abderites; they lived a considerable distance to the west, in the vicinity of Mount Pangaion and the Strymon River.

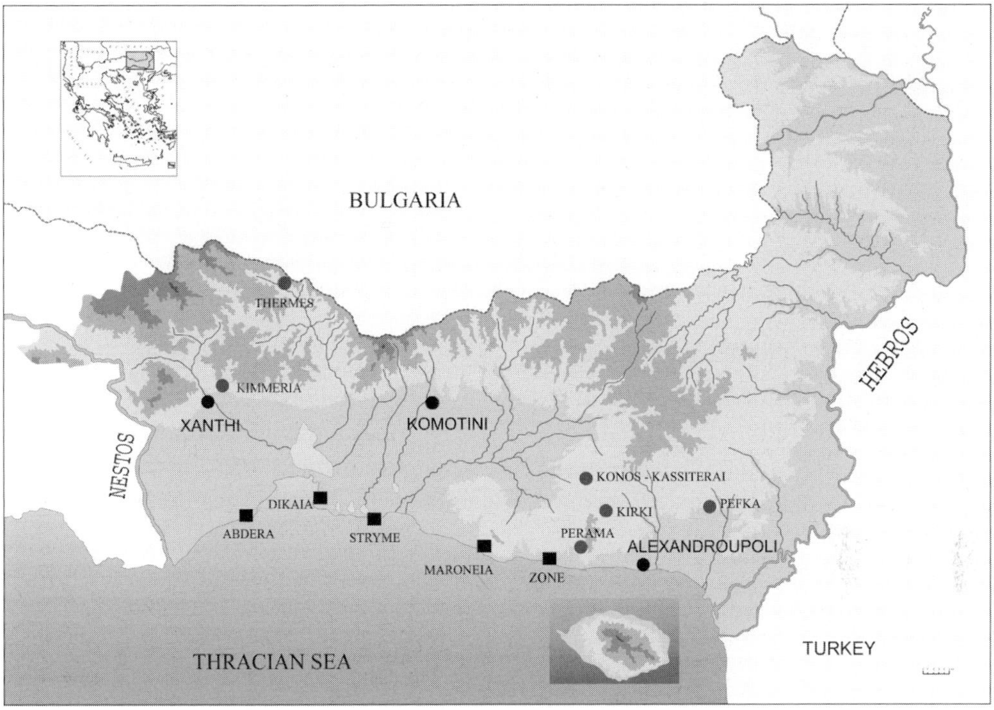

Fig. 8.5. Map of the Greek colonies (squares) and sites with precious metals (circles) mentioned in the text. The Hebros and Nestos rivers and the modern cities of Xanthi, Komotini, and Alexandroupoli are also shown. Darker shading indicates higher elevation.

Fig. 8.6. Abdera: vases from the archaic cemetery.

The continual flooding of the Nestos river resulted in the gradual filling of the bay with silt, forcing the Abderites to transfer their city further to the south, near the open sea, in the fourth century BC (Syrides and Psilovikos 2004, 351–354; Triandaphyllos 2004, 261–269). The acropolis and the new city enclosure were built there. Under the acropolis, they built a pier with large cornerstones to protect the main harbour. A second harbour with a pier was on the east side of the city. Remnants of the two piers still survive underwater. The filling in of the bay was a purely natural event, according to the results of geological studies. However, a future geo-morphological study should examine whether harbours and other sewer and drainage systems built by the settlers contributed to the elimination of the gulf, and to what degree.

Enormous quantities of building materials were needed to rebuild the extensive walls, piers, and public and private buildings. The nearby Mandra region had ancient limestone quarries, in which the quarry faces and beds for extracting stone are still visible. The bulk of the material was derived from this site, but we do not know for certain when the quarries were in use. Traces of quarrying have also been found on other nearby hills.

Agricultural production, especially the cultivation of grapes and cereals, was a basic factor in the development of the economy from the start (Pindar 25–26, 60). These products were intended for exports as well as for local consumption. It is therefore reasonable to conclude that extensive areas were deforested to obtain the large plots of land necessary for cultivation.

Apart from the main highway networks leading inland and to nearby cities, many rural roads must have been opened to facilitate access to the fields and to transport products. Thucydides mentions the road from Abdera to Istros, a journey which a young man in good physical condition could cover in 11 days (Thucydides 2.97.1–3).

Fishing enjoyed a prominent place in the city's economy. Athenaeus mentions the famous '*kestreis*', the pikes of Abdera, and the cuttlefish caught between Abdera and Maroneia (Athenaeus 7.77 (307b), 7.124 (324b)). Ever greater expanses of forest had to be cut down on the banks of the neighbouring rivers and lakes, and even on the northern hills of Rhodope, in order to provide timber, firewood, and ships for fishing and war.

The lavish series of silver and gold coins, which entered circulation around 520/15 BC and were widely used in the distant lands of the east, along with the city's great contributions to the Athenian alliance, attest that the city had access to sources of precious metals (IThrAeg, 173). Near the village of Kimmeria in Xanthi, where a metal mine has been in operation in recent years, chemical and micro-stereoscopic analyses confirmed the presence of gold and silver in the rocks. (Vavelidis *et al.* 1992, 297–308). Alluvial gold was also discovered in the local waterfall. It is thus possible that these sources were being mined in antiquity, and that there may even have been wells and tunnels which have been destroyed by the more recent exploitation of the site.

Fig. 8.7. Abdera: Clazomenian sarcophagus of Troilos.

The presence of slag from the smelting of metals, and the analyses of gold grains from the villages of Thermes and Kalotycho in Xanthi and of alluvial gold grains from the Kompsatos River, which has the same source, all indicate that gold and silver may have been mined in these regions of Rhodope (see Fig. 8.5) (Vavelidis 1995, 207–209). After all, the economic relationships that developed with the Thracians of the hinterland would have involved the trade in precious metals, which are abundant even today in the northernmost section of the Rhodope mountain range, in the territory of modern Bulgaria.

One characteristic feature of the extensive cemeteries of Abdera are the scattered burial mounds, isolated or in clusters, erected to cover the sarcophagus burials of wealthy individuals and families. The construction of the mounds began in the late sixth to early fifth centuries BC and continued until the late fourth to early third centuries BC (Kallintzi 1997, 828–831; 2004, 274–276) (Fig. 8.7). Therefore, the graves belong to the Teos settlers, who began to bury their dead in mounds, with rich grave goods as soon as their economic situation improved (Fig. 8.8).

Stryme

In the absence of epigraphic information, the ruins of a fortified city on the peninsula of Molyvoti, which date to the fifth and fourth centuries BC, have been identified with Stryme, which is mentioned in the sources as a colony or emporion of Thasos (Stefanus Byzantius: Strymi; Souda: Strymi) (see Fig. 8.5). Herodotus' information about the geographical site of the city is unclear (7.108–109). If the literary testimony concerning the strife between Thasians and Maronites in the middle of the seventh century BC is accurate, the city must have already existed before then (Harpocration, Archilochus F 146, Filochorus (FGrHist 328) F 43 (128)). But the oldest pottery samples can be dated only to the late sixth or early fifth centuries BC. The city was destroyed *c.* 350 BC, possibly as a result of an alliance between the Maronites and Philip II (Bakalakis 1967, 145).

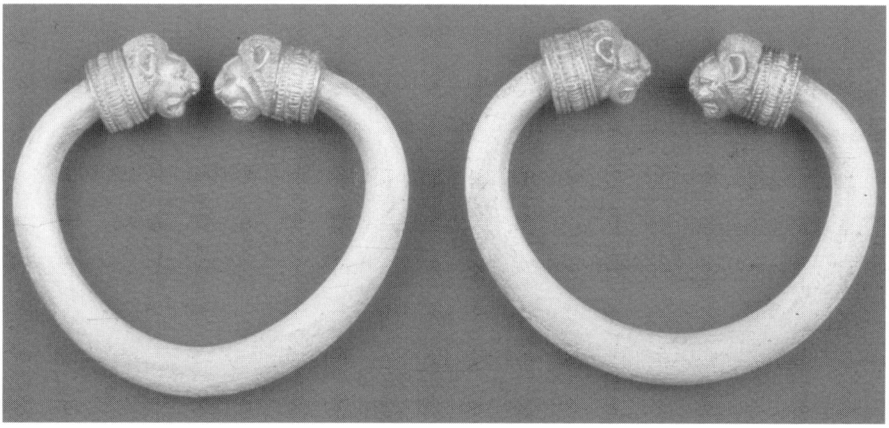

Fig. 8.8. Abdera cemetery: silver bracelets.

In literary sources, Stryme appears as an island (Souda: Strymi) which later joined with the neighbouring shoreline to become the modern-day peninsula. A systematic geo-morphological study could verify this information and detect possible interventions by the inhabitants which accelerated the fusion of the island with the mainland. The city's economy was mainly based on cultivation of grain in the nearby fertile plains, as well as on trade with the native inhabitants of the region.

The lack of drinking water led the residents to construct a public work which is rather significant from a technical and hydraulic perspective, and which is comparable to the 'Eupalinian aqueduct' of Samos, though it is much smaller (Bakalakis 1967, 38–45). On the modern shore of the archaeological site, which was created after the erosion of a large piece of land into the sea, we may discern the mouths of three tunnels leading to underground aqueducts. The two L-shaped tunnels are probably the northern part of the original four-sided aqueduct. The water would seep through the soft stone and, guided by conduits carved in the rock, it would gather in the wells that were placed at intervals along the bottom of the tunnels. The water was pumped up through surface wells, which were located directly above the underground wells. The third mouth belongs to a simple tunnel of a similar type, leading to a rectangular reservoir.

One transformation in the natural landscape of the area, extending north of the ancient city, is the construction of large burial mounds for interment of wealthy individuals, as in the Abdera cemetery. The tombs that have been excavated date to the second half of the fifth century BC (see Fig. 8.9) (Triandaphyllos 1992, 655–667; 2000, 87–104).

Maroneia

Maroneia was founded by Chian colonists in the land of the Kikones before the middle of the seventh century BC (Skymnos, 676–678) (Fig. 8.5). Strabo mentions Xantheia, Maroneia, and Ismaros as cities of the Kikones (7a. 1. 44). The acropolis on the summit of Ismaros mountain, Aghios Georgios, and the walls that extend to the shore, have been identified with Ismaros or Ismara (Triandaphyllos 1987–90, 302). In lexicographical sources, Maroneia is identified with Ismaros, the Homeric city of the Kikones (Souda: oinos ismarikos).

The information in Herodotus about the geographical location of the city is unclear. The ruins on the southwestern sides of Ismaros mountain, from the peak of Aghios Athanasios to the harbour of Aghios Charalambos, were identified, based on epigraphic evidence, with the Maroneia of Hellenistic, Roman, and Byzantine times. One critical problem for researchers is the absence of finds from the archaic period. If the location of Ismaros has been determined correctly, and since Maroneia and Ismaros are identified in the written sources, then it is possible that the first colonists settled in the Aghios Georgios area. When they later decided to expand their city to a larger, more comfortable size, they transferred it to the location of Hellenistic and Roman Maroneia. They may alternatively have settled in another neighbouring site that still

Fig. 8.9. Stryme: white-ground lekythos from a fifth-century BC tomb.

remains unknown. Since Maroneia has been inhabited for so long, it is also possible that we have not yet discovered the archaic strata, or that these strata are in an as yet undetermined location. Future excavations will confirm or disprove these hypotheses.

It has been suggested that the mythological cycle of Maron, a priest of Apollo who lived in the god's sacred grove in Ismaros, his meeting with Odysseus, the appearance of the horse as a symbol of Maroneia, and the cult of Maron and Apollo constitute evidence signifying peaceful relations and co-existence between the Kikones and the Greek colonists (Triandaphyllos 1987–90, 302, 312).

The imposing acropolis of Aghios Georgios, the palatial building, the walls circling the area down to the shore, and the megalithic gate were constructed out of the hard local igneous rock, which is a pluton composed of monzonite. At the Kouvouki site, traces of quarrying and stonecutting have been detected (Melfos and Vavelidis 2000, 67–70). In other locations, the large boulders common to the region bear traces of having been worked. Incisions, into which wedges were inserted and struck until a chunk of stone was broken off, are visible (Fig. 8.10). There is also evidence of working on the two monolithic pillars of the gate in the western wall. The acropolis and the walls of Ismaros have not been dated with precision. The early Iron Age pottery leads us to date the quarrying and the erection of the walls to the ninth and eighth centuries BC (Triandaphyllos 1987–90, 302).

Fig. 8.10. Stones with traces of quarrying.

Fig. 8.11. The theatre of Maroneia.

The acropolis and walls of Hellenistic Maroneia were built in the middle of the fourth century BC. The walls, along with their circular and rectangular towers, are built from local gneiss and crumbling granite. They enclose a large area, from the peak of Aghios Athanasios all the way down to the sea, where there was a harbour with a quay and a pier (Lazaridis 1971, 41–42; Tsimbidis-Pentazos 1971, 102–104, 110). The theatre and the mosaic floor of one house are the famous monuments of the ancient city (Figs 8.11, 8.12).

The city's economy was based on agriculture (particularly the cultivation of olives and grapes) and animal husbandry – occupations still practised to the present day. Maroneia was famous in antiquity for horse breeding. Until recently, experienced Maronites tamed the wild horses that lived in the Ismaros region. The gentle slopes and plateaus around the city would have been deforested very early on to be converted into olive groves and vineyards.

The appearance of the place name 'Maroneia' in the Laurion area, where artisans and metalworkers from Maroneia had settled, attests to the Maronites' involvement in exploiting the metal ore in the Ismaros and Rhodope regions (Kakavoghiannis 2005, 89). The circulation of coins from the end of the sixth century BC, the payment of taxes to the Athenian alliance beginning in 454 BC, and the appearance of numismatic types of the city in the coins of Thracian kings all indicate that Maroneia had access to sources of metal.

Fig. 8.12. Maroneia: mosaic floor of one house.

Fig. 8.13. Maroneia: crowning member of a grave stele.

Metalliferous deposits containing gold have been discovered along the Lissos and Makropotamos rivers and their tributaries, as well as in the Xylagani area. The gold appears as small flakes or isolated grains, or mixed with quartz and iron pyrite (Vavelidis 2001, 24–33). In the Konos-Kassiterai area, in the Sapai district, mine galleries have been discovered, but there is no evidence of their precise date. These mines were probably for extracting gold and silver, as the metal that appears in this region consists of mixtures of gold with tellurium and silver (Vavelidis 2001, 34–37).

At Ktismata Hill (Mal-Tepe), south of Aghios Georgios, a mining well was discovered with three gradually descending spiral galleries (Triandaphyllos 1987–90, 304; 1973, 463–464). Chemical analysis has shown that the metal ore contains iron and manganese, as well as other elements which have a negative impact on the smelting of the iron-rich ore. A lekanis-shaped vessel found at the entrance of the largest gallery dates to the middle of the second century BC. Potsherds discovered at the bottom of the well date to the same century (Papastamataki *et al.* 2001, 617–631). The mine may have been abandoned due to the lack of extractable copper, or the presence of harmful elements which prevented the successful smelting of iron. At the shore of the Marmaritsa site, east of Aghios Charalambos, iron deposits appear in the marble. The extraction of iron from this site in modern times suggests the possibility of similar activity in antiquity.

There is no testimony about the roads leading from Maroneia inland or to neighbouring cities. Herodotus (7.109) mentions one road near the sea, which was followed by one of the three divisions of Xerxes' army in order to stay in touch with the ships sailing along the coast. This road went through the pass as Akra Maroneias, where a stone-paved path from the Ottoman period is still preserved (Triandaphyllos 1987–90, 303).

Between Maroneia and Aghios Georgios, at the site of Marmaritsa, six marble quarries have been discovered. The marble is coarse-grained, white to whitish-grey in colour, and in some areas consists of large asbestite crystals (Melfos and Vavelidis 2000, 70–76). The stone was extracted from large gradated surfaces, beginning from the top and working down to the bottom. The extraction technique followed the geological and tectonic features of the stone. It is estimated that over 4,500 m^3 of marble were mined, to be used in the construction of buildings, architectural members, sculptures, and inscribed stelae (Fig. 8.13). It is not known when the quarry first went into operation, but it may be linked to the city's peak period in the fourth century BC, when extensive construction was being performed. The quarries remained in use during Hellenistic and Roman times.

In the artificial riverbed of the Lissos River, near the village of Mikro Doukato, a region that lay within the limits of the broader Maroneia's territory, tombs have been discovered which provide interesting information about the relations between colonists and locals. Based on the pottery and bronze fibulae, the tombs have been dated to the first half of the sixth century BC. The same region has yielded pottery of the well-known Psenicevo and Cepina types, familiar from Bulgaria, which date to before the establishment of the settlers. The presence of Ionian pottery, some of which is related to the pottery of Thasos, along with finds following Balkan and particularly Thracian cultural traditions, indicates that the inhabitants of the Thracian settlement that was near the cemetery remained there even after the settlers arrived. The finds from the tombs reveal for the first time the co-existence of Greek and Thracian cultural elements, and therefore the early influence of Greek art (Triandaphyllos 1983, 194–196).

Zone

Zone appears in the sources as a city of the Kikones located on the western edge of the shore of Doriskos, near the cape of Serreion (Herodotus, 7.59. Stephanus Byzantius: Zoni). It is mentioned, along with Drys, as one of the *emporia* along the continental coast opposite Samothrace (Skylax 67). It is situated in a beautiful natural spot, the southern foothills of the Zonaia mountain, whose oak forests were associated with Orpheus. The region was praised by the poets Apollonius Rhodius (Argonautica 1.23–34) and Nicander (Theraica 458–462).

Based on the large number of coins found in excavations, Zone has been identified with the ruins of the ancient settlement until now known as Mesembria (see Fig. 8.5). Herodotus mentions Mesembria as a *polis* (7.108), and also mentions Zone in another passage (7.59). Jugs with incised decoration, cups with beveled rims, bronze fibulae, and many sherds of handmade pottery bearing incised and grooved decoration were found at the site of the old necropolis. All these finds date from the mid-eighth to the mid-seventh century BC (Vavritsas 1966, 70; 1967, 93–94; Triandaphyllos 1987–90, 306–307) and indicate that a Thracian settlement existed before the founding of Zone at the end of the seventh century BC. In light of this, it has been suggested that the name of the Thracian settlement of Mesembria was retained as the name of the new city, which was later renamed to Zone, explaining why it no longer appears in the sources (Triandaphyllos 1987–90, 308). Of course, there is also a conflicting view, namely that Mesembria was much further west, at the site of the present-day beach of Petrota (Tsatsopoulou 1996, 922). The peaceful co-existence of Greeks and Thracians is attested by inscriptions written in Greek characters in the Thracian dialect, as well as Thracian names.

Excavations have brought to light parts of the city wall, the sanctuary of Apollo, the sanctuary of Demeter, streets, private residences, professional spaces, and the walled settlement in the southwest quadrant of the city. The finds testify that the city was inhabited from the archaic period to the third century BC, when its decline set in (Tsatsopoulou 1997, 615–630).

The large quantities of materials necessary to rebuild the city were extracted from local quarries. Two ancient quarries have been discovered. The first is along the shore, at the Moussá Vrysi site, approximately 2 kilometres west of the city. This was a limestone quarry. The second was found on a hilltop about a kilometre northwest of the city. This was a quarry for calc-schist and grey marble. The limestone is particularly hard and ranges in colour from orange-pink to pinkish-white. It was mined over open gradated surfaces, with access from south to north. The extraction technique was simple, and followed the geological and tectonic features of the stone. Over the entire period of the mine's exploitation, over 4,000 m^3 were removed, and used in the construction of the fortification, buildings, and architectural members. The extraction of limestone must have started in the late seventh century BC, as is attested by a portion of the western wall, which is built out of this limestone, in the Lesbian masonry style (Vavelidis 2001, 69–72).

The intricate gold and silver jewellery found in tombs (Figs 8.14, 8.15), the extensive trade relations attested by the finds, and the series of bronze coins all confirm access to metal ores or to trade in precious metals. Geological studies have shown that there are gold veins along the Hebros and Arda rivers in Bulgaria, which supply these rivers with gold. There is testimony that alluvial gold was extracted from the Hebros in the early nineteenth century (Vavelidis 2001, 19–23).

In Kirki, where metal mines have been in operation in recent years, older mineshafts have been discovered, which cannot be dated due to the collapse of their walls. Since analysis has shown a very high content of gold and silver, it is quite likely that they were used to extract these metals (Vavelidis *et al.* 1989, 350–365; Vavelidis 2001, 37–38).

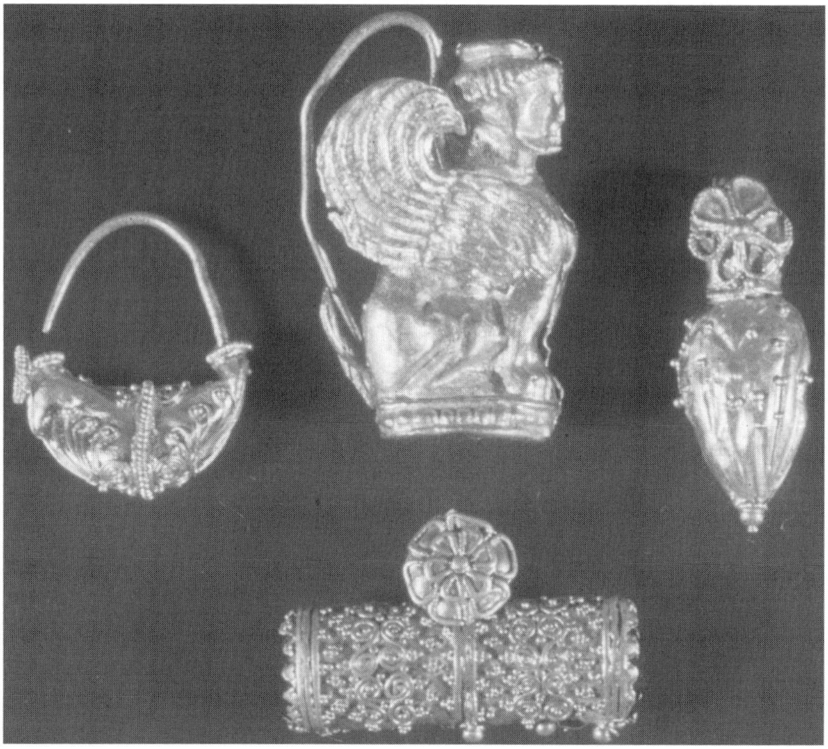

Fig. 8.14. Zone cemetery: gold jewellery.

In the Pefka area, veins of silver, lead and zinc ore have been discovered. Lead and zinc was intensively extracted during the 1950s using shafts and wells (Vavelidis 2001, 38–40).

In the Perama area, and on Mavrokorfi, there are also deposits rich in precious metals, which have recently attracted the close interest of a gold mining corporation (Vavelidis 2001, 40–41).

The gold and silver finds prove that the inhabitants of Zone had a profound expertise in metalworking. But to prove whether the metal was extracted from the above sites, specialized analyses of lead, osmium and, rhenium isotopes will have to be conducted, since the processed metal retains the same ratio of isotopes as the original ore (Vavelidis 2001, 51).

Conclusion

This has been a very brief survey of the evidence, but it has shown that the intensive exploitation of wealth-producing sources by the Greek colonies to achieve rapid economic development affected the natural environment of the region irrevocably. The evidence presented here cannot adequately cover such important subjects as the foundation of the Greek colonies, the activities of the colonists, the effects on the natural environment, and the relations between the colonists and the native inhabitants of the region. Researchers will continually return to the questions and problems posed by these areas of research. This article has shown that it is crucial that geological and geo-morphological studies be conducted in all the coastal colonies, in order to help answer questions relating to the environment and the exploitation of

Fig. 8.15. Zone cemetery: silver votive plaque.

natural resources, and that such studies should go hand in hand with historical and archaeological investigations.

Abbreviation

IThrAeg = Inscriptiones antiquae parties Thraciae quae ad ora maris Aegaei sita est.

Bibliography

Agelarakis, A. (2004) The Clazomenian Colonization Endeavor at Abdera in Retrospect: Evidence from the Anthropological Record. In A. Moustaka, E. Skarlatidou, M.-C. Tzannes and Y. Ersoy (eds) *Klazomenai, Teos and Abdera: metropoleis and colony. Proceedings of the International Symposium held at the Archaeological Museum of Abdera, Abdera, 20–21 October 2001*, 327–349. Thessaloniki, University Studio Press.

Bakalakis, G. (1967) Ανασκαφή Στρύμης. Επιστημονική Επετηρίς Φιλοσοφικής Σχολής Πανεπιστημίου Θεσσαλονίκης, παραρτημα 13, Θεσσαλονίκη, Αριστοτελειον Πανεπιστημιον Θεσσαλονικησ.

Kakavoghiannis, E. (2005) Μέταλλα εργάσιμα και συγκεχωρημένα. Η οργάνωση της εκμετάλλευσης του ορυκτού πλούτου της Λαυρεωτικής από την Αθηναϊκή Δημοκρατία. Δημοσιεύματα του Αρχαιολογικού Δελτίου αρ. 90. Αθήνα.

Kallintzi, D. (1997) Έθιμα ταφής στα αρχαία Άβδηρα. Ταφικές πρακτικές και εθιμικές πράξεις από τα μέσα του 6ου ως τα μέσα του 3ου αι. π.Χ. In D. Triandaphyllos and D. Terzopoulou (eds) Αρχαία Θράκη, Πρακτικά του 2ου Διεθνούς Συμποσίου Θρακικών Σπουδών, Σεπτέμβριος 1992, 807–839. Κομοτηνή.

Kallintzi, D. (2004) Abdera: Organization and Utilization of the Area Extra Muros. In A. Moustaka, E. Skarlatidou, M.-C. Tzannes and Y. Ersoy (eds) *Klazomenai, Teos and Abdera: metropoleis and colony. Proceedings of the International Symposium held at the Archaeological Museum of Abdera, Abdera, 20–21 October 2001*, 271–289. Thessaloniki, University Studio Press.

Koukouli-Chryssanthaki, Ch. (1997) Η αρχαϊκή πόλη των Αβδήρων, Β. Αρχαιολογικές έρευνες. In D. Triandaphyllos and D. Terzopoulou (eds) Αρχαία Θράκη, Πρακτικά του 2ου Διεθνούς Συμποσίου Θρακικών Σπουδών, Σεπτέμβριος 1992, 715–734. Κομοτηνή.

Koukouli-Chryssanthaki, Ch. (2004) The Archaic city of Abdera. In A. Moustaka, E. Skarlatidou, M.-C. Tzannes and Y. Ersoy (eds) *Klazomenai, Teos and Abdera: metropoleis and colony. Proceedings of the International Symposium held at the Archaeological Museum of Abdera, Abdera, 20–21 October 2001*, 235–248. Thessaloniki, University Studio Press.

Lazaridis, D. (1971) Μαρώνεια και Ορθαγορία. Αρχαίες Ελληνικές πόλεις 6. Αθηναϊκός Τεχνολογικός Όμιλος – Αθηναϊκό Κέντρο Οικιστικής. Αθήνα.

Melfos, V. and Vavelidis, M. (2000) Η κατεργασία του λίθου και η λατομική δραστηριότητα κατά την αρχαιότητα: ίχνη λατόμευσης στη Μαρώνεια του Νομού Ροδόπης. Θεσσαλονικέων Πόλις 2, 63–76.

Papastamatakis, A., Orfanos, V., Dimitriou, D., Triandaphyllos, D. and Karadima, Ch. (2001) Ένα άγνωστο μεταλλείο στη Μαρώνεια Κομοτηνής. In Y. Bassiakos, E. Aloupi and Y. Facorellis (eds) Archaeometry Issues in Greek Prehistory and Antiquity, 617–632 Athens, Hellenic Society for Archaeometry.

Skarlatidou, E. (1987) Ανασκαφή στο αρχαϊκό νεκροταφείο Αβδήρων. Το Αρχαιολογικό Έργο στη Μακεδονία και Θράκη 1, 421–429.

Skarlatidou, E. (2004) The Archaic Cemetery of the Clazomenian Colony at Abdera. In A. Moustaka, E. Skarlatidou, M.-C. Tzannes and Y. Ersoy (eds) *Klazomenai, Teos and Abdera: metropoleis and colony. Proceedings of the International Symposium held at the Archaeological Museum of Abdera, Abdera, 20–21 October 2001*, 249–259. Thessaloniki, University Studio Press.

Syrides, G., Psilovikos, A. (2004) Geoarchaeological Investigations in the Area of Ancient Abdera. In A. Moustaka, E. Skarlatidou, M.-C. Tzannes and Y. Ersoy (eds) *Klazomenai, Teos and Abdera:*

metropoleis and colony. Proceedings of the International Symposium held at the Archaeological Museum of Abdera, Abdera, 20-21 October 2001, 351–359. Thessaloniki, University Studio Press.
Triandaphyllos, D. (1973) Αρχαιολογικόν Δελτίον, Χρονικά Β3, 463–464.
Triandaphyllos, D. (1980) Les monuments mégalithiques en Thrace occidentale. Pulpudeva 4, 145–163.
Triandaphyllos, D. (1983) Αρχαϊκό νεκροταφείο στη Δυτική Θράκη. *Annuario della Scuola Archeologica di Atene* LXI N. S., XLV, 179–207.
Triandaphyllos, D. (1985) Les sanctuaires en plein air dans la region des Cicones. *Thracia Pontica* 3, 129–134.
Triandaphyllos, D. (1987–1990) Η Θράκη του Αιγαίου πριν από τον ελληνικό αποικισμό. Θρακική Επετηρίδα 7, 297–322. = (1991) La Thrace égéenne avant la colonisation grecque. *Thracia Pontica* 4, 283–308.
Triandaphyllos, D. (1990) Οχυρωματικοί περίβολοι στην ενδοχώρα της Αιγαιακής Θράκης. Μνήμη Δ. Λαζαρίδη. Πόλις και χώρα στην αρχαία Μακεδονία και Θράκη, Πρακτικά Αρχαιολογικού Συνεδρίου, Καβάλα 1986, 683–693, Figs 1–11. Θεσσαλονίκη.
Triandaphyllos, D. (1992) Ανασκαφή τύμβων στο νεκροταφείο της Αρχαίας Στρύμης. Το Αρχαιολογικό Έργο στη Μακεδονία και Θράκη 6, 655–667.
Triandaphyllos, D. (2000) La nécropole de la colonie thasienne de Strymé. In *Pratiques Funéraires dans l' Europe des XIIIe - IVe siècles av. J.-C.* Actes du IIIe Colloque international d' Archéologie funéraire, Tulcea 1997, 87–104.
Triandaphyllos, D. (2004) Abdera: the Classical and Hellenistic Cities. In A. Moustaka, E. Skarlatidou, M.-C. Tzannes and Y. Ersoy (eds) *Klazomenai, Teos and Abdera: metropoleis and colony. Proceedings of the International Symposium held at the Archaeological Museum of Abdera, Abdera, 20-21 October 2001*, 261–269. Thessaloniki, University Studio Press.
Tsatsopoulou, P. (1996) Μεσημβρία-Ζώνη 1987–1997. Το Αρχαιολογικό Έργο στη Μακεδονία και Θράκη 10, 917–926.
Tsatsopoulou, P. (1997) Η ανασκαφική έρευνα στη Μεσημβρία του Αιγαίου την τελευταία Δεκαετία. D. Triandaphyllos & D. Tertsopoulou (eds) Αρχαία Θράκη, Πρακτικά του 2ου Διεθνούς Συμποσίου Θρακικών Σπουδών, Σεπτέμβριος 1992, 615–630 Κομοτηνή.
Tsimbidis-Pentazos, E. (1971) Αρχαιολογικαί έρευναι εν Θράκη. Πρακτικά της Αρχαιολογικής Εταιρείας, 87–101.
Tsimbidis-Pentazos, E. (1972) Προϊστορικαί ακροπόλεις εν Θράκη. Πρακτικά της Αρχαιολογικής Εταιρείας, 86–93.
Vavelidis, M. (1995) A new occurrence of placer gold in the Kompsatos River, Northern Greece. In J. Pašava, B. Křibek and K. Žák (eds) *Mineral Deposits: From Their Origin to Their Environmental Impacts*, 207–09. Rotterdam, CRC Press.
Vavelidis, M. (2001) Μελέτη χρυσών, αργυρών και λίθινων αρχαιολογικών ευρημάτων από τις ανασκαφές της αρχαίας Μεσημβρίας-Ζώνης. Τελική Έκθεση Ερευνητικού Έργου. Θεσσαλονίκη. Unpublished.
Vavelidis, M., Filippidis, A., Michailidis, K. and Evangelou, E. (1989) The polymetallic ore mineralization of the Kirki area. *Geologica Rhodopica* 1, 350–365.
Vavelidis, M., Michailidis, K., Christofides, G. and Boboti-Tsitlakides I. (1992) Geochemical study of placer gold and the gold-bearing skarn-type mineralization of Kimmeria area, Xanthi district, NE Greece. *Geologica Rhodopica* 2, 297–308.
Vavritsas, A. (1966) Ανασκαφή Μεσημβρίας Θράκης. Πρακτικά της Αρχαιολογικής Εταιρείας, 67–70.
Vavritsas, A. (1967) Ανασκαφή Μεσημβρίας Θράκης. Πρακτικά της Αρχαιολογικής Εταιρείας, 93–94.

9

Orgame necropolis in the Black Sea area

Vasilica Lungu

Orgame, Argamum in Roman times, was one of the first Greek colonies founded in the Black Sea area by colonists from Ionia, most probably from Miletus. The foundation, placed on the present day Dolojman Cape, dates to about the middle of the seventh century BC, very close to the date of the foundation of Istros on the Western shore of Pontus Euxinus (Fig. 9.1). Istros, situated approximately 27 kilometres in a straight line south of Orgame, was the main Ionian city in the West Pontic area, with a continuous history from the seventh century BC to the seventh century AD (Avram 2003; Alexandrescu 2005), and is better known from literary sources, epigraphic finds, extensive excavations, and detailed studies, than is Orgame. This site was abandoned at the beginning of the seventh century AD, too (Fig. 9.2) (Adamesteanu 2001; 2003). Today the Greek and Roman site of ancient Orgame remains free of modern buildings and this offers good opportunities for developing systematic research of the site.

The first excavations there were made before the Second World War, between 1926 to 1932 (Nicorescu 1944), within the Roman fortified area; the second stage of excavations started in 1965, inside the Greek and Roman city (Coja 1972; 1986; 1990; 2005). Excavations conducted on a limited scale in the city, covering *c.* 2.5 hectares, have uncovered only small parts of the fortified area, a few buildings, particularly of Late Roman period, which overlap some Greek remains of Archaic, Classical, and Hellenistic periods (Adamesteanu 2003). More extensive digs were started from the 1990s onwards. These are still continuing, and have now been extended to the necropolis.

The necropolis of Orgame stretches out towards the West just close to the city (Lucian of Samosate, *Charon* 22, noted that the *necropoleis* were normally placed in front of the cities). It was identified by rescue excavation in 1988 and since 1990 excavations

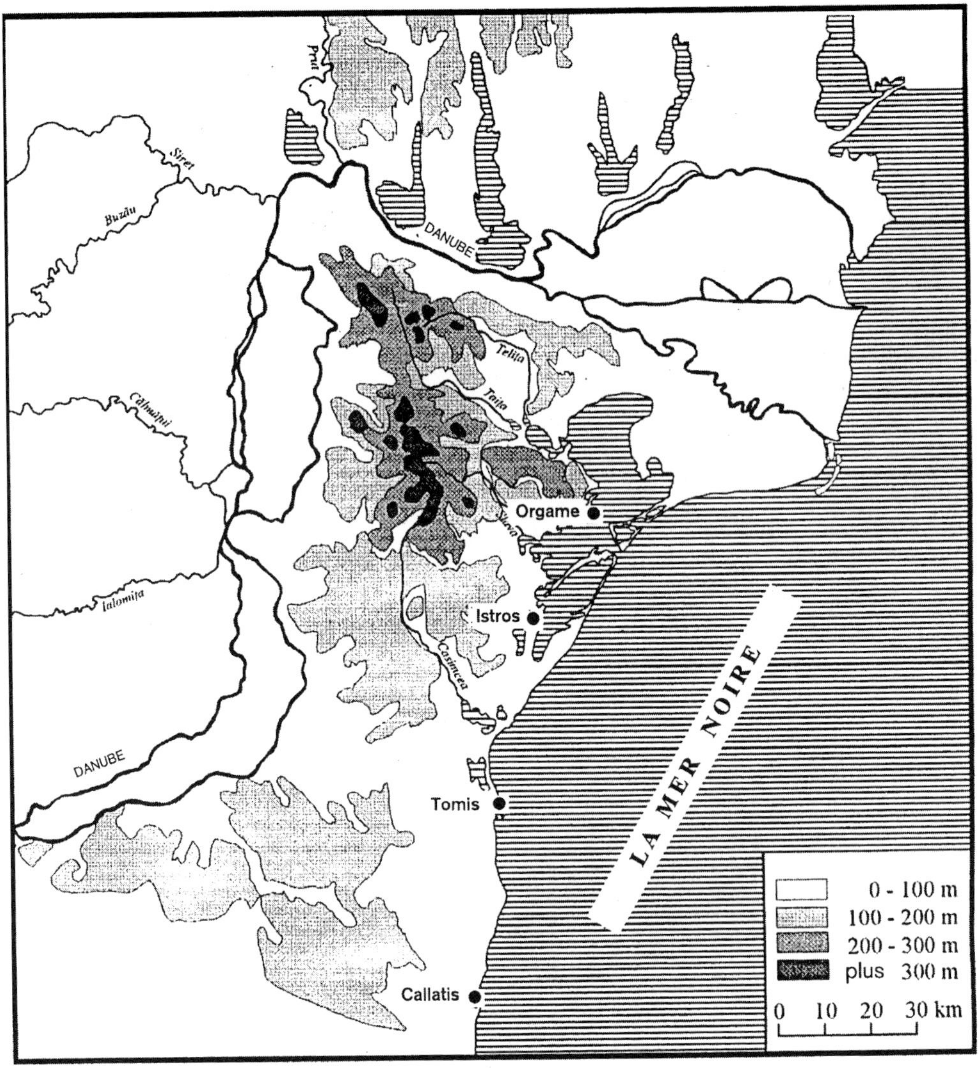

Fig. 9.1. Map of the western Black Sea.

have regularly been undertaken on a large scale in various areas throughout the promontory. The necropolis seems to have been in use throughout the lifetime of Greek Orgame: the earliest finds date back to the second part of the seventh century BC, some of them to the sixth, but those belonging to the fourth and third centuries BC are in a majority (Canarache 1957; Lungu 1995; 1996; 1999; 2000a; 2000b; 2000–2001; 2002a; 2002b; 2003; 2004a; 2006; 2007). Most of the latter are concentrated in three main burial areas (Fig. 9.3). Two main gaps are registered in the chronology of the excavated tombs: the first one is between the second part of the sixth and the fifth century BC, and the second one from the second part of the third century BC to the Roman period.

Fig. 9.2. Orgame, city and necropolis.

The burial areas and funerary rites

The first area, the so-called central cemetery (Fig. 9.3, *Secteur* I), located near the middle of the funerary area, contains tombs ranging from the beginning of the fourth to the third century BC. Primary cremation tombs, attested from the beginning of the necropolis, continue into the Classical and Hellenistic period. More frequently, however, some form of secondary depositions of the cremated remains in the soil seems to have been practised (Fig. 9.4). The custom of urn-burial should be mentioned here: the vase was set directly in the ground and covered by a small tumulus. Most of the time, amphorae, *pithoi*, *kraters* and handmade urns were used for adult burials. It was also a common practice to bury infants in pots or under large fragments of broken jars; both domestic and transport vessels could be used for this purpose. Young children were as a rule cremated and then deposited in ceramic vessels, like *hydriai* (Figs 9.5, 9.6), which were buried either separately in the necropolis, or within smaller tombs located close to adult tombs of larger size.

The second cluster of tombs corresponds to a small area located in the northwestern part of the city, close to the Heroon (Fig. 9.3, *Secteur* II) (Lungu 2000a, 112, fig. 1). It includes at least two cremations *in situ* and eleven secondary cremation tombs, all investigated. The cremated remains had been placed on the ancient layer on a surface protected by stone circles and covered by small tumuli. An infant tomb in an archaic Lesbian amphora (*enchythrismos*) investigated in this area represents the only example of this practice in the necropolis. At a short distance to the West, one

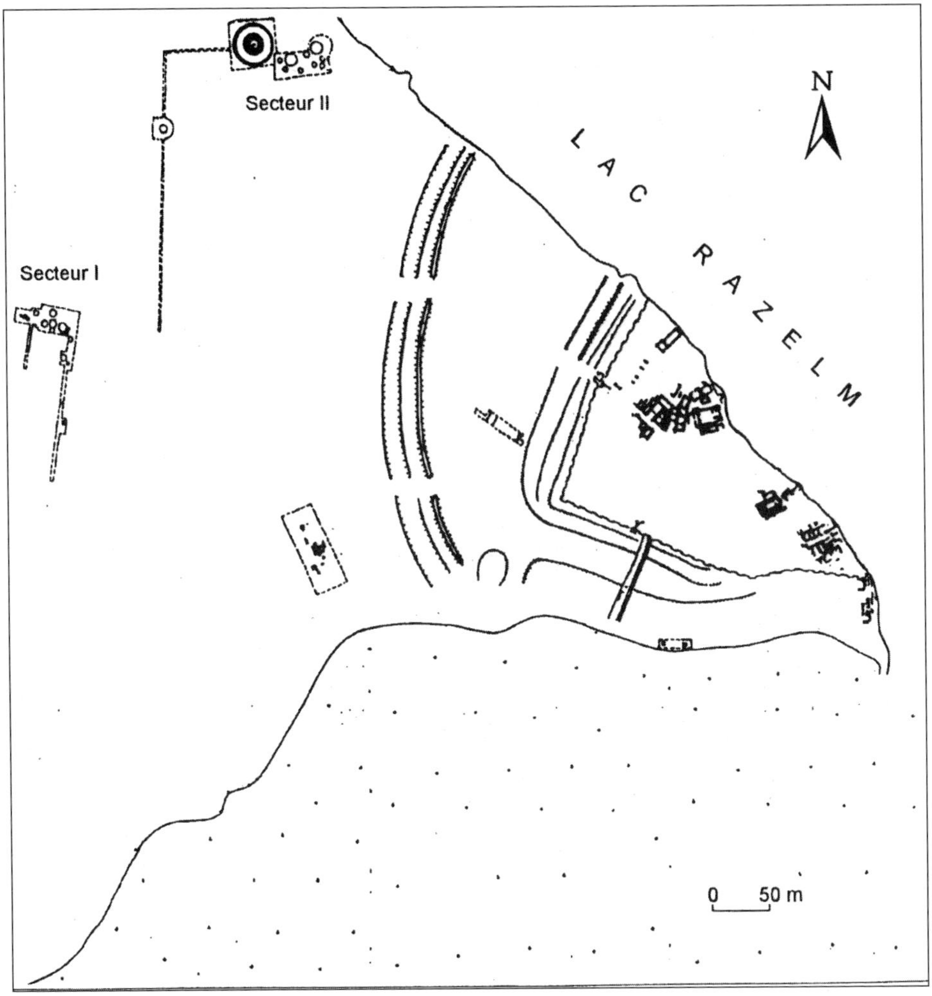

Fig. 9.3. Plan of the excavations, with Sectors I and II.

pit grave was found, within which were inhumations belonging to adults of various ages, possibly belonging to a minority ethnic group in the population. Three further tombs of the third century BC and a cenotaph complete this grouping. All these tombs form a special sector of the necropolis developed close to the settlement. However, we do not believe that there is just a simple correlation between distance and date, but the choice of location was presumably not arbitrary. The cremation tombs date to between the third quarter of the seventh century and the middle of the sixth century BC. The inhumation tomb is without offerings except one arrowhead belonging of the latest layer, and probably dated to the fifth century BC (Lungu 2000a, 117, fig. 5).

The third burial plot was identified halfway between the first two on the southern slope of the promontory, and is still being excavated. The tombs discovered there

Fig. 9.4. Tumulus T07, secondary deposition.

belong to the Hellenistic period and reveal common features with the first location. It is during this period that the tombs in Orgame are best attested.

At Orgame, the tumulus is the most permanent funerary monument, and its position and shape reveal the importance of funerary practices in preserving social status. Its use also spread in other Greek areas in different times (Pelon 1976; Coldstream 1977, 226; Kurtz and Boardman 1971, 183–186, 282–283; Machowski 2007, 51–62). At Orgame, tumuli of various sizes cover individual cremation tombs, which are normally surrounded by stone circles and are clustered in groups of two or more tombs. It may be assumed from the amount of labour needed for their construction, and their often richer grave-goods, that at least some of them were intended for persons of special status. In many respects these assemblages resemble those of Istros (Alexandrescu 1966, 133–294), and, some, those of Berezan (Solovyov 1999, 79–84, fig. 60), Olbia (Skudnova 1988, 10), Apollonia Pontica (Panayotova and Nedev 2003), Abdera (Kallintzi 2004, 15), Macedonia (Andronikos 1964), and Ionian necropoleis such as Samos (Boehlau 1898, 33, fig. 20). In comparison with other Ionian colonies in the Black Sea area which have produced fairly considerable numbers of graves, the sequence of the archaeological evidence from Orgame is much more limited. Some other analogies were in the indigenous necropoleis in the vicinity, for example, Sabangia (Simion 2003, 360, fig. 2a), Enisala (Simion 2003, 362, figs 6–7) and Celic Dere (Simion 2003, 237–246).

Fig. 9.5. Inventory of a child urn-tomb.

Fig. 9.6. Pelike from the inventory of tumulus TXIII93.

The commonest rite is cremation, a rite which seems to be common in Greek religion (Kurtz and Boardman 1971, 73–74; Furley 1981, 27–33). The seventh and sixth century cremation tombs, as well as those of the fourth and third centuries, are considerably better attested than other types and might well represent the initial core of the Orgame community. Some of the Orgame cremations were simple surface pyres with the body completely burnt *in situ* and the tomb built over the pyre, covered by a tumulus and surrounded by a stone ring. These were usually the biggest and often have particularly plentiful grave goods, which were there to distinguish their occupants from those who were buried in the smaller tumuli. Throughout the Archaic to Hellenistic periods, most burials are secondary cremations with human remains set directly on the ancient soil. Urn-burials are restricted to a few individual cremations deposited in vases. The ash urns were placed in the same type of burial with stone enclosure. Cremations are also reported at Istros and Tomis, as well as on indigenous sites such as Enisala or Celic Dere, while cemeteries on Berezan, at Olbia and Apollonia Pontica, which mainly use the inhumation rite, contain only few cremations.

Among the other types of burials at Orgame, accounting for a very small proportion of the graves, were the *enchytrismos* burials in amphorae, the cenotaphs and the collective inhumation burial in a pit cut into the rock (Lungu 2000a, 117, fig. 5). This latter tomb was used for at least four or five successive inhumations. The last burials there are of two skeletons, male and female, both orientated east–west. The multiple-inhumation made a significant appearance close to the archaic area on the summit at the Northern limit of the promontory and it may be compared with some other similar interments, earlier in date and identified closer to the dwelling area: a pit with 13 skeletons belonging to the tenth–ninth centuries BC has been investigated under the wall of the Greek fortification (Ailincăi *et al.* 2003, 307–324; Ailincăi *et al.* 2006, 81–107).

The predominant pattern of the necropolis, however, is represented by cremation tombs and the emergence of a social group which defined itself in burial by building larger tombs with sacral fittings like altars, sacrificial pits or trenches for keeping funerary offerings.

Both sexes are represented, and there are also children as well as adults. There is important evidence for the different treatment of child burials in different periods: the very young children were inhumed in amphorae, the older ones cremated. The *enchythrismos* burial attested in the Archaic necropolis completely disappears in the fourth and third centuries and is replaced by a normal cremation tomb. With only one exception, all other child burials were cremations, with occasional use of urns. In the case of these cremations, the division between children and adults is not always very clear. The distinction for the most part must rely on tomb type and size, or on the goods present in the tomb. This is however sufficient to show specific features, particularly a low infant and child mortality.

Offerings

As a rule each tomb contained funerary offerings, the only exception being one of the cenotaphs. One notable feature of earlier tombs as well as of the later ones is the variability of their offerings records, including artefact types from various different origins. The majority of the offerings are represented by pottery from various centres of manufacture, which implies a variety of contacts (for example, amphorae from Lesbos, Clazomenae, and Samos, a North-Ionian ring askos, and Milesian 'Middle Wild Goat II', grey ware). It is generally accepted that the colonization was undertaken within pre-existing networks of trade – and this could explain the different origin of many goods. There is no reason to read ethnic differences in the use of available vessels in the tombs. But the scarcity of Milesian products in the earliest tombs poses an interesting question about the relationship between the earliest settlers and the mother city.

From the third quarter of the seventh to the first half of the sixth century, the necropolis of Orgame shows significant interest in the disposal of ceramic vessels in the tombs, in terms of variety of shapes as well as quantity: for example, amphorae, jars, *kraters*, pelikes, bowls, kantharoi, gutti, pyxides, and lekythoi (Lungu 2004, 85–97). Only in the fourth century do vessels and other goods become more prominent and varied. From this period come the richest grave offerings, in particular those of very large numbers of amphorae, which must also have involved considerable expenditure and ostentation (Figs 9.7, 9.8) (Lungu 1995, 231–263). This provides a striking contrast

Fig. 9.7. Tumulus TIV90.

with the poverty of the metal objects found in the tombs, rarely going beyond a fibula, a *strigilium*, some coins and arrow heads. These are associated with the adult tombs. Even rarer is jewellery, examples of which are a ring in an adult tomb, and a pendant and an earring which appear together in an adolescent tomb. Other types of personal ornaments and armament are almost totally non-existent. So, the quantity of metals in the tomb is relatively low and also quite constant during the four centuries, between the seventh/sixth and the fourth/third centuries BC. Even taking into account that the Heroon was robbed – only a small scrap of gold attests to the deposition of precious metal here (Lungu 2002a, 136, fig. 4) – the inhabitants of Orgame evidently had no great enthusiasm for the deposition of metal objects in their tombs.

The domestic character of the pottery in the Orgame tombs, is very pronounced, especially at the end of the Classical and beginning of the Hellenistic period. The repetitive presence of some shapes like fish-plates and jugs in tombs may mean that, except in a few cases, the offering practices followed strictly religious rules. Most of the vases are of fine quality; some are not.

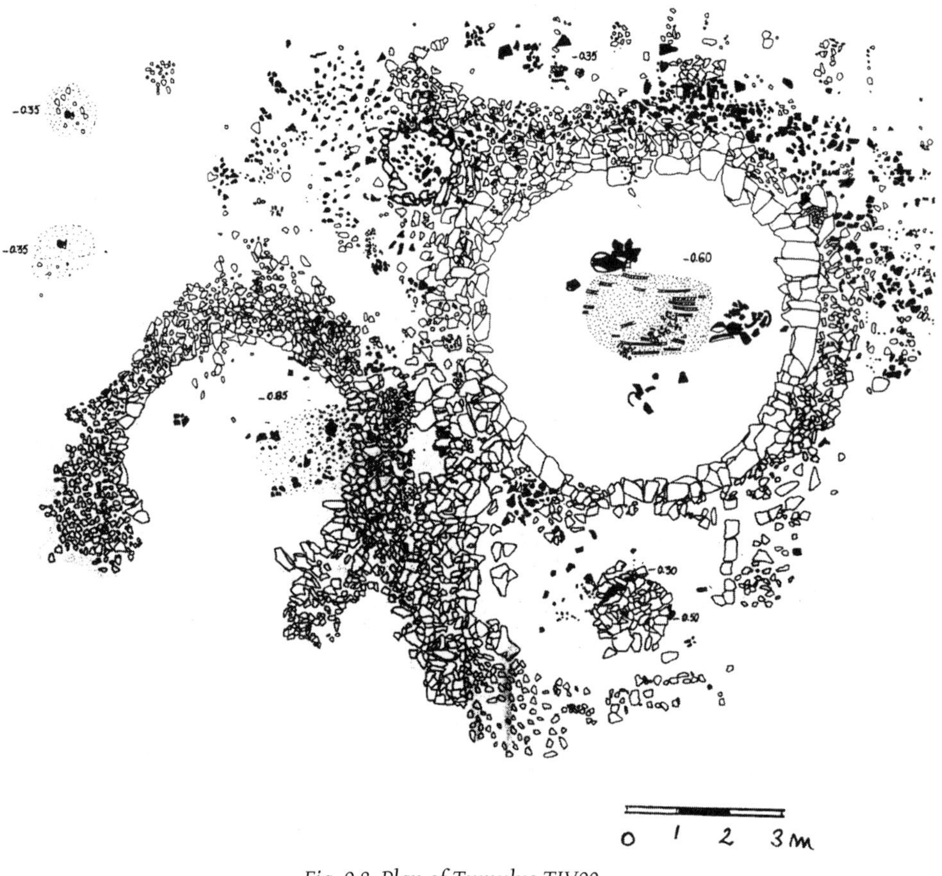

Fig. 9.8. Plan of Tumulus TIV90.

Rarely some form of grave-marker may have been provided. Two examples have so far been found: a fragment of stone stele and a rectangular marble stele (Lungu 2004b). The fact that there are only two examples noted among the hundred or so graves at Orgame, is consistent with them being reserved for special tombs.

Family plots

It is likely that cremation was used by the population of Orgame in general, which may indicate that the community was relatively affluent. The tombs are clustered in family plots and kinship (Morris 1987, ch. 5) obviously had a role in organizing funeral plots (Fig. 9.9). The number of graves each cluster contains varies from four to ten individual tombs of varying sizes, in the investigated area. There are enough plots excavated at Orgame to prove this to be a particular norm of this necropolis. The clustering of tombs around the biggest tomb of the plot implies a desire to establish some sort of hierarchic relationship inside the family plots (Fig. 9.9). Some of these familial plots from Orgame had similarities with tomb assemblages in other sites, like those in the tumulus Γ of Boulokalyva, Thessaly (Blackman 1999, 71–72, fig. 87), dating from PG to Archaic period, or the other ones in the tumulus of Kamenica (Albania) (Beko 2004, 40–41, particularly fig. 4), which contains graves of the late seventh and sixth centuries BC.

While the location of family plots along the roads would primarily reflect practical convenience, the present interpretation of the archaeological evidence emerging from Orgame necropolis could suggest that it was developed according to a regular plan,

Fig. 9.9. General view of the Orgame necropolis.

implying a concept of foundation. But Orgame is not the only Greek colony to indicate regular planning. Some evidence of planned plots is apparent about a century later in Istros (Adamesteanu 1967, 374 f.; *cf.* Alexandrescu 1999, 62, n. 21).

Ritual practices and Ancestor cults

The family tombs frequently have further commemorative offerings outside them. Such rites could be observed in the case of most of the investigated tombs and could be evidence of annual commemorations in honour of the dead. Funerary inscriptions from elsewhere mention this practice (McLean 2002, 260–278). Some of the archaic tombs have stone-built low circular platforms placed outside the tomb on the stone enclosure; these platforms have been interpreted as ground altars or *escharai* for a cult of the dead. Burkert, followed by Antonaccio, proposed that the function of the circular platforms was for funerary feasting (Burkert 1985, 192; Antonaccio 1995, 206). Offering pits were closely associated with some burials of the fourth and third centuries BC (Lungu 1995, 234 and fig. 2). The inventory of these included vessels for libations of wine and water such as amphorae and pouring vessels (on ancient libations, see Versnel 1994, 62–63). Burning offerings outside the tomb, which were also left on the stone circles during commemorative occasions, was also a widespread custom at Orgame.

Some Archaic tombs received new offerings in the fourth and third centuries BC, particularly of Greek amphorae, and this evidence suggests the veneration of the families' founders who died some centuries before (*cf.* Antonaccio 1995, 252–254).

The Heroon

Tumulus TA95 has received most of our attention (Figs 9.3 and 9.10) in recent years. It was the main monument excavated in the seasons 1995–2002, and some general considerations and finds associated with the Hero-Tomb have been published regularly (Lungu 2000a, 108–110; 2000b, 67–87; 2000–2001, 171–188; 2002b, 3–17; 2006; 2007, 337–382).

The tumulus stands on top of the ancient level of limestone slabs on the north side of the necropolis, about 500 m to the west of the urban settlement, not far from the later Roman gate. This tomb contains a central pyre (about 8 m in diameter) formed around a cremation pit cut into the rock (measuring 2.50/3.0 × 1.48 m). The remains of the pyre – an impressive wooden construction – and some vessels surrounding the pyre have been identified *in situ* (Fig. 9.11). Finds included fine pottery, namely: one Ionian cup (Villard-Vallet A2), probably of Samian or Milesian origin (Fig. 9.12) (Lungu 2000b, 82 a, b; 2000–2001, 178, fig. 6; Kerschner 2006, 236, figs 11, 11 a, b), and one fragmentary filleted cup (Villard-Vallet A1), several transport amphorae of both Clazomenian and Lesbian types, oinochoai, as well as one handmade vase. In terms of the chronology of this material, the limits given by the pottery point to a short period, confined to the middle and third quarter of the seventh century BC. The ritual of the vases deposited around the wooden pyre corresponds to that attested by Homer in his description of Patroclus's funeral (Homer *Iliad* 23, 167–168; Lungu 2008). The trench was used widely for centuries for ritual offerings to the dead.

Fig. 9.10. Structure TA95, the heroon.

Fig. 9.11. View of the heroon pyre.

Fig. 9.12. Cup of the heroon.

The prominent location, the large dimensions and the construction of this tumulus differed obviously from other tombs situated to the immediate east of the necropolis, as well as from tombs in other Greek necropoleis of the Black Sea. Compared with all other excavated tombs of the necropolis, this tomb displays most impressive proportions. It has a complex structure, combining a tomb and a circular trench of offerings, on a surface of 42–43 m. It is about three times larger than the largest of the tombs and 20 times larger than the smallest of the tombs excavated inside the necropolis. Indeed, this is one of the largest archaic monumental tombs found anywhere in the Greek colonial area of the Black Sea.

The trench deposits contain remains of cremations and vessels in connection with the ritual practice of periodic commemoration covering a long chronological span. Finds date from the seventh to the third centuries BC, including pottery from Archaic, Classical, and Hellenistic Greek periods, as well as some distinctive handmade vases, contemporaneous with the imported vases. These vessels were often similar to those of the grave goods found in the common tombs of the necropolis, but they include well-dated characteristic pieces. The tomb, although robbed, is still associated with important quantities of grave goods. All this evidence points towards an identification of this tomb as the locus for hero cult – perhaps the cult of the *oikist*.

The earliest vessels inside the trench (after the mid-seventh century BC) are contemporaneous with the contents of the pyre and suggest the start of the cult of *oikist* immediately after the tumulus construction until the middle of the third century BC. The deposits consist mainly of pottery and fragments of painted tiles (Lungu 2000b, 83, figs 8–9), but also include a few metal objects and fragments of games board (Fig. 9.13). These pieces have numerous resonances with Greek painted vases with famous Greek heroes, such as Achilles and Ajax, in games scenes (Fitta 1997, 157–161; Kurke 1999, 248–272), and imply the idea of competitions (*agones*) related to funeral games (Burkert 1985, 193: 'The burial of an important figure was followed by an *agon*...').

The most frequent finds are ceramic vessels related to drinking, such as amphorae, jugs, some *krater* fragments, and drinking cups suitable for the commemoration of a hero (Ekroth 1999). The majority were imported vases, with a few handmade wares. Amphorae formed the lion's share of the contents of the trench; they were used both for practical purposes and as status symbols. The presence of many amphora stamps will affect the

Fig. 9.13. Game board fragment.

dates of all classes of pottery found with them in the trench. The study of these may have an impact on the current suggested chronology of the hero cult practices here. These stamps may take the final phase of hero cult later in absolute terms than that currently proposed, viz. around the second quarter of the 3rd century BC. This historical record of the hero cult is supported by the presence of many *graffiti*. These were all incised after the pots were fired and their content made sense according to the religious rules of the Greek city. The language of the *graffiti* seems generally to be in the Ionian dialect, but most of them show variations in the text and style of the inscription. One of them shows the second part of a name finished by - *OXEŌ* (Fig. 9.14). First of all, we can think of a personal name such as Phloxis (Floci/j, Athens, 5th *c.* BC, IG I[3] 461, 36.), but we could also suggest the restoration of the name *Loxias*, as *epiclesis* of Apollo, *i.e.* Apollo *Loxias*, *–ies*, with Ionian form of Genitive in *-eō* (Herodotus. I.91; Liddell and Scott 1958, 1061; Pindar, *Isth.* VII.9; *Frg. Paian* VI, ep.1; *Parthen.* II. 36. Frei-Lüthy 1978, 61; Dougherty-Glenn 1988, 113: '...poetic Apollo as oracular god at Delphi is called Loxias, the oblique one'; Malkin 1987, 17–29).

The founders of new cities were normally worshipped (Farnell 1921, 361–372; Boehringer 1996). At Orgame, his cult could be associated with the god of the Pontic colonization, Apollo. This evidence seems to support the Malkin hypothesis concerning the interdependency between the cult of *oikist* and the 'collective beginnings' in Greek colonies (Malkin 2002, 211). It is certainly a practice in the sixth century BC, as is revealed by literary sources (Herodotus 6.38; Thucydides 5.11).

Fig. 9.14. Vessel fragment with OXEŌ graffito.

The Hero in this tomb therefore could be the *oikist* of the colony in Orgame who was honoured after his death until the third century BC. For the second part of the sixth to the fifth century BC the evidence is very scarce.

Conclusions

To sum up, the main features of Orgame necropolis – tomb types, family plots, spatial distribution, post-burial commemorative rites, hero cult – were sufficiently conservative for many centuries that any alteration could have an impact. The funeral practices which began in the earliest years of the colony and became increasingly prevalent over the seventh and sixth centuries, and then the fourth and third centuries, were part of a set of customs typical for Orgame necropolis.

In Orgame, where tumuli appeared at the first stages of the necropolis and multiplied at different times during its existence, the plan of tumulus construction varied, some contained impressive features, others were less impressive. It should be noted that the tumuli generally contained single burials, a notable exception being the multiple-inhumation tomb. There is thus no exclusive association of this set of practices with foreign types of tomb in Orgame. Cremation tombs of different dimensions protected by stone rings were established there as canonical or 'normative burial practice'.

The Heroon and the rise of hero cult at Orgame can be explained through the activity of a new colony – establishing its borders and legalizing its presence in this land (de Polignac 1984). The hero cult activity increased there towards the fourth and third centuries BC and there is a perceptible change at Orgame. Graves either become more elaborate or richer in goods, and unusual features of all sorts – libation-pits, grave markers or offerings at the archaic tombs – occur during this period. It is in this context that the Heroon received new artefacts (like tiles) and the hero cult was perhaps revitalized. The appearance of numerous *graffiti*, containing vocabulary typical of dedications, certainly seems to add new elements to the cult.

In the light of the finds of the fourth and third centuries BC in archaic tombs placed close to the Heroon we suggest that these new offerings correspond to a further stage of veneration of the dead, *i.e.* the veneration of symbolic family founders in traditional locations. Hero cult practices in connection with the oldest tombs are common in the Greek world (Morris 1988, 750–761). In the case of Orgame, this activity could be interpreted as a result of pressure exercised upon the existing social system, and this may be as a result of the Macedonian expansion to the North.

In the same period, the middle of the fourth century BC, a sanctuary of the dead is built on the west hill at the limit of the necropolis in the sector of the Basilica IV. We excavated there, in the seasons 1993–1995, 2002 and 2007, a structure connected between them: a square building, with the entrance on the south side, some offerings pits, one of them published (Lungu 2004c, 217–228), and an underground central hall communicating with the exterior by two built wells occupied a large area surrounded by a large ditch. It is not possible to reach firm conclusions until the excavations are complete. But, one could speculate that the fourth-century cult activities were addressed to the founder of the colony and to the ancestors of some important families of the city, may be the oldest ones, as the archaeological evidence is already enabling us to associate the cult activities here with those at the Heroon and the tombs of Archaic period. The underground central hall communicated with the outside by means of two wells built in different manners, and the offerings burned on a large surface close to one of them could connect these remains even to the particular practices of a Necromanteion.

At this relatively early stage of investigation, the relationship between this necropolis and other Ionian necropoleis is difficult to gauge. Instead, we should look around for an explanation of the evidence – and there seems no need to go further afield than Istros, where cremation in tumuli was a very common rite, becoming increasingly restricted to the elite. The comparison between the mortuary behaviour at Istros and Orgame offers some similarities which can be explained in terms of comparable social structures, while the necropolis of inhumation at Istria Bent situated in the *chora* of Istros is completely different, but more Greek in its features (Teleagă and Zirra 2003). While the Istros evidence is rather more complicated than that from Orgame, nevertheless it does seem to show evidence of close interactions between the two colonies.

The cremation burials at Orgame are not identical with those of Istros, nevertheless they are very close in their main characteristics – shallow pyres, stone circles, tomb-pyres, secondary cremations. This close connection, in the fourth century at least, is demonstrated by the appearance of coins from Istros in some of the tombs at Orgame. Moreover, the proportion of cremation versus inhumation at Orgame and Istros is higher than for any other Pontic Greek sites. An earlier cooperation between these both at the beginning of their foundations cannot be archaeologically recognized because of the relative lack of excavations in the earliest (mid-sixth century) tombs at Istros (*e.g.* Alexandrescu 1966, 143–146 – tumulus XX, dated *c.* 560–550 BC). The present evidence suggests that an *oikist* could be archaeologically recognized at Orgame, but we cannot yet draw firm conclusions about the status of Orgame in relation to Istros. One of the possibilities is emphasized by Alexandrescu's theory concerning the foundation of Istros 'en deux temps' (Alexandrescu 1999).

As concerns the burial practices in the colonies of Istros and Orgame and how they relate to those of the mother-city, Miletus there is very little information (Forbeck 2001/2002, 55–64, with bibliography). Nevertheless, the few burials of relevant date which have been found there are chamber or tiles tombs, and it seems that the burial practices of Istros and Orgame did differ greatly from those of Miletus. It seems clear that there were divergent practices between these colonies and their mother city, but this need not be interpreted as evidence of hostility. Rather, the civic and religious particularities of burial in Orgame and Istros may indicate that both colonies deliberately constructed their own independent identities from the moment of foundation. The significant features of the necropolis of both these cities are therefore to be explained with reference to the social circumstances in the colonies themselves and by their relationship with the cultures of new lands in which they were located (Kurtz and Boardman 1971, 317).

Φλοχὶ

Bibliography

Adameşteanu, D. (1967) *Histria II (comptes-rendus)*, Archaeologia Clássica 19.2, 374–380.

Adamesteanu, M. M. (2001) *Orgamé/Argamum*, Tulcea, International Conference of Economics and Management.

Adamesteanu, M. M. (2003) Orgame. In D. V. Grammenos and E. K. Petropoulos (eds) *Ancient Greek Colonies in the Black Sea I*, 341–388. Publications of the Archaeological Institute of Northern Greece, Thessaloniki.

Ailincăi, S., Mirițoiu, N. and Soficaru, A. (2003) O gropă cu oseminte umane atribuită culturii Babadag descoperită în nivelul precolonial de la Orgame (com. Jurilovca, jud. Tulcea). *Arheologia Moldovei* XXVI, 307–24.

Ailincăi, S., Mirițoiu, N. and Soficaru, A. (2006) A Pit with Human Remains attributed to the Babadag Culture discovered in Pre-Colonial Level at Orgame. In M. Manucu-Adamesteanu (ed.) *Orgame/Argamum Supplementa 1. A la recherche d'une colonie, Actes du Colloque International, 40 ans de recherches archéologiques a Orgame/Argamum, Bucarest-Tulcea-Jurilovca, 3-5 octobre 2005*, 81–107. Bucarest, Editions AGIR.

Alexandrescu, P. (1966) *Histria II. Necropola tumulară. Săpături 1955-1961*. Bucarest, Editura Acamediei R. S. R.

Alexandrescu, P. (1999) *L'aigle et le dauphin. Etudes d'archéologie pontiques*. Bucarest-Paris, Editura enciclopedică.

Alexandrescu, P. (2005) *Histria VII. La zone sacrée d'époque grecque (Fouilles 1915-1989)*. Bucarest-Paris, Editura Academiei Române.

Andronikos, M. (1964) *Vergina. The Prehistoric Necropolis and the Hellenistic Palace*, SIMA XIII. Göteborg, Astrom Edition.

Antonaccio, C. (1995) *An Archaeology of Ancestors. Tomb Cult and Hero Cult in Early Greece*. Maryland, Rowman & Littlefield.

Avram, A. (2003) Histria. In D. V. Grammenos and E. K. Petropoulos (eds) *Ancient Greek Colonies in the Black Sea*, 279–340. Publications of the Archaeological Institute of Northern Greece, Thessaloniki.

Beko, L. (2004) *The Iron Age Tumulus at Kamenica* (Albania). In P. Cabannes and J.-L. Lamboley (eds) *L'Illyrie Méridionale et l'Epire dans l'Antiquité IV, Actes du IVe colloque international de Grenoble (10-12 octobre 2002)*, 40–41. Paris, Editions De Boccard.

Blackman, D. (1999) Archaeology in Greece 1998–99, *Archaeological Reports*, 45 (1998–1999), 1–192.

Boehlau, J. (1898) *Aus Ionischen und Italischen Nekropolen: Ausgrabungen und Untersuchungen zur Geschichte der nachmykenischen griechischen Kunst*. Leipzig, Teubner.

Boehringer, D. (1996) Zur Heroisierung historischer Persönlichkeiten bei den Griechen. In M. Flacher, H.-J. Gehrke and E. Heinrich (eds) *Retrospektive, Konzepte von Vergangenheit in der griechisch-römischen Antike*, 37–61. Munich, Biering & Brinkmann.

Burkert, W. (1985) *Greek Religion*. Cambridge, Mass., Harvard University Press.

Canarache, V. (1957) *Importul amforelor ştampilate la Histria*. Bucarest, Editura Academiei Republicii Populare Romine.

Coja, M. (1972), Recherches dans un établissement pontique peu connu et observations sur son territoire. In M. Nystazopoulou-Pelekidou and T. Jochalas (eds) *Actes du IIe Congrès International des études du sud-est européen, Athenes, 7-13 mai, 1970*. Tome II: Histoire, 267–274. Athens, Association Internationale des Études du Sud-Est Européen.

Coja, M. (1986) Les fortifications grecques dans les colonies de la côte ouest du Pont Euxin. In P. Lerriche and H. Tréziny (eds) *La fortification dans l'histoire du monde grec, Actes du Colloque International, Valbonne, décembre 1982*, 95–103. Paris, Centre National de la Recherche Scientifique.

Coja, M. (1990) Greek Colonists and Native Populations in Dobruja (Moesia Inferior): The Archaeological Evidence. In J.-P. Descoeudres (ed.) *Greek Colonists and Native Populations*, Proceedings of the First Australian Congress of Classical Archaeology, Sydney 1989, 157–168. Oxford, Oxford University Press.

Coldstream, J. N. (1977) *Geometric Greece*. London, Methuen.

Dougherty-Glenn, C. L. (1988) *Apollo, Ktisis and Pindar. Literary representations of archaic city foundations.* PhD, Princeton University.

Ekroth, G. (1999) *The Sacrificial Rituals of Greek Hero-Cults in the Archaic to the Early Hellenistic Periods.* PhD, Stockholm University.

Farnell, L. R. (1921) *Greek Hero Cults and Ideas of Immortality*. Oxford, Clarendon Press.

Fitta, M. (1997) *Spiele und Spielzeug in der Antike.* Stuttgart, Theiss.

Forbeck, E. (2001–2002) Die Nekropolen von Milet. Grabtypologie und Bestattungsbräuche von vorarchaischer bis römischer Zeit. In H. Işkan and F. Işikm (eds) *Güneybati Anadolu'da mezar tipleri ve ölü kültü*, Lykia VI, 55–64. Antalya, Akdeniz University.

Frei-Lüthy, C. (1978) *Der Einfluss der griechischen Personennamen auf die Wortbildung*. Heidelberg, C. Winter Universitaetsverlag.

Furley, W. D. (1981) *Studies in the use of fire in Ancient Greek Religion*. Salem, N.H., Ayer.

Kallintzi, K. (2004) Abdera: Organization and Utilization of the Area extra-muros. In A. Moustaka, E. Skarlatidou, M.-C. Tzannes and Y. Ersoy (eds) *Klazomenai, Teos and Abdera: Metropoleis and Colony. Proceedings of the International Symposium held at the Archaeological Museum of Abdera, 20–21 October 2001*, 271–89. Thessaloniki, University Studio Press.

Kerschner, M. (2006) Zum Beginn und zu den Phasen der griechischen Kolonisation am Schwarzen Meer. *Eurasia Antiqua* 12, 227–250.

Kurke, L. (1999) *Coins, Bodies, Games, and Gold. The Politics of Meaning in Archaic Greece.* Princeton, Princeton University Press.

Kurtz, D. and Boardman, J. (1971) *Greek Burial Customs*. London, Thames and Hudson.

Lungu, V. (1995) Une tombe du IVe siècle av. J.-C. dans la nécropole tumulaire de la cité d'Orgamé. *Argamum, Peuce* 9, 231–263.

Lungu, V. (1996) Archaeological Data and Literary Sources about the Funerary practices from the North- and West-Pontic Greek Cities. *Proceedings of the 13th International Congress of Prehistoric Sciences*, 745–752. Forli, A.B.A.C.O. Edizioni.

Lungu, V. (1999) Remarques sur la chronologie des timbres thasiens à propos d'une tombe du IVe siècle av. J.-C. In Y. Garlan (ed.) *La production et le commerce des amphores anciennes en mer Noire, Actes du Colloque international, Istanbul, 25–28 mai 1994*, 71–80. Aix-en-Provence, Publications de l'Université de Provence.

Lungu, V. (2000a) Pratiques funéraires et formes d'organisation sociale dans la nécropole de la cité grecque d'Orgamé. In G. Simion and V. Lungu (eds) *Tombes tumulaires de l'Âge du Fer dans le Sud-Est de l'Europe, Actes du IIe Colloque International d'Archéologie Funéraire, (Tulcea 1995)*, 101–117. Tulcea, Institut de Recherches Éco-Muséologiques.

Lungu, V. (2000b) La tombe d'un héros et l'organisation de la nécropole d'une cité milésienne du Pont-Euxin. In V. Lungu (ed.) *Pratiques funéraires dans l'Europe des XIIIe-IVe s. av. J.-C., Actes du IIIe Colloque International d'Archéologie Funéraire, (Tulcea 1997)*, 67–85. Tulcea, Institut de Recherches Éco-Muséologiques.

Lungu, V. (2000–2001) La tombe d'un Héros et l'organisation de la nécropole d'une cité milésienne du Pont Euxin: le tumulus T A95 d'Orgamé. *Talata* XXXII-XXXIII, 2000–2001, 171–188.

Lungu, V. (2002a) Tombs, Texts and Images: Fire in Greek Funeral Ritual. In D. Gheorghiu (ed.) *Fire in Archaeology. Papers from a session held at the European Association of Archaeologists. Sixth Annual Meeting in Lisbon 2000*, BAR International Series 1089, 133–142. Oxford, BAR.

Lungu, V. (2002b) Hero Cult and Greek Colonization in the Black Sea Area. *Revue des études sud-est européennes* XL 1–4, 3–17.

Lungu, V. (2003) On the etymology of Orgame. A Greek colony on the West Black Sea. *Revue des études sud-est européenes* XLI 1–4 103–09.

Lungu, V. (2004a) Vessel structures – Social structures in Orgame Necropolis, in *Peuples, Etats et Nations dans le sud-Est de l'Europe, Actes du IXe Congrès International des Etudes du Sud-Est Européen, 30 août - 4 septembre, Tirana 2004*, 85–97. Bucarest, Anima.

Lungu, V. (2004b) Iconographie et société antique: à propos d'une stèle funéraire d'Orgamé. *Peuce* II (XV), 49–60.

Lungu, V. (2004c) Un dépôt d'amphores thasiennes du IVe siècle av. J.-C. à Orgamé. In J. Eiring and J. Lund (eds) *Transport Amphorae and Trade in the Eastern Mediterranean, Actes of the International Colloquium at the Danish Institute at Athens, (September 26–29, 2002)*, Monographs of the Danish Institute at Athens, Vol. 5, 217–228. Aarhus, Aarhus University Press.

Lungu, V. (2006) Les tumuli comme repères du territoire de la cite grecque d'Orgamé. In M. Manucu-Adamesteanu (ed.) *Orgame/Argamum Supplementa 1. A la recherche d'une colonie, Actes du Colloque International, 40 ans de recherches archéologiques à Orgame/Argamum, Bucarest-Tulcea-Jurilovca, 3-5 octobre 2005*, 117–139. Bucarest, Editions AGIR.

Lungu, V. (2007) Nécropoles grecques du Pont Gauche: Istros, Orgame, Tomis, Callatis. In D. V. Grammenos and E. K. Petropoulos, (eds) *Ancient Greek Colonies in the Black Sea 2*, BAR International Series 1675 (I), 337–382.

Lungu, V. (2008) Les funérailles de Patrocle et les plus anciennes nécropoles ioniennes de la mer Noire. In O. Özbek (ed.) *Funeral Rites, Rituals and Ceremonies from Prehistory to Antiquity: Proceedings of an International Workshop "Troas and its Neighbours", Çanakkale October 2-6, 2006*, 153–170. Istanbul, Institut Français d'Etudes Anatoliennes Georges- Dumezil.

Machowski, W. (2007) *The barrows of the Iron Age in Mainland Greece, Cyprus and the Aegean Islands.* Studies in Art and Civilizations 10, Krakow.

Malkin, I. (1987) *Religion and Colonization in Ancient Greece*, Leiden-New York-Copenhagen-Cologne, Brill.

Malkin, I. (2002) Exploring the Validity of the Concept of 'Foundation': A visit to Megara Hyblaia. In V. B. Gorman and E. W. Robinson (eds) *Oikistes. Studies in Constitutions, Colonies, and Military Power in the Ancient World offered in Honor of A. J. Graham*, 195–225. Leiden-Boston-Cologne, Brill

McLean, B. H. (2002) *An introduction to Greek Epigraphy of the Hellenistic and Roman Periods from Alexander the Great down to the Reign of Constantine (323 B.C.-A.D. 337).* Ann Arbor, University of Michigan Press.

Morris, I. (1987) *Burial and Ancient Society.* Cambridge, Cambridge University Press.

Morris, I. (1988) Tomb Cult and the Greek Renaissance. *Antiquity* 62, 750–761.

Nicorescu, P. (1944) Les basiliques byzantines de Dolojman. *Bulletin de la Section Historique* XXV.1, 95–101. Bucarest.

Panayotova, C. and Nedev, D. (2003) Apollonia Pontica. In D. V. Grammenos and E. K. Petropoulos, (eds) *Ancient Greek Colonies in the Black Sea I*, 123–140. Publications of the Archaeological Institute of Northern Greece, Thessaloniki.

Pelon, O. (1976) *Tholoi, tumuli et cercles funéraires.* Athens, École Française d'Athènes.

Polignac, F. de (1984) *La naissance de la cité grecque: cultes, espace et société VIIIe-VIIe siècles avant J.-C.* Paris, Éditions la Découverte.

Simion, G. (2003) *Culturi antice în zona Gurilor Dunarii.* Cluj-Napoca.

Skudnova, V. M. (1988) *Arhaicheskii nekropol' Ol'vii.* Leningrad, Iskusstvo.

Solovyov, S. L. (1999) *Ancient Berezan. The Architecture, History and Culture of the First Greek Colony in the Northern Black Sea*. Leiden-Boston-Cologne, Brill.

Teleagă, E. and Zirra, V. (2003), *Die Nekropole des 6.-1. Jhs.v. Chr. von Istria Bent bei Histria: Archaologische Untersuchungen zur Bevolkerung in der westlichen Schwarzmeerregion.* Rahden, Germany, Verlag Marie Leidorf.

Versnel, H. S. (1994) *Transition and Reversal in Myth and Ritual*, 2nd ed. Leiden-New York-Cologne, Brill.

10

Transformations of landscape use in the Lower Dnieper region

Valeria Bylkova

The study of the ways in which Greek settlers integrated into existing landscapes or created new ones seems a fertile approach to the problem of colonization and Greek/ native relations (Owen 2005). An examination of the specific situations, formed in each individual region where Greek settlers had been present, may be suggested on the basis of the archaeological data that has emerged over recent decades. In spite of a variety of views and methods, which makes a comparison of information rather difficult (Osborne 2004), regional studies nevertheless demonstrate a broad pattern and establish the local situation in more detail (Bilde and Stolba 2006). Ethnic characteristic cannot be determined absolutely by the material culture but one can correlate settlement patterns to populations through the archaeological evidence.

Differences between inland and coastal settlements have been observed in the area of Greek colonization: the more coastal (outer) sites of indigenous population display more significant Greek impact than the more inland (inner) ones (Coja 1990; Antonaccio 2005, 98; Maslennikov 2005; Avram 2006, 65, fig. 3). In contrast with other territories, the Lower Dnieper region allows the possibility of inspecting the development of an atypical situation in which the Greeks were initially the only settled population with developed agriculture. Archaeological data indicate an apparent absence of any settlements in the region under review throughout the Archaic and the Early Classical periods. The forms of cultural contacts between Greek and Barbarian populations in the lower course of the Dnieper valley were different in Archaic, Late Classical, and Hellenistic periods (Bylkova 2005). The influence of Greek colonization over this region was less impressive in comparison with other areas of the north coast of the Black Sea, and no Greek city was ever founded in the lower reach of the Dnieper. This territory did not become the object of Greek colonization during the Archaic period.

The eastern frontier of the Archaic Olbian chora was marked by the shrine of Demeter on the cape of Hyppolaios, which was mentioned by Herodotus [IV.53.6]. This border was definitely fixed by the Archaic settlement at Stanislav 1, located to the west of the cape (Vinogradov 2002), and no monument of so early a date is known to the east of this settlement. Greeks had settled rather late in this region which belonged to nomads. Settlements and scattered finds form the basis for this study and they are dated from the Late Classical period. Kinburn peninsula held a special position in the left bank of the Dnieper and it is here alone that the temporary craft productions were developed by Greeks during the Archaic period (Kryzhitskij *et al.* 1989, 22).

The Lower Dnieper region is a part of the Northern Black Sea coast lowlands. This is a territory in which the differences between two natural sub-zones has always been revealing. This region belongs to a zone of true steppe with several sub-zones and is characterized by variety of landscapes (Krivulchenko 2005). Settlements are located in several sub-zones according to physical-geographic regionalization: in the Black Sea coast Central Steppe and Lower Bug-Dnipro there is Lowland of Dry Steppe (Atlas 1978; 2000). The northern sub-zone (Middle/Central Steppe landscapes) is less dry and very warm, and the southern sub-zone (Southern–Dry Steppe) is very dry and temperate hot. The northern sub-zone coincides with an area of the most fertile cernozems (black soils), which consist of more than 4.5% humus. The Bonitet (account) of this soil is defined as 57 (Kotovskij *et al.* 1998, 60–61). The southern sub-zone is characterized by dark chestnut-coloured soils with a humus content up to 2.5%. The Bonitet of this soil comes to 45. As in the other lowlands, the Lower Dnieper region lacks mineral raw materials.

This differentiation of the South-Steppe and Middle-Steppe landscapes, which had existed both in prehistoric and historic times, determines the peculiarities of the use of the natural environment by different populations. Cartography of the archaeological monuments in the region under review demonstrates the extension of all types of site to diverse landscape areas (Fig. 10.1). Greeks here were probably not limited in choice of territory but the settlement pattern indicates that they preferred a familiar coastal environment to the inner territory with its favourable wet climate, black soils and solid Neogene limestone. We can use archaeological evidence to compare the situation in the inner and the outer areas of region under review, which demonstrate distinctions both in the cultural types and in the principles of landscape use by the two groups of populations. The location of settlements in the landscape demonstrates the different spatial principles of Greeks and Scythians, determined first of all by the different lifestyles. Since the mode of life of the Greeks and Scythians was fundamentally different, the Greek settlers mainly settled here in a naturally-constructed, not a culturally-constructed, landscape.

The inner part of the Lower Dnieper region (Middle or North Steppes) is a centre of so-called Scythia Magna, or Classical Scythia. It was an area where settlements with developed stone buildings had existed in the Late Bronze Age (Sharafutdinova 1961, 13). These were constructed by the earliest truly settled agricultural population, but one cannot see any links between those sites and the Scythian ones. Later the region

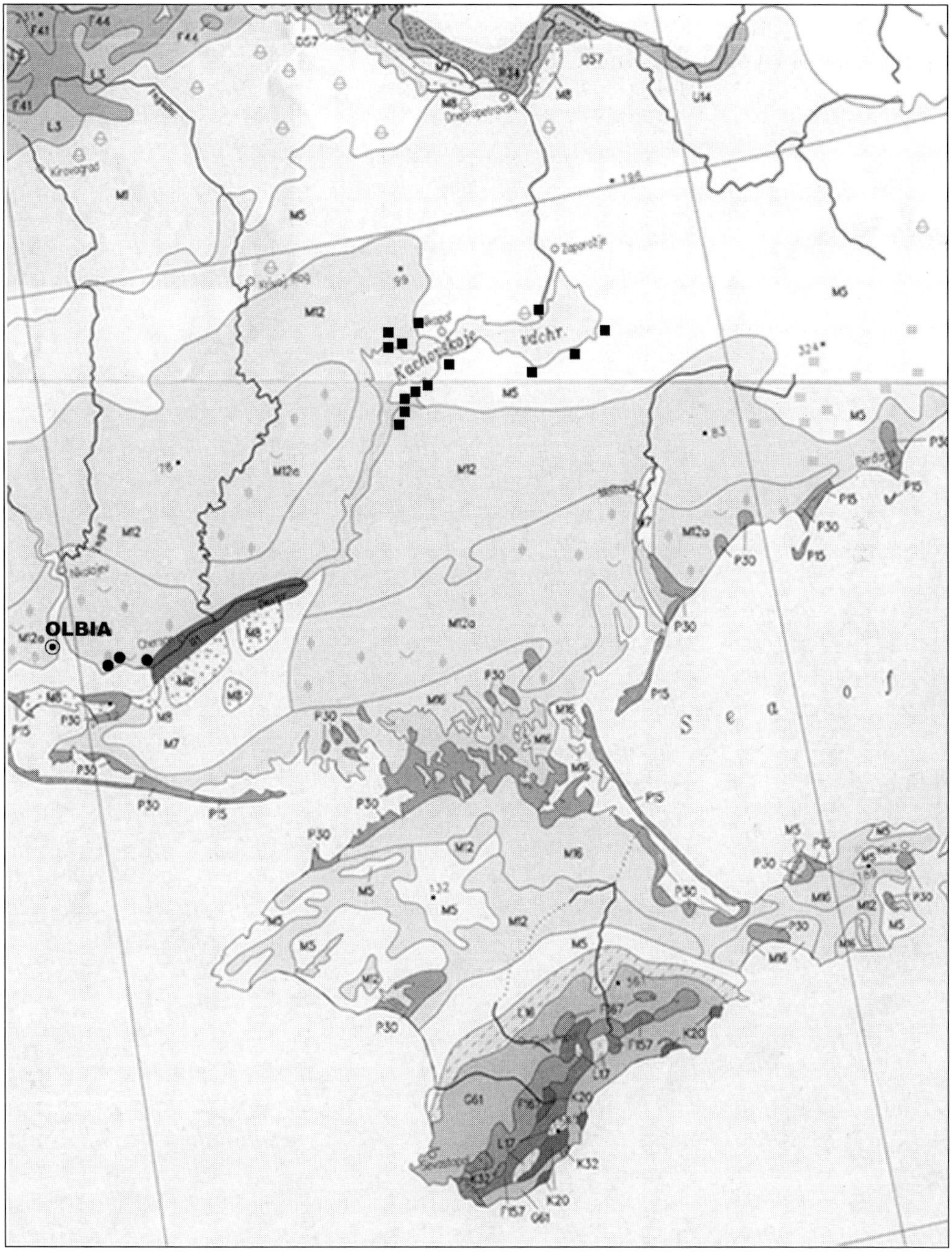

Fig. 10.1. The Crimea and southern Ukraine, with different ecological zones and sites mentioned in the text.

was dominated by nomadic Scythians with burial-mounds as the main archaeological monuments. The area where the first Scythian settlements had been founded was constantly occupied by Scythian nomad tribes; the Scythian burial-mounds are concentrated here, and large groups – and even fields – of mounds are located here. The materials obtained are totally representative of a Scythian culture: stone sculpture, bronze cauldrons, typical weapons and horse bridle, and handmade pottery are found. The earliest long-term inland settlements of the Early Iron Age arose from the end of the fifth to the middle of the fourth centuries (Bylkova 2005a, 225–227). This period is the least well known in the transition of Scythia in the Steppe region (Alekseev 2003, 237).

The Scythian group of settlements is completely within area No. M5 of the sub-zone of herb-grass steppes of lowland-colline types (Fig. 10.1), according to a map of natural European vegetation (Bohn *et al.* 2000, 64, 138, blat. 6, 9). The Middle sub-zone of the steppe is characterized by greater precipitation than the southern sub-zone. Wood vegetation, black soil, and wet ravines are specific to this area. 'Water forests' – plavni – had covered a significant area on the left bank of Dnieper-river. The 'Kamenskij Pod' in antiquity had been an area of forests with large water-meadows (Ijevlev 1991). These water-forests still served as a source of succulent fodder for livestock during drought in the 19th century (Afanasjev-Chuzhbinskij 1863). The water in the Dnieper remained clean enough until the twentieth century (Evarnitskij 1890, 32). Underground water could also have been in use in antiquity.

The right bank of Dnieper is higher and the left one is lower and slopes more. There are four terraces above the valley of the river. Scythian settlements are sited on the banks of the tributaries, side-channels and branches of the Dnieper (Fig. 10.2). Most of the settlements are concentrated on the left bank, on the Konka River and the smaller tributaries, but others are on the right bank, on the Pidpil'na-River and its tributaries. A headland position alongside tributaries and side-channels, sloping to water is characteristic for these sites (Fig. 10.3). Scythian settlements are scattered in this landscape without special preparation of space. They are usually small, 1–4 hectares in area, with a few notable exceptions (Bylkova 2007a, 41). The fortified settlement at Kamenskoe is more than 1,000 ha and is surrounded by earth ramparts and ditches (Grakov 1954).

As for mineral raw materials, Neogene limestone is distributed on the right bank of Dnieper River. Brown iron ore, a limonite, was easily accessible in the sub-zone of the Middle-Steppe. Traces of iron production – such as ore, slag, obtained metal, and pit-kilns – have been discovered in the inner Scythian settlements. A smith could make a small quantity of metal from bog ore in smith-kilns by the crucible method (Olgovskij 1987). Copper craft is also well known in Kamenskoe fortified settlement (Grakov 1954, 115–136; Gavriljuk 1999).

These Scythian settlements have specific features which distinguish them from those of the neighbouring tribes. They are highly disorganized. Cultural layers and building remains can be fixed only on some parts of their territory which are less densely built up. In those parts of the settlements where dwelling and household structures are concentrated, there is no trace of systematic planning, with buildings of different types and sizes scattered haphazardly. Ethnographically, a similar picture may be observed at the beginning of sedentarization, where the scattered distribution of their houses identifies the settlements of recently settled nomads (Cribb 1990, 156–161).

In the inner Scythian settlements house construction takes the form of pit structures (the smaller less deeply dug out) and ground level wattle and daub dwellings of irregular shape. These range in size from 4–5 to 150 m^2. Uniformity of building had not been developed. The remains of wattle and daub walls and clay plaster are constantly encountered on these sites and they attest the existence of ground level structures of various functions with such walls. Their earth walls were 1.4 to 2.5 m in height. Some of them consisted of a rectangular room with rounded corners and an oval stepped entrance (Bylkova 2007, 304–306, figs 32.5; 32.6). As for hearths, they take the form of small, round or oval, clay platforms or alternatively shallow pits. They are found within semi-pit and other structures, but also outside them. The hearths also had been heated with wood or, rarely, with bones.

The Scythians had never made use of mud-brick, nor roof tiles. Several examples of stone construction were noted in excavations at the Scythian settlement Pervomaevka 2 (Bylkova 2007a, 47, 185, fig. 32). Irregular shaped stones of different size were laid out together with broken bones and ceramic sherds as a kind of small paving. A special stone line was laid also along the border of this settlement. This 'masonry' was irregular – large slabs had been mingled with small stones. Its width was 0.4–0.8 m, and height 0.3–0.4 m. Solid Neogene limestone outcrops immediately alongside the inner settlements. The Scythians exploited the stone for numerous tools, sometimes for supporting earth mounds, but not for house-building. Wood remained the main building material.

Fig. 10.2. Terraces above the Dnieper River, a common location for Scythian settlement.

Fig. 10.3. Headland on the Dnieper River estuary.

Special places for cult practice have not been identified in the inner settlements. Occasional cult activity may be assumed on the basis of finds in several pits: animal bones were laid in anatomic order on the bottom, reminiscent of an offering. A complex of clay objects, including a male figurine and 'scones', was found in a pit in the Pervomaevka 2 settlement. Similarities with the Forest-Steppe zone settlements of agricultural tribes (Shramko 1999) suggest possible impact from the north. But no traces of Greek cult practice were found – no altars, terracotta, or graffiti. B. N. Grakov noted that a distinctive feature of the Kamenskoe fortified settlement was the absence of ash; in only one case was ash found in a dwelling (Grakov 1954, 62–63). This observation was confirmed for the Scythian settlements excavated subsequently. The Scythians did not designate special places or receptacles for the collection of domestic ash, as was customary among agricultural peoples.

The Scythians used the landscape according to their nomadic economy and lifestyle. The nomadic economy was based on stock-breeding; bones of cattle and horses predominate among the finds in the Scythian settlements (Zhuravlev 1991). Crop-growing was secondary with millet and barley as main crops (Pashkevich 2000). Meljukova (1989, 114) explains the process of Scythian partial sedentarization as a result of Greek impact, which spread over tribes neighbouring Greek settlements, but this cannot be the same for hinterland. E. H. Minns was one of the first scholars to suggest that there may have been settlements among both the agricultural and the nomadic Scythians, drawing ethnographic analogies from the cultures of nomadic people who had special places for trade, craft, and capital centres (Minns 1913, 15, 52). It looks as if there are no grounds to assert that Scythian settlements were founded under the influence of Greeks. One cannot fix significant observable changes in Scythian culture as a result of these contacts. The Scythians did not try to transform the steppe to arable land despite being located on fertile soil. The explanation should rather be sought in the character of the nomadic economy. All three types of nomadic stock-breeding were linked more or less with crop-growing (Andrianov 1985, 54; Markov 1981). The inner Scythian settlements represent a different level of material cultural remains in comparison with the outer sites which are described below. Some changes in the structure of material were connected with use of Greek amphoras, as wine was constantly carried to the inner territory. Although the Scythians were familiar with wine and exotic imports, their normal everyday lifestyle had not changed under Greek impact. Nor were weaving looms, potters' wheels, lead craft, building, or the ritual practice of Greeks incorporated into the culture of the inner Steppe population of this region. The inner Scythian settlements and the outer Greek ones had been founded synchronously in the Late Classical period; there are no reasons whatsoever to explain a sedentarization of Scythians as a result of Greek colonization.

The outer part of the region under review had been a territory where Greek settlers began to cultivate virgin land and where non-Greek settlements were absent. Greek settlements were located on the right bank of Dnieper, in the mouth of the river. In antiquity the Dnieper and the Southern Bug, where Olbia and her chora were founded, had a common delta. Later this part of Dnieper River transformed into the Dnieper liman (Brujako and Karpov 1992, 95–96, fig. 1). With respect to physical geography divisions (Kotovskij *et al.* 1998, 109; Atlas 2000, XLI) the outer settlements of the Lower Dnieper region are located in the same area of the South-Steppe as the Olbian sites, in the Lower Bug-Dnipro Lowland with chestnut soils on loess layers. This area was completely and continuously occupied from the very beginning of the fourth century BC. The outer settlements fit well with an area No. M 12A of West Pontic grass steppes (Bohn *et al.* 2000, 65, 139, blatt 9), as do all the Olbian chora settlements (Fig. 10.1). The settlements are found on the right bank of the lower reaches of the Dnieper. There were the forests in the Dnieper estuary in the first millennium BC (Ardamatskaja *et al.* 1987, 8). Archaeological evidence, including wild animal bones that were found in the outer settlements, confirm that forest types were predominant over steppe types (Zhuravlev 1991, 84–85, table 5). One can suggest that the total dominance of steppe types among wild animals in the settlements, dated from the first century BC to the third century AD, demonstrates a depletion of these forests. Such a modification of landscape is considered to be a result of negative human activity (Buchinskij 1963). Small rivers had been transformed into dry ravines. The Black Sea littoral in this region is formed by rock of 4–5 levels of stability that create conditions for a high speed of abrasion of both surface and underwater areas of the coastline. Colonization everywhere was accompanied by clearing of land for cultivation, including the burning and logging of forests. As a result erosion intensified and the hydrological regime changed (Kryzhitskij 1995, 17–18).

The Greeks had started to develop the lands in the southern part of the region at the same time as the Scythians had founded their first settlements. All the outer settlements had occupied high banks cut by ravines. The most convenient places for fishing and sailing were chosen: in the eighteenth century these same places were chosen for the building of new ports and wharfs. The river bank is gently sloped and convenient for building. Advantages of this sub-zone consist in large land area, suitable places for quays, a wealth of fish, different types of clay and outcrops of Paleogene limestone (although not of the best quality). The dark chestnut-coloured soils are not as fertile as the black soils in the inner Middle-Steppe subzone, where solid stone and ores were also widespread, but the outer South-Steppe sub-zone is more similar to the usual Greek environment. Indeed, Greeks in the Lower Dnieper region used a landscape in a customary way and they organized their settlements accordingly.

The outer settlements extended along the bank of the river, their length never less than twice their width, with an area usually of 2 to 4 hectares. One site is sizeable with fortification walls enclosing some 10 ha (Buiskikh 1989). There were several periods of building in all the settlements, and all of them were inhabited permanently by the population from the same archaeological culture. All of these settlements are densely built-up with elements of systematic planning. A regular plan was laid out at a very early stage of settlement. A distribution of structures can be traced both along the shoreline and on a line running inland from the bank. The distance between synchronous dwellings is a minimum of 5–10 m. Non-dwelling structures were also located on land adjacent to the settlement. All buildings in the outer settlements were made of limestone and mud brick with tiled or clay and reed roofs. Yard pavings were made from limestone slabs in combination with amphora sherds. Despite the difficulties connected with building on loess layers, a variety of structure forms were used, including high level constructions (Bylkova 2007, 299–302, figs 32.2; 32.3; 32.4). One can trace a consistency in the use and quarrying of stone by inhabitants of outer settlements during all periods of their existence. In contrast with Scythian settlements, ash was important both in building and in ritual practice. The above-ground and semi-dugout dwellings of these settlements were surrounded by storage-pits, trash-pits, household structures, cisterns, and so on. Both the building type and peculiarity of finds produce the evidence of independent individual *oikoi*, which composed these settlements.

Traces of constant cult activity were found in all the outer settlements. The location of ritual places gives an evidence of domestic cults: home altars and terracotta were found in or near dwellings; graffiti with gods' names are also known. Especially popular was the worship of Demeter and Dionysus. Some places may be connected with common cult practice. Two mounds of ash were discovered in the Glubokaja Pristan' settlement, 1.2 m and 2 m high (Buiskikh 1993, 80–82). They were located

22 m apart in two ancient gullies. Taking into account the depth of these gullies, the thickness of these accumulations of ash increases to 4 m and 2.8 m. The ash mound was constructed from ash with layers of burned clay and crushed stone. All the material encountered in them shows the traces of the action of fire. It includes clay 'loaves', anthropomorphic statuettes, terracotta fragments and graffiti, including a dedication to Apollo. Judging by the date of the ceramics, the ash piles were established at the time of the settlement's foundation and continued in use until the cessation of life there (Buiskikh 1993, 80–82). The ash with archaeological finds filled in a small natural ravine gully, excavated in the Usad'ba Litvinenko settlement (Bylkova 2002), can be connected with the same custom of accumulating ash in special places, even if an ash mound was not constructed. In the Belozerskoe settlement such large, specially designated ash piles were absent, but the habit of depositing ash separately from other refuse, in pits originally used for storing foodstuffs, may be observed. The fine ash of this fill contains a great quantity of finds, including specific artefacts of fired and unfired clay – 'loaves', 'cakes', beads and weights. 'Ash piles' were discovered both in the chora near Olbia and in more distant settlements (Golovachova and Rogov 2002; Nosova 2002; Kotzura 2006), but they are unknown at Scythian steppe settlements.

At the outer settlements the numerous remains of different fishes, net-weights, bone needles for making nets, and anchor stones for boats demonstrate the importance of fishing as distinct from the inner Scythian settlements. The herd composition also offers two different lines with predominance of goats and sheep (40%) in the outer settlements (analyses by O. P. Zhuravlev). Inspection of the paleobotanical remains, made by G. A. Pashkevich, reveals wheat and barley as main crops. The productive activity of population of the outer settlements can be seen in the usual domestic craft, remains of lead production, and rare traces of iron production without professional specialization.

The complexities of determining the ethnic characteristic of outer population are the same as in other regions of the Black Sea littoral, where the relationships between Greek and 'indigenous' populations are being studied. There were no ethnical or cultural entities found in the settlements of Olbian chora, though taking into consideration a presence of non-Greek types of material culture in the settlements and in Olbia herself, one can presume that some representatives of indigenous tribes adopted a Greek lifestyle (Kryzhitskij *et al.* 1989, 147; 1999, 410–411). One point of view represents the situation in the Lower Bug region in the Classical period as a transformation of non-Greek settlements into Hellenized ones. To confirm this suggestion a popular 'dugout dwellings argument' is adduced along with changes in the building tradition. According to Marchenko, in the first half of the fourth century BC dugouts and semi-dugouts dominated, and only in the Early Hellenistic period planning, construction and building materials were changed under Greek influence (Marchenko 2005, 119, 123, 126). In the outer settlements in the Lower Dnieper region one can trace a quite different situation. There both above-ground and dugout structures were discovered, but they differ from Scythian ones by type, building materials, and arrangement. All Greek building materials and types of structures also were in use in outer settlements of the region under review from their foundation; the same was true for material culture and economy. Therefore, landscape and environment corresponded to the needs of Greek settlers. Being among the inhabitants of the outer settlements, non-Greeks did not form a principle component of their culture – that remained Greek.

Dugout dwellings, indeed, are represented both in the inner and in the outer territories. The types of dugout constructions, which are specific to the outer settlements, do not coincide with Scythian types from the inner settlements. The adaptation to unfamiliar natural conditions called forth new features in the culture of the Greeks, but the essential foundations of their existence were preserved even in these remote regions. The finds *in situ* within semi-dugouts exhibit the usual range of artefacts, and do not suggest a special function or ethnic character. We, thus, have no reason to link the use of dugout structures in the outer territory with the presence of Scythians. In the Lower Dnieper region inner and outer settlements were even characterized by two different sets of handmade ware, which is often considered as a significant local non-Greek feature. And if we take into account the fact that dugouts appeared in the Olbian chora in the Archaic period, when there were no Scythian settlements in steppe at all, then the connection with the Scythians of Steppe zone becomes quite untenable. Research has shown that even the easternmost 'frontier' outer settlements, where it was anticipated that greater reciprocal influences between cultures might be encountered, are not at all like the settlements of the Scythians themselves that are located in the inner part of the region under review. One may suggest that indigenous population could be included into inner settlements, but physical anthropological analyses of the corresponding finds from two settlements and that T. A. Nazarova (Institute of Archaeology, National Academy of Science of Ukraine, Kiev) and E. V. Veselovskaja (Laboratory of Anthropological Reconstruction, Russian Academy of Science, Moscow) had made for excavations reports, demonstrate that the inhabitants of outer territory belong to classic gracile Mediterranean type.

This proposed overview demonstrates *two lines of landscape use* by two population groups living in the region. Details of the landscape changes in the Lower Dnieper region have just begun to be studied, but some of them may be explained by arrival of Greek settlers. A different way of life within the inner Scythian territory in comparison with the outer settlements explains the different character of the archaeological remains. There are no reasons to regard the outer population of South-Steppe sub-zone as a Hellenized indigenous population. Hellenization may be seen here only as a result of including some people of Scythian origin among the inhabitants of the outer settlements. Although the inner and outer settlements were contemporaneous, their foundations were conditioned by different factors, reflected in the choice of environments. We find no similarity, archaeologically, in the character of inner and outer sites, not even to the extent that one might speak of significant cultural influence. The important difference consists in a principle of choice of landscape zone for settlement and in the results of exploiting that zone.

Diachronic changes in the distributions of settlements in the Lower Dnieper region may be traced throughout Hellenistic and Roman times. The next stage in existence of settled life in the Lower Dnieper region is dated from the second half of the second century BC to the third century AD (Bylkova 2007a, 111–114). During the Late Hellenistic period new non-Greek populations had settled here. It was a period of migrations and intensive cultural interactions; this time a significant Greek impact to the inner territory is visible archaeologically. The South-Steppe sub-zone, as before, was occupied by a mainly Greek population (or population of Greek cultural tradition) (Kryzhitskij *et al.* 1989, 215–216). The new population of the Middle-Steppe sub-zone were interested in other environments than the earlier Scythians and site location attest to these changes. Now the absolute majority of inner settlements is situated in plot M 12 of Grass steppes (Bohn *et al.* 2000, 64, 138, blat. 6, 9), mostly on the right bank of the Dnieper. Both non-Greek and Greek features are traced in building, fortification, and lifestyle. Mixed style in planning and building the inner settlements go together with use of new materials (Kryzhitskij 1982). The combination of building methods, construction and components demonstrate the formation of a Greek-non-Greek fortification (Koltukhov 1999, 99). Stone had acquired a great significance, so outcrops of Neogene limestone were under constant use. Agriculture and fishing played an important part in life of this population. A specific feature of these new inner settlements is existence of ash accumulations, such as ash mounds and ash fills of gullies.

Thus, in the first stage of Greek settlement in the Lower Dnieper region only the outer territories (in the South-Steppe sub-zone) had been influenced by Greek settlers. The cultural and natural landscape in the inner areas (the Middle-Steppe sub-zone) had not been changed under Greek impact. Comparison between the Greek and Scythian spheres in the Lower Dnieper region shows major differences in the environment, in the choice of natural resources for exploitation, and in the topography, planning, and construction of the settlements themselves. One can demonstrate changes in the inner part of the Lower Dnieper region only during the Late Hellenistic period when new non-Greek populations had settled here. This time a strong Greek impact is apparent in inner zone, including landscape use. Settlement location and the main characteristics of the culture of their inhabitants during Classical and Early Hellenistic period demonstrate co-existence in the region under review of two different types of populations in two different landscapes.

Abbreviations

Altas 2000 = *Atlas of Ukraine* (2000) Kyiv, Institute of Geography, National Academy of Science of Ukraine.

Atlas 1978 = *Atlas prirodnyh uslovij i estestvennyh resursov Ukrainskoj SSR* (1978). Moscow.

Bibliography

Afanasjev-Chuzhbinskij, A. A. (1863) *Poezdka v Juzhnuju Rossiju. Part 1. Ocherki Dnepra.* Sankt-Peterburg.

Alekseev, A. Yu. (2003) *Chronografija Evropeiskoj Skifii.* Sankt-Peterburg, State Hermitage.

Andrianov, B. V. (1985) *Neosedloe naselenie mira (istoroko-etnograficheskoe issledovanie).* Moscow, Nauka

Antonaccio, C. M. (2005) Excavating Colonization. In H. Hurst and S. Owen (eds) *Ancient Colonizations. Analogy, Similarity and Difference*, 97–113. London, Duckworth.

Ardamatskaja, T. B., Zelinskaja, L. M., Umanets, O. Yu. and Fedorenko, A. P. (1987) Chernomorskij zapovednik. In *Zapovedniki SSSR: Zapovednimi Ukrainy i Moldavii.* Moscow, Mysl'.

Avram, A. (2006) The Territories of Istros and Kallatis. In P. G. Bilde and V. F. Stolba (eds) *Surveying the Greek Chora. Black Sea Region in a Comparative Perspective. Black Sea Studies, 4*, 59–80. Aarhus, Aarhus University Press.

Bilde, P. G. and Stolba, V. F. (eds) (2006) *Surveying the Greek Chora. Black Sea Region in a Comparative Perspective. Black Sea Studies, 4.* Aarhus, Aarhus University Press.

Bohn, U., Gollub, G. and Heettwer, Ch. (2000) *Karte der naturlichen vegetation Europas.* Bonn, Bad Godesberg.

Brujako, I. V. and Karpov, V. A. (1992) Drevnjaja geografija i kolebanija urovnja morja (na primere severo-zapadnoj chasti Chernomorskogo bassejna v antichnuju epokhu) *Vestnik drevnej istorii.*2, 87–97.

Buchinskij, I. E. (1963) *Klimat Ukrainy v proshlom, nastojashchem i budushchem.* Kyiv, Gossel'khozizdat.

Buiskikh, S. B. (1989) Issledovanija v urochishche Glubokaja Pristan' In *Tezisy dokladov Vsesojuznoj konferentsii, posvjashchennoj 90-letiju so dnja rozhdenija professora B. N. Grakova*, 23–24. Zaporozh'e, Institut arkheologii AN SSSR, Moscow State University, Zaporozh'e State University.

Buiskikh, S. B. (1993) Eskhary Glubokoj Pristani. In S. B. Okhotnikov (ed.) *Drevnee Prichernomor'e*, 80–82. Odessa, Odesskoe arkheologicheskoe obshchestvo, Odesskij arkheologicheskij.

Bylkova, V. P. (2002) Osnovni rezul'taty doslidgen' poselennja "Sadyba Lytvynenka" (Stanislav 2). In *Arheologichna zbirka 2*, 120–132, Kherson.

Bylkova, V. P. (2005) The Lower Dnieper region as an Area of Greek/Barbarian Interaction. In D. Braund (ed.) *Scythians and Greeks. Cultural Interactions in Scythia, Athens and the Early Roman Empire (sixth century BC - first century AD)*, 131–147. Exeter, Exeter University press.

Bylkova, V. P. (2005a) The Chronology of Settlements in the Lower Dnieper Region (400–100 BC). In L. Hannestad and V. Stolba (eds) *Chronologies of the Black Sea Area in the Period c. 400–100 BC (Black Sea Studies, 3)*, 217–247. Aarhus, Aarhus University Press.

Bylkova, V. P. (2007) Scythian and Olbian settlements in the Lower Dnieper region In R. Westgate, N. Fisher and J. Whitby (eds) *Building communities: House, Settlement and Society in the Aegean and Beyond*, British School at Athens Studies 15, 297–306.

Bylkova, V. P. (2007a) *Nizhnee Podneprov'je v antichnuju epokhu (po materialam raskopok poselenij).* Kherson, Kherson State University.

Coja, M. (1990) Greek Colonists and Native Populations in Dobruja (Moesia Inferior): The Archaeological Evidence. In J.-P. Descoeudres (ed.) *Greek Colonists and Native Populations. Proceedings of the First Congress of Classical Archaeology held in honour of Emeritus Professor A. D. Trendall*, 157–168. Canberra, Humanities Research Centre and Oxford, Clarendon Press.

Cribb, R. (1990) *Nomads in Archaeology.* Cambridge, Cambridge University Press.

Evarnizkij, D. I. (1890) *Volnosti zaporozhskikh kozakov. Istoriko-topograficheskij ocherk.* Sankt-Peterburg.

Gavriljuk, N. A. (1999) *Istorija ekonomiki Stepnoj Skifii VI-III vv. do n. e.* Kyiv, Institut arkheologii, National Academy of Science (Ukraine).

Golovachova, N. V. and Rogov, Ye. Ya. (2002) Sel'skij hram i zol'nik u poselenija Kozyrka 11 na hore Ol'vii. In *Bosporskij fenomen. Pogrebal'nyje pamjatniki i svjatilishcha.P.* 2, 41–44. Sankt-Peterburg, State Hermitage.

Grakov, B. N. (1954) *Kamenskoje gorodishche na Dnepre. Materialy i issledovanija po arheologii SSSR*, 54. Moscow.

Ijevlev, M. M. (1991) Paleogeograficheskaja obstanovka v rajone Nizhnego Podneprov'ja v IV veke do n. e. In A. Ju. Alekseev, Murzin V. Yu. and Rolle R. *Chertomlyk*, 311–318. Kyiv, Naukova.

Koltukhov, S. G.(1999) *Ukreplenija Krymskoi Skifii.* Simferopol', Sonat.

Kotovskij, I. M., Alifanov, O. P., Bojko M. F. *et al.* (1998) *Priroda Khersonskoj oblasi: fiziko-geografichnyj narys* Kyiv, Fitosotsiotsentr.

Kotzura, A. G. (2006) Votivy Kosharskogo zol'nika, svjazannye s remeslennym proizvodstvom i promyslami. In *Drevnee Prichernomor'e*, VII, 104–110. Odessa, Odessa National University, Odessa Archeological Society.

Krivulchenko, A. I. (2005) *Sukhi stepy Prichornomor'ja ta Pryazov'ja: landshafty, galogeohimija grunto-pidgruntja.* Kyiv, Gidromax.

Kryzhitskij, S. D. (1982) *Zhilyje doma antichnykh gorodov Severnogo prichernomor'ja.* Kyiv, Naukova dumka.

Kryzhitskij, S. D. (1995) Pro vplyv zmin otochujushchego seredovyshcha na istorychnyj rozvytok Ol'vijskoi derzhavy *Arheologija*, 2, 13–25.

Kryzhitskij, S. D., Buiskikh, S. B., Burakov, A. V. and Otreshko, V. M. (1989) *Sel'skaja okruga Ol'vii.* Kyiv, Naukova dumka.

Kryzhitskij, S. D., Rusyaeva, A. S., Krapivina, V. V., Leipunskaya, N. A., Skrzhinskaya, M. V. and Anokhin V. A. (1999) *Ol'vija. Antichnoe gosudarstvo v Severnom Prichernomor'je.* Kyiv, Institut arkheologii NAN Ukrainy.

Marchenko, K. K. (2005) *Greki i varvary Severnogo Prichernomor'ja v skifskuju epohu (ed.)* Sankt-Peterburg, Aleteja.

Markov, G. E. (1981) Skotovodcheskoje khozjajstvo i kochevnichestvo. *Definizii i terminologija Sovetskaja etnografija*, 4, 83–94.

Maslennikov, A. A. (2005) The Development of Graeco-Barbarian Contacts in the Chora of the European Bosporus (Sixth-First Centuries). In D. Braund (ed.) *Scythians and Greeks. Cultural Interactions in Scythia, Athens and the Early Roman Empire (sixth century BC – first century AD)*, 153–166. Exeter, Exeter University Press.

Meljukova, A. I. (1989) *Stepi evropejskoj chasti SSSR v skifo-sarmatskoje vremja (ed.).* Moscow, Nauka.

Minns, E. H. (1913) *Scythians and Greeks. A Survey of Ancient History and Archaeology on the North Coast of the Euxine from the Danube to the Caucasus.* Cambridge, Cambridge University Press.

Nosova, L. V. (2002) O kul'tovykh zol'nikakh antichnyhk poselenij Severo-Zapadnogo Prichernomor'ja (v svjazi s raskopkami Kosharskogo arheologicheskogo kompleksa) In *Bosporskij fenomen. Pogrebal'nyje pamjatniki i svjatilishcha.P. 2*, 62–68. Sankt-Peterburg, State Hermitage.

Olgovskij, S. Ya. (1987) Social'no-ekonomicheskaja rol' Kamenskogo gorodishcha. In E. V. Chernenko (ed.) *Skyfy Severnogo Prichernomor'ja*, 48–53. Kyiv, Naukova.

Osborne, R. (2004) Configuring the landscape. In F. Kolb (ed.) *Chora und Polis. Schriften des Histrischen Kollegs. Kolloquien 54*, 369–374. Munchen, R. Oldenbourg Verlag.

Owen, S. (2005) Analogy, Archaeology and Archaic Greek Colonization. In H. Hurst and S. Owen (eds) *Ancient Colonizations. Analogy, Similarity and Difference*, 5–22. London, Duckworth.

Pashkevich, G. A. (2000) Paleoetnobotanicheskie issledovanija skifskikh pamjatnikov stepnoj zony Severnogo Prichernomor'ja. In V. I. Guliaev and V. S. Olkhovskiy (eds) *Skify i sarmaty v VII-III vv. do n. e. Paleoekologija, antropologija i arheologija*, 101–109, Moscow, Institut arheologii RAN.

Sharafutdinova, I. M. (1961) Novi pam'jatki epokhi piznjoi bronzy v Nizhnjomu Podniprov'I *Arkheologichni pamjatki URSR 10*, 12–25. Kyiv, Institut arkheologii.
Shramko, B. A. (1999) Glinjanye skul'ptury Lesostepnoj Skifii. *Rossijskaja arheologija* 3, 35–49.
Vinogradov, Y. A. (2002) Gorodishche Stanislav (osnovnye itogi issledovanij 1982, 1988–91 gg.). In *Arheologichna zbirka 2*, 88–106. Kherson, Kherson Regional Museum.
Zhuravlev, O. P. (1991) Zhivotnovodstvo i okhota u naselenija skifskihk gorodishch Nizhnego Podneprov'ja. In *Problemy arheologii Severnogo Prichernomor'ja (k 100-letiju osnovanija Khersonskogo muzeja drevnostej)*, 75–86, Kherson, Kherson Regional Museum.

11

Borysthenes and Olbia: Reflections on the character of contacts between Greeks and Natives during the initial stage of colonization

Sergey Solovyov

The initial stage of Greek penetration into Scythia occurred from the middle to the last quarter of the seventh century BC. This chronological framework is determined by the first Greek imports found in the northern Black Sea hinterland and by the foundation of Greek settlements in the coastal zone, which more or less corresponds to the information from ancient authors on the Greek colonization of Northern Pontus (Vinogradov *et al.* 1990). The archaeological evidence, which used to be associated with this date, can be divided into two groups by provenance. One group includes finds of archaic Greek pottery in the sites and tombs of the indigenous population which inhabited the steppe and forest-steppe zones of Scythia. The other group embraces the Greek ceramic imports of two coastal sites – those on Berezan Island and on the coast of the Taganrog Gulf (Fig. 11.1).

A review of archaeological evidence from Berezan has definitely shown that relevant archaeological materials actually consist of a very small group of painted Greek vessels (Solovyov 2007, 38–40). These comprised mostly of SiA Id (after Kerschner and Schlotzhauer 2005) and jugs and plates (so-called stemmed dishes), accompanied by a number of North Ionian bird bowls dating not earlier than 630 BC and isolated finds of Proto-Corinthian pottery, with some of Linear *kotyle* dating to 650–630 BC. Handmade local ceramics originating in the forest-steppe of Scythia were also recovered, including tulip-shaped pots of the Late Chyornyi Les culture, which were decorated with applied decoration separated by fingerprints with pierced holes (Fig. 11.2).

In contrast, the Taganrog collection of seventh century Greek imports consists mainly of several dozen sherds of East Greek bird bowls and jugs (Kopylov and Larenok 1994). But we should not forget that this collection was mainly formed of artefacts found on the sea shore. First attempts have just recently been made to investigate ancient cultural layers submerged by the sea (Dally and Larenok 2002).

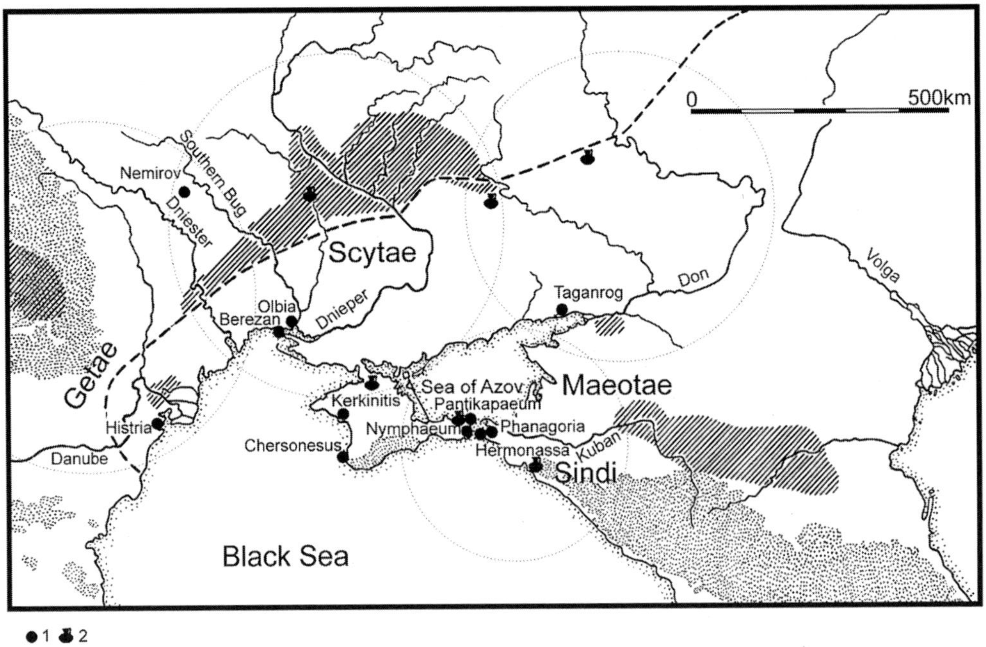

Fig. 11.1. The map of the Northern Black Sea area: 1 – Greek and local sites; 2 – Scythian tombs with Greek pottery of the seventh century BC

The presence of both imported and local pottery cannot be used as an argument for the presence of both Greeks and natives before around 630 BC. In the immediately following decades of the seventh century, the pottery seems to reflect a time of comparative stability for the site as a trading emporium for the northern Black Sea coast. The reasons for, and processes of, Greek penetration into the Northern Black Sea now have been widely discussed (Koshelenko and Kuznetsov 1998; Tsetskhladze 1994; 1998; Solovyov 2007; Domanskii and Marčenko 2007). The appearance of Scythians on the coast has also been explained by the specific character of their economy and the seasonal dependence on cattle breeding (Gavrilyuk 1999, 138–139).

The recent archaeometric analysis of Greek pottery from Berezan provides some observations on the ethnic composition of the traders and their trading habits. The late seventh century BC imported pottery was generally dominated by South Ionian, mainly Milesian products, while the market in the sixth century BC was dominated by North Ionian products. The mutable partition between South Ionian and North Ionian products can reflect a free market or can also indicate changes in the origin of probably newly arrived settlers (Posamentir 2006, 161–162, Figs 2–4; Posamentir and Solovyov 2006, 127).

Nevertheless, the small number and typological homogeneity of Greek imports and handmade pottery of the seventh century might signify the irregularity and the short duration of first contacts between Greeks and natives (Solovyov 1998, 208–12;

Fig. 11.2. Greek (Inv. B90.21, B172, B69.29, B254, B83.19, B451, B69.60) and local (Inv. B69.217) pottery of the first stage of colonization from Berezan.

2007, 41). They needed plenty of time for getting better acquainted with each other. More than a quarter of the century passed before the first traces of their permanent and joint residence on Berezan appeared – the cultural layer and dwellings in the settlement area and the burials in the necropolis (Solovyov 1999, 3–4).

On the basis of archaeological materials from Berezan and other places in the Northern Pontic area where Greeks were active, it can be stated that the development of the coastal zone of the Black Sea-Azov Basin could not have been accomplished by the ancient Greeks without their being well-acquainted with the geographical conditions, natural resources, and demography of the colonized regions. The development was accomplished by small groups of seafarers – adventurers and traders, who were mostly Ionians. They were interested in new sources of raw materials – first of all copper and iron – and, probably, in obtaining foodstuffs for their home cities, which were burdened by internal social and economic problems and struggles against external enemies (Solovyov 2007).

Contacts with the local population of the northern Black Sea littoral were undoubtedly an important part of the colonization process (Marčenko 2005). Numerous archaeological data testify that the most simple and widespread pattern of interaction was the accidental meeting of Greek seafarers with nomads and semi-settled populations, who lived in the steppes and forest-steppes of Scythia, and used the water-meadows of Borysthenes and Hypanis, as well as northern coast of Lake Maeotis, as winter pastures for their cattle. Under favourable circumstances (such as peaceful and easygoing interactions, the absence of external threat or mutual benefits) these casual meetings gradually developed into steady, regular and most likely seasonal contacts. The areas around Berezan (on the northern Black Sea shore) and Taganrog (on the northern coast of the Sea of Azov) became the epicentres of such contacts (Solovyov 2004).

Without a doubt, the widespread development of trade dominated relations between Greeks and natives in these places. The same could be inferred from handicraft production, which initially also had a seasonal character. The best example of such a seasonal craft site is at Yagorlyk on the Dnieper delta not far from Berezan (Fig. 11.3). The remnants of temporary iron, bronze and glass-making workshops, dated from the seventh century BC, have been found on the site (Ostroverkhov 1979). New evidence of bronze-making and pottery-manufacturing workshops has recently been uncovered on Berezan, dating as early as the early sixth century BC (Domanskii and Marčenko 2007).

Greek merchants and the tribal leaders of nomadic and semi-settled Scythians could have initiated this kind of interaction. To be successful, the Greeks probably had to receive the approval of the local leaders. This could be obtained in different ways: by providing occasional gifts, by making temporary agreements and by paying regular tribute. The majority of seventh century Greek imports found in the Scythian burials must have been such gifts.

Seasonal moorings were certainly erected at other coastal points, protected from bad weather and the threat of sudden attack. Most probably these were the places

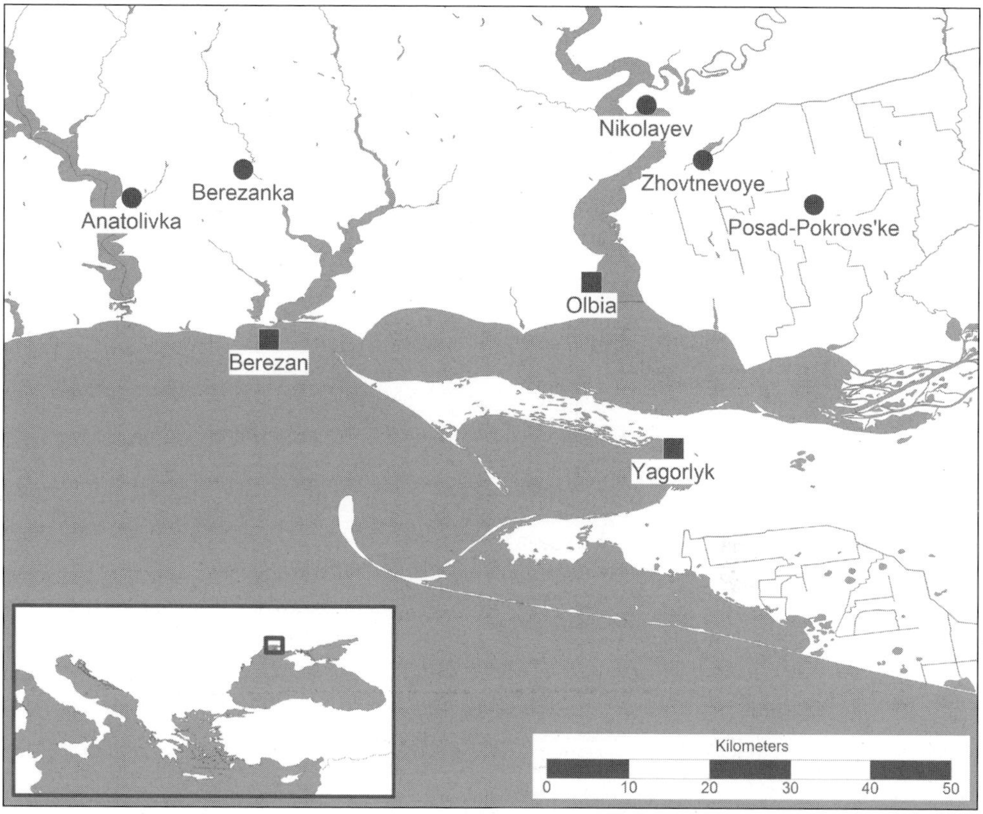

Fig. 11.3. Map of the Dnieper-Southern Bug estuary with key sites. Circles indicate modern cities, squares indicate ancient settlements.

identified in the Greek *periploi* of Pontus. By the end of the seventh and the early sixth centuries BC these locations began to be transformed into permanent settlements with a mixed Greek and native population. The archaeological sites on both banks of the Cimmerian Bosporus probably fall into this category; for example those of Panticapaeum and Hermonassa (Tsetskhladze 1997, 44–49, 55–57).

The last decade of the seventh century BC saw the appearance of the first Greek settlements proper; trading stations or ports-of-trade on the northern Black Sea coast that completely changed the character of cultural interactions between Greeks and Scythians. Though the number and composition of finds of the Greek pottery in the hinterland changed little in comparison with that of the previous stage, the ceramic assemblages of coastal settlements, in contrast, became numerically significant and typologically various (Kopeikina 1986, 28–37). The main feature of the coastal settlements became a mixture of the Greek and local traditions in all their cultural variety. A vivid example is that of the Berezan settlement (Solovyov 1999) (Fig. 11.4).

The Berezan settlement, known in the ancient world initially by the name Borysthenes, was the first link in a chain of Greek city-states, which appeared on the northern coast of the Pontus in the Archaic period. Together with those other city-states, Borysthenes became an active participant in the cultural and trading expansion of the ancient Greeks into Northern Pontus and in the transmission of Greek culture to the vast territory of forest-steppe and steppe Scythia. Borysthenes

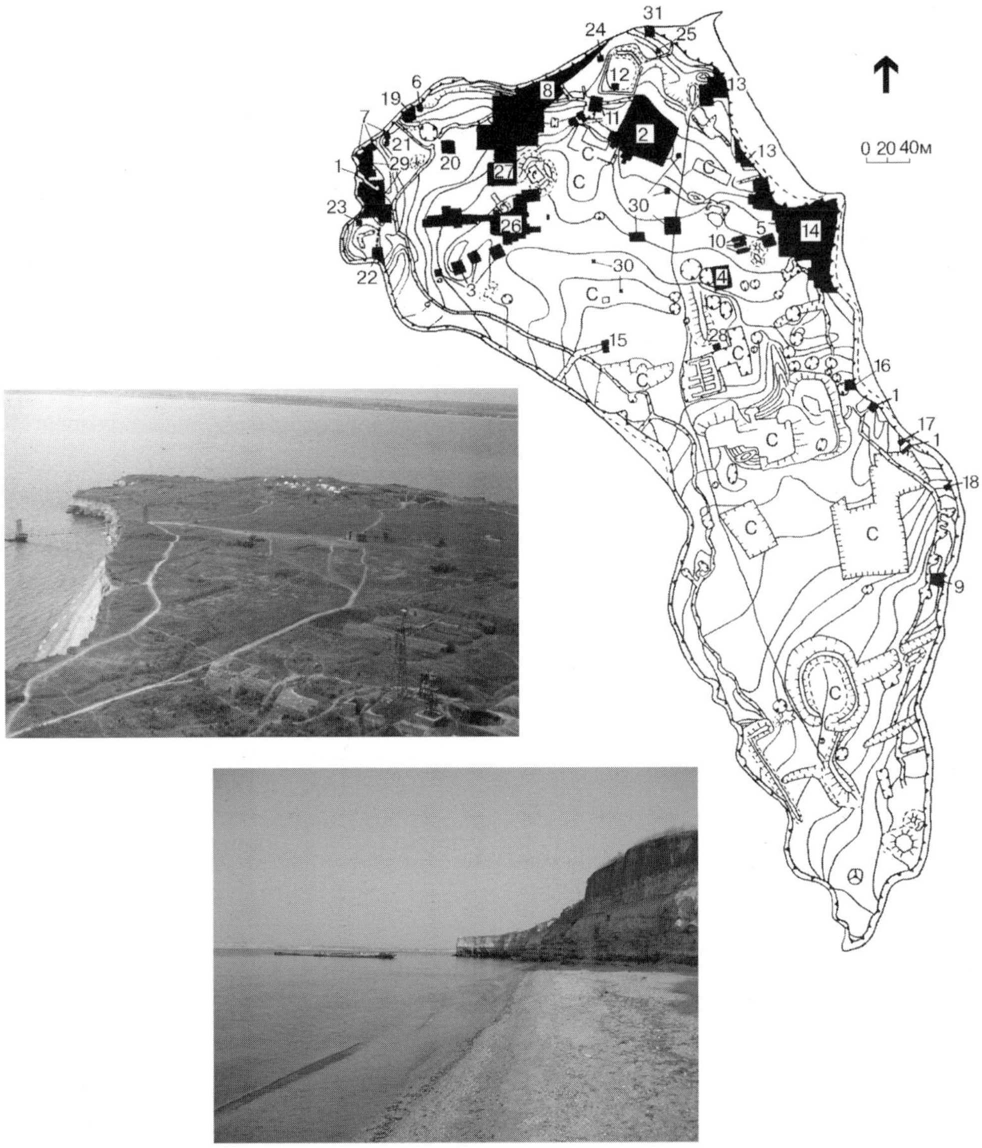

Fig. 11.4. Map and views of the Berezan Island.

became a powerful 'magnet', drawing the representatives of the indigenous population into its economic and political influence and also due to its advantageous position at the mouth of two major rivers of Scythia, the Borysthenes and the Hypanis. Natives, in turn, left numerous traces of their presence in the material and spiritual culture of Berezan.

The settlement was founded on a peninsula in full conformity with the Greek colonial practice. However, during the vast majority of its existence the settlement was built up by the use of dugout (semi-subterranean) dwellings, which were made in accordance with the local house-building traditions (Fig. 11.5). They were built half-in and half-out of the earth in an area occupying from 5 to 16 m^2. These buildings were architecturally crude, characterized by simplicity of construction and interior layout. The basic distinction among dugout constructions lies in the form of dwellings: the layout may be quadrangular, oval or circular. The duration of their functioning averaged from 5 to 12 years. Nearly 250 such dwellings have been found up to the present time. The composition of dwellings varied in different parts of the settlement (Fig. 11.6). The north-western section was dominated by dugouts of circular and oval layouts. In contrast, the eastern section was dominated by dugouts of quadrangular shape. The central area of the settlement was clear of domestic architecture at that time, but is likely to have contained associated structures, such as storage pits.

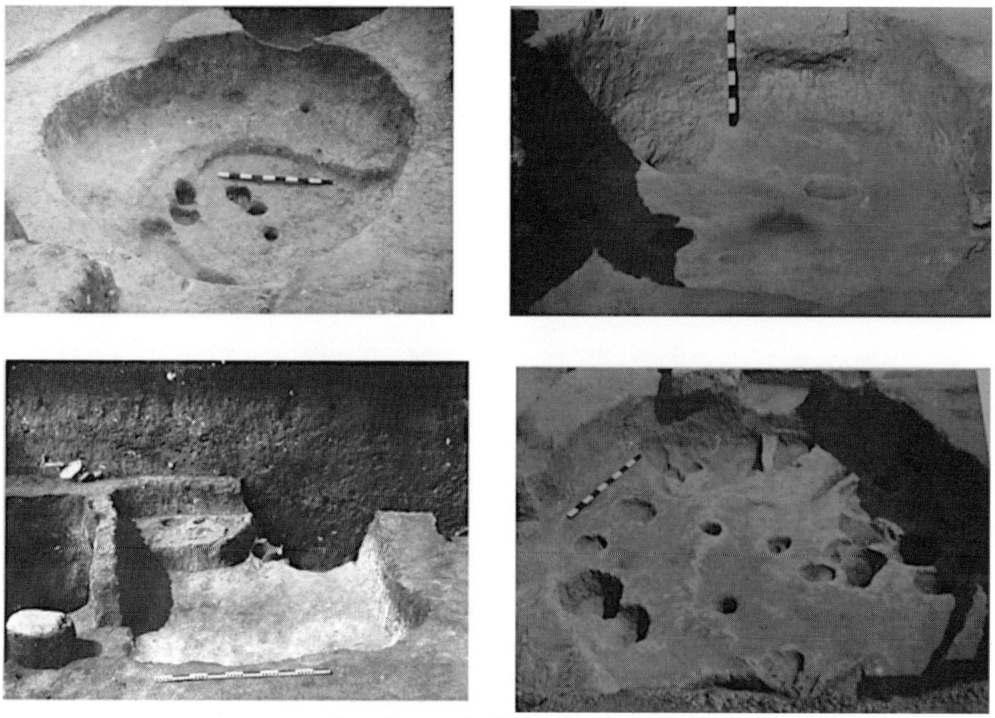

Fig. 11.5. Archaic dugout dwellings of the Berezan settlement.

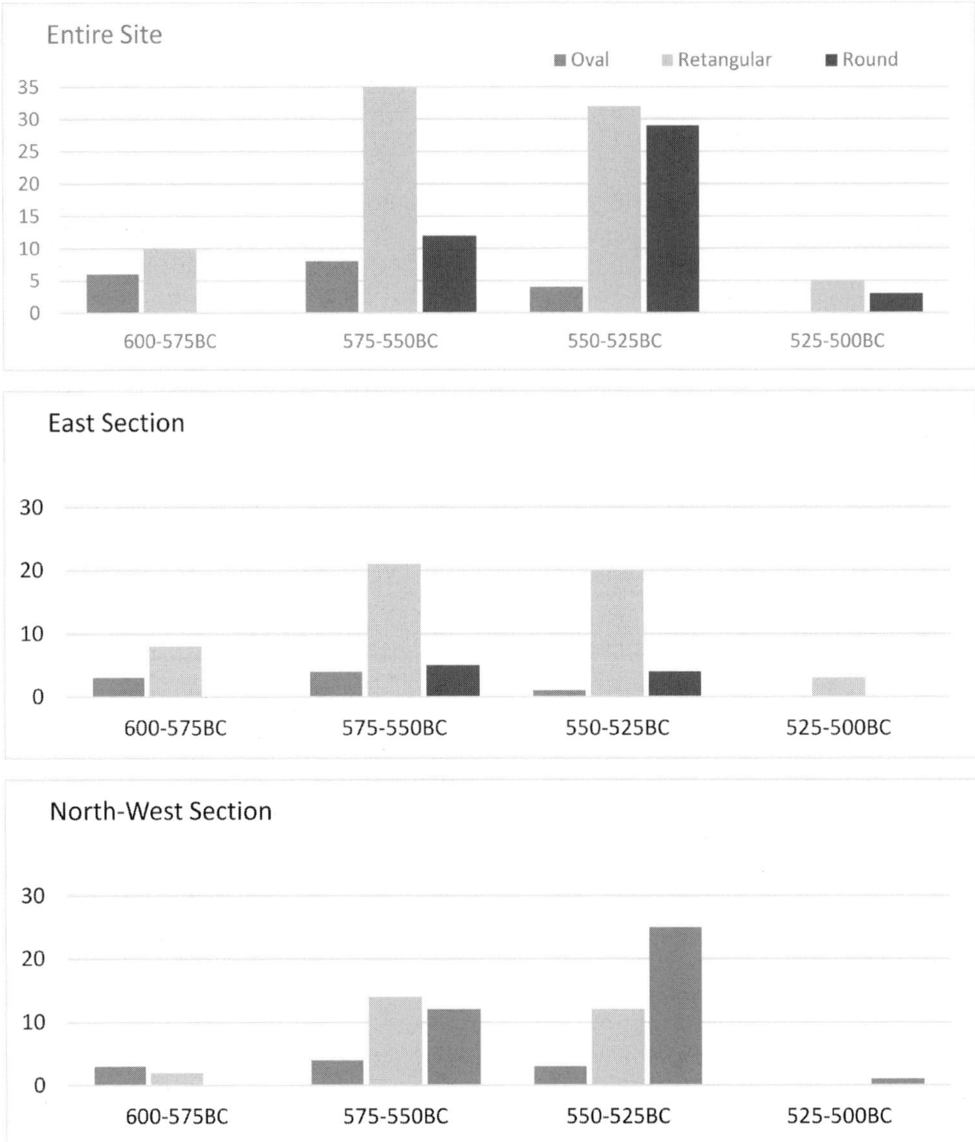

Fig. 11.6. Dynamics of Berezan dugouts varied by layouts.

The building practices of the first inhabitants of Berezan were determined mainly by local traditions of dugout construction, shown by not only the morphological characteristics of the Berezan dugouts, but also by the spatial arrangement of the settlement, which developed haphazardly, with no regulation of construction, and was shaped exclusively by the elementary rules of communal living and by the conditions of economic activity. Resting on dugout construction, the urbanization of the Berezan settlement could not be fully realized in principle (Solovyov 1996).

Nevertheless, the strongest local tradition is attested by handmade pottery, which consists of varied typological groups and represents a stable complex of various categories of vessels (Marčenko 1988; Senatorov 2005) (Fig. 11.7). First of all, it is comprised of coarse kitchenware, decorated with applied decoration separated by finger-prints with pierced holes, and tableware with incised ornamentation, reflecting the ceramic traditions characteristic of forest-steppe Scythian cultures of the Early Scythian period. Other table pottery, which has polished surface decorated with both incised and combed ornaments, was characteristic of the Kizil-Koba (or early Taurian) culture in the Crimean peninsula, which dated, respectively, from the eighth to the first half of the sixth century BC, and from the second half of the sixth to the first half of fourth century BC. The appearance of such pottery on Berezan is dated as early as the second quarter of the sixth century BC (Solovyov 1995). The coarse jars and bowls with fluted surface, which appeared in Berezan at the same time attest the presence of population either derived from the Northern Thrace or strongly influenced by the Thracian culture.

On the whole, the statistical analysis of ceramic assemblages from the Berezan dugouts has shown that fragments of Greek trade amphorae made up the largest proportion of finds (up to 80% of all pottery fragments). Excluding amphorae, the ratio of imported Greek ware to handmade pottery was approximately 80% to 20%. In some areas the proportion of handmade pottery increased by 10–20%.

So, one can assume that certain particular features of the construction of dugouts at Berezan, which at first glance appear accidental (especially the three layout types of dwellings, changes in the frequency of their occurrence in separate areas of the settlement, and the apparent absence of construction regulations in general), in fact directly reflected the diversity of the local culture. The fact of this heterogeneity became clear primarily as a result of the observed combination of specific characteristics of Berezan dugouts with other features of daily life for the Berezan inhabitants. Most important in this regard was the combination of dugout features with the types of handmade pottery widely used in everyday life and discovered in the fill inside dugouts (Fig. 11.8). In places where circular dugouts were concentrated, pottery related to that of the middle Dniester region, which seemed to be under the strong influence of Thracian culture, tended to predominate. In parts of Berezan occupied by rectangular and to some extent oval structures, a different type of handmade pottery predominated. This other type can be linked only to the pottery of the middle Dnieper region, which was settled by forest-steppe Scythian tribes.

Cultural differences between the groups of natives, who (willingly or unwillingly) ended up residing in the lower Bug River region, can be seen not only in the type of dwellings or in ceramic assemblages, but also in other details of everyday life at Berezan (Solovyov 2005, 126–135). Particularly important in this regard are cult objects, types of work tools, weapons, and adornments. All of those have been found in great quantities at Berezan and the great majority of which are linked to local cultures. The first craft workshops, which appeared at Berezan and in its vicinities at the same time, made bronze and iron products of local types.

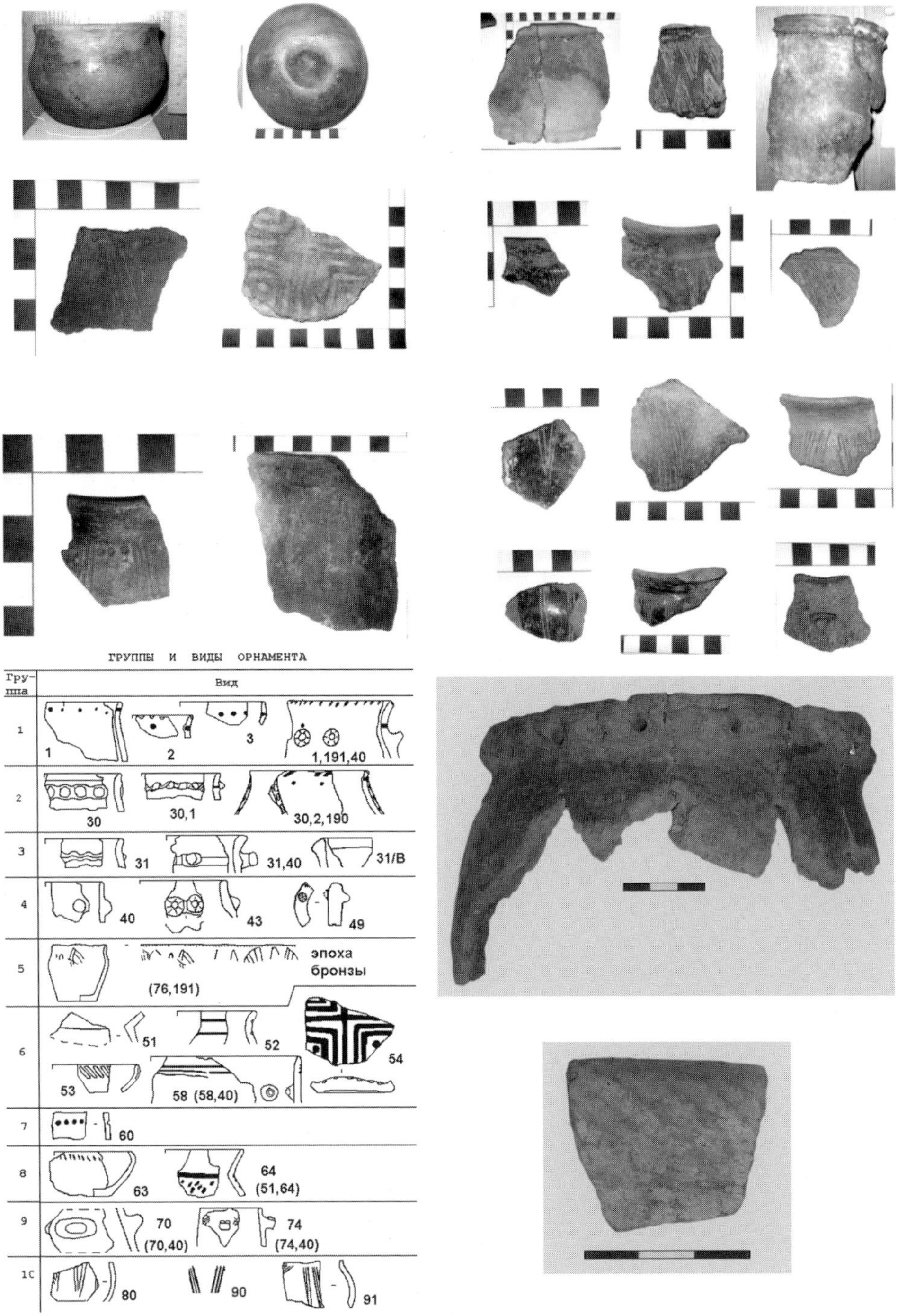

Fig. 11.7. Archaic handmade pottery of the Berezan settlement.

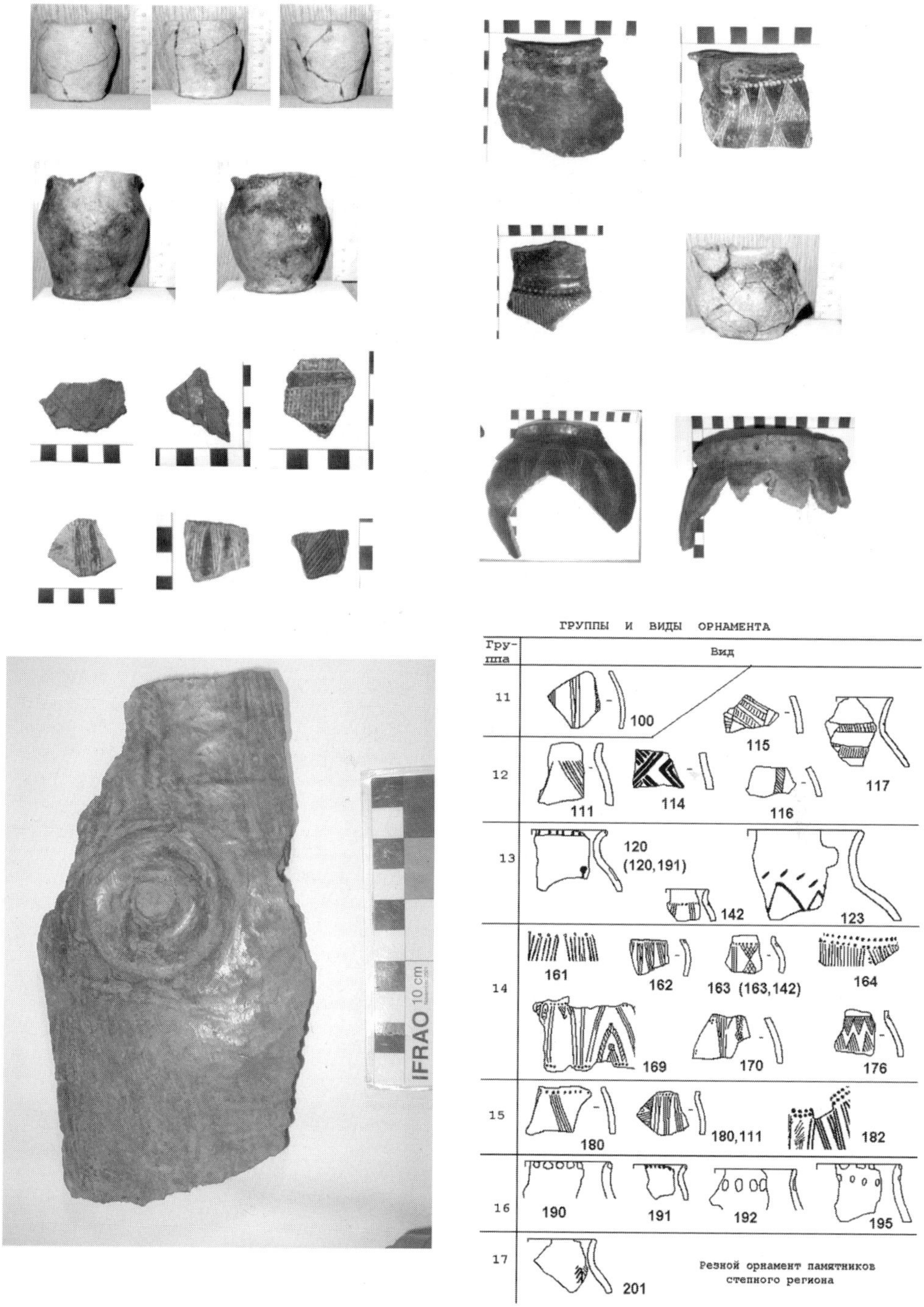

Fig. 11.7. (Continued)

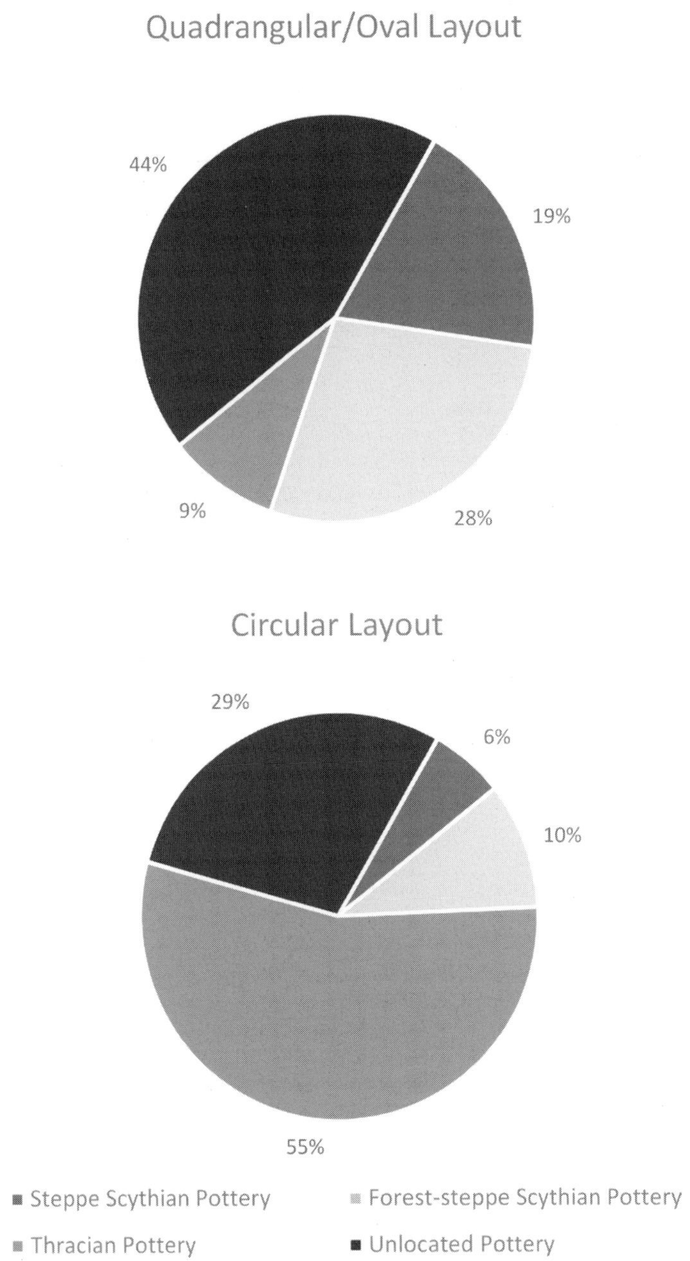

Fig. 11.8. Composition of hand-made pottery from Berezan dugouts varied by layouts.

Therefore, in my opinion, there is no doubt that most of the more visible features of the culture of Berezan during the first three quarters of the sixth century BC were rooted in the local cultures of the northern Black Sea. However, it is also clear that some part of Berezan culture must have belonged to the Greek colonists, whose existence in this region is of course without doubt.

The statistical analysis of ceramic assemblages from dugouts has shown that the fragments of trade amphorae from Clazomenai, Chios, Lesbos, and Miletus made up the largest part of the numerous finds, followed by those of imported Greek ware. The composition of Greek table pottery at that time was dominated by North Ionian products. This ceramic material showed a surprisingly limited variety of shapes and at the same time a surprising amount of almost identical objects, and among them a high number of 'extraordinary' shapes such as *askoi*, *alabastra*, and *lydia*. On the whole the spectrum of shapes is dominated by table amphorae, jugs, *kraters*, plates or stemmed dishes, and drinking cups. The latter, in turn, composed of well-known types of the North Ionian area, such as bird-, rosette-, meander-, lotus-, eye-, banded-ware-, and animal-frieze bowls. The South Ionian pottery of that time is represented by the so-called Ionian cups and Fikellura pottery. It is worth noting that the Berezan settlement also became one of the most important places of discovery for the Aeolian *dinoi* of the so-called London Dinos Group (Posamentir 2006, 161–164, figs 4, 10, 11).

Other groups of Greek pottery were composed of Early Corinthian *aryballoi*, *kotylai* and *pyxides* (Bukina 2008), Chiot chalices and *lekanai* (Ilina 2005), Clazomenian *kraters* and jugs (Ilina 2010), as well as of Attic black-figure vessels, of which the earliest examples are dated to the first quarter of the sixth century, including the workshops of Sophilos, the Gorgon Painter, the Komast Group and the Polos Painter (Smith 2008; Petrakova 2005). The overall number of Athenian black-figure imports increases towards the middle of the century.

The first Greek settlers could probably use any part of the dugout constructions as temporary dwellings (Solovyov 2008). One of the most notable features of such buildings is the stone basement arranged around all the sides of a pit (Solovyov 1999, 59–63, figs 43, 44, 46). The above ground parts of the wall were constructed of mud bricks. The lower row of the masonry consisted of large polygonal slabs placed sideways. The dwellings were one-chambered; however, interior spaces were divided into two 'halves' with separate functions: living and food-preparation areas, where stoves and hearths were located (Fig. 11.8). Moreover, the inhabitants of the dugouts also used portable braziers. Finds from these buildings consist, as usual, mainly of fragments of amphorae from various manufacturing centres of Ionia and Greece. Both decorated and cooking pottery is well represented too.

Among the numerous and diverse archaic burials in the Berezan necropolis (Fig. 11.9) only a few can be dated to the first half of the sixth century BC. Most of these were cremations and child interments in vases (Vinogradov and Domanskii 1996). At the same time, an appreciable absence of a large number of early Greek graves may also indicate a rather small proportion of Greeks among the first settlers on Berezan. The necropolis materials attest that the number of Greek colonists grew sharply in the second half of the sixth century BC. More than half of the Greek burials were dated to that time.

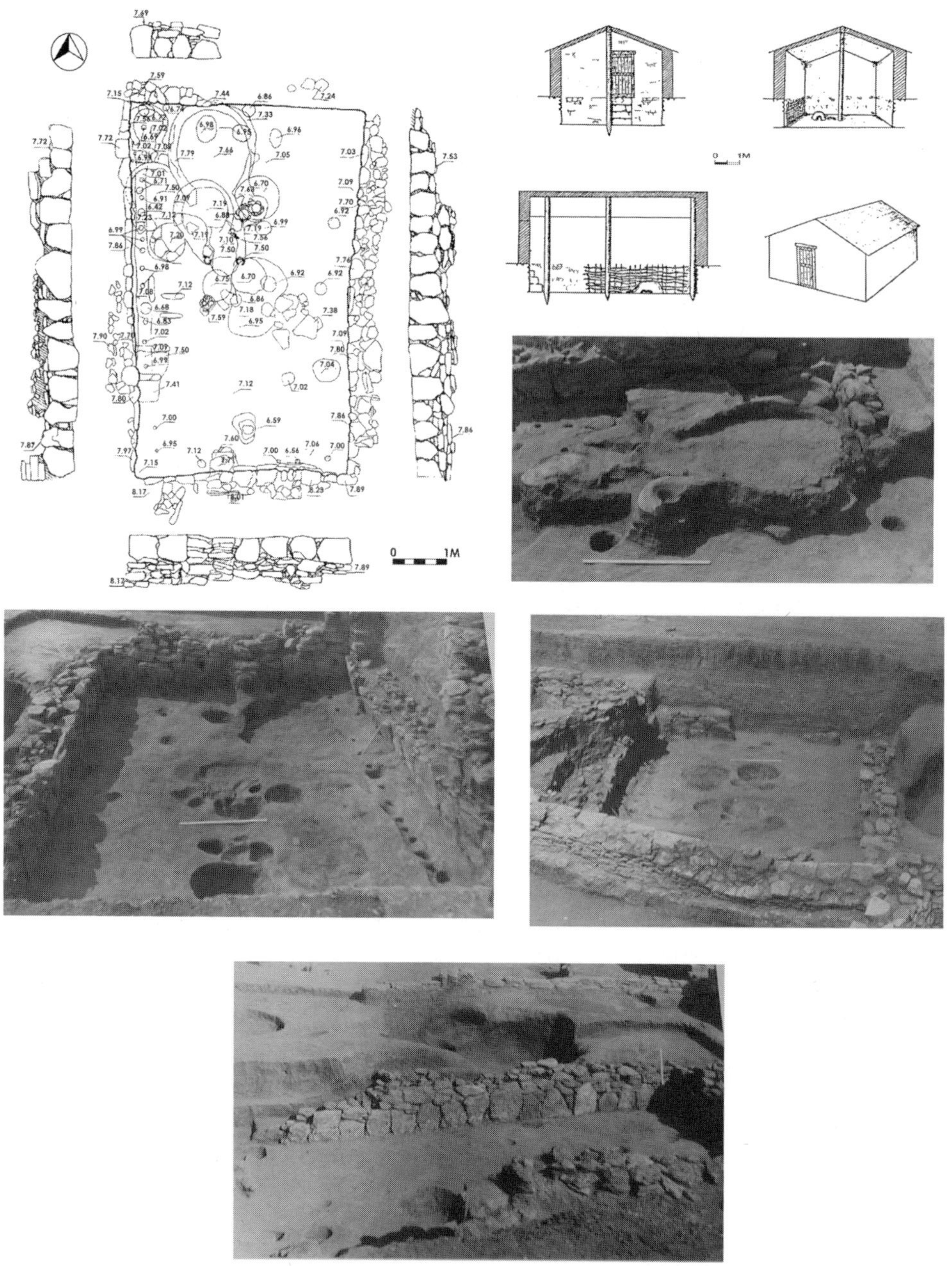

Fig. 11.9. Berezan dugout 41 of the second quarter of the sixth century BC.

These cultural features of the Berezan settlement during the first 60–70 years indicate that its main function was as a trading-craft centre. Although this was probably initiated by the interest of Greeks in trading with natives, the interest in such trade was probably mutual.

It is worth noting that when the Greeks, in addition to their trade affairs, engaged in the political organization of the Dnieper-Bug estuary (Solovyov 2001), the Berezan settlement was purposefully transformed into the typical Greek city and Borysthenes *polis*, in which non-Greeks formed the main part of rural population. It is improbable that this could have taken place without the consent of local tribal leaders. These fundamental changes in the architectural and cultural aspects of Berezan settlement took place in the third quarter of the sixth century BC.

Over a very short time the whole territory of the settlement was built up with above-ground homes of, generally, Greek types. This was preceded by preparatory work to fill the dugouts and storage pits, and to level the surface of areas designated for above ground construction (Solovyov 1999, 64–79).

The newly erected houses had an area of 100 to 260 square meters and consisted of a few living and household rooms that were grouped around an interior courtyard (Fig. 11.10). Depending on their designated purpose, the rooms held stoves, hearths, braziers, heating systems of a fireplace type, paving, and drains. In the courtyards, partially paved with fragments of pottery and small stones, there were located wells, root cellars, altars, and drains. The houses were most likely one-storeyed, although the wall construction of Berezan buildings would not prevent the construction of a second floor. The quality of the construction work varied and seemed to depend on the wealth of the home-owner. On the whole, construction techniques were of a fairly high level.

The architectural appearance of the Berezan houses indicates the urban character of construction. All the dwellings were grouped into blocks of eight or more houses (Fig. 11.11). The area of such a block approached 0.2 hectares. The size and placement of the blocks were regulated by a developed network of streets, which was evidently established from the beginning by an approximately regular plan. Regulation of the area of the settlement occupied by above-ground buildings evidently did not extend to the outskirts, where right up to the beginning of the fifth century BC dugout construction continued, although to a significantly lesser extent than before (Fig. 11.12). Only a very small number of the former dwellers of Berezan evidently remained living on the peninsula. These people were possibly involved in construction work at the new city or had some other relationship with the newcomers.

That the new settlers of Berezan possessed a political organization of the *polis* type also seems difficult to doubt. By the end of the first third of the fifth century BC, Borysthenes had reached the greatest extent that it ever attained. The construction work at Borysthenes reached its peak, which undoubtedly gave it the characteristic features of a classical city.

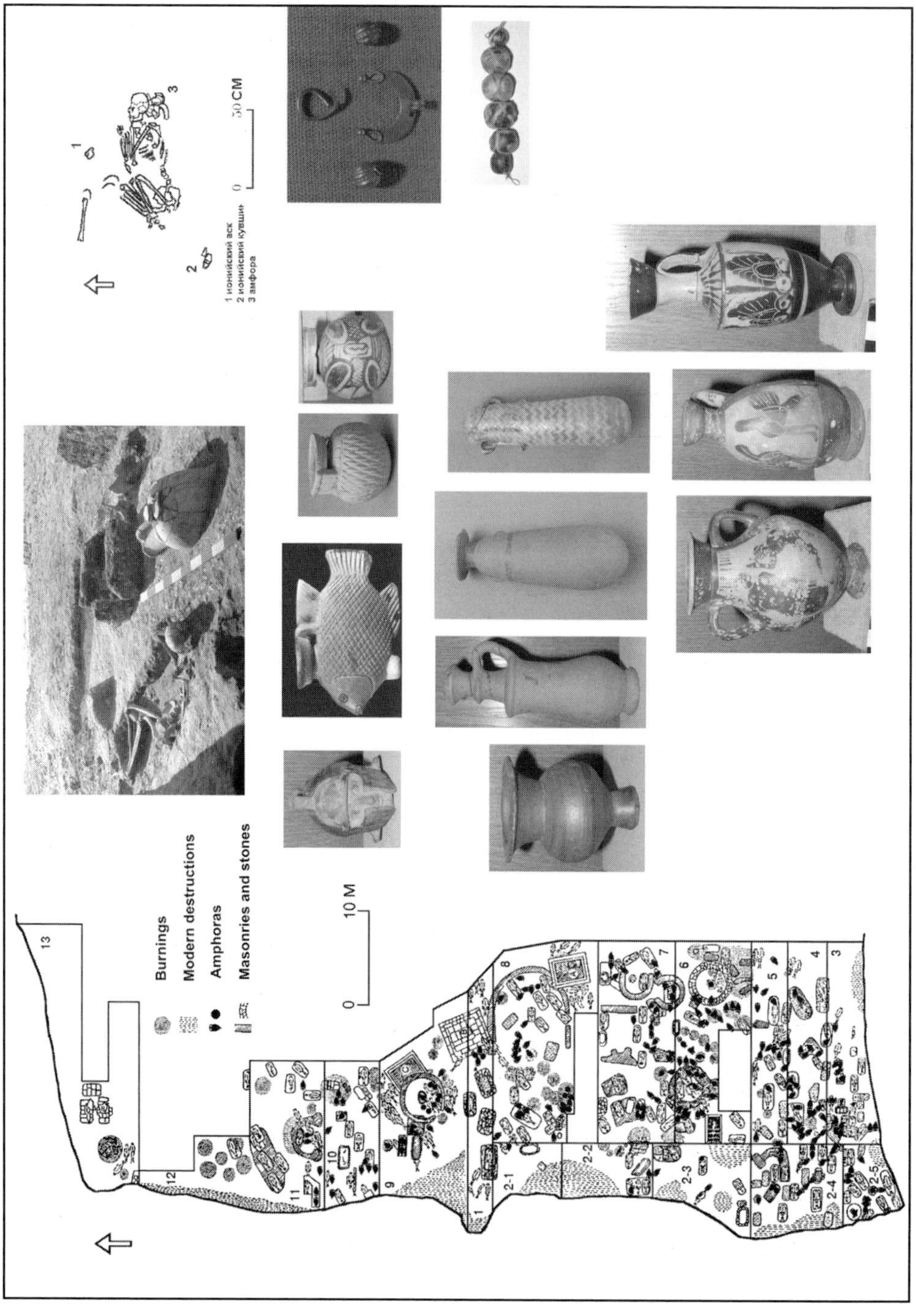

Fig. 11.10. The map of the Berezan necropolis excavated by G. L. Skadovskii (after Lapin 1966).

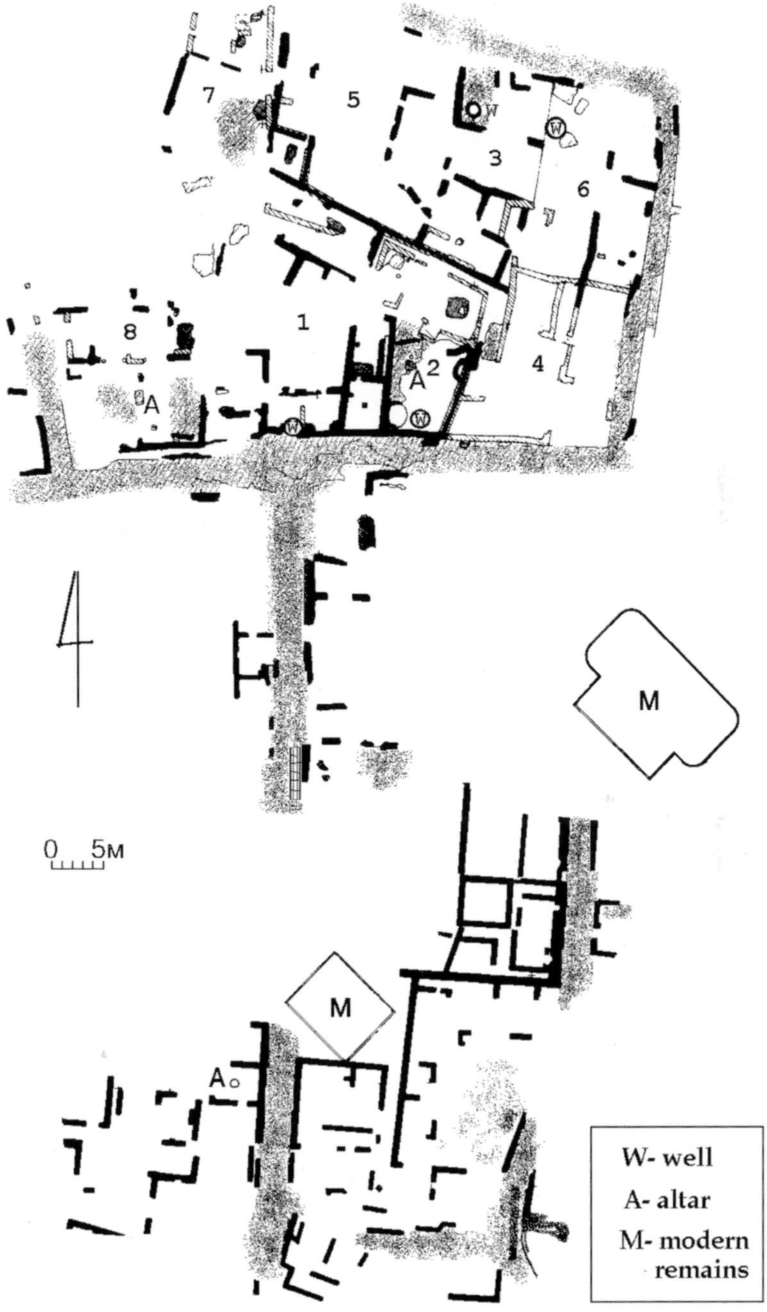

Fig. 11.11. The map of the Late Archaic residential area B of Borysthenes.

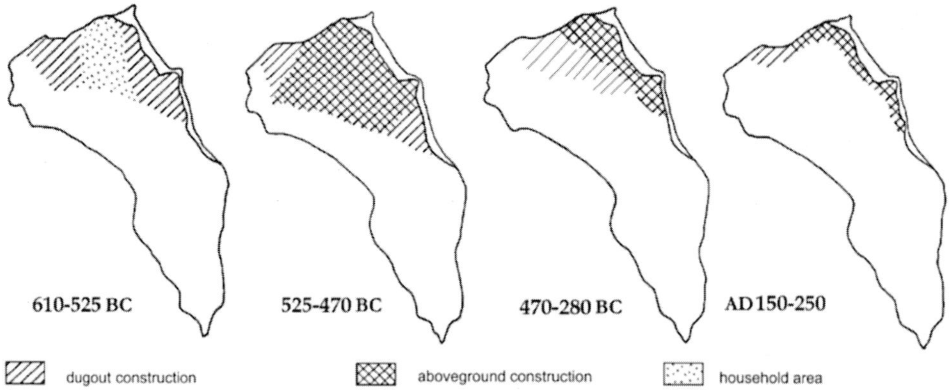

Fig. 11.12. Dynamics of residential construction in Berezan.

In the last quarter of the sixth century BC fundamental changes developed in practically the entire cultural sphere of the Berezan settlement (Solovyov 1999, 64–97). Substantial changes occurred in the composition of the ceramic complex of the settlement. Most significant was the growth of wheel-made pottery, both cooking and table wares. From this time forward, most of this pottery consisted of products from Athenian workshops. Among other pottery forms stemmed cups taper off in quantity during the later years of the sixth and the early years of the fifth centuries BC, only to be replaced to some extent by *skyphoi*; *lekythoi* also increase in popularity in the years around 500 BC (Smith 2008). Attic products gradually supplanted Ionian pottery in the daily life of Borysthenes' citizens, although the amphorae produced by Ionian potters were excluded from this process. It is well known that wine was in huge demand in the marketplaces of the northern Black Sea region, sought after by both Greeks and natives. The amount of handmade pottery in the ceramic complex of Berezan declined substantially in comparison with earlier times. In addition, the composition of such pottery also changed: many specialized forms disappeared, but handmade imitations of Greek originals became frequent.

One further very important change of this time consisted in the fact that the spiritual life of Borysthenes inhabitants now took on typically Greek characteristics. Primary among these characteristics are traces of Greek cults. Attributable materials, which were discovered in above-ground houses, included remnants of fixed and portable altars, numerous graffiti on vessels, and dedications to various deities of the ancient Greek pantheon, cultic terracotta, stone statuettes, and stone and clay lamps. The single known cult construction on Berezan – the temple of Aphrodite – was erected at the same time (Nazarov 2001; Kryzhytskii 2001). The first Borysthenes coins were issued at this time (Solovyov 2006); these were cast of bronze in the shapes of arrowheads and dolphins, and in shape a large proportion combined images of both an arrowhead and a head of tuna. One of the earliest jewellery workshops with bronze punches in the Northern Pontus has been revealed at Berezan (Treister and Solovyov 2004).

The as yet unexcavated part of the Berezan necropolis mainly belongs to the same time (Vinogradov and Domanskii 1996). From the second half of the sixth to the first half of the fifth century BC, 90% of burials were inhumations in simple funeral pits with quadrangular or oval shapes. Most of the skeletons found in them were laid extended on their backs, oriented with the head, as a rule, to the northeast or northwest. In this group 33% of the deceased were buried crouched and laid on one side. It is possible to associate these with the indigenous population of the Northern Pontic area, although the question of the ethnicity of crouched burials recovered from the necropolis of Ancient Greek cities, is still rather far from a final conclusion. Apart from these crouched burials, the rest of the bodies were buried according to Greek funeral rites. The location of the cemetery of the indigenous population remains unknown.

All of the features that we saw earlier were specific to Berezan (dugout construction, handmade pottery, elements of local cults), one can find in the culture of the later Borysthenes agricultural population, which was heterogeneous and Hellenized. From the later sixth century the indigenous population was mainly used in developing agriculture in the Borysthenes *chora*. Natives, both farmers and settled nomads, under the influence of Greek economy and political organization, became dependent on the Greek community, which granted them lands on lease and allowed bartering at the city markets. The semi-dependent status of natives is attested by archaeological data from *chorai* of the Ionian Northern Pontic cities. One form of non-economic coercion was slavery. The epigraphic evidence such as lead letters from Berezan and Phanagoria (Vinogradov 1971; 1998) and Herodotus mention the slaves, most probably non-Greek in origin, among the population of early Greek colonies in the Northern Pontic region.

The aspiration for marking the borders of the state territory was realized through the creation of several boundary sanctuaries (Buiskikh 2004), such as those of the sacred grove of Achilles in the Beykush settlement and the altars of Heracles and the Mother of the Gods in Hylaia. The main such altar most likely was that of the sanctuary of Apollo the Healer in Olbia, which at that time obviously was just the part of Borysthenes *polis*. Olbia was settled by a mixed population of both Greek and natives, attested by the dugout construction and handmade pottery discovered in the settlement. However, owing to social strife within Borysthenes, already by the last quarter of the sixth century BC Olbia had become an independent city-state (Solovyov 2001).

In this period, after the arrival of a significant group of new colonists, Olbia became the centre for the worship of Apollo Delphinion. The social conflict between the first settlers and the newcomers took the form of a religious dispute between worshippers of Apollo the Healer and Apollo Delphinion. It is reflected in the Apollo Didyma oracle found on Berezan (Rusyaeva 1986). According to its contents, the recovery of social peace in the region was owed to Apollo. It was reached due to the worship of both hypostases of the god. The territory of the *polis* was divided between the new city-states, which became those of Borysthenes and Olbia (Solovyov 2001).

from the forest-steppe Scythia into the process of occupying the lower Bug River region. Based on certain features of their culture (particularly building practice and the making and decorating of handmade pottery), the forest-steppe Scythian groups were drawn mainly from two areas, those of the middle Dniester and middle Dnieper regions.

The culture of the nomadic Scythian population, which is also reflected in archaeological materials, probably comprised a third component of indigenous culture. Owing to specific characteristics of the nomadic way of life, the steppe-Scythian culture was very heterogeneous and included components of those cultures with which the nomads came into contact.

At the end of the first third of the fifth century BC the cultural and historical situation in the Northern Black Sea region underwent fundamental changes because of the Scythian expansion to the west (Marčenko and Vinogradov 1989). The areas of nomad activity had come very close to the Greek colonies in the northwestern Black Sea area. In that period of political and military instability in Scythia, some portions of the urban, and possibly rural, population of Borysthenes may have moved into Olbia. From that time the decline of the Berezan settlement gradually began. The later existence of ancient Berezan is the history of an ordinary agricultural and fishing settlement not very visible against the background of the other villages of Olbia *polis*, a settlement which had rather better fortune.

Bibliography

Buiskikh, S. B. (2004) Svyatilishcha extra-urban epokhi gretskoi kolonizatsii Nizhnego Pobuzhya. *Arkheologiya* 3, 3–14.

Bukina, A. (2008) *Corinthian Aryballoi. Corpus Vasorum Antiquorum Russia* Fasc. XIV, The State Hermitage Museum Fasc. VII. Roma, L'Erma di Bretschneider.

Dally, O. and Larenok, P. A. (2002) Taganrog. Eine griechische Siedlung im Dondelta. In J. Fornasier and B. Böttger (eds) *Das bosporanische Reich*, 86–91. Mainz, von Zabern.

Domanskii, Y. V. and Marčenko, K. K. (2007) K voprosu o bazovoi funktsii pervonachalnogo Borisfena. In I. V. Tunkina (ed.) ΕΥΧΑΡΙΣΤΗΡΙΟΝ, 22–7. St-Petersburg, Nestor-Istoriya.

Gavrilyuk, N. A. (1999) *Istoriya ekonomiki Stepnoi Skifii 6–3 vv. do n.e.* Kiev, Institut Arkheologii NAN Ukrainy.

Ilina, Yu. I. (2005) Khiosskaya keramika iz raskopok na ostrove Berezan. In S. L. Solovyov (ed.) *Borysthenes - Berezan. The Hermitage Archaeological Collection* I, 70–173. St Petersburg, The Hermitage Publishing House.

Ilina, Yu. I. (2010) Klazomenskaya keramika iz raskopok na Berezani. In S. L. Solovyov (ed.) *Borysthenes - Berezan. The Hermitage Archaeological Collection* II. St Petersburg, The Hermitage Publishing House, 141–170.

Kerschner, M. and Schlotzhauer, U. (2005) A New Classification System for East Greek Pottery. *Ancient West and East* 4.1, 1–56.

Kopeikina, L. V. (1986) Raspisnaya keramika arkhaicheskogo vremeni iz antichnykh poselenii Nizhnego Pobuzhya i Podneprovya kak istochnik dlya izucheniya torgovykh i kulturnykh svyazei. *Arkheologicheskii Sbornik Gosudarstvennogo Ermitazha (Archaeological Collection of the State Hermitage)* 27, 27–47.

Kopylov, V. P. and Larenok, P. A. (1994) *Taganrogskoe poselenie.* Rostov-upon-Don, Gefest.

Koshelenko, G. A. and Kuznetsov, V. D. (1998) Greek Colonisation of the Bosporus. In G. R. Tsetskhladze (ed.) *The Greek Colonisation of the Black Sea Area, Historical Interpretation of Archaeology* (*Historia* 121), 249–264. Stuttgart, Franz Steiner.

Kryzhytskii, S. D. (2001) Khram Afrodity na Berezani. *Vestnik Drevnei Istorii (Journal of Ancient History)* 1, 165–175.

Kryzhitskii, S. D., Buiskikh, S. B. and Otreshko, V. M. (1990) *Antichnye poseleniya Nizhnego Pobuzhya (arkheologicheskaya karta)*. Kiev, Naukova Dumka.

Lapin, V. V. (1966) *Grecheskaya kolonisatsiya Severnogo Prichernomorya*. Kiev, Naukova Dumka.

Marčenko, K. K. (1988) *Varvary v sostave naseleniya Berezani i Olvii vo vtoroi polovine 7 - pervoi polovine 1 v. Do n.e.* Leningrad, Nauka.

Marčenko, K. K. (2005) Osnovnye aspekty i resultaty izucheniya greko-varvarskikh kontaktov i vzaimodeistvii v Severnom Prichernomorie skifskoi epokhi. In K. K. Marčenko (ed.) *Greki i varvary Severnogo Prichernomoriya v skifskuyu epokhu*, 12–26. St Petersburg, Aleteya.

Marčenko, K. K. and Domanskii, Ya. V. (1981) Antichnoe poselenie Staraya Bogdanovka-2. *Arkheologicheskii Sbornik Gosudarstvennogo Ermitazha (Archaeological Collection of the State Hermitage)* 22, 62–75.

Marčenko, K. K. and Domanskii, Ya. V. (1986) Antichnoe poselenie Kutsurub-1. *Arkheologicheskii Sbornik Gosudarstvennogo Ermitazha (Archaeological Collection of the State Hermitage)* 27, 48–61.

Marčenko, K. K. and Domanskii, Ya. V. (1991) Kompleks veshchestvennykh nakhodok na antichnom poselenii Kutsurub-1. *Arkheologicheskii Sbornik Gosudarstvennogo Ermitazha (Archaeological Collection of the State Hermitage)* 31, 57–76.

Marčenko, K. K. and Vinogradov, Ju. A. (1989) The Scythian Period in the Northern Black Sea Region (750–250 BC). *Antiquity* 63 (241), 803–813.

Nazarov, V. V. (2001) Svyatilishche Afrodity v Borisfene. *Vestnik Drevnei Istorii (Journal of Ancient History)* 1, 154–165.

Ostroverkhov, A. S. (1979) K voprosu o syrievoi baze remeslennogo proizvodstva v raione Dneprovskogo i Bugskogo limanov. *Vestnik Drevnei Istorii (Journal of Ancient History)* 3, 115–126.

Petrakova, A. (2005) Attic Black-Figure and Bilingual Drinking Cups. CVA The State Hermitage Museum Fasc. III. Roma, L'Erma di Bretschneider.

Posamentir R. (2006) The Greeks in Berezan and Naukratis. A Similar Story? In A. Villing and U. Schlotshauer (eds) *Naukratis: Greek Diversity in Egypt*, 159–167. London, The British Museum.

Posamentir R. and Solovyov S. L. (2006) Zur Herkunftsbestimmung archaisch-ostgriechischer Keramik: die Funde aus Berezan in der Eremitage von St. Petersburg. *Istanbuler Mitteilungen* 56, 103–128.

Rusyaeva, A. S. (1986) Milet - Didimy - Borisfen - Olviya. Problemy kolonizatsii Nizhnego Pobuzhya. *Vestnik Drevnei Istorii (Journal of Ancient History)* 2, 25–64.

Senatorov, S. N. (2005) Lepnaya keramika poseleniya na ostrove Berezan iz raskopok Gosudarstvennogo Ermitazha 1963–1991 gg. In S. L. Solovyov (ed.) *Borysthenes - Berezan. The Hermitage Archaeological Collection* I, 174–351. St Petersburg, The Hermitage Publishing House.

Smith, T. J. (2008) Athenian Black-figure Pottery from Berezan. In S. L. Solovyov (ed.) *Borysthenes - Berezan. The Hermitage Archaeological Collection* II. St Petersburg: The Hermitage Publishing House.

Solovyov S. L. (1995) Lepnaya keramika s reznym geometricheskim ornamentom Berezanskogo poseleniya. *Arkheologicheskii Sbornik Gosudarstvennogo Ermitazha (Archaeological Collection of the State Hermitage)* 32, 31–9.

Solovyov S. L. (1996) Periodizatsiya zhilogo stroitelstva antichnoi Berezani. *Arkheologicheskie vesti (Archaeologica News)* 4, 153–163.

Solovyov S. L. (1998) Archaic Berezan: Historical-Archaeological Essay. In G. R. Tsetskhladze (ed.) *The Greek Colonisation of the Black Sea Area* (*Historia* 121), 205–227. Stuttgart, Franz Steiner.

Solovyov S. L. (1999) *Ancient Berezan. The Architecture, History and Culture of the First Greek Colony in the Northern Black Sea* (*Colloquia Pontica* 4). Leiden, Boston, Cologne, Brill.

Solovyov, S. L. (2001) On the History of the City-States in the Lower Bug Area: Borysthenes and Olbia. In J. Boardman, S. L. Solovyov and G. R. Tsetskhladze (eds) *Northern Pontic Antiquities in The State Hermitage Museum* (*Colloquia Pontica* 7), 113–126. Leiden, Boston, Cologne, Brill.

Solovyov S. L. (2004) Greki i varvary Severnogo Prichernomorya: tipy kontaktov. Bosporan Readings V, 333–337. Kerch, Demetra.

Solovyov, S. L. (2005) Borisfen-*Berezan. Nachalo antichnoi epokhi v Severnom Prichernomorie. Catalogue of exhibition.* St Petersburg, Ars.

Solovyov, S. L. (2006) Monetary Circulation and the Political History of Archaic Borysthenes. *Ancient Civilisations from Scythia to Siberia* 12.1–2, 63–74.

Solovyov S. L. (2007) Ancient Greek Pioneering at the Northern Black Sea Coastal Area in the Seventh Century BC. In S. Mitchell and G. Erkut (eds) *The Black Sea: Past, Present and Future* (*BIAA Monograph* 42), 37–44. Istanbul, British Institute at Ankara.

Solovyov, S. L. (2008) "Dom kolonista" v arkheologicheskom kontekste arkhaicheskoi Berezani. *Trudy Gosudarstvennogo Ermitazha (Proceedings of The State Hermitage Museum)* 41.

Treister, M. Yu. and Solovyov, S. L. (2004) Bronze Punches from Berezan. *Ancient West and East* 3.2, 365–375.

Tsetskhladze, G. R. (1994) Greek Penetration of the Black Sea. In G. R. Tsetskhladze and F. De Angelis (eds) *The Archaeology of Greek Colonisation*, 111–135. Oxford, Oxbow Books.

Tsetskhladze, G. R. (1997) A Survey of the Major Urban Settlements in the Kimmerian Bosporos. In M. H. Hansen (ed.) *Yet More Studies in the Ancient Greek Polis* (*Historia* 117), 39–82. Stuttgart, Franz Steiner.

Tsetskhladze, G. R. (1998) Greek Colonisation of the Black Sea Area: Stages, Models, and Native Population. In G. R. Tsetskhladze (ed.) *The Greek Colonisation of the Black Sea Area, Historical Interpretation of Archaeology* (*Historia* 121), 9–68. Stuttgart, Franz Steiner.

Vinogradov Ju. G. and Domanskij Ja. V. (1996) Berezan' archaïque à la lumière des dernières déccouvertes. In O. D. Lordkipanidzé and P. Lévêque (eds) *Sur le traces des Argonautes*, 291–296. Paris, Presses Universitaires Franc-Comtoises.

Vinogradov, Ju. G., Domanskij, Ja. V. and Marčenko, K. K. (1990) Sources écrites et archéologiques du Pont Nord-Ouest. Analyse comparative. In O. Lordkipanidze and P. Lèvêque (eds) *Le Pont-Euxin vu par les Grecs*, 121–139. Paris, Presses Universitaires Franc-Comtoises.

Vinogradov, Yu. G. (1971) Drevneishee grecheskoe pismo s ostrova Berezan. *Vestnik Drevnei Istorii (Journal of Ancient History)* 4, 74–100.

Vinogradov, Yu. G. (1998) The Greek Colonisation of the Black Sea Region in the Light of Private Lead Letters. In G. R. Tsetskhladze (ed.) *The Greek Colonisation of the Black Sea Area, Historical Interpretation of Archaeology* (*Historia* 121), 153–178. Stuttgart, Franz Steiner.

12

Polis, *Chora* and the development of the colonial landscape in the Lower Bug region

Sergej Bujskikh and Alla Bujskikh

Olbia Pontica was established at the northern part of the inhabited Greek world between the end of the seventh and the beginning of the sixth century BC, and from the very beginning she was designated by the colonists as a centre for the future state and its territory (Fig. 12.1). Large and small settlements of different types, separate farms, and arable lands for agricultural activity and cattle-breading were located on this territory. All of these created the agricultural zone of the *polis* and the single political and economic system 'city – *chora*' and '*polis* – *chora*'. The development and co-existence of the *chora* and *polis* was closely connected, moreover, to the colonial conditions of settlement in the Northern Black Sea littoral. This link between the city and the territory can be pointed to as the best argument for *polis* organization of the newly established colony. Both city and territory reflected the main stages of *polis* development, its development and flourishing, crises and decline. This can also be proven by looking at the dynamics of the spatial development of settlements in the region of the Lower Bug: 107 settlements belong to the archaic period, 152 to the Classical and Hellenistic periods, and 64 to the period of the first centuries BC (Kryjickij and Bujskich 1999, 286).

In spite of the differences in the total number of settlements during the three main periods of the Olbian *polis* existence, the distribution of the agricultural settlements around Olbia was concentrated in the same areas from the sixth century BC until the third century AD. This territory of triangular shape was delimited by the Bug, Dnieper, and Berezan estuaries and the left bank of the Dnieper estuary. These boundaries framed the territory, and created a permanent territory of the Olbian *chora* and the Olbian state in the Lower Bug region during nearly 1,000 years of its existence. The dimensions of the agricultural zone for all these periods are approximately 55 km from west to east by 45 km from north to south. That means that the borders of the state were established from the earliest times with an eye to the future growth of the

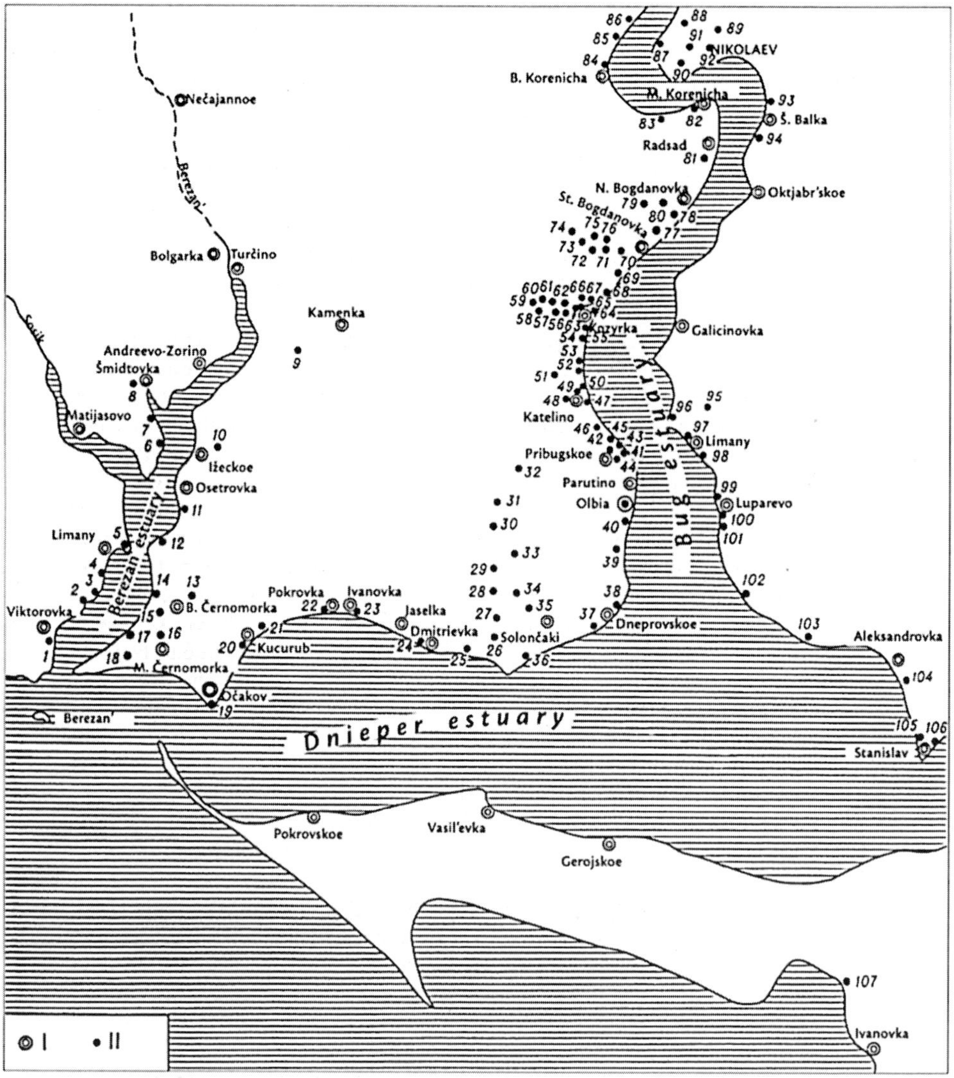

Fig. 12.1. Map of the Olbian chora in the archaic period, showing the location of 107 settlements in the Lower Bug region (Kryzhitskij et al. 1999). I: Modern settlements; II: Ancient settlements.

polis, and the Olbian citizens protected them during the entire long period of their state development. The organization of a *chora* as a necessary part of the Olbian *polis* started in the context of the colonial exploration of the region. The success of this colonial activity was supported by the total absence of any permanent indigenous population in this region in the second half of seventh century to the sixth century BC (S. Buyskikh 2007, 24).

The starting point of the colonization of the Lower Bug by Ionian Greeks was the middle of the seventh century BC, or in accordance with Eusebius, 647/646 BC when

Borysthenes (*i.e.* the settlement on Berezan island) was founded (Euseb. *Chron.* P. 95 b Helm). To our minds, Borysthenes was a middleman trade centre with hinterland in the earliest period and was an emporion without its own *chora* (S. Bujskikh 2005a, 164). The second, no less important function of Borysthenes can be seen in the developed local craft using different coloured metals, perhaps produced for export to *metropolia* (Domanskij and Marčenko 2003, 35).

In contrast, the latest research indicates that Olbia was founded at the end of the first quarter or the turn between first and second quarters of sixth century BC. It was the second Greek *apoikia* (after Borysthenes) sent by Milesians to the northwestern part of the Pontic region. As we have said above, to our minds, from the very beginning it was laid out as the centre of the future *polis*, with its own territory for intensive agricultural development. We can also now conclude that almost all the necessary locations for key urban structures were reserved during the process of the spatial organization of the new colony.

First of all, the natural defenses were used well. The city of Olbia was established on a high two-terrace plateau of triangular shape surrounded by two deep ravines from the north and the west, and the river from the east. In the Upper city of Olbia, the areas to be used for public centres, including locations for cult practice, were reserved in the central and perhaps southern parts of the site, and the first temenos, known as the western temenos, and dedicated mainly to Apollo Hietros, was organized almost as soon as Olbia was founded. Regular cult activity in the western temenos also started in the second quarter of the sixth century BC (Rusyaeva 1994; 1999, 76–77). The presence of a sacred zone and the earliest graffiti with dedications to Apollo Hietros, found both in Olbia and Borysthenes, allow us to conclude that the religious festivities of the new civil community had to be organized in Olbia, at the western temenos. This was perhaps even the main reason why Olbia was chosen as the centre for the new city-state (Rusjaeva 1986, 52). The agora and the second temenos, known as the eastern temenos, and dedicated mainly to Apollo Delphinius, were thought not to have appeared until the end of the sixth century BC (Karasjov 1964, 27ff.). More recent research puts this at the beginning of the fifth century BC. In any case, their locations were also free from any dwellings, and from the very beginning until the first centuries AD were excluded from the inhabited zone.

The agora, situated close to the eastern temenos, received its first pavement at the beginning of the fifth century BC. This pavement indicates its primary function as a place for public meetings of the civil community (Martin 1956, 268; Kenzler 2000, 27ff.). We can only surmise that the agora in Olbia had the same functions as in her mother-city, changing with time. As we have seen, it is possible to conclude that the special separation of a large part of the city territory for public centres and sacred zones started from the earliest period of a city's existence, and was part of colonization practice. The land distribution in the city was organized both for domestic use and public activity. In spite of the absence of early defensive buildings, we can conclude that the urban organization of the *polis* passed through almost all the necessary stages, well known from the literary tradition (see A. Bujskikh 2005, 24f.). This *polis* organization and the familiar Greek urban development was the distinctive feature of the newly founded colony, and separated its inhabitants from the local populations of the surrounding area.

The first main types of dwellings were dugouts – structures partly cut into the clay subsoil to a depth of nearly 0.5–1.2 m with mud-brick walls above ground. These structures can be considered a phenomenon of the Greek colonization of the entire Northern Pontic region. Their appearance and wide and quick distribution – nearly 500 of these structures are known in the northwestern area alone – can be explained by climatic conditions, and the geological structure of the subsoil which consists of clay with a total absence of bed-rock (or a deep natural level of bed-rock as on Berezan Island). To our minds, therefore, the natural conditions of the territory in Olbia dictated the character of the main construction type of dwellings in the initial period of *polis* existence (A. & S. Bujskikh 2001, 667–669).

The first above-ground stone buildings in the city were represented by constructions connected with cult – altars of Ionian type (mainly rectangular and round) and small temples *in antis* erected no earlier than the end of the third quarter of the sixth century BC. Indeed, in both the urban centres of the Olbian *polis* – in Olbia and Borysthenes (Berezan), temple building began at the same time. In Borysthenes, a special temenos was laid out, separated from the inhabited area by a wall, with a temple (perhaps to Aphrodite) *in antis*, and a round altar (Nazarov 2007, 541ff.). The parallel appearance of two *temenoi* in Olbia and Borysthenes could allow us to conclude that both urban structures developed *poleis* city-centres. However, the determination of the political organization of the *polis* of Olbia or Borysthenes is much more complicated than this. As we said above, we maintain that only Olbia had *polis* status in a political sense, and that the earliest settlement in Berezan was organized as an emporion (S. Bujskikh 2005c, 164; Kerschner 2006, 242–243).

The modern chronology of the archeological finds from Olbia allows us to conclude that along the boundaries of the future agricultural *chora*, and therefore of the *polis*, a system of special sacred zones appeared at the same time as the city. The development of the *chora* in the sixth and fifth centuries BC was exactly within the frames demarcated by the *extra-urban* sanctuaries. These sanctuaries may be seen as the creation of a special system of colonial sacred places around the city. This system had the main purpose of organizing divine protection for the inhabited territory. The border protectors of the *polis* to the south and southwest were Achilles (Leuke Island and Tendra), the Mother of the Gods, Borysthenes, Herakles and Hecate (Kinburn); to the east was Demeter (Cap of Hippolaios), and to the west was Achilles (Cap of Bejkush) (S. Bujskikh 2005a, 194).

The latter sanctuary has been very well excavated by the archaeological researchers (S. Buyskykh 2005b; 2006b). An area of more than 2,000 m^2 was excavated, and nearly 200 different sacred archaeological deposits and more than 100 graffiti with dedications to Achilles were found. Amongst the built structures in this sanctuary, there were (mainly underground, partly or completely carved into soil) pits for sacrifices, *favissae*, *bothroi*, niches, various types of grottoes, imitating rocky caves, buildings for ritual actions and sacred meals, and other remains above ground such as altars, sacred pavements and ovens. All the built structures excavated in Bejkush *extra-urban* sanctuary, reflect one of the facets of the complicated process of Greek colonization, and allow us to conclude concerning the skillful and successful adoption of Greek traditional cult practice to the conditions of the new region. The closest similarities with the sacred buildings and objects from Bejkush are in the buildings of the same period at the Western temenos (Rusyaeva 1994, 96ff.), and in the earliest buildings from the eastern temenos in Olbia. All of them give perfect examples of the ritual usage of underground or carved structures. They were not only for habitation or household purposes, as was previously presumed (S. Bujskich 2006b, 146; 2006c, 118).

It was also necessary for the long-time survival of the state that it be well supplied with natural resources. The natural resources of the Lower Bug region were helpful for all the activities of the civil community. That is why it was important that the colonists developed for themselves forms of animal husbandry, and that they also developed the fertile lands of the territory for diverse functions, judging what was most useful and productive in the new climatic and geological conditions. Agriculture, cattle-breeding, and all kinds of handicraft were developed in the same intensive manner, supported by fishing for freshwater fish and hunting. The main indication of the Greeks' exploration of the region after the foundation of Olbia is the appearance of numerous agricultural settlements. These also allow us to conclude concerning the primary position of agriculture in the entire region (Lapin 1966, 183, 235).

The settlements created a long chain along the shores of the river estuaries or the small steppe rivers which flowed into them. All of them were situated on high plateaux, often on the top of capes, but usually near sources of drinking water, as that was the first and most pressing need. This was one of the reasons why any kind of defensive buildings were absent in the initial period, and the entire region was inhabited and explored in a peaceful manner.

The Greek colonial *chora* in the Lower Bug was delimited by the *extra-urban* sanctuaries. This region passed through three main stages in its spatial development (S. Bujskich 2006c, 116–122). In the first stage (second quarter to the middle of the sixth century BC) the territory reached the littorals of the Berezan estuary, the right littoral of the Dnieper estuary, and the southern part of the right bank of the Bug estuary up to Olbia. In the second stage (the second half of the sixth century BC) the chain of the Greek settlements reached the territory of the modern town of Nikolaev. Beginning from the third quarter of the sixth century BC the Greek *polis* in the Lower Bug region can be seen as Olbian, as it is possible to consider it with the help of the famous inscription on the bone plaque found in Berezan (Rusyaeva 1986, 262–264). After this action Borysthenes became a permanent part of the Olbian *polis*. This means that, starting from last quarter of the sixth century BC the borders of the Olbian chora became the official borders of the Olbian state in the Lower Bug region (S. Bujskich

2006c, 116). At the common level of everyday life; the social, economic, and cultural development of the city and countryside seems to be almost the same. The typical built structures (dugouts and semi-dugouts), inside the city and elsewhere carry on almost exactly the same with the same number of ceramic and other finds, including table and cooking wares, special pots and vessels, terracottas, graffiti, children toys, weapons, and coins (A. & S. Bujskikh 2001; 2007).

Solovyov's approach (Solovev 1998; Solovyov 1999, 42–43, 63) which limits the *typical* finds to handmade pottery only, and therefore concludes that the finds bear the typical characteristics of barbarian population presence, is not productive (A. Bujskikh 2001, 626f.; A. & S. Buiskikh 2001, 680–681; S. Bujskikh 2006b, 112, n. 9; 2006c, 121; 2007, 23ff.). Both local and Greek artifacts were usual for the Greek colonial culture in the northwestern part of the Black Sea littoral. Dugouts from Olbia and the territory of its agricultural zone are similar in the peculiarities of their construction. But they also give evidence of the realities of the everyday life of the colonists in the new climatic and geological conditions. Dugouts were the distinctive visible features of the Greek colonization of the region. But the deeper context of this process was the aim of creating and supporting the conditions for the normal existence of a *polis* community with the necessary social structure; something completely unknown in this part of the world.

The new series of Olbian agricultural settlements in the Lower Bug region appear in the beginning of the fifth century BC. Their appearance can be considered not only as a new wave of colonization, but also as an internal colonization, connected with the further development of the state territory and demographic changes inside the state. The inhabited territory increased with the joining of the right bank of the Bug estuary and the deep steppe ravines. This means that during the third stage of colonization (the first quarter of the fifth century BC) the Olbian *chora* possessed its maximum territory. Inside this territory it is now possible to subdivide some regions with different economic specializations and productive development – agricultural, cattle breeding, and handicraft specialization for internal consumption and imports to the barbarian hinterland.

One of the most interesting regions of the *chora* was located in the Adzhigol ravine (Kryzhitskij *et al.* 1999, 20–23; Nr 25–36), an area connected mainly with cattle breeding. Here there was an organized, well developed settlement structure, consisting of twelve settlements: eight shepherds' temporary shelters, two settlements of medium size, and two large permanent settlements. In the estuary of this ravine, on its right side, a common necropolis for this micro-region of the *chora*, Maritzin, was found (Ebert 1913, 1ff.). For decades in Russian language historiography this necropolis was taken as proof of barbarian (Scythian nomads) presence in the region from the end of the sixth century BC (Il'inskaja and Terenozhkin 1983, 198–199). Only now do we consider these graves to belong to the Greek inhabitants of this region of Olbian *chora* (S. Bujskich 2005c, 164ff.).

While we are looking at this central part of Olbian *chora*, we need to re-examine another idea of Solovyov. His main argument here concerns the demarcation of the borders of two *poleis* for the late Archaic period (the Olbian *polis* and the Borysthenes *polis*), which he argues were both bordered by the Adzhigol ravine (Solovyov 1999, 96–97, footnote 62; 2001, 118–120). To our minds, this idea is wrong and must be completely denied, because we support the conception of only one *polis* in existence in all the periods – the Olbian *polis*.

The basic inhabited unit of the Greek colonial *chorai* in the Lower Bug region in the sixth century to the beginning of the fifth century BC was an *oikos* (S. Bujskich 2006c, 118), consisting of a varied number of separated households in each of the settlements. This pattern was first noted during the archaeological research on the settlement Čertovatoe-7 (S. Bujskich 2006c, 118–119) and was later proven with examples of some other settlements. Every *oikos* was nearly 0.5 hectares square, and consisted of an inhabited centre and a surrounding zone for household related purposes. Every inhabited centre included a central dugout dwelling (approximately 12–15 m^2), and three to five other smaller dugouts and semi-dugouts, surrounding the central one (approximately 6–9 m^2). The household structures included up to between ten and twelve pits (mainly for grain, and later used for rubbish accumulation), one or two cisterns and some other secondary buildings. The *oikoi* were not closely arranged, but were located at some distance from each other. Perhaps, this was deliberate, and was connected with the necessary demands of hygiene or the problems of land usage inside the settlement. We would like to underline that a widespread building practice – in the layout of separate dwellings, and in their overall dimensions – was found which was accomplished with the help of the metrological standard from Ionia, or the region of Miletus – Samos (A. & S. Bujskikh 2001, 672–673).

The number of *oikoi* within each settlement depended on the dimensions of each settlement. The smallest ones included only one *oikos*. The settlements of middle size (from 2–3 up to 5–8 hectares) contained between four and sixteen households. The large settlements (agglomerations of approximately 50–70 hectares) contained between approximately 100 and 160 *oikoi*. Such a settlement structure has a lot of analogues in *metropolia*, where diminutive settlements ('Einzelhaussiedlung' 0.2–0.5 hectares), consisted of one household, settlements of medium size (5–10 hectares), agglomerations with irregular inner planning (40–60 hectares) or settlements with regular planning systems, existed at the same time on the territories of Greek city-states (Lang 1996, 56–62; Lohmann 2007, 375ff.).

During the last stage of the Greek colonization in the Lower Bug region, after the last quarter of the sixth century BC, there were some important changes in Olbia and her *chora*. Dugout houses, inhabited by two generations of colonists, were swapped completely for above ground houses built from mud-bricks on stone socles (A. Bujskikh 2017, 10). To begin with these houses had a simple one-chamber plan of square or nearly square shape, with a lower part, carved into a level of subsoil. This can be considered to be a continuation of the dugout building tradition. Only later, after the middle of the fifth century BC were these houses transferred into Greek houses of usual type with inner courts surrounded by separate rooms. A lot of them had cellars under the ground floor levels, and that became a distinctive feature of the Greek house-building tradition in Olbia and in the Northern Black Sea littoral in general until late-Roman times. In the middle of the fifth century BC the eastern temenos, where the large central altar was erected and dedicated to Apollo Delphinius, received the leading position among the sacred zones in the city.

At the end of the first third of the fifth century BC inhabitation of the majority of settlements stopped, and their population was concentrated mainly in Olbia. This was the main reason why in the second third of the fifth century BC the agricultural territory of *polis* collapsed, and the *polis* was left with only territory enough to support the city inhabitants with the necessary products (such as grain). There is no real archaeological proof for the point of view that the collapse of Olbian *chora* was due to nomadic (Scythian) migration, or that they created a kind of protectorate (Vinogradov 1989, 90ff.). In spite of the reduction of the *chora's* dimensions, the city expanded rather quickly. The reasons for this are better found in the economic and social development of the city, and not in the military and political sphere. This change was closely connected with the culmination of the process of Olbian *polis* organization involving the concentration of the population and the other resources together and the intensive building in the main urban centre (S. Bujskich 2006c, 122).

It is therefore possible to conclude that the Olbian *polis* created its *chora* in the frames of the entire Lower Bug region. The close similarities and principles of formation of the inhabited structures in the Olbian *chora* and in the metropolis were not fortuitous. In fact this gives us an opportunity to re-examine an idea, expressed earlier, about the unplanned and random character of the organization of Olbian settlements in the sixth and fifth centuries BC in the context of Greek colonization in the whole region (Kryjickij, and Bujskih 1999, 274; Kryzickij 2006, 99ff.). The total spread of the *oikos* unit can be used to prove an idea of the special subdivision in founding, building and spatial development of the Lower Bug agrarian settlements in the period of colonization. On the other hand, this pattern can be connected with the centralized activity of the Olbian *polis* in the total exploration of her agrarian territory. The main boundaries of this territory were established in the second quarter of the sixth century BC as soon as Olbia was founded (A. Buyskykh 2005; S. Bujskikh 2005a; 2006a).

The initial exploration of the *chora* and its natural resources was a well agreed programme with several stages, and was not finished until the beginning of the fifth century BC. Later, because of the building of the large urban *polis*-centre, the dimensions of the agrarian zone were reduced to the minimum necessary. The model of large *chora* was realized in practice for the second time in the last third of the fifth century until the first quarter of the fourth century BC (S. Bujskikh 2006c, 122). At this time, the Olbian chora again had all the necessary features of Greek agricultural structures in the North Pontic littoral and in the Mediterranean. We hope that the new excavations will bring forth new archaeological materials to contribute to the better understanding of the processes of the development of the Greek colonial *chora* in the Lower Bug region.

Bibliography

Bujskikh, A. V. (1999) L'Architecture religieuse des villes grecques du littoral Nord-Pontique aux VIe – Ve siècles av. N.e., In O. Lordkipanidze and P. Lévêque (ed.) *Religions du Pont-Euxin. Actes du VIIIe Symposium de Vani (Colchide) 1997*, 52–60. Paris, Diffusion les Belles Lettres.

Bujskikh, A. V. (2001) Review of G. R. Tsetskhladze (ed.) *The Greek Colonisation of the Black Sea Area: Historical Interpretation of Archaeology*. Fr. Steiner Verlag. Stuttgart 1998. Historia Einzelschriften 121. 336 S., *Eurasia Antiqua*, 7, 623–629.

Bujskikh, A. V. (2005) Die Gründung von Olbia im Lichte jüngster archäologischer Untersuchungen, *Eurasia Antiqua*, 11, 15–35.

Bujskikh, A. V. (2007) The Earliest East Greek Pottery from Olbia Pontica. In J. Cobet, V. Graeve, W. D. Niemeier and K. Zimmerman (eds) *Frühes Ionien. Eine Bestandsaufnahme. Panionion - Symposium Güzelçamlı 26. IX–1. X. 1999*, Milesische Forschungen, 5, 499–510. Mainz, Philipp von Zabern.

Bujskikh, A. V. (2017) From Dugouts to Houses: Urban Development in Late Archaic Olbia Pontica. In M. Mărgineanu-Cârstoiu (ed.) *Caiete ARA* 8, 5–17.

Buiskikh, A. V. and Buiskikh S. B. (2001) I siti di Olbia e della sua *chora* nel periodo della colonizzazione greca. In *Problemi della chora coloniale dall' Occidente al Mar Nero. Atti del XL Convegno di Studi sulla Magna Greca. Taranto, 29. IX–3. X. 2000*, 667–682. Taranto, Istituto per la storia e l'archeologia della Magna Grecia.

Bujskikh, S. B. (2005a) Les sanctuaries *extra-urbains* à l'époque de la colonization grecque dans le Bug méridional. In D. Kacharava, M. Faudot and E. Geny (eds) *Pont-Euxin et polis. Actes du Xe Symposium de Vani*, 181–202. Besançon, Presses universitaires de Franche-Comté.

Bujskikh, S. B. (2005b) The Beykush Sanctuary of Achilles from the Greek Colonisation Period in the Lower Bug Region. In J. Bouzek and L. Domaradzka (ed.) *The Culture of Thracians and their Neighbours*. British Archaeological Reports International Series 1350, 201--207. Oxford, Archaeopress.

Bujskikh, S. B. (2005c) Antičnoe poselenie Adzigol – 1 bliz Ol'vii, *Starozytnosti Stepovogo Pryčornomor'ja i Krymu*, 12, 164–189.

Bujskikh, S. B. (2006a) Die kolonialen Heiligtümer der archaischer Zeit in Olbia. In S. Conrad, R. Einicke, A. E. Furtwängler, H. Löhr and A. Slawisch (eds) *Pontos Euxeinos: Beiträge zur Archäologie und Geschichte des antiken Schwarzmeer- und Balkanraumes*, Schriften des Zentrums für Archäologie und Kulturgeschichte des Schwarzmeerraumes, 10, 265–274. Langenweißbach, Beier & Beran.

Bujskikh, S. B. (2006b) Kap Bejkuš – Kap des Achilleus: eine Kultstätte des göttlichen Heros im Mündunggebiet des Bug. In J. Hupe (ed.) *Der Achilleus Kult im nördlichen Schwarzmeerraum*, Internationale Archäologie, 94, 111–153.

Bujskikh, S. B. (2006c) Die *chora* des pontischen Olbia: Die Hauptetappen der räumlich-strukturellen Entwicklung. In P. G. Bilde and V. F. Stolba (eds) *Surveying the Greek Chora*, Black Sea Studies, 4, 115–139. Aarhus, Aarhus University Press.

Bujskikh, S. B. (2007) Contacts between Greeks and Non-Greeks on the Lower Bug in the sixth and fifth Centuries BC, in *Proceedings of the British Academy*, 142, 23–33.

Domanskij, J. V. and Marčenko, K. K. (2003) Towards Determining the Chief Function of the Settlement of Borysthenes. In P. G. Bilde, J. M. Højte and V. F. Stolba (eds) *The Cauldron of Ariantas: Studies Presented to A N. Ščeglov on the Occasion of His 70th Birthday*, 29–36. Aarhus, Aarhus University Press.

Ebert, M. (1913) *Ausgrabungen auf dem Gute Maritzyn, Gouv. Cherson (Süd-Russland).* II Teil, *Prähistorische Zeitschrift*, Band 5, Heft 1–2, 1–80.

Il'inskaja, V. I. and Terenozhkin, A. I. (1983) *Skifija VII–IV vv. do n. e.* Kiev, Naukova Dumka.

Ivantchik, A. I. (2006) Book review of E. K. Petropoulos (2005) *Hellenic Colonization in Euxeinos Pontos. Penetration, early establishment, and the problem of the «emporion» revisited.* BAR International Series 1394. Oxford, Archaeopress. In *Ancient Civilizations from Scythia to Siberia*, vol. 12, Nr. 3–4, 330–336.

Karasjov, A. N. (1964) Monumental'nye pamjatniki ol'vijskogo temenosa (Monumental buildings at Olbian temenos). In V. F. Gajdukevič, *Ol'vija. Temenos i agora*, 27–130. Moskva-Leningrad, Nauka.

Kenzler, U. (2000) Vom dörflichen Versammlungsplatz zum urbanen Zentrum. Die Agora im Mutterland und in die Kolonien. In F. Krinzinger (ed.) *Die Ägäis und das westliche Mittelmeer. Beziehungen und Wechselwirkungen 8. bis 5. Jh. v. Chr.* Wien, Verlag der Österreichischen Akademie der Wissenschaften.

Kerschner, M. (2006) Zum Begin und zu den Phasen der griehischen Kolonisation am Schwarzen Meer, *Eurasia Antiqua*, 12, 227–50.

Kryžickij, S. D. (2006) The Rural Environs of Olbia: Some Problems of Current Importance. In P. G. Bilde and V. F. Stolba (eds) *Surveying the Greek Chora*, Black Sea Studies, 4, 99–114. Aarhus, Aarhus University Press.

Kryjickij, S. D. and Bujskih, S. B. (1999) La dynamique d'aménagement du territoire rural d'Olbia Pontique. *Bulletin de Correspondance Hellenique,* Suppl. 34, 273–288.

Kryzhitskij, S. D., Bujskikh, S. B. and Otreshko, V. M. (1999). *Antičnye Poselenija Nizhnego Pobuzh'ja (Archeologičeskaja Karta).* Kiev, Naukova Dumka.

Lang, F. (1996) *Archaische Siedlungen in Griechenland. Struktur und Entwicklung.* Berlin, Akademie Verlag.

Lapin, V. V. (1966) *Grecheskaya kolonisatsiya Severnogo Prichernomorya (Greek Colonization of the Northern Black Sea Coast).* Kiev, Naukova Dumka.

Lohmann, H. (2007) Die Chora Milets in archaischer Zeit. In J. Cobet, V. Graeve, W. D. Niemeier and K. Zimmerman (eds) *Frühes Ionien. Eine Bestandsaufnahme. Panionion - Symposium Güzelçamli 26. IX-1. X. 1999*, Milesische Forschungen, 5, 363–392. Mainz, Philipp von Zabern.

Martin, R. (1956) *L'urbanisme dans la Grèce antique.* Paris, Editions A. et J. Picard.

Nazarov, V. V. (2007) A Temenos of the 6th Century BC. at Berezan. In J. Cobet, V. Graeve, W. D. Niemeier and K. Zimmerman (eds) *Frühes Ionien. Eine Bestandsaufnahme. Panionion - Symposium Güzelçamli 26. IX-1. X. 1999*, Milesische Forschungen, 5, 541–550. Mainz, Philipp von Zabern.

Petropoulos, E. K. (2005) *Hellenic Colonization in Euxeinos Pontos. Penetration, early establishment, and the problem of the «emporion» revisited.* British Archaeological Reports International Series 1394. Oxford, Archaeopress.

Rusyaeva, A. S. (1986) Milet - Didimy - Borisfen - Ol'viya - Problemy colonizatsii Hizhnego Pobuzh'ya (Miletos - Didyma - Borysthenes - Olbia. Problems of the Colonization in the Lower Bug Region), *Vestnik drevnej istorii,* Nr. 2, 225–264.

Rusyaeva, A. S. (1994) Investigations of the Western Temenos of Olbia, in *Ancient Civilizations from Scythia to Siberia*, vol. I, Nr. 1, 80–102.

Rusyaeva, A. S. (1999) Les *temene* d'Olbia à la lumière de son histoire au Vie siècle av.n.è., In O. Lordkipanidzé and P. Lévêque (ed.) *Religions du Pont-Euxin. Actes du VIIIe Symposium de Vani (Colchide),* 75–84. Paris, Diffusion les Belles Lettres.

Solovyov, S. L. (1998) Archaic Berezan: Historical - Archaeological Essay. In G. R. Tsetskhladze (ed.) *The Greek Colonisation of the Black Sea Area: Historical Interpretation of Archaeology* (Historia Einzelschriften 121), 205–225. Stuttgart, Franz Steiner Verlag.

Solovyov, S. L. (1999) *Ancient Berezan* (Colloquia Pontica, 4), Leiden-Boston-Cologne, Brill.

Solovyov, S. L. (2001) On the History of the City-States in the Lower Bug Area: Borysthenes and Olbia. In J. Boardman, S. L. Solovyov and G. R. Tsetskhladze (eds) *Northern Pontic Antiquities in the State Hermitage Museum*, Colloquia Pontica, 7, 113–125. Leiden, Brill.

Vinogradov, Yu. G. (1989). *Politicheskaya istoriya Ol'viyiskogo polisa VII-I vv. do. n.e. (Political History of the Olbian Polis VII-I centuries B.C.E)*, Moscow, Nauka.

13

Colonial landscapes and colonial interactions in Skythia and the Euxeinos Pontos

Elias K. Petropoulos

The appearance of the ancient Greeks along the shores of the Euxeinos Pontos and their subsequent settlement in this region form one part of the historical phenomenon known as 'Greek colonization' (on the various permutations and connotations of the term, see Gosden 2006, 1–6; also Osborne 1998, 251–252, 268; de Angelis 1998, 539–548; van Dommelen 2002, 121–122; Dietler 2005, 33–55; Malkin 2005b, 60–61). From the eighth century BC onwards, the ancient Greeks had already begun to settle the Western Mediterranean, with the Euboeans as pioneers (D'Agostino 2006, 201–206; Greco 2006, 171), proving themselves worthy successors of the Mycenaeans around the Mediterranean (Petropoulos 2005, 100; 2008; Vanschoonwinkel 2006, 94). On the basis of archaeological evidence, the Euboeans touched on the shores of the Eastern Mediterranean from as early as the tenth century BC; in the West, their first colonies were founded somewhat later (Lemos 2005, 58). The Euboeans acquired considerable experience of new settlements and communication with non-Greek speaking peoples. Such contacts with the 'other' helped the Euboeans cultivate their ethnic identity (Thomas and Conant 1999, 134–143; Mitchell 2006, 414–418); they also helped native peoples cultivate their own identity (for example, see Dominguez 2002, 70; 2006b, 446–456; Gosden 2006, 65–72). After establishing new commercial relations around the entire Mediterranean basin, colonists soon took advantage of trading opportunities, even before the official establishment of the first Greek settlement on Pithekoussai (D'Agostino 2006, 217).

It is customary to speak of 'pre-colonial' relations between Greeks and natives (Malkin 1998, 10–14, 74–81; 2002, 151; Morel 2006, 367; D'Agostino 2006, 226; Greco 2006, 183; Kirigin 2006, 57), whenever numbers of Greek pottery sherds are found in a region outside continental Greece and wherever a Greek settlement followed in the same area (Carter 2006a, 52; D'Agostino 2006, 215–216, 226; Kirigin 2006, 57). These

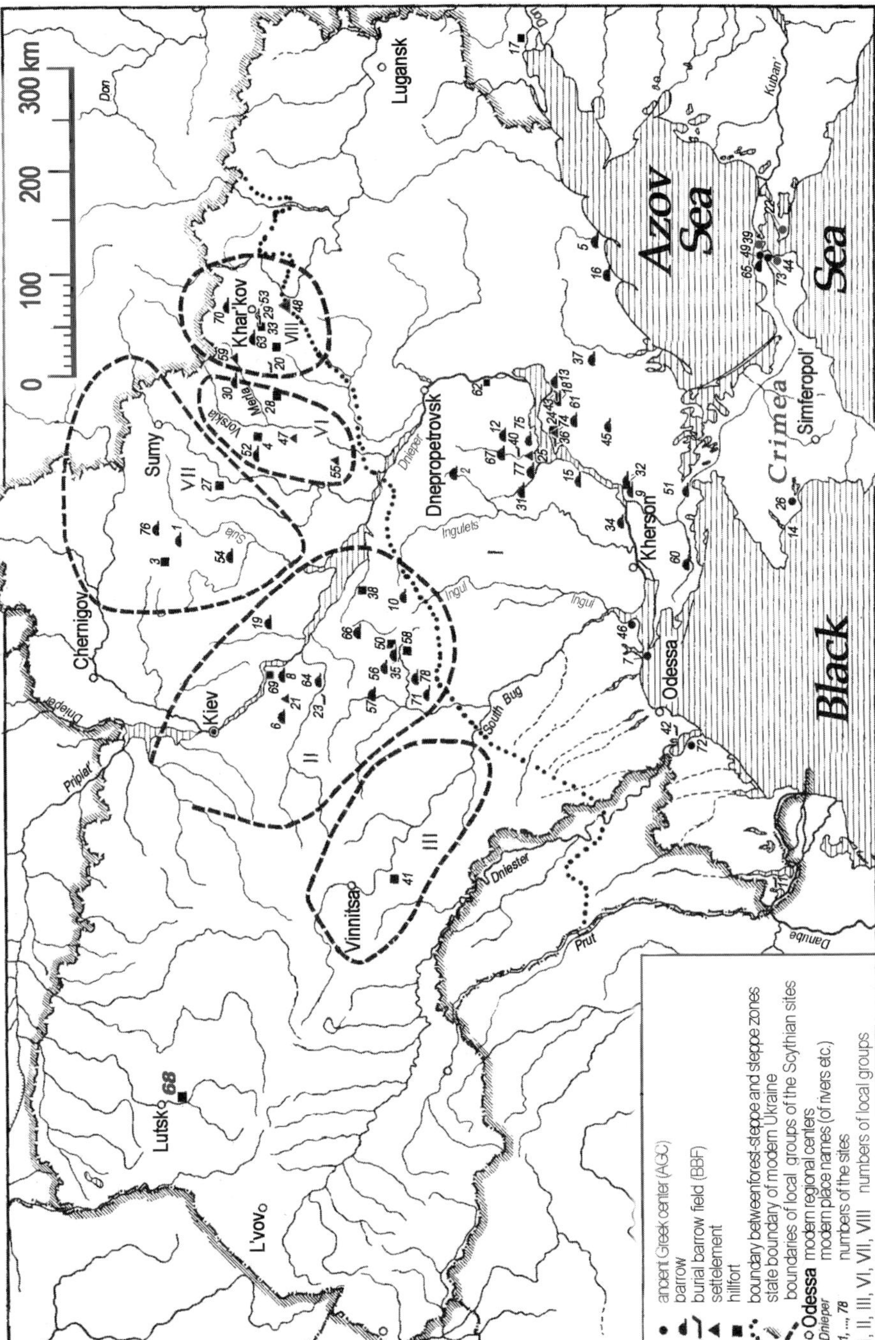

Fig. 13.1. Map of the Scythian sites in the Northern Black Sea area showing the distribution of Greek imports (by Gavrilyuk 2007, 663–664).

from their starting point in the Lower Dnieper (Fig. 13.1) (Gavrilyuk 2007, 631). This apparently occurred after the colonists determined that no Scythian settlement had yet been built in the neighbouring steppe.

Not all scholars agree with this reconstruction of events, and some endeavour to prove that merchants from the forest-steppe tribes were accustomed to descend to the Lower Dnieper and the Bug Rivers regions for salt and fish long before the appearance of Ionian Greek settlers (Boltrik 2000, 122–124). It has even been claimed that Greeks were neither able to visit, nor resilient enough to inhabit this region, noted even today for its harsh climate. Indeed, Herodotus (IV, 28) and other ancient writers describe the region's cold weather. However, when describing the demographics of the Scythian interior, Herodotus also observes the following:

> The Budinians are a great and numerous nation; the eyes of all of them are very bright, and they are ruddy. They have a city built of wood, called Gelonos. The wall of it is thirty furlongs in length on each side of the city; this wall is high and all of wood; and their houses are wooden, and their temples; for there are among them temples of Greek gods, furnished in Greek fashion with images and altars and shrines of wood; and they honour Dionysos every two years with festivals and revels. *For the Gelonians are by their origin Greeks, who left in past times their emporia to settle among the Budinians;* and they speak a language half Greek and half Scythian. But the Budinians speak not the same language as the Gelonians, nor is their manner of life the same (Herodotus IV, 108).

Russian and Ukrainian archaeologists have hypothesized (Rybakov 1979, 153; Shramko 1975, 119; 1987, 156–164; Melyukova 1989, 47–48) that the ancient settlement of Gelonos mentioned by Herodotus is to be identified with a settlement in the Scythian forest-steppe called Belsk, near the mid-point of the Vorskla River in the Ukraine (see Gavrilyuk 1999; see also Braund 2005, 5–6 and Rousyaeva 1999, 93–96). In a study of the antiquities from this settlement, to which study he devoted many years of his life, the archaeologist Boris A. Shramko made the material recovered from Belsk available to scholars. The Belsk settlement encompasses nearly 4,000 hectares, with sturdy fortified walls extending to a length of more than 36 km (Murzin and Rollet 1997, 12; Murzin 2005, 35–37). Given these dimensions, one can only imagine what sort of settlement Belsk was, and what kind of political power was needed to collect the necessary materials and manpower to erect such fortifications. And Belsk is not the only instance of ancient Greeks living with natives (for further information and updated bibliography, see Petropoulos 2005; in a recent article, A. Avram supports the idea that such mixtures did not have an ethnic character, but rather that they were '*une connotation sociale*' 2007, 249).

Let us now return to the South Russian region. The situation suggested by the earliest Greek pottery discovered in the forest-steppe is that of the initial phase of Greek colonization in the northern Black Sea region (as opposed to its eastern and western sides). As I have tried to show elsewhere (Petropoulos 2005, 3–74), visits by Greek settlers to the forest-steppe region of Scythia encompassed its entire geographic expanse, and included sites at a great distance from one another. Archaeological investigation has demonstrated that this pottery belonged to Greeks, who for whatever reason remained, even if briefly, in the forest-steppe. Some archaeologists believe that in the seventh century BC *Nemirovskoye gorodishe* (Nemirovo) was a sort of Greek '*post of trade*' of the Boristhenitai (the Greek settlers on the island of Berezan), from which Greek merchants could conduct trade with the inhabitants of the forest-steppe hinterland (Martchenko 2005, 59–62). The peak of this 'early and relatively short-term' importation falls in the last quarter of the seventh century BC (Vakhtina 2000, 216). Something of a stir was created in archaeological research by the fact that most early examples of Greek pottery from the early Archaic period were uncovered in the Scythian forest-steppe, whereas logically one would have expected this to occur along the coastal zone, where Greek settlements were located. This is in contrast with Etruscan imports in southern France, where trade was largely a coastal phenomenon (Dietler 1997, 279; Malkin 2002, 155), just as it was in Iberia (Dominguez 2002, 68–87).

Dietler has shown that ancient Etruscan and Greek traders and colonists did not move far inland from the coast, and traders were therefore restricted to selling their products in places on or near the coast, with natives promoting such products further inland (Dietler 1995; 1997). But why was this? And why is the picture the archaeological evidence paints for South France and Iberia so different from that along the northern coast of the Euxeinos Pontos? One point needs to be taken into account when considering the contrasting cases. In the first case, *i.e.* in South France (and Iberia), it has been shown that the coastal zone was densely inhabited; hence, there was no reason for traders to transport themselves or their wares further inland, since these could reach distant places in Northern Europe through internal distribution and reselling among natives.

Such was not the case with the Euxeinos Pontos, however. Modern archaeological research indicates that the entire steppe zone (including the coast) was uninhabited. How, therefore, could ancient Greek traders circulate their wares? Did they wait for trading caravans from the forest-steppe to appear and negotiate with their members (as seems to be the conclusion drawn by Boltrik 2000, 124)? If this were the case, one has difficulty imagining that representatives of the local aristocracy participated in these trading caravans from the forest-steppe to the coast in order to obtain fish or salt. Furthermore, there is mention of not just one or a few pots in native forest-steppe settlements, but of large quantities of pottery, and these at sites very remote from the coast, extending across a large part of the forest-steppe down to the end of the seventh century BC (Gavrilyuk 2007, 630–631, 655–656; see also Petropoulos 2005, 3–74). It is also believed that these Greek objects were not goods intended for trade, but gifts by the first Greek settlers to distinguished representatives of the Scythian nobility (Gavrilyuk 2007, 656; cf Petropoulos 2004, 34–35; Vakhtina 1999, 25–26; Graham 1984, 6). Thus the two cases (South France/Iberia – Scythia) are quite distinct as regards the population distribution of natives during the period in question.

And even in the case of Iberia, matters do not seem entirely certain, to judge from recent archaeological data. Here I have in mind Castulo, a centre far inland in Upper Andalusia, where sometime between the late fifth and early fourth century

BC we can observe almost every type of Greek pottery, including types not normally found in coastal centres and shapes known only in the Greek city of Emporion (Dominguez 2006a, 467–469). Following Dominguez, might we suspect that here we had the creation of a *sui generis* 'port of trade' during this period, comparable to the settlement of Pistiros in Thrace (Domaradzka 2005, 19; Herman Hansen 2006, 22–23) or that of Gelonos (Belsk) in Scythia? While this issue requires further discussion, what at present seems significant is that in Spain between the late fifth and early fourth centuries BC, ancient Greeks were in a position to penetrate far inland in order to facilitate trade with indigenous inhabitants, and to live side by side with them, developing and securing collaboration that benefited both parties.

The situation in the remaining Black Sea regions

Let us now consider the situation on the other sides of the Euxeinos Pontos region during the initial colonization period. In the western area, the archaeological evidence proves the generally peaceful and friendly tenor of Milesian colonization; in connection with certain locations scholars sometimes speak of 'cooperation' between colonists and natives (Avram 2003, 290; Manuçu-Adameşteanu 2003, 367–368; Nedev and Panayotova 2003, 100–101, 109; Minchev 2003, 218), implying the mutual interests of colonists and members of the native aristocracy (Frost 1982, 280–289; Porojanov 1986, 158–165; Hind 1992–93, 84; Lazarov 1984, 63–68; Porogeanov 1984, 69–75; Fol 1996, 2–3) who anticipated enrichment through their dealings with these new inhabitants from Ionia. In this respect some scholars speak of Thracian sea power (*thalassocracy*) in the mid-second millennium BC and accept pre-colonial contacts (Minchev 2003, 215). Acquisition of 'exotic' customs allowed local elites to place themselves on an equal footing with the Greek aristocracy (D'Agostino 2006, 208–212, 217). We find in many ancient writers remarks that testify to a similar cooperation between ancient Greek colonists and autochthonous peoples living in numerous areas around the Mediterranean (Osborne 1996, 238–239; Dominguez 2005, 94; Morel 2006, 365–366, 375, 388–389).

With respect to the Euxeinos Pontos, for example in Histria, we note that while the shoreline was uninhabited before Histria was established, the natives themselves created a settlement there following the arrival and establishment of the first Ionian colonists, once again suggesting peaceful co-existence and cooperation between the two ethnic groups during the archaic period (Avram 2003, 292; 2006, 63; a similar situation is found in Orgame: Manuçu-Adameşteanu 2003, 352–353). At this point I might note a disagreement expressed by Vassilika Lungu during my presentation at the Symposium. She believes that recently uncovered archaeological evidence would indicate these sites were inhabited when the first Greek colonists appeared (for a similar opinion, see Martchenko and Vakhtina 2001, 144–145, where it is stated that during their initial colonizing efforts in the Lower Danube in the mid-seventh century BC, the Greek settlers encountered a powerful union of tribes under the leadership of Scythian aristocrats). We shall look forward to reading more about this hypothesis when the evidence is published in detail. In a recent article, M. Damyanov (2007, 9) states that, to date, archaeological research along the western Black Sea coast has not revealed a single instance of continuity between an Early Iron Age Thracian layer and subsequent archaic Greek layers. Perhaps the Greeks' determination to establish commercial relations with natives – not only along the coastal zone, but in the hinterland as well – led them to pursue a systematic policy of amicable co-existence that was successfully applied in many places in the Mediterranean, for example in the Iberian peninsula (Dominguez 2006a, 434–435, 448), in Emporion (Dominguez 2005, 99; Miró i Alaix 2006, 21) and in the Marseilles region (Morel 2006, 388–389). According to the archaeological evidence (D'Agostino 2006, 215–217), the *symposion*, shared by immigrants and natives, played a decisive role in determining their mutual relations.

Along the eastern coast of the Black Sea, there are no early (*i.e.* seventh century BC) Greek settlements observed (Gabelia 2003, 1216–1224; Lordkipanizde 2003, 1313–1321), probably because of strong resistance by natives. A permanent Greek presence was established only in the late seventh–early sixth centuries BC (Gabelia 2003, 1220; Lordkipanidze 2003, 1312ff.). For the Ochamchire (Gyenos?) settlement, available evidence attests to peaceful penetration by the Greeks into the Ochamchire Bay. It is presumed that the indigenous population joined the Greek settlement from the earliest stage of its foundation (Kvirkvelia 2003, 1287–1288). A similar situation seems to be discernible in Pichvnari (Vickers and Kakhidze 2004, 152–202).

On the southern coast, archaeological research has not advanced sufficiently to permit us to form a clear idea about Greek-barbarian contacts during the period of colonization. However, the first Milesian establishment in Sinope, on the isthmus connecting Boztepe to the mainland, may be approximately dated to the latter part of the seventh century BC (Doonan 2003, 1381–1382; 2006, 52), though ancient written sources speak of an earlier settlement here. In the opinion of archaeologists, the main reason why the Greeks did not manage to establish themselves in the southern Pontos before the mid-seventh century BC was the powerful presence of the Kimmerians (Atasoy 2003, 1338–1339).

Changing landscapes and identification

We might mention here the question posed by John Bintliff (2006, 23) and even expand upon it: 'What were the "native"-colonial interactions and their relations in the *chora*' (or in the Greek *apoikiai* or settlements themselves)? In seeking an answer to this question, I believe that the following is of interest: if there were no inhabitants in the coastal regions when the Greeks arrived (as the current evidence suggests), then why did they not build their settlements ashore from the first moment, instead of preferring peninsulas and isthmuses or small islands near the coast, presumably for protection and fortification (Osborne 2005, 12), and only after the passage of some decades move onto the mainland to build colonies proper? In the Euxeinos Pontos, almost all early Greek settlements confirm this: the settlement on the Berezan peninsula (older) and the subsequent establishment of Olbia after *c.* 50–60 years,

Apollonia (which archaeologists have found to be the product of collaboration between Greeks and natives), Orgame, Histria, and Sinope.

The Tauric peninsula provides one notable exception. According to the archaeological evidence and ancient written testimony, when the first Greek settlement on the Herakleian peninsula occurred in the last quarter of the sixth century BC (Nikolaenko 2006, 153–154), the southwest Crimea was inhabited by bearers of the Kizil-Koba civilization (Taurians) and (probably) by Scythians (Petropoulos 2005, 122; Carter 2006b, 186, 193).

Of course, the mere fact of an initial settlement in a naturally fortified location does not prove the eventual physical presence of natives who may have made the colonists' life difficult, including resorting to battle (we recall here that the ancient sources relate a number of similar cases in the wider Euxeinos Pontos area). Such settlements might imply a standardized colonization policy, demonstrating a uniform means of operation in a totally unknown region that was for the most part inhospitable. The Greeks established city-states from the eastern coast of the Black Sea to Spain in the Western Mediterranean as maritime colonies with a 'ship-to-shore' perspective, expressed in their typical site choices (offshore islands, promontories) and in negotiations with hinterland populations, for whom beaches and offshore islands often seemed peripheral. The beach thus served as a less-threatening middle ground for both Greeks and natives (Malkin 2005a, 5) (I would like to thank Professor Irad Malkin for having directed my attention to this point during my oral presentation at the symposium). Such choices may also imply the colonists' reservations and mistrust towards their new neighbours, even when the latter seemed friendly. The colonists took measures to protect their settlements even in cases where the natives posed no serious threat.

Another issue, directly related to the previous one and falling within the overall discussion concerning the nature of contacts between Greek immigrants and indigenous populations, is the discovery in almost every early Greek settlement in the northern Pontos of dugout or semi-dugout structures, together with the question of how these are to be interpreted (see Petropoulos 2005, 36–41). Similar pits have been uncovered on the eastern coast of the Pontos, where 'to the earliest period of the history of the town could be ascribed wooden constructions of semi-dugout type' (Kvirkvelia 2003, 1286), as well as the western Pontos (Avram 2003, 291, 323; 2006, 61). The question that has remained unanswered for some decades, and which continues to arouse considerable debate, is whether such pits served as abodes for the first immigrants from Ionia or as warehouses intended for storing numerous products, cereals in particular. With respect to the idiosyncratic type of the first houses in the colonies of the northern Pontos, I would like to point to some new evidence that may shed further light on this question.

Some researchers believe that during the early phase of colonisation in the Circumpontic region (*i.e.* from the mid-seventh century BC to approximately 500 BC, or possibly somewhat earlier), Greek settlers lived in dugouts and semi-dugouts, while the transition to stone dwellings on the surface occurred later; others disagree with this interpretation of the evidence. The hypotheses of both are based on archaeological material that is often hard to interpret. In his recent work, S. Bujskikh (2005, 3–21) offered strong support for the view that one cannot dispute the authenticity of this type of initial abode in the Greek settlements of the Euxeinos Pontos. After offering a critique of the opposing arguments, particularly those of Solovyov, Bujskikh enumerated examples of the use of similar abodes for Greek immigrants in other regions of the Mediterranean where colonization occurred, arguing that all were Greek.

A number of circular dugout huts from modern excavations in the *chora* of the ancient Greek colony of Metapontion (in Incoronata) in South Italy display striking similarities (Carter 2006a, 58–68) to what is currently known from the Berezan settlement and the *chora* of Olbia (Bylkova 2000, 27ff.; Kryzhytskyy and Krapivina 2003, 514–524). The dugout and semi-dugout dwellings at Metapontion contain 'varying proportions of imported Greek pottery, locally made indigenous wares, some handmade, some wheel-made, and a hybrid wheel-made "colonial" pottery using Greek shapes and eclectically chosen Greek motifs' (Carter 2006b, 193), *i.e.* exactly what is observed in similar constructions in Berezan, Olbia (Kryzhytskyy *et al.* 2003, 399, 428–429, 467) and other settlements of the Lower Bug River region (S. Bujskikh 2005, 11–12).

The argumentation employed among scholars over the identity of the owners of such pits is complex, but there appear to be three basic views: a) the dugout was a purely local (*viz.*, Northern Black Sea) traditional dwelling that Greek colonists borrowed from natives for the construction of temporary houses; b) such constructions were Greek; and c) there were different traditions co-existing independently of one another. A detailed account of the various approaches has been given by S. Bujskikh (2005, 3–12). The nature of the dispute among archaeologists dealing with the *chora* of Metapontion is similar (Carter 2006a, 58–84), while regarding the *chora* of Histria one must reserve conclusions (Avram 2006, 63).

Discussion becomes even more heated in the attempt to solve one further riddle. How are we to interpret the presence of handmade pottery (often displaying features of native pottery, and therefore not cited in the literature as Greek or Greek-made) unearthed in large quantities alongside (genuinely) Greek pottery and other characteristic objects in abodes of this type in every shore settlement (Kryzhitskiy *et al.* 1999, 83) of the Northern Black Sea as well as inland, *e.g.* in the rural settlements of the Lower Dniester (Ochotnikov 2006, 86)? It is common for handmade pottery in Greek settlements to lead archaeologists to conclude that natives were living alongside Greek immigrants (for example, Kryzhitskij 2005, 128; Morel 1984, 125; Kirigin 2006, 26); natives are considered to have been the purveyors and users of such pottery (Boltrik 2000, 123–124; Solovyov 1999, 42–47; Senatorov 2005, 174–249; Martchenko 2005, 62; Avram 2006, 63; Sekerskaya 2007, 477). But what is to prevent us from hypothesizing that the immigrants from Ionia (or from any other Greek metropolis) also made such pottery to meet their everyday needs, and so as not to be obliged to wait for natives to supply them? Why need the presence of handmade pottery call forth thoughts of possible intermarriages between Greek settlers and women from local families (for example, Morel 2006, 365–366; D'Agostino 2006, 224)? Here, I would like to note two examples that have not have been highlighted in scholarly discussion.

Archaeological excavation at the site of Karabournaki in Thessaloniki has uncovered a number of semi-dugout spaces, normally beehive-shaped, more rarely rectangular, hewn into natural soil of hard, yellowish, clay (Petropoulos 2005, 38–41). Some of these semi-dugouts consist of two spaces communicating with one another through a small opening. Their brick and stone superstructure probably continued above the earth's surface. Within these spaces were found traces of clay hearths and storage pots, cooking vessels, and other objects. Professor M. Tiverios draws a parallel between these structures and those of later years known as 'the dwellings of Slavs'. The latter are referred to in the miracles of St Dimitrios as *kasai*, 'coffins'; they were semi-dugout huts built of wood and earth. Evidence that they were habitations led Professor Tiverios to consider whether in this manner a number of ancient sources that claim the ancient Phrygians dwelt below ground might be confirmed (Tiverios *et al.* 1998, 225). From other ancient sources, we learn that comparable habitations also existed in Macedonia and were called *argilai*; Strabo uses the same word to denote the underground habitations of the legendary Kimmerians (V, 4, 5).

Noteworthy is the fact that according to the archaeological evidence available, the semi-dugout houses at Karabournaki pre-date the above-ground dwellings. There seems no doubt that during the archaic period this was the most important harbour along the Thermaic Gulf; 'luxury' pottery and other products arrived here from all the major centres of the ancient Greek world and the East, whence they were transported inland. In some cases, the two types of structure may have been in use simultaneously, or some of the semi-dugouts may have been re-used by the inhabitants of the 'stone' dwellings. The archaeologist's observations clearly indicate the period of use for these two construction types as the seventh and sixth centuries BC, a chronology coinciding with the colonizing activity of the Ionian Greeks. Recent archaeological research has shown that the phase with older stone walls is to be dated after the end of the eighth century BC (Petropoulos 2005, 38–41). In short, precisely the same picture is presented in the Chalkidike as that presented by the archaeological data coming from Greek settlements in Metapontion and the northern Euxeinos Pontos and dating from the mid-seventh century to *c.* 530 BC.

From these observations, there emerges the hypothesis that the Eastern Greeks, particularly the Ionians, before immigrating to the northern Euxeinos Pontos and founding colonies there from the mid-seventh century BC onward, had contacts (perhaps even settlements) in Central Macedonia from the early seventh or possibly the late eighth century BC. They were familiar with semi-dugouts or dugouts, which could be employed as dwellings, confirming the view of S. Bujskikh (2005, 7–8) that Ionian settlers brought the tradition of such constructions with them from the motherland. The differentiation in the traditions of dugout and semi-dugout constructions between Greeks and locals is well-illustrated in the Belozyorskoye settlement and the *chora* of Olbia, where the two traditions co-existed (Bylkova 2000, 30). Recourse to such habitations appears to have been standard practice for the Greek colonists in places with a climate colder than that of their native environment; such structures facilitated their survival during their initial presence in the new land (Avram 2003, 323; Kryzhytskyy and Krapivina 2003, 522; Malyshev 2007, 927).

Our second example concerns the use of similar constructions for residences in modern times, at the beginning of the seventeenth century when America was being colonized by Europeans. The Dutch immigrants who settled at the site of contemporary Manhattan 'disembarked and stood defenceless before the towering pines. For shelter initially they dug square pits in the ground, lined them with wood, and covered them with bark roofs (a minister, who arrived a few years later, when proper houses were being built, sneered at the "hovels and holes" in which the first arrivals "huddled rather than dwelt")' (Shorto 2004, 44).

It seems to me reasonable to imagine that the dugout is a construction that is not the achievement of any one particular group, but which indicates something more profound. I think that in all probability the dugout was a universal device, a result of humans' efforts to survive in difficult conditions irrespective of their cultural origins or era. Its copyright seems to belong to humanity in general (the same conclusion was reached during the Roundtable Discussion Panel at the end of the Symposium). However, since the issue of dugout and semi-dugout constructions also relates to the origins of the founders of many Greek settlements, and bears on a number of issues in this discussion, *e.g.* Graeco-barbarian relations, I think endeavouring to arrive at some final solution may be a necessary evil. Here I would add that I agree with Carter that 'a closer comparative study might lead to a better understanding of both [*i.e.*, Incoronata & Berezan] of these groups of early settlers' (2006a, 65), as well as all ancient colonial Greek settlements across the Mediterranean and Euxeinos Pontos where such dugout dwellings have been found to date.

Finally, as regards the handmade pottery found in these pits in the Greek settlements of the Black Sea, especially in Berezan, recent studies have shown that the possibility of local production of painted pottery should be seriously considered (A. V. Bujskikh 2005, 185). There are indications for local production of painted fine-ware pottery of the Ionian style among the pottery from Berezan stored in the State Hermitage of St Petersburg (Posamentir 2006, 164–166). Since the colonists were apparently able to make their own fine wares, why exclude the possibility of their also having produced handmade pottery to meet everyday needs? In Greece itself, coarse cooking ware was not made on the potter's wheel from the sixth to the fourth century (Sparkes 1996, 77–78); it is possible the newcomers followed this tradition. Unless we suppose that domestic pottery decorated in the Ionian style served for cooking and other everyday needs (*i.e.* that the first colonists had the means to dine on costly decorated pottery, while living – in all probability – in dugouts or semi-dugouts), I believe it reasonable to assume that the colonists were obliged to make simple, handmade pottery to satisfy urgent and everyday needs. This would have freed them from depending on natives for such wares, though exchanges involving handmade pottery cannot be ruled out (Martchenko 1988, 77). The presence of representatives from the forest-steppe of the middle Dnieper in Olbia and Berezan has repeatedly been established (Boltrik 2000, 123, with references). Nevertheless, the evidence suggests that there are clear differences between the handmade pottery used by Olbian Greeks (common to all settlements of the later agricultural area of the same city) and that found in contemporary Scythian settlements of the lower Dnieper. This has been shown by modern excavations at the Belozyorskoye settlement, viewed until recently as Scythian (Bylkova 2000, 33–34).

Conclusions

Today there is a need for a comparative study of the colonization phenomenon on the basis of the evidence available from the Mediterranean and the Euxeinos Pontos and for detailed study of individual issues. This may lead us to sounder conclusions and a fuller understanding of numerous aspects of the Greek colonization phenomenon. Although we cannot speak of 'patterns' in Greek colonization, the more evidence archaeological investigation brings to light, the more common points we will discern regarding how the colonists addressed practical issues, even in regions very distant from each other. A good example of such a practical issue is the dugout. Similar constructions have been uncovered in several places of the ancient (and not only the ancient) *oecumene*, which leads us to suspect they may be a diachronic human invention designed for coping with challenging climactic conditions. The presence of such constructions in the Euxeinos Pontos, especially in its northwestern area, may not have been an exclusive prerogative of Scythians or natives, *i.e.* non-Greeks; rather, it seems that both Greeks and non-Greeks had understood the utility of such abodes before their first contact with one another. For the moment, I do not think we can say with certainty to whom the handmade ceramic sherds discovered in the dugout or semi-dugout constructions belonged; nonetheless, these too comprise important evidence that should become the object of detailed comparative study.

On the other hand, we observe that at least with regard to Scythia, Greek decorative pottery of high quality is attested from the first moment of the Greeks' establishment and is found in native settlements quite distant from the Greek littoral settlements. Perhaps this allows us to suppose that native handmade pottery also made its way to Greek settlements through trade. The Greek presence in remote forest-steppe native settlements should no longer be questioned; this in turn suggests the absence of permanently established settlements in the steppe zone during the period of Greek colonisation, *i.e.* from the mid-seventh century until at least the late seventh – early sixth century BC, as well as the importance of contacts with native peoples for the Greeks, regardless of how far they were from the newly founded Greek settlements. Apart from establishing their settlements, the Greeks appear to have simultaneously sought out native populations and established contacts with them. Such contacts seem to have played a vital role in the lives of both natives and colonists. This active seeking out of contacts, similarly, might suggest the extensive scope of the Ionian colonisation enterprise – at least in the North Black Sea region – as well as the timely organization of participants. We are not speaking here of 'vagabond' Robinson Crusoes who landed on the shores of the Pontos by mistake, owing to powerful winds or poor sailing. I am convinced the Ionians were acting in accordance with a well-organized plan (Petropoulos 2005; for similar conclusions see Osborne 1998, 261; Kirigin 2006, 43ff.).

The period of pre-colonial contacts was a fundamental prerequisite for migratory activity and the eventual decision to settle a given region. The evidence suggests that such a period was necessary for both the Greeks and Phoenicians. During this period, information was collected as several previously unknown regions were discovered. The vital role of archaeological excavation at the sites of ancient Greek and autochthonous settlements is thus evident, encouraging us to further research and in-depth comparative study of the colonisation phenomenon across the entire Mediterranean and the Black Sea regions.

Abbreviations

BABesch – Bulletin Antieke Beschaving. Annual Papers on Classical Archaeology.
RA – Российская Археология (Russian Archaeology). Moscow.
VDI – Вестник Древней Истории (Journal of Ancient History). Moscow.

Acknowledgments

I would like to extend my thanks to Professor A. Dominguez for valuable information, as well as for his kindly agreeing to read and offer timely observations on the entire manuscript. My thanks to Professor John Papadopoulos of UCLA for reading the entire manuscript and offering many valuable observations and suggestions for improvement.

Bibliography

Angelis, F. de (1998) Ancient Past, Imperial Present: the British Empire. In T. J. Dunbabin's *The Western Greeks*. *Antiquity*, vol. 72.277, 539–549.

Atasoy, S. (2003) Amisos. In D. V. Grammenos and E. K. Petropoulos (eds) *Ancient Greek Colonies in the Black Sea*. Publications of the Archaeological Institute of Northern Greece, No 4, vol. I., 1331–1377. Thessaloniki.

Avram, A. (2003) Histria. In D. V. Grammenos and E. K. Petropoulos (eds) *Ancient Greek Colonies in the Black Sea - 2*. British Archaeological Reports International Series 1675, vol. I., 279–340. Oxford, Archaeopress.

Avram, A. (2006) The Territories of Istros and Kallatis. In P. Guldager Bilde and V. F. Stolba (eds) *Surveying the Greek Chora: Black Sea Region in a Comparative Perspective*. Black Sea Studies, 4, 59–80. The Danish National Research Foundation's Centre for Black Sea Studies. Aarhus, Aarhus University Press.

Avram, A. (2007) Kallatis. In D. V. Grammenos and E. K. Petropoulos (eds) *Ancient Greek Colonies in the Black Sea - 2*. British Archaeological Reports International Series 1675, vol. I, 239–286. Oxford, Archaeopress.

Bintliff, J. (2006) Issues in the Economic and Ecological Understanding of the *Chora* of the Classical *Polis* in its Social Context: A View From the Intensive Survey Tradition of the Greek Homeland. In

P. Guldager Bilde and V. F. Stolba (eds) *Surveying the Greek Chora: Black Sea Region in a Comparative Perspective*. Black Sea Studies, 4, 13–26. The Danish National Research Foundation's Centre for Black Sea Studies. Aarhus, Aarhus University Press.

Blázquez Martinez, J. M. (2004) *Origines* финикийской колонизации в западном Средиземноморье и Тартессийское царство. Состояние проблемы (*Origines finikiyskoy kolonizatsii v zapadnom Sredizemnomorye i Tartessiyskoe tsarstvo. Sostoyaniye problemy*). In *VDI, No 4*, 13–29.

Boltrik, Yu. V. (2000) Основной торговый путь Ольвии в Днепровское Лесостепное Правобережье (*Osnovnoy torgoviy pout Olvii v Dneprovskoye Lesostepnoe Pravoberezhye*). *RA, No 1*, 121–130.

Bujskikh, A. V. (2005) Новая землянка VI в. до н.э. в Ольвии: новый взгляд на старые проблемы (*Novaya zemlyanka VI v. do n.e. v Olvii: noviy vzglyad na stariye problemy*). In *The Phenomenon of Bosporan Kingdom: Problems of Correlation Written & Archaeological Sources*. Proceedings of the International Conference. St. Petersburg. The State Hermitage Museum Editors House, 183–6.

Bujskikh, S. B. (2005) Земляночное домостроительство эпохи колонизации Северного Причерноморья (на примере Нижнего Побужья) [*Zemlyanotchnoye domostroitelstvo epokhi kolonizatsii Severnogo Pritchernomorya (na primere Nizhnego Pobouzhya)*]. *Bosporos Studies*, Vol. IX, 3–21. Sifmeropol-Kerch, 3–31.

Braund, D. (2005) Introduction. In Braund, D. (ed.) *Scythians and Greeks: Cultural Interactions in Scythia, Athens and the Early Roman Empire (sixth century BC - first century AD)*, 1–12. Exeter, University of Exeter Press.

Bylkova, V. P. (2000) О культурных традициях населения Нижнего Поднепровья скивского времени (*O koultournykh traditsiyakh naseleniya Nizhnego Podneprovya skifskogo vremeni*). *RA, No 2*, 26–39.

Carter, J. C. (2006a) *Discovering the Greek Countryside at Metaponto*. Ann Arbor, The University of Michigan Press.

Carter, J. C. (2006b) Towards a Comparative Study of *Chorai* West and East: Metapontion and Chersonesos. In P. Guldager Bilde and V. F. Stolba (eds) *Surveying the Greek Chora: Black Sea Region in a Comparative Perspective*. Black Sea Studies, 4, 175–205. The Danish National Research Foundation's Centre for Black Sea Studies. Aarhus, Aarhus University Press.

D'Agostino, B. (2006) The First Greeks in Italy. In G. R. Tsetskhladze (ed.) *Greek Colonisation: An Account of Greek Colonies and Other Settlements Overseas*. Vol. I, 201–237. Leiden-Boston, Brill.

Damyanov, M. (2007) Dionysopolis, its territory and neighbours in the pre-Roman times. In D. V. Grammenos and E. K. Petropoulos (eds) *Ancient Greek Colonies in the Black Sea - 2*. British Archaeological Reports International Series 1675, vol. I, 1–36. Oxford, Archaeopress.

Daragan (2004) Хронология Жаботинского поселения (*Khronologiya Zhabotinskogo poseleniya*). In *The Phenomenon of Bosporan Kingdom: Problems of Chronology and Dating*. Proceedings of the International Conference. St. Petersburg. The State Hermitage Museum Publishing House. Vol. II, 211–216.

Dietler, M. (1995) The Cup of Gyptis: Rethinking the Colonial Encounter in Early-Iron-Age Western Europe and the Relevance of World-Systems Models. *Journal of European Archaeology* (1995) 3.2, 89–111.

Dietler, M. (1997) The Iron Age in Mediterranean France: Colonial Encounters, Entanglements, and Transformations. *Journal of World Prehistory*, vol. 11.3, 269–358.

Dietler, M. (2005) The Archaeology of Colonisation and the Colonisation of Archaeology: Theoretical Challenges from an Ancient Mediterranean Colonial Encounter. In G. J. Stein (ed.) *The Archaeology of Colonial Encounters: Comparative Perspectives*. School of American Research advanced seminar series, 33–68. Santa Fe; Oxford.

Domaradzka, L. (2005) Graeco-Thracian Relations in the Upper Maritsa Valley (5th–4th Centuries BC) (based on epigraphic evidence). In J. Bouzek and L. Domaradzka (eds) *The Culture of Thracians and Their neighbours*. Proceedings of the International Symposium in Memory of Prof. Mieczyslaw Domaradzki, with a Round Table "Archaeological Map of Bulgaria". British Archaeological Reports International Series 1350, 19–26. Oxford, Archaeopress.

Dominguez, A. J. (2002) Greeks in Iberia: Colonialism Without Colonisation. In Cl. L. Lyons and J. K. Papadopoulos (eds) *The Archaeology of Colonialism*, 65–95. Los Angeles, The J. Paul Getty Trust.

Dominguez, A. J. (2005) Греки в Иберии и контакты с туземным миром (*Greki v Iberii i ikh kontakty s touzemnym mirom*). *VDI, No 4*, 88–107.

Dominguez, A. J. (2006a) Greeks in the Iberian Peninsula. In G. R. Tsetskhladze (ed.) *Greek Colonisation: An Account of Greek Colonies and Other Settlements Overseas*. Vol. I, 429–505. Leiden-Boston, Brill.

Dominguez, A. J. (2006b) Hellenic Identity and Greek Colonisation. In *Ancient West and East*, vol. 4.2, 446–457.

van Dommelen, P. (2002) Ambiguous Matters: Colonialism and Local Identities in Punic Sardenia. In Cl. L. Lyons and J. K. Papadopoulos (eds) *The Archaeology of Colonialism*, 121–147. Los Angeles, The J. Paul Getty Trust.

Doonan, O. (2003) Sinope. In In D. V. Grammenos and E. K. Petropoulos (eds) *Ancient Greek Colonies in the Black Sea*. Publications of the Archaeological Institute of Northern Greece, vol. II, 1379–1402. Thessaloniki.

Doonan, O. (2006) Exploring Community in the Hinterland of a Black Sea Port. In P. Guldager Bilde and V. F. Stolba (eds) *Surveying the Greek Chora: Black Sea Region in a Comparative Perspective*. Black Sea Studies, 4, 47–58. The Danish National Research Foundation's Centre for Black Sea Studies. Aarhus, Aarhus University Press.

Dougherty, C. (1993) *The Poetics of Colonisation: From City to Text in Archaic Greece*. Oxford-New York, Oxford University Press.

Fol, A. (1996) Thracia Pontica-Twenty years later. In *Colloquia Pontica*, 1, 1–12.

Frost, H. (1982) Stone anchors as Clues to Bronze Age Trade Routes. In M. Lazarov *et. al.* (eds) *Thracia Pontica I: La Mer Noire et le Monde Méditerranéen*, 280–289. Sofia, Centre d'Histoire Maritime et d'Archeologie Sous-Marine.

Gabelia, A. N. (2003) Dioscourias. In D. V. Grammenos and E. K. Petropoulos (eds) *Ancient Greek Colonies in the Black Sea*. Publications of the Archaeological Institute of Northern Greece, vol. II, 1215–1265. Thessaloniki.

Gavrilov, A. V. (2006) Theodosia and its *Chora* in Antiquity. In P. Guldager Bilde and V. F. Stolba (eds) *Surveying the Greek Chora: Black Sea Region in a Comparative Perspective*. Black Sea Studies, 4, 249–308. The Danish National Research Foundation's Centre for Black Sea Studies. Aarhus, Aarhus University Press.

Gavrilyuk, N. A. (1999) История экономики Степной Скифии VI-III вв. до н.э. (*Istoriya ekonomiki Stepnoy Skifii VI-III vv. do n.e.*). Kiev, Институт археологии НАН Украины.

Gavrilyuk, N. A. (2007) Greek Imports in Skythia. In D. V. Grammenos and E. K. Petropoulos (eds) *Ancient Greek Colonies in the Black Sea - 2*. British Archaeological Reports International Series 1675, vol. I., 627–676. Oxford, Archaeopress.

Gonzalez de Canales, F., Serrano, L. and Llompart, J. (2006) The Pre-colonial Phoenician Emporium at Huelva ca. 900–770 BC. In *BABesch* 81, 13–29.

Gosden, C. (2006) *Archaeology and Colonialism: Cultural Contact from 5000 BC to the present*. Cambridge, Cambridge University Press.

Graham, A. J. (1984) Commercial Interchanges between Greeks and Natives. *Ancient World* (10. 1&2), 3–10.

Grammenos, D. V. and Petropoulos, E. K. (2003) (eds) *Ancient Greek Colonies in the Black Sea*. Publications of the Archaeological Institute of Northern Greece, No 4. Volumes I+II. Thessaloniki.

Grammenos, D. V. and Petropoulos, E. K. (2007) (eds) *Ancient Greek Colonies in the Black Sea - 2*. British Archaeological Reports International Series 1675. Volumes I+II. Oxford, Archaeopress.

Greco, E. (2006) Greek Colonisation in Southern Italy: A Methodological Essay. In G. R. Tsetskhladze (ed.) *Greek Colonisation: An Account of Greek Colonies and Other Settlements Overseas*. Vol. I, 169–200. Leiden-Boston, Brill.

Grigoryev, D. V. (1998) К вопросу о военно-политической ситуации на Боспоре в конце VI – первой половине V в. до н.э. (*K voprosu o voenno-polititcheskoy situatsii na Bospore v kontse VI - pervoy polovine V v. do n.e.*). In *Journal of Historical, Philological and Cultural Studies*, Moscow-Magnitogorsk, vol. 5, 38–43.

Guldager Bilde, P. and Stolba, V. F. (2006) (eds) *Surveying the Greek Chora: Black Sea Region in a Comparative Perspective*. Black Sea Studies, 4. The Danish National Research Foundation's Centre for Black Sea Studies. Aarhus, Aarhus University Press.

Herman Hansen, M. (2006) *EMPORION*: A Study of the Use and Meaning of the Term in the Archaic and Classical Periods. In G. R. Tsetskhladze (ed.) *Greek Colonisation: An Account of Greek Colonies and Other Settlements Overseas*. Vol. I, 1–39. Leiden-Boston, Brill.

Hind, J. G. F. (1992/1993) Archaeology of the Greek and Barbarian People around the Black Sea (1982–1992). *Archaeological Reports*, 80–92.

Inadze, M. (1999) The Navigation and Trade on the Southern and Eastern Coasts of the Black Sea in 8th–7th c. BC. In *Dziebani. The Journal of the Centre for Archaeological Studies of the Georgian Academy of Sciences*. Supplements. I. "Trade on the Black Sea in the Archaic and Classical Periods: Historical Perspective of the Silk Road." Abstracts of Papers of the 9th International Symposium on the Ancient History and Archaeology of the Black Sea Area (Vani, 20–23 September 1999). Tbilisi, 52.269–63.

Katyushin, Ye. A. (2003) Theodosia. In D. V. Grammenos and E. K. Petropoulos (eds) *Ancient Greek Colonies in the Black Sea*. Publications of the Archaeological Institute of Northern Greece, No 4, vol. I, 645–695. Thessaloniki.

Kirigin, Br. (2006) *PHAROS: The Parian Settlement in Dalmatia. A study of a Greek Colony in the Adriatic*. British Archaeological Reports International Series 1561. Oxford, Archaeopress.

Koshelenko, G. A. and Kuznetsov, V. D. (1998) Greek Colonisation of the Bosporus. In G. R. Tsetskhladze (ed.) *The Greek Colonisation of the Black Sea Area. Historical Interpretation of Archaeology*, 249–263. Stuttgart, Franz Steiner Verlag.

Kryzhitskiy, S. D. (2005) Olbia and the Skythians in the Fifth Century BC: The Skythian 'Protectorate'. In D. Braund (ed.) *Scythians and Greeks: Cultural Interactions in Scythia, Athens, and the Early Roman Empire (sixth century BC - first century AD)*, 123–130. Exeter, University of Exeter Press.

Kryzhitskiy S. D. (2006) The Rural Environ of Olbia: Some Problems of Current Importance. In P. Guldager Bilde and V. F. Stolba (eds) *Surveying the Greek Chora: Black Sea Region in a Comparative Perspective*. Black Sea Studies, 4, 99–114. The Danish National Research Foundation's Centre for Black Sea Studies. Aarhus, Aarhus University Press.

Kryzhitskiy, S. D. and Krapivina, V. V. (2003) Olbian Chora. In D. V. Grammenos and E. K. Petropoulos (eds) *Ancient Greek Colonies in the Black Sea*. Publications of the Archaeological Institute of Northern Greece, No 4, vol. I, 507–561. Thessaloniki.

Kryzhitskiy, S. D., Rousyaeva, A. S., Krapivina, V. V., Leypunskaya, N. A., Skrzhinskaya, M. V. and Anokhin, V. A. (1999) Ольвия. Античное государство в Северном Причерноморье (*Olvia. Antitchnoe gosoudarstvo v Severnom Pritchernomorye* – Olbia. Ancient State in the Northern Black Sea Littoral). Kiev, Институт археологии НАН Украины.

Kryzhitskiy, S. D., Krapivina, V. V., Leypunskaya, N. A., and Nazarov, V. V. (2003) Olbia-Berezan. In D. V. Grammenos and E. K. Petropoulos (eds) *Ancient Greek Colonies in the Black Sea*. Publications of the Archaeological Institute of Northern Greece, No 4, vol. I, 389–505. Thessaloniki.

Kulikov, A. Vl. (2007) Akra and its Chora. In D. V. Grammenos and E. K. Petropoulos (eds) *Ancient Greek Colonies in the Black Sea - 2*. British Archaeological Reports International Series 1675, vol. II, 1023–56. Oxford, Archaeopress.

Kvirkvelia, G. (2003) Gyenos. In D. V. Grammenos and E. K. Petropoulos (eds) *Ancient Greek Colonies in the Black Sea*. Publications of the Archaeological Institute of Northern Greece, No 4, vol. II, 1267–1296. Thessaloniki, Archaeological Institute of Northern Greece.

Lapin, V. V. (1966) Греческая колонизация Северного Причерноморья (*Gretcheskaya kolonizatsiya Severnogo Pritchernomorya*). Kiev, Наукова думка.

Lazarov, M. (1984) La navigation le long du littoral Thrace du Pont Euxin avant la colonisation grecque. In *Dritter Internationalen Thrakologischer Kongress*, vol. II. Sofia, Staatliche Verlag Swjat.

Lemos, I. (2005) The Changing Relationship of the Euboeans and the East. In A. Villing (ed.) *The Greeks in the East*. The British Museum Research Publication No. 157, 53–60.

Lordkipanidze, O. D. (2003) Phasis. In D. V. Grammenos and E. K. Petropoulos (eds) *Ancient Greek Colonies in the Black Sea*. Publications of the Archaeological Institute of Northern Greece, No 4, vol. II, 1297–1329. Thessaloniki.

Malkin, I. (1998) *The Returns of Odysseus: Colonisation and Ethnicity*. Berkeley-Los Angeles-London, University of California Press.

Malkin, I. (2002) A Colonial Middle Ground: Greek, Etruscan, and Local Elites in the Bay of Naples. In Cl. L. Lyons and J. K. Papadopoulos (eds) *The Archaeology of Colonialism*, 151–181. Los Angeles, The J. Paul Getty Trust.

Malkin, I. (2005a) Introduction. In I. Malkin (ed.) *Mediterranean Paradigms and Classical Antiquity*, 1–12. London-New York, Routledge.

Malkin, I. (2005b) Networks and the Emergence of Greek Identity. In I. Malkin (ed.) *Mediterranean Paradigms and Classical Antiquity*, 56–74. London-New York, Routledge.

Malyshev, A. A. (2007) Torikos and the South-Eastern Periphery of the Bosporan Kingdom (7th c. BC – 3rd c. AD). In D. V. Grammenos and E. K. Petropoulos (eds) *Ancient Greek Colonies in the Black Sea - 2*. British Archaeological Reports International Series 1675, vol. II, 927–950. Oxford, Archaeopress.

Manuçu-Adameşteanu, M. (2003) Orgame. In D. V. Grammenos and E. K. Petropoulos (eds) *Ancient Greek Colonies in the Black Sea*. Publications of the Archaeological Institute of Northern Greece, No 4, vol. I, 341–388. Thessaloniki.

Martchenko, K. K. (1988) Варвары в составе населения Березани и Ольвии (*Varvary v sostave naseleniya Berezani i Olvii*). Leningrad, Наука.

Martchenko, K. K. (2005) Греки и варвары Северо-Западного Причерноморья второй половины VII – первой четверти V вв. до н.э. (*Greki i varvary Severo-Zapadnogo Pritchernomorya vtoroy poloviny VII - pervoy tchetverti V vv. do n.e.*). In *idem* (ed.) Греки и вавpвары Причерноморья в скифскую эпоху (*Greki i varvary v skifskuyu epokhu*), 42–136. St. Petersburg, Aleteya,.

Martchenko, K. K. and Vakhtina, M. Yu. (2001) «Древняя Скифия» в Северо-Западном Причерноморье ('Drevyaya Skifiya' v Severo-Zapadnom Pritchernomorye). *VDI, 4*. 141–145.

Maslennikov, A. A. (2005) The Development of Graeco-Barbarian Contacts in the Chora of the European Bosporos (Sixth – First Centuries). In D. Braund (ed.) *Scythians and Greeks: Cultural Interactions in Scythia, Athens, and the Early Roman Empire (sixth century BC – first century AD)*, 153–66. Exeter, University of Exeter Press.

Melyukova, A. I. (1989) География и этнография Скифии в трудах советских учёных (*Geografiya i etnografiya Skifii v trudakh covetskikh utchonykh*). In *idem* (ed.) Степи европейской части СССР в скифо-сарматское время (*Stepi yevropeyskoy tchasti SSSR v skifo-sarmatskoye vremya*), 40–48. Moscow, Nauka.

Minchev, A. (2003) Odessos. In D. V. Grammenos and E. K. Petropoulos (eds) *Ancient Greek Colonies in the Black Sea*. Publications of the Archaeological Institute of Northern Greece, No 4, vol. I, 209–278. Thessaloniki.

Miró i Alaix, M. T. (2006) *La ceràmica Àtica de figures roges de la ciutat grega d' Emporion*. Monografies Emporitanes 14. Museu d'Arqueologia de Catalunya Empúries.

Mitchell, L. G. (2006) Ethnic Identity and the Community of the Hellenes: A Review. *Ancient West and East*, vol. 4.2, 409–420.

Morel, J.-P. (1984) Greek Colonisation in Italy and the West: Problems of evidence and interpretation. In *Crossroads of the Mediterranean*. Archaeologica Transatlantica II. Louvain-la-Neuve, 123–161.

Morel, J.-P. (2006) Phocaean Colonisation. In G. R. Tsetskhladze (ed.) *Greek Colonisation: An Account of Greek Colonies and Other Settlements Overseas*. Vol. I, 359–428. Leiden-Boston, Brill.

Murzin, V. Yu. (2005) Key points in Skythian History. In D. Braund (ed.) *Scythians and Greeks: Cultural Interactions in Scythia, Athens, and the Early Roman Empire (sixth century BC – first century AD)*, 33–38. Exeter: University of Exeter Press.

Murzin, V. Yu. and Rollet, R. (1997) Совместные украинско-немецкие археологические исследования в Бельске (*Sovmestniye oukraisko-nemetskiye arkheologitcheskiye issledovaniya v Belske*). In *Summarized Papers of the International Conference "New pages of the ancient history of South Ukraine" 3–8 November*. Nikolaev, 1997, 12–13.

Nedev, D. and Panayotova, K. (2003) Apollonia Pontica: End of the 7th – 1st centuries BC. In D. V. Grammenos and E. K. Petropoulos (eds) *Ancient Greek Colonies in the Black Sea*. Publications of the Archaeological Institute of Northern Greece, No 4, vol. I, 95–155. Thessaloniki.

Nikolaenko, G. M. (2006) The *Chora* of Tauric Chersonesos and the Cadastre of the 4th–2nd Century BC. In P. Guldager Bilde and V. F. Stolba (eds) *Surveying the Greek Chora: Black Sea Region in a Comparative Perspective*. Black Sea Studies, 4, 151–174. The Danish National Research Foundation's Centre for Black Sea Studies. Aarhus, Aarhus University Press.

Ochotnikov, S. B. (2006) The Chorai of the Ancient Cities in the Lower Dniester Area (6th Century BC–3rd Century AD). In P. Guldager Bilde and V. F. Stolba (eds) *Surveying the Greek Chora: Black Sea Region in a Comparative Perspective*. Black Sea Studies, 4, 81–98. The Danish National Research Foundation's Centre for Black Sea Studies. Aarhus, Aarhus University Press.

Osborne, R. (1996) *Greece in the Making (1200–479 BC)*. Routledge History of the Ancient World. London- New York, Routledge.

Osborne, R. (1998) Early Greek Colonisation? The Nature of Greek Settlements in the West. In N. Fisher and H. van Wees (eds) *Archaic Greece: New Approaches and New Evidence*, 251–269. Swansea, Duckworth with The Classical Press of Wales.

Osborne, R. (2005) Urban Sprawl: What is Urbanization and Why does it Matter? In R. Osborne and B. Cunliffe (eds) *Mediterranean Urbanization, 800–600 BC*. Proceedings of the British Academy, 126, 1–16. Oxford, Oxford University Press.

Pavlopoulou, A. (1997) Η ελληνική μυθολογική παράδοση περί ηρώων και ο αφηρωισμός των Θρακών βασιλέων. In D. Triantafyllos and D. Terzopoulou (eds) *2e Symposium International des Études Thraciennes: Thrace ancienne: époque archaïque, classique, hellénistique, romaine, (Komotini, 20–27 Septembre 1992)*, 168–72. Komotini, Edition de l'Association Culturelle de Komotini.

Petropoulos, E. K. (2004) Colonial Encounters in the Black Sea Region: Dating Problems of the Earliest Kimmerian Bosporos Greek Cities. In *The Phenomenon of Bosporan Kingdom: Problems of Chronology and Dating*. Proceedings of the International Conference. St. Petersburg. The State Hermitage Museum Publishing House. Vol. I, 33–41.

Petropoulos, E. K. (2005) *Hellenic Colonisation in Euxeinos Pontos: Penetration, Early Establishment, and the Problem of the 'Emporion' Revisited*. British Archaeological Reports International Series 1394. Oxford, Archaeopress.

Popov, D. (1999) Тракология (*Trakologiya*). Sofia, Izd-Vo "Lik".

Porogeanov, K. (1984) Navigation et Commerce de la population du littoral européen de la mer Noire de la Thrace Ancienne avec les peuples de la Méditerranée Orientale (XVI-XII s. av. J. C.). In *Dritter Internationalen Thrakologischer Kongress*, vol. II, 67–75. Sofia, Staatliche Verlag Swjat.

Porojanov, K. (1986) Les relations entre les colonies grecques et les états thraces du littoral occidental de la mer Noire VII-V s. av. n. e. In M. Lazarov *et. al.* (eds) *Thracia Pontica III: Les Thraces et les colonies grecques. VII-V s. av. n.e.* Table Ronde sur les ancres anciennes, 158–65. Sofia, Centre d'Histoire Maritime et d'Archeologie Sous-Marine.

Posamentir, R. (2006) The Greeks in Berezan and Naukratis: A Similar Story? In A. Villing and U. Schlotzhauer (eds) *Naukratis: Greek Diversity in Egypt*. Studies on East Greek Pottery and Exchange in the Eastern Mediterranean. The British Museum Research Publication No. 162, 159–167.

Redina, Ye. (2005) Scytho-Thracian Cultural Contacts in the North-western Black Sea Littoral. In J. Bouzek and L. Domaradzka (eds) *The Culture of Thracians and Their neighbours*. Proceedings of the International Symposium in Memory of Prof. Mieczyslaw Domaradzki, with a Round Table "Archaeological Map of Bulgaria". British Archaeological Reports International Series 1350, 231–38. Oxford, Archaeopress.

Rousyaeva, A. S. (1998) К вопросу об основании ионийцами Ольвии (*K voprosu ob osnovanii ioniytsami Olvii*). In *VDI, No 1*, 160–170.

Rousyaeva, A. S. (1999) Проникновение эллинов на территории украйнской лесостепи в архаическое время (К постановке проблемы) [*Proniknoveniye ellinov na territorii oukraynskoy lesostepi v arkhaitcheskoye vremya (k postanovke problemy)*]. In *VDI, No 4*, 84–97.

Rybakov, B. A. (1979) Геродотова Скифия (*Gerodotova Skifiya*). Moscow, Наука.

Salkin, A. E. (2007) Bizone. In D. V. Grammenos and E. K. Petropoulos (eds) *Ancient Greek Colonies in the Black Sea - 2*. British Archaeological Reports International Series 1675, vol. I, 37–50. Oxford, Archaeopress.

Samoylova, T. L. (2007) Tyras: The Greek City on the River Tyras. In D. V. Grammenos and E. K. Petropoulos (eds) *Ancient Greek Colonies in the Black Sea – 2*. British Archaeological Reports International Series 1675, vol. I, 435–470. Oxford, Archaeopress.

Sekerskaya, N. M. (2007) The Ancient City of Nikonion. In D. V. Grammenos and E. K. Petropoulos (eds) *Ancient Greek Colonies in the Black Sea - 2*. British Archaeological Reports International Series 1675, vol. I, 471–506. Oxford, Archaeopress.

Senatorov, S. N. (2000) Кизил-кобинская керамика VIII – первой половины VI в. до н.э. из Нимфея (*Kizil-kobinskaya keramika VIII - pervoy poloviny VI v. do n.e. iz Nimfeya*). In S. L. Solovyov and G. R. Tsetskhladze (eds) Taman Antiquity 3: Greeks and Natives in the Cimmerian Bosporos (7th – 1st Centuries BC). Summarized Papers of the International Conference Taman, Russia, 9–16 October 2000, 85–88. St. Petersburg, The Hermitage Museum Publisher.

Senatorov, S. N. (2005) Местная керамика из колонии на острове Березань (*Mestnaya keramika iz kolonii na ostrove Berezan*). In S. L. Solovyov (ed.) *Borysthenis - Berezan: The Hermitage Archaeological Collection I*, 174–239. St. Petersburg: The Hermitage Publishing House.

Shorto, R. (2004) *The Island at the Center of the World: The Epic Story of Dutch Manhattan and the Forgotten Colony That Shaped America*. New York-London-Toronto-Sydney-Auckland, Vintage Books.

Shramko, B. A. (1975) Крепость скифской эпохи у с. Бельск – Город Гелон (*Krepost skifskoy epokhi ou s. Belsk-Gorod Gelon*). In Скифский мир (*Skifskiy mir*), 117–125. Kiev, Наукова думка.

Shramko, B. A. (1987) Бельское городище скифской эпохи. Город Гелон (*Belskoye gorodishe skifskoy epokhi. Gorod Gelon*). Kiev, Наукова думка.

Sokolova, O. Yu. (2003) Nymphaeum. In D. V. Grammenos and E. K. Petropoulos (eds) *Ancient Greek Colonies in the Black Sea*. Publications of the Archaeological Institute of Northern Greece, No 4, vol. II, 759–802. Thessaloniki.

Solovyov S. L. (1999) *Ancient Berezan: The Architecture, History and Culture of the First Greek Colony in the Northern Black Sea*. Colloquia Pontica 4. Leiden, Brill.

Sparkes, B. A. (1996) *The Red and the Black. Studies in Greek Pottery*. London, Routledge.

Thomas, C. G. and Conant, C. (1999) *Citadel to City-State: The Transformation of Greece, 1200–700 BC*. Indiana, Indiana University Press.

Tiverios M., Manakidou E. and Tsiafaki D. (1998) – Μ. Τιβέριος, Ε. Μανακίδου, Δ. Τσιαφάκη. Ανασκαφικές έρευνες στο Καραμπουρνάκι κατά το 1998: Ο αρχαίος οικισμός. – In: AEMTh, 12. 223–230.

Vakhtina, M. Yu. (1999) К вопросу о начальном периоде культурных контактов между эллинами и варварами на территории Северного Причерноморья (K vorposu o natchalnom periode koultournykh kontaktov mezhdou ellinami i varvarami na territorii Severnogo Pritchernomorya). In G. A. Koshelenko (ed.) *VI* чтения памяти В. Д. Блаватского. К *100*-летию со дня рождения, [*Summarized Papers in honor of Pr. V. D. Blavatskiy*], 25–26. Moscow, Наука.

Vakhtina, M. Yu. (2000) Греческая столовая керамика VI вю до н.э. из раскопок Немировского городища в Побужье (Gretcheskaya stolovaya keramika VI v. do n.e. iz raskopok Nemirovskogo gorodisha v Pobuzhye). In Zuev, V. Yu. (ed.) ΣΥΣΣΙΤΙΑ: Papers of the Conference in Honorem Yu. V. Andreev, 209–217. St. Petersburg, Aleteya.

Vakhtina, M. Yu. (2004) О начале распространения южно-ионийского керамического импорта в варварский мир Северного Причерноморья (*O natchale rasprostraneneiya yuzhno-ioniyskogo deramitcheskogo importa v varvarskiy mir Severnogo Pritchernomorya*). In *The Phenomenon of Bosporan Kingdom: Problems of Chronology and Dating.* Proceedings of the Interantional Conference, Vol. II, 204–211. St. Petersburg, The State Hermitage Museum Publishing House.

Vanschoonwinkel, J. (2006) Mycenaean Expansion. In G. R. Tsetskhladze (ed.) *Greek Colonisation: An Account of Greek Colonies and Other Settlements Overseas.* Vol. I, 41–113. Leiden-Boston, Brill.

Vickers V. and A. Kakhidze (2004) Pichvnari. Results of Excavations conducted by the jointed British-Georgian Pichvnari Expedition. Volume 1. *Pichvnari 1998–2002. Greeks and Colchians on the East Coast of the Black Sea. Part 1: Text.* Oxford, The Ashmolean Museum, University of Oxford and the Batumi Archaeological Museum.

Vinogradov, Yu. A. (2000) К проблеме становления древнегреческих городов в районе Боспора Киммерийского (*K probleme stanovleniya drevnegretcheskikh gorodov v rayone Bospora Kimmeriyskogo*). In Zuev, V. Yu. (ed.) ΣΥΣΣΙΤΙΑ: Papers of the Conference in Honorem Yu. V. Andreev, 227–232. St.Petersburg, Aleteya.

Vinogradov, Yu. A., Butyagin, A. M., Vakhtina, M. Yu. (2003) Myrmekion-Porthmeus: Two “small” towns of Ancient Bosporus. In D. V. Grammenos and E. K. Petropoulos (eds) *Ancient Greek Colonies in the Black Sea.* Publications of the Archaeological Institute of Northern Greece, No 4, vol. II, 803–840. Thessaloniki.

Vinogradov, Yu. A., Martchenko, K. K. (2005) Периодизация истории Северного Причерноморья в скифскую эпоху (*Periodizatsiya istorii Severnogo Pritchernomorya v skifskyuy epokhu*). In K. K. Martchenko (ed.) Греки и вавpвары Причерноморья в скифскую эпоху (*Greki i varvary v skifskuyu epokhu*), 27–41. St. Petersburg, Aleteya.

Zadnikov, S. A. (2004) К вопросу о развитии античного импорта в лесостепи (по материалам новых исследований Бельского городища) [*K voprosu o razvitii antitchnogo importa v lesostepi (po materialam novykh issledovaniy Belskogo gorodisha)*]. In Проблемы истории и археологии Украины. Материалы V Международной научной конференции посвящённой 350-летию г. Харькова и 200-летию Харьковского национального университета им. В. Н. Каразина. 4–6 ноября 2004 года. (*Proceedings of the Scientific Conference Problems in History and Archaeology of the Ukraine*), 33–34. Kharkov, V. N. Karazin Kharkiv National University.

Zinko, V. N. (2006) The *Chora* of Nymphaion (6th century BC – 6th century AC). In P. Guldager Bilde and V. F. Stolba (eds) *Surveying the Greek Chora: Black Sea Region in a Comparative Perspective.* Black Sea Studies, 4, 289–308. The Danish National Research Foundation’s Centre for Black Sea Studies. Aarhus, Aarhus University Press.

14

Colonial location: Olbia on the Hypanis

David Braund

Olbia might seem to be in the wrong place, specifically on the bank of the wrong river. For Olbia was commonly known around the Greek world as 'Borysthenes', the Greek name for the mighty river Dnieper. The name suggested that it stood on the Dnieper, just as the other Pontic colonies at Phasis, Tyras, and Istros were located on the estuaries of rivers of those same names. Of course, this was not simply a Pontic phenomenon, though the rivers of the region did impress Mediterranean Greek sensibilities (Hdt. 4. 82). Outside the Black Sea, it will suffice to recall Gela in Sicily at the mouth of the River Gelas. But Olbia did not stand on the river Borysthenes, the Dnieper. It was located on the estuary of the ancient river Hypanis, the modern Bug. Accordingly, an Olbian at large in the Greek world might well describe himself as a citizen of Olbia 'on the Hypanis'. We happen to have an instance from Chalcedon on the south coast of the Black Sea (Merkelbach 1980, no. 4.13, albeit partially restored). In Olbia itself, citizens described themselves as 'Olbiopolitans', announcing the prosperity of their community, for 'Prosperity' is what 'Olbia' means in Greek.

The general Greek tendency to refer to Olbia by the name Borysthenes requires explanation. And that explanation no doubt should include the fame of the Dnieper and its relative proximity to the city. In particular, the fact that the estuary of the Bug joins that of the Dnieper (albeit well below Olbia) will also have been relevant. At the same time, we should note the tendency of the name 'Borysthenes' to proliferate in and beyond that estuary, where it is applied not only to Olbia but also to the islands of Berezan and (further afield) apparently even to Leuke (Blavatskiy 1968; *cf.* Hind 2005). In general, it is easy to overstate the obscurity of these places even among the better-informed in the Greek world at large (*pace* West 2003; 2007), but we may well suspect that there was a real sense in which close distinctions about the geography of the margins of Greek culture were of minimal interest to most in the Mediterranean world.

The whole issue is both clarified and extended by Herodotus' remarks on Olbia. His primary concern in this part of his *Histories* is with Scythians and Scythia, exploring how local geography and concomitant lifestyles enabled a pastoralist society to defeat a Persian invasion which the unreflecting might well take to be the irresistible irruption of a more advanced and more powerful culture (Braund 1998). However, the Greek cities were of minimal interest to him: many are not mentioned at all, while others feature only fleetingly. Olbia receives far more attention than any of the other cities of the region, for two key reasons. First, Herodotus seems to have visited the city and gained most of his information about Scythia and Scythians during his sojourn there (Braund 2007). Even those who insist that he did not in fact visit the city tend to allow that he had acquired hard information about it from other writers (West 2007). Secondly, Herodotus deploys Olbia as a location for cultural interaction between Greeks and Scythians. The story of Scyles is of course set in Olbia, where it is built upon tension between processes of integration and alienation (further Braund 2008). And the parallel story of Anacharsis, built around the same tension, is located in Olbian Hylaea and seems to be an Olbian origin-story for the cult of the Great Mother there (Hartog 1988; Braund 2007). It seems that Olbia provided a convenient location for Herodotus to explore his favourite theme of problematic cultural interactions, specifically for Greeks and Scythians.

Meanwhile, we must understand that Herodotus' account of the region is profoundly polemical. His claim – sometimes made explicit (*e.g.* 4.108–9) – is to have at his disposal better knowledge than is currently available elsewhere. Of course, his suggestion that he visited Olbia serves to bolster that claim, as also his allusions to local informants, including even Scythians, as well as a royal representative or agent, Tymnes. In that context, it is no great surprise to find Herodotus holding forth on the naming of Olbia as Borysthenes. His assertions are both clear and correct, authenticated by the epigraphy of Olbia itself. We should not be distracted by the fact that occasional Olbiopolitans may appear as 'Borysthenites' when moving around the Greek world at large (*e.g. Fouilles de Delphes*, 207.4; *Bulletin Épigraphique* 1958, 327): that was an understandable response to general Greek usage. In fact, Herodotus demonstrates his superior grasp of the local situation by stating that the people of Olbia call themselves 'Olbiopolitans'. And that their city stands on the Hypanis (Bug), not the Borysthenes (Dnieper). Further, he explains, the people of Olbia use the term 'Borysthenites' not to describe themselves, but to denote those who live along the river Borysthenes. However, since Herodotus is writing for a broad Greek audience, he prefers to refer to Olbia and its people as Borysthenes and Borysthenites, (*e.g.* 4.54), except when paying specific attention to the issue of terminology.

In that way Herodotus displays the same constructive polemic that he shows elsewhere in his account of the northern Black Sea region. In surveying Scythia, Herodotus applies a more careful and exclusive model of 'Scythianness' than was usual in the Greek world even after his time. Similarly, in surveying the local identities in and around Olbia, he is concerned to apply more precise labels and characterizations than were usual. Vague notions that Olbia was somehow located on the river Borysthenes could not survive the incisive analysis of a Herodotus who was well informed about local particularities.

At the same time, however, Herodotus' account of the river Borysthenes is glowing on the subject of its many advantages:

> Fourth, the River Borysthenes, which is the greatest of these rivers after the Ister and, in my view, is the most productive not only of the Scythian rivers, but of all the others too, with the exception of the Egyptian Nile. For with that river no other is comparable. However, of the other rivers, the Borysthenes is the most productive, providing the most beautiful and nourishing pastures for livestock as well as the finest fish in great numbers. Its water is very sweet to drink and flows pure where others are murky. The finest crops grow along its course, while where no crops are planted the deepest grass grows. Salts are deposited naturally at its mouth in abundance. Enormous spineless fish (which they call antikaioi) are available for salt-pickling, as well as many other remarkable creatures.
>
> As far as the Gerrhus region, a voyage of forty days upstream, the river-course is known, flowing from the north-wind. But no-one can say anything about the land through which it flows above that. However, it seems to flow through an empty land to the land of the Scythian farmers. For these Scythians range along its banks for a voyage of ten days. It is only about this river and the river Nile that I can say nothing with regard to their sources; neither – in my view – can any of the Greeks. (Hdt. 4.53)

Even among the rivers of the Black Sea, whose wonders Herodotus appreciates (4.82), the Borysthenes appears as quite outstanding, albeit smaller than the Danube. For neither the Danube nor the Don receive this kind of focus and laudation. The Bug is not neglected, but it is very much overshadowed by its neighbour. In consequence, a fresh and important question arises from the ashes of the terminological debate. Given the multiple attractions of the river and its renown around the Greek world, why was Olbia not located there? In what sense(s) was Olbia's location on the Bug more attractive and viable for settlement?

Choices about places

By and large, civic traditions about the settlement of communities tend to be stories of sudden creation, as if a key decision by Greek settlers established a city in a place where until that crucial moment there had been nothing. Such Big Bang accounts of colonial settlement, commonly with supernatural involvement, served to provide the later community with an origin which was both grand and ordained (for critiques, see *e.g.* Braund 1994, 73–87; Osborne 1998; Gosden 2004; Owen 2005). Accordingly, where we find Greeks considering colonial locations, discussion tends to be conducted in that spirit of grandeur. So much is to be expected, perhaps, of theorists like Plato and Aristotle. However, the rather more practical (though not unphilosophical) Xenophon can expatiate in much the same way on the attractions of a colonial location, specifically at Calpe on the south coast of the Black Sea in

Bithynia. The location offered some defensibility, a fine bay, and a mid-way location on the sea-route between Heraclea and Byzantium as well as excellent, well-watered land, woods, and crops. But (crucially) Xenophon observes also the abiding reason for *not* settling there: the ferocious hostility of the local Bithynians, who are said to inflict all manner of vicious abuse upon such Greeks as fall into their hands (Xen. *Anab.* 6. 4. 2–3).

Xenophon's Bithynians are an important reminder that decisions about Greek settlement had at least to take full account of indigenous inhabitants. That of course can spoil a good story. Chalcedon is a case in point (Hdt. 4.144; *cf.* Merkelbach 1980). For Chalcedon could be mocked as the 'City of the Blind', because its location was evidently inferior to that of Byzantium, nearby across the Bosporus in Europe. Herodotus states that this sobriquet was the invention of the remarkable Persian general Megabazus, who was tasked with subjugating Thrace for Darius (*cf.* 5. 1–2). In literary terms, the remark serves to round off Herodotus' account of Darius' Scythian campaign, recalling (in circular fashion) the remarkable blinded slaves of the Scythians who had figured in its beginning (4.2). More importantly, Megabazus' quip depends on acceptance of the simple truth of the (problematic) proposition that Chalcedon's foundation happened 17 years before that of Byzantium. Modern scholars tend to accept the fine chronology and offer two kinds of explanation for Chalcedon's priority. They are not mutually exclusive: namely, the difficulty of founding the city of Byzantium among hostile Thracians and the attractions of the site of Chalcedon, especially as a port of call (Malkin and Shmueli 1988). It was much more satisfactory for most in antiquity to enjoy the notion of Chalcedon as the 'City of the Blind'. We are left to speculate about how the people of Chalcedon told their own story. Certainly, Herodotus' version was not the only one, to the extent that another tradition ascribes his quip to Apollo himself, through a Delphic oracle (Strabo, 7. 6. 2; *cf.* Tac. *Ann.* 12. 63).

Herodotus relates a foundation-narrative of Cyrene which deals with a comparable problem in terms of local agency. Here it is not the force of the local inhabitants, but their deceptiveness, which accounts for the location of the colony at Cyrene and not at a place which might seem to offer a greater agrarian potential by virtue of its rainfall, at a place where there was a 'hole in the sky'. Local guides had deliberately taken Greek settlers past this place at night, so that they would not appreciate its attractions, wanting it for themselves. Deception was not straightforwardly reprehensible in archaic Greek thought. Indeed, it might even be regarded as heroic, rather as with Odysseus, for example (Krentz 2000). However, an indigenous ability to deceive was no doubt less than welcome. This story of foundation not only contributes to an explanation of the location of Cyrene, but also suggests a measure of anxiety in interactions there. Meanwhile, we should also pause to observe that Herodotus' narrative shows a Cyrene which emerged from a stuttering process of settlement which began elsewhere in the region (*cf.* Malkin 2003).

Another way to accommodate local participation in a grand foundation-story was to focus more on status than on ethnicity. Accordingly, some such stories place emphasis upon the role – even the initiative – of local kings. After all, Homeric poetry had shown kings offering land and women to heroic Greeks (*cf.* Coldstream 1993). The later city could interpret a king's decision to accommodate Greeks as his proper appreciation of the special value of a Greek presence, culturally, economically, and militarily. We have already observed the Olbian story of Scyles (set in the earlier fifth century), which shows – self-servingly – a local king eager for Greek culture. As for foundation-stories, Hyblon and Amasis stand out, hosting Megara Hyblaea and Naucratis (*e.g.* Hall 2007). In the Black Sea, the fact that a 'grandson of Aeetes' was ruling Phasis was a key consideration, perhaps an encouragement, for settlement there by Xenophon's forces (Braund 2005). At Heraclea Pontica the colonial process seems to have involved the helotization of the ordinary members of the local population, the Mariandyni: we may wonder about the role of their rulers, who may well have been complicit in that process.

For once we start to move away from grand foundation-narratives, we find a much more fractured picture. After all, there is every reason to suppose that Greek participation was also fragmented. In most circumstances, there was no viable alternative to some form of cooperation between settlers and local populations. The inchoate community could not afford to be hostile and exclusive towards all its neighbours all of the time. Nor is it obvious why it should attempt to follow such a dangerous path. Inevitably, we must deal in a priori probabilities, because we have no archaic account of the establishment of a settlement, while later accounts are driven by the self-images of more established colonies, more concerned with their present situations than with the details of their elusive pasts. The merest glance at the later circumstances of Greek settlements around the Black Sea (not to mention other locations) shows how important to these cities were their relationships with local populations. For example, Xenophon shows Trapezus living comfortably with friendly Colchian farmers close by, while in a state of low-intensity war with hostile locals in the mountains above the city (Drilae: Xen. *Anab.* 5. 2. 2). Even the strongest city of this region, Sinope, had to reckon with Corylas, a powerful Paphlagonian king behind the city, whose friendship could not be relied upon (Xen. *Anab.* 5. 5. 12). All along this coast, Xenophon shows cities which have poor communications by land and are orientated overwhelmingly upon the sea. Meanwhile, also at Olbia, although the steppe landscape of the hinterland and its river-networks were quite unlike the hinterland behind most of the south coast of the Black Sea, it was travel, transport, and communication by sea and estuary that was most important for the emerging colonial communities.

The location of Olbia

A priori consideration of the establishment of settlements in the northwestern Black Sea must acknowledge the fact that the later history of the region was a shifting matrix of complex relationships between cities and non-Greek peoples, especially pastoralists. The Protogenes inscription of the later third century BC is only the best known of a set of similar inscriptions showing agreements, tensions and hostilities between cities and pastoralists here (Braund 2007). The hypothesis of some form of 'Scythian protectorate' over the city of Olbia, entailing Scythian control of the city in the fifth century, has been comprehensively demolished (Kryzhitskiy 2005). However, we should retain an awareness, nevertheless, that Olbia was permanently engaged in diplomacy with its powerful pastoralist neighbours.

At the same time, we must recall also that the cities of the region were themselves rivals: Greek settlers had to cope not only with non-Greeks but also with other Greeks, whose cultural affinity was no guarantee of support or cooperation. There is every reason, therefore, to suppose that in the northwestern Black Sea (as usual also elsewhere around the Greek world) the process of settlement entailed engagement with a complex indigenous situation. Not only local topography, but also local powers and cultures will have been central to the choice of location. In particular, local attitudes towards incomers will have been of fundamental importance, so that 'choice' of location was not the unencumbered decision of Greek colonists. Indeed, it is possible that most of this choice was not only conditioned by local topography, but driven (conceivably even dictated) by local interests. It is worth noting the later claim that the re-foundation of Olbia (after a Getic sack) was inspired by Scythians (Dio Chrys. 36. 5).

Of course, the notion of empty land has been important to notions of colonization in a variety of ways across the centuries (*e.g.* Gosden 2004). In regard to Olbia, it has commonly been claimed in modern scholarship that Greek settlement in the region was indeed conducted in an empty landscape. However, although this orthodoxy still has its supporters, it must at least be heavily qualified. For example, it has been suggested that something is amiss with our understanding of the archaeological record, especially with regard to Early Iron Age chronology (Lapin 1966, 55–58, while developing the case for empty land). However, without subverting chronological norms, we must at least appreciate that a landscape which may seem to have been empty, was more probably a rather busy environment. For at the time when settlement on the lower Bug was developing through the seventh and sixth centuries BC, the hinterland of the wooded steppe was experiencing a dynamic process of urbanization, with the emergence of large, well-defended settlements. Between these settlements and the lower Bug was not only steppe-land, but also a large river system, whose archaeological record indicates significant exchange between pre-colonial local cultures (Boltrik 2000, 122). In view of these waterways, in particular, we should not be surprised if the earliest local pottery in Olbia shows significant similarities with pottery of the wooded steppe (Marchenko 2005). Nor should we be surprised to find that some fine pottery made in the Greek world in the late seventh century found its way north (Vakhtina 2007a). Meanwhile, there were also the land-routes followed by pastoralists in later centuries and presumably earlier too, exploiting the grass and other natural resources. The salt available at the coast was an undoubted attraction (Hdt. 4.53, quoted above, with Dio Chrys. 36.3 on salt-winning).

Chronologies – absolute and relative – remain matters of concern across the region, since they rely so much upon the presence or absence of Greek wares in the archaeological record. Accordingly, close chronologies are especially problematic, not much helped by the questionable dates and data provided in the written tradition (Hall 2007, 100–106). Meanwhile, the progress of archaeology at Olbia in particular is edging its chronology earlier through the discovery of further examples of early imported pottery (A. V. Bujskikh 2007 and *pers. comm.*). Of course, such imports entail a series of problems. On the one hand, we are left to wonder how quickly pottery made in the Aegean came to Olbia and/or into the interior. On the other hand (and more importantly), the appearance of small quantities of imported pottery tells us much less than we might wish. For there is every likelihood that there was significant Greek contact with a place or region before such pottery was brought and deposited in the archaeological record there. We must acknowledge the appearance of local places and related names in the earliest extant Greek literature, while Homeric poetry serves to confirm the existence of Argonautic stories before Homer (with or without the northwestern Black Sea). While the *Odyssey* offered a conceptual framework for travel and settlement in the western Mediterranean (Malkin 1998), Argonautic tales offered a similar framework, *mutatis mutandis*, for the Black Sea region (Braund 1994, esp. 11–39).

In particular, we should not be seduced by the argument that Greek knowledge of a region was only possible *after* the establishment of substantial settlements there, or by misleading assertions about the completeness of our archaeological knowledge. The process of settlement no doubt gave particular causes and impetus to Greek quests for knowledge about a region, but all forms of travel, planning, and passing presence in a region also prompted interest and inquiry. In the Black Sea, we must also recognize that archaeology remains incomplete at all major settlements, while at some of the most important – such as Sinope – we have almost no archaeological knowledge of the colonial period whatsoever (Braund 2005a, *contra* West 2002). In addition, as the present discussion serves to illustrate, we cannot expect to have much (if any) hard archaeological knowledge about the pioneering frontiersmen who were the beginnings of the colonial process.

On the usual view (which may well be right) Greek settlement on Berezan was established in the later decades of the seventh century BC, while the Greek presence at Olbia came a few decades later (Marchenko 2005). Close to the south of Olbia on the shore of the Bug estuary was another settlement, also adjudged to be Greek, established around 600 BC (Kryzhitskiy *et al.* 1990). Meanwhile, also in this early phase, was a curious settlement south of the Bug-Dnieper estuary, at Yagorlyk on Kinburn spit. This was a location remarkable for its concentration of metalworking (and apparently also glass-working). Yet it was also a small settlement, which is regularly regarded as a place of temporary – perhaps seasonal – occupation (Ostroverkhov 1978; Kryzhitskiy *et al.* 1999, 37). Quite unclear is the relationship between these locations, though it is often supposed that settlers moved from Berezan to Olbia. It is supposed (quite rightly, perhaps) that settlement spread from Berezan (almost certainly a promontory, though now an island) to the east bank of the estuary of the river Berezan and soon onwards, *c.* 600–550, to the west bank of the Bug estuary (including Olbia), after which it developed on both sides of the Bug and extended northwards above Olbia (Kryzhitskiy *et al.* 1999, 37). However, while this broad dynamic is plausible enough, we should be alert for what may be particular exceptions. For example, at Shirokaya Balka (some 4.5 km south of Olbia along the coast), a variety of quite early imported pottery has been observed – including both amphorae and fine-ware – which might even take the settlement a little earlier than 600 BC (Kryzhitskiy *et al.* 1990, 25–26, preferring a date close after 600). Meanwhile, fundamental work on imported pottery (especially fine-ware) at Olbia has shown a single fragment of seventh-century Middle Wild Goat Style. It has been well observed that the hypothesis that Berezan came earlier is supported by the absence from Olbia of most pre-600 pottery, which is relatively abundant on Berezan (A. V. Bujskikh 2007). Even so, the 'foundation-date' for Olbia is edging earlier: a sanctuary was established there by *c.* 580–560 (A. V. Bujskikh 2007, 504, superseding Rusyayeva 2006, long in press). The future discovery of more early pottery is considered unlikely by the current excavators (*e.g.* Kryzhitskiy *et al.* 1999, 44), but the possibility cannot be ruled out completely. Perhaps more important, we need also to consider the (in)significance of imported pots. How much pottery did pioneers bring with them? How long could a pioneering presence persist at Olbia (or elsewhere) without such imports? In principle, at least, proto-Olbia may have had no great desire for seventh-century 'bird-bowls' and the like. The society, economy, and taste of early Berezan may have been substantially different from the culture of Olbia. In sum, there are imponderables and there is a need for caution and reflection, given the state of our evidence. However, as a working hypothesis, the orthodox notion of a decades-long process of extension from Berezan into the interior remains valuable and valid enough.

In all this there are important implications for the question of choice of site. We have observed the key role played by local powers (especially the pastoralist rulers) in that process of choice. The marked tendency for archaic settlement on the lower Bug to be located on the west bank of the river may well reflect local attitudes, which will have varied according to place and political grouping. However, while we can make inferences about locals, we must also reflect upon the notion of 'Greek', which is usual in discussions of this region. The search for ethnicities has engendered a vigorous and polarized debate. This has been useful in prompting close consideration of the evidential base. In consequence, it has been established that the form of a dwelling allows no reliable inferences about the ethnicity of those who lived in it (S. B. Bujskikh 2007). Less clear is the significance of handmade pottery, for which much has been claimed. At least some of it seems to indicate non Greek involvement in the colonial process (Marchenko 2005; but see *contra* S. B. Bujskikh 2007). Meanwhile, a priori consideration of the colonial process in the northwest Black Sea tends strongly to suggest that many of the women of the developing settlements were probably drawn from non-Greek society, including women from the urbanized wooded steppe. For burial-practices of the wooded steppe seem to have been transferred to elite burials in archaic Olbia (Rusyayeva 2007). That would accord well with the strong tendency of colonial traditions to present the process of colonization as the act(s) of males, drawing their women from the local environment. This is a key issue for our whole understanding of the colonial process, which continues to resist clear-cut answers from archaeological enquiry (Coldstream 1993; *cf.* Shepherd 2005, rather pessimistically).

A version of the post colonialist concept of hybridity is helpful here (see *e.g.* Malkin 1998, 15–16; Antonaccio 2003; Owen 2005, 16). What kind of 'Greeks' were these early individuals and groups who inhabited and moved about the region from the seventh century BC and possibly earlier? And what kind of families did they have? Of course, the established community at Olbia was eager to assert its Greekness as part of a grand foundation-story which has not survived, but which will have started in Miletus and given a large role to Apollo. But such stories give no real access to the pioneers, adventurers, dealers, robbers, desperadoes, and chancers who made lives for themselves in the region, whether in the short term or permanently. For these were the frontiersmen who gave initial impulses to the process of settlement. These risk-takers were able to find a place for themselves in the region, at the coast and probably also in the hinterland.

Such men were key to choices about places, but they are hard to find. Archaeologically, they have left scant traces. For the literary tradition, they were beneath consideration and perhaps beneath contempt. However, remarkably enough, there is some evidence about them, problematic though it may be. Although rather later, Herodotus is helpful. He refers to 'the Greeks dwelling in the Scythian land', distinguishing them from the Greeks of the Black Sea. These men (tellingly, with Scythians) are cited as informants on the Neurian wolf-men of the deep interior (Hdt. 4.105). Further, he also states that Greeks from the coastal trading-centres (including Olbia) penetrated as far into the hinterland as the Argippaei. Here too they are mentioned in tandem with Scythians (Hdt. 4.24). The tendency for frontiersmen to push into the interior (especially to the more familiar world of the wooded steppe beyond the steppe proper) no doubt encouraged Herodotus to believe that a settlement had been established in the wooded steppe (Gelonos) by Greeks who had long ago moved north from trading centres of the Black Sea coast; there they were partially assimilated to local culture (Hdt. 4.108–109). We need not be detained by the (un)reality of Herodotus' conception of the origins of this community, which has still to be located (*pace* the classic Shramko 1987). Far more interesting is the fact that Herodotus' experience of Olbia and his informants attracted him to that very conception. Evidently, Herodotus' knowledge of Olbia was such as to make the Greek creation of a Gelonos entirely plausible. It may well be that Herodotus had met men engaged in the trade which cut across the hinterland between Olbia and the Don (Medvedev 1997). Or others who travelled north. For a burnished jar has survived almost complete in an archaic pit at Nemirovo, north in the hinterland above Olbia. The pottery-assemblage at Nemirovo suggests that the jar was made on site. Its body bears a number of random scratchings, but there is a concentration of marks scratched onto a section of its shoulder. Upon its discovery, these marks were taken to be a Greek inscription, specifically an invocation (Grakov 1959). Thereafter, the jar has been displayed in the Hermitage Museum, where autopsy explains the reservations of some Russian scholars about the reality of the inscription (I am grateful to A. Alekseyev, G. Smirnova and M. Vakhtina). Now, at any rate, the most that can be discerned is the possibility of two or three Greek letters (a name perhaps?), but it is quite possible that these are no more than a collocation of random marks. In sum, the jar offers some uncertain encouragement to the view that men who knew Greek letters were to be found in archaic Nemirovo. Given the presence of Greek amphorae and fine-ware at the site, that would be no great surprise (Smirnova 1998; Vakhtina 1998; 2007; 2007a). After all, we happen to be told that a Scythian king had a Greek wife (from Istros) around 500 BC: her son (Scyles) may not have been the only Scythian to pick up a little Greek. Meanwhile, we must also consider the taste for fine-ware at Nemirovo and other locations in the hinterland. We can do no more than make inferences about the ways in which that taste emerged and about the forms it may have taken. What (if anything) did the inhabitants of Nemirovo think about this pottery, or do with it? At any rate, it is right to acknowledge and consider the function of these artefacts in the development of 'Graeco-Scythian' art, driven by north–south interaction and movements by a range of participants in all directions (Vakhtina 2005).

While different groups might well assert their ethnic and cultural identities, there is every reason to believe that the early frontiersmen of the northwest Black Sea and its hinterland developed a complex of multiple identities which enabled them to live and prosper in this changing environment. By the fifth century, there were 'Greek Scythians' living around Olbia, as Herodotus terms the Callippidae (4.17). The origins of these people are presumably to be located at least in the sixth century, if not the seventh or even earlier. Meanwhile, on Herodotus' account, Olbia was a place where one could find not only the occasional philhellenic Scythian king, but also a substantial Scythian presence at the gates (which seems routine in Scyles' story) and a Scythian royal administrator, presumably representing his master's interests in the city, whether as a resident or a visitor there. It is no surprise to find the adoption of Scythian-style names among the elite of the city. Accordingly, we are left to wonder how far the assertion of exclusivity (which Herodotus stresses as a Scythian trait: 4.76) may have been a response to a widespread process of acculturation. At any rate, it is easy enough to understand why Greeks of the Mediterranean regarded the self-proclaimed Greeks of Olbia and elsewhere in the Black Sea as somehow not properly Greek at all (Braund 1997). It is also easy to understand why there was so much disagreement about who was and who was not a Scythian (Hdt. 4.81; 108–109).

Therefore, the emergence of Olbia as the location for the main community of the region was a consequence primarily of the engagement of a broadly 'hybrid' population with a local situation with which it was already familiar. Its knowledge and experience could only set the tone for any impulses from the Mediterranean, or from settlements further afield around the Black Sea. In that sense the very notion of a 'local' population becomes unwieldy, since it must include not only simple polarities (Greeks-Scythians, agriculturalists-pastoralists), but also hybrid groupings, well exemplified by the Callippidae, whom Herodotus perceived as an amalgam of two ethnicities and two economies and lifestyles. In more traditional terms, we must at least recognize the impact of experience at Berezan for the development of Olbia, if the accepted chronological and historical development from the one to the other is to be accepted. At the same time, the very notion of choice should not draw our attention away from the evolutionary element of this process. We may be sure that choices of location were substantially responses to local realities (geographical, political, and economic). Moreover, that some initiatives prospered (as at Olbia), while others faded (as Berezan, Shirokaya Balka) or failed completely (as at Yagorlyk).

Olbia was like many of the other settlements on the Bug, in that it benefited from natural defences. The shores of the lower Bug are set along with ravines which run from west and east down to the river. For this geographical idiosyncrasy occurs on the east bank too, as, for example, at Skel'ka. Meanwhile, we should observe the recurrence of the term Balka (Ravine) among the toponyms of the region. However, of the several plateaus formed by these ravines, the site of Olbia offered the most extensive (I am grateful to A. V. and S. B. Bujskikh for discussion of these matters). Moreover, most of its circumference was protected by ravines, although these were imperfect, subsequently augmented by additional defences (S. B. Bujskikh 1991). The fact that Olbia and the majority of other settlements clustered on the west bank of the Bug seems to be best explained by the socio-political system there. The west bank seems to have offered an environment (including the Callipidae) which was more welcome for settlement than the east bank, where the physical environment seems to have been much the same. Further, it is worth noting that the distribution-pattern of the archaic settlements on the east bank of the Bug shows a cluster across the river from Olbia. There is evidence from later periods to suggest that the Bug may have been fordable near Olbia (Boltrik 2000, 126). The level of water in the estuary has risen substantially since antiquity, so that (although claims abound) we have only a general notion of Olbia's port and insufficient knowledge of the water-course in general to convince everyone that a ford existed.

The Bug itself offered a direct route north into the wooded steppe (and south from it), while the Dnieper described a lazy arc eastwards which will not have been welcome to those heading north. Accordingly, Herodotus believed that he knew the source of the Bug, while the upper course of the Dnieper was unknown (4.52–53). The delta of the Dnieper was also problematic, marshy, and beset with mosquitoes. In the archaic period, the Bug was the shortest route to the most vibrant sector of the wooded steppe in archaic times, where archaic Greek imports certainly found their way (*e.g.* Bondar 1955, esp. 62, Fig. 1). All the more so, when we consider the role of the river Ingulets in connecting the Bug with the west bank of the Dnieper (Boltrik

lazy bend eastwards. At the same time, passage up the Bug included a nodal point of routes across Scythia at Exampaeus, where exchange was facilitated and power was expressed and memorialized by at least one Scythian king (Ariantas: Hdt. 4.81). From a perspective in Olbia, the Dnieper was close enough, but throughout the city's history it was kept rather apart, always marginal to Greater Olbia (Braund 2007; Bylkova in this volume). By the fifth century, the Dnieper's rich resources had brought substantial 'Scythian' settlement. Its course was not only an interface with the lofty and perhaps rebarbative Royal Scythians, but was also dangerously close to the well-guarded burials of the Scythian kings. At least (and this is what matters most) that is what they told Herodotus in Olbia.

For we may be sure enough that by Herodotus' day the Olbiopolitans had already woven grand stories about its foundation by Milesian settlers and no doubt a supernaturally-inspired choice of its site. Herodotus does not relay these stories, except insofar as the Olbian version of the death of Anacharsis amounts to the creation of an Olbian cult for the Great Mother in Hylaea. He knew that all colonial foundations had such stories, while the Black Sea colonies were of scant interest to him in themselves. He was much more interested in the challenging world of the Scythians and their particular customs, so that the only sustained discussion of origins in his account of the Black Sea region in Book Four of his *Histories* is the disquisition on Scythian origins with which he opens the book, together with the origins of some of the other peoples of the region whom the Scythians summoned to a council of war against the invasion of the Persians (4.99ff., especially the Sauromatians and the Geloni). These stories of foundation entailed not only sharp disagreements (*e.g.* between Scythian and Pontic Greek notions of Scythian origins), but also some sense that movement, settlement, and cultural interaction could indeed generate hybrid cultures. The 'hybridization' caused (on Herodotus' story: 4.108–109) by the arrival of Greeks among the Scythian-like Budini raised and continues to raise a series of questions about what had happened during the emergence of the Callippidae and of Olbia itself, about the nature of hybridity on the lower Bug and about the emergence of Olbia as a self-proclaimed Greek city.

Bibliography

Antonaccio, C. (2003) Hybridity and the cultures within Greek culture. In C. Dougherty and L. Kurke (eds) *The cultures within ancient Greek culture*, 57–76. Cambridge, Cambridge University Press.

Blavatskiy, V. D. (1968) ΒΟΡΥΣΘΕΝΙΣ, *Vestnik Drevnei Istorii* 4, 119–22.

Boltrik, Yu. V. (2000) Osnovnoy torgovyy put' Ol'vii v Dneprovskoye lesostepnoye pravoberezh'ye, *Rossiyskaya Arkheologiya* 9, 121–130.

Bondar', N. N. (1955) Torgovyye snosheniya Ol'vii so Skifyey v VI-V vv. do n.e., *Sovietskaya Arkheologiya* 23, 58–80.

Bowersock, G. W. (1992) "Les Grecs 'barbarises'" *Ktema* 17, 249–257.

Braund, D. (1997) Greeks and barbarians: the Black Sea region and hellenism under the early Roman empire". In S. Alcock (ed.) *The early Roman empire in the east*, 121–136. Oxford, Oxbow Books.

Braund, D. (1998) Herodotus and the problematics of reciprocity. In C. Gill, N. Postlethwaite and R. Seaford (eds) *Reciprocity in ancient Greece*, 159–80. Oxford, Oxford University Press.

Braund, D. (2005) Pericles, Cleon and the Pontus: the Black Sea in Athens *c.* 440–421. In D. Braund (ed.) *Scythians and Greeks: cultural interactions in Scythia, Athens and the early Roman empire*, 81–99. Exeter, University of Exeter Press.

Braund, D. (2005a) Reflections on Eumelus' Black Sea region. In D. Kacharava, M. Faudot and E. Geny (eds) *Pont-Euxin et polis. Actes du Xe symposium de Vani*, 99–112. Franche-Comte, Presse Universitaire.

Braund, D. (2007) Greater Olbia: ethnic, religious, economic and political interactions in the region of Olbia *c.* 600–100 BC. In D. Braund and S. D. Kryzhitskiy (eds) *Classical Olbia and the Scythian world*, 35–75. Proceedings of the British Academy 142, Oxford, Oxford University Press.

Braund, D. (2008) Scythian laughter: conversations in the northern Black Sea region in the fifth century BC. In P. Guldager Bilde (ed.) *Meetings of cultures in the Black Sea region: between conflict and coexistence*, 347–368. Aarhus, Aarhus University Press.

Bujskikh, A. V. (2007) The earliest East Greek pottery from Olbia Pontica. In J. Cobet, V. von Graeve, W.-D. Niemeier and K. Zimmermann (eds) *Frühes Ionien. Eine Bestandaufnahme*, 499–510. Milesische Forschungen, 5, Mainz.

Bujskikh, S. B. (1991) *Fortifikatsiya Ol'viyskovo gosudarstva*. Kiev, Naukova Dumka.

Bujskikh, S. B. (2007) Contacts between Greeks and non-Greeks on the lower Bug in the sixth and fifth centuries BC. In D. Braund and S. D. Kryzhitskiy (eds) *Classical Olbia and the Scythian world*, 35–75. Proceedings of the British Academy 142, Oxford, Oxford University Press.

Coldstream, J. N. (1993) Mixed marriages at the frontiers of the early Greek world, *Oxford Journal of Archaeology* 12, 89–107.

Gavrilyuk, N. A. (1999) *Istoriya ekonomiki stepnoy Skifii 6–4 vv. do n. e.*, Kiev, Институт археологии НАН Украины.

Gosden, C. (2004) *Archaeology and colonialism*. Oxford, Oxford University Press.

Grakov, B. N. (1959) Grecheskoye graffito iz Nemirovskovo gorodishcha, *Sovietskaya Arkheologiya* 1, 48–54.

Hall, J. M. (2007) *A history of the archaic Greek world*. Oxford, Blackwell.

Hartog, F. (1988) *The mirror of Herodotus*. English transl, Berkeley, University of California Press.

Hind, J. (2005) Berezan: the ancient and modern names. In S. L. Solovyov (ed.) *Borisfen-Berezan: arkheologicheskaya kollektsiya Ermitazha*, 26–31. St. Petersburg, The Hermitage Publishing House.

Krentz, P. (2000) Deception in archaic and classical Greek warfare. In H. van Wees (ed.) *War and violence in ancient Greece*, 167–200. UWICAH, London, Duckworth.

Kryzhitskiy, S. D. (2005) Olbia and the Scythians in the fifth century BC: the Scythian "protectorate". In D. Braund (ed.) *Scythians and Greeks: cultural interactions in Scythia, Athens and the early Roman empire*, 123–130. Exeter, University of Exeter Press.

Kryzhitskiy, S. D., Bujskikh, S. B. and Otreshko, V. M. (1990) *Antichnyye poseleniya nizhnevo Pobuzh'ye (arkheologicheskaya karta)*. Kiev, Naukova Dumka.

Kryzhitskiy, S. D., Rusyayeva, A. S., Krapivina, V. V., Leypunskaya, N. A., Skrzhinskaya, M. V. and Anokhin, V. A (1999) *Ol'viya*. Kiev, Institute of Archeology of the National Academy of Sciences of Ukraine.

Lapin, V. V. (1966) *Grecheskaya kolonizatsiya Severnovo Prichernomor'ya*. Moscow, Naukova Dumka.

Malkin, I. (1998) *The returns of Odysseus: colonization and ethnicity*. Berkeley, University of California Press.

Malkin, I. (2003) "Tradition" in Herodotus: the foundation of Cyrene. In P. Derow and R. Parker (eds) *Herodotus and His World: Essays from a Conference in Memory of George Forrest*. Oxford, Oxford University Press.

Malkin, I. and Shmueli, N. (1988) The "City of the Blind" and the Foundation of Byzantium. In I. Malkin and R. Hohlfelder (eds) *Mediterranean cities. Historical perspectives*, 21–36. London, Cass.

Marchenko, K. K. (2005) Greki i varvary Severo-Zapadnovo Prichernomor'ya skifskoy epokhi. In K. K. Marchenko (ed.) *Greki i varvary severnovo Prichernomor'ya v skifskuyu epokhu*, 42–136. St. Petersburg, Aleteja.

Medvedev, A. P. (1997) Ol'viyskiye torgovye puti i stepen' dostovernosti etnogeograficheskikh dannykh Gerodota *Arkheologiya* 4, 24–28.

Merkelbach, R. (1980) *Die Inschriften der Kalchedon*. Inschriften Kleinasiens, Bonn.

Nenquin, J. (1961) *Salt: a study in economic prehistory*. Bruges, De Tempel.

Osborne, R. (1998) Early Greek colonization? The nature of Greek colonization in the west. In N. Fisher and H. van Wees (eds) *Archaic Greece: new approaches and new evidence*, 251–270. London, Duckworth.

Ostroverkhov, A. S. (1978) Pro chornu metalurgiyu na Yagorlits'komu poselenni, *Arkheologiya* 23, 26–35.

Owen, S. (2005) Analogy, archaeology and archaic Greek colonization. In H. Hurst and S. Owen (eds) *Ancient Colonizations: analogy, similarity and difference*, 5–22. London, Duckworth.

Rusyayeva, A. S. (1999) Proniknoveniye ellinov na territoriyu Ukrainskoy lesostepi v arkhaicheskoye vremya (k postanovkye problemy), *Vestnik Drevnei Istorii* 4, 84–97.

Rusyayeva, A. S. (2006) Stroitel'nyye ostatki khramov. In V. N. Zinko (ed.) *Drevneyshiy temenos Ol'vii Pontiskoy*, 32–42. MAIET suppl.2, Simferopol.

Rusyayeva, A. S. (2007) Religious interactions between Olbia and Scythia. In D. Braund and S. D. Kryzhitskiy (eds) *Classical Olbia and the Scythian world*, 91–100. Oxford, Oxford University Press.

Shepherd, G. (2005) Dead men tell no tales: ethnic diversity in Sicilian colonies and the evidence of the cemeteries, *Oxford Journal of Archaeology* 24, 115–136.

Shramko, B. A. (1987) *Bel'skoye gorodishche skifskoy epokhi.Gorod Gelon*. Kiev, Naukova Dumka.

Smirnova, G. I. (1998) Skifskoye poselen'ye na Nemirovskom gorodishche: obshchiye dannyye o pamyatnikye, *Materialy po Arkheologii, Istorii, Etnografii Tavrii* 6, 77–121.

Taylor, T. (2001) Believing the ancients: quantitative and qualitative dimensions of slavery and the slave trade in later prehistoric Eurasia, *World Archaeology* 33, 27–43.

Vakhtina, M. Yu. (1998) Osnovnyye kategorii grecheskoy importnoy keramiki iz raskopok Nemirovskovo gorodishcha, *Materialy po Arkheologii, Istorii, Etnografii Tavrii* 6, 122–139.

Vakhtina, M. Yu. (2005) Grecheskoye isskustvo i isskustvo Yevropeyskoy Skifii. In K. K. Marchenko (ed.) *Greki i varvary severnovo Prichernomor'ya v skifskuyu epokhu*, 297–399. St. Petersburg, Aleteja.

Vakhtina, M. Yu. (2007) Grecheskaya arkhaicheskaya keramika iz raskopok Nemirovskovo gorodishcha i Pobuzh'ye. In S. A. Skoriy (ed.) *Ranniy Zalizniy Vik Evraziy*, 49–51. Kiev-Chigirin, Institute of Archeology of the National Academy of Sciences of Ukraine.

Vakhtina, M. Yu. (2007a) Archaic East Greek pottery from Nemirovo. In J. Cobet, V. von Graeve, W.-D. Niemeier and K. Zimmermann (eds) *Frühes Ionien. Eine Bestandaufnahme*, 511–18. Milesische Forschungen, 5, Mainz.

West, M. L. (2002) 'Eumelos': a Corinthian epic cycle? *Journal of Hellenic Studies* 122, 109–133.

West, S. R. (2000) Herodotus in the North? Reflections on a colossal cauldron, *Scripta Classica Israelica* 19, 15–34.

West, S. R. (2003) The most marvellous of all seas: the Greek encounter with the Euxine, *Greece and Rome* 50, 151–167.

West, S. R. (2007) Herodotus and Olbia. In D. Braund and S. D. Kryzhitskiy (eds) *Classical Olbia and the Scythian world*, 77–90. Oxford, Oxford University Press.

15

'Greek' colonization: The view from Ionia

Alan M. Greaves

Introduction

The work of the Greek Colonization and European Development project will serve to synthesize and analyze a great deal of information from across the Greek colonial world. In recent years in the areas of the Black Sea and the western Mediterranean in particular there have been rapid advances in the amount of data available on the origins and nature of Greek colonial settlement, which will be usefully synthesized and analyzed by the Cambridge team and, thanks to advances in GIS technology, it will be possible to interrogate this information in innovative ways. Although archaeological work on the colonial *metropoleis* of the Greek heartland has not stopped in the meantime, the rapid advances in our understanding of the archaeology of the regions that were colonized and the opening up of the Black Sea to western scholars have served to focus much academic attention away from the *metropoleis* and onto the colonies, where it has largely remained. We have now long since passed the point at which we know more about the colonies than we do about many of the *metropoleis* that supposedly founded them. As a result, there is the possibility that the axis between the two will become dislocated and we will start to view the colonial world merely as a *koinē* created by the Greek *metropoleis*, but essentially unconnected to them.

In response to the papers presented at the Cambridge symposium, and included in this volume, I would like to take this opportunity to briefly direct our attention towards the *metropoleis* of Ionia because I believe this approach, and this region, have the potential to raise a number of issues worthy of further academic consideration in light of our new, greater knowledge of the Greek colonial world. In doing so I hope to offer new perspectives that draw us into re-evaluating our assumptions about the causes and processes of the Greek colonial phenomenon and thereby bring about a more informed consideration of *metropolis*-colony relationships.

Ionia is a good test-bed for studies of Greek colonization because, on the basis of both literary tradition and archaeological evidence, it is generally agreed to have been the region of Greece that was most active in the overseas expansion of the archaic period (eighth to sixth centuries BC). Ionia was home to several colonial *metropoleis*, including the most important and prolific of them all – Miletos. Other Ionian *metropoleis* included Phokaia, Samos, Kolophon, Klazomenai, Teos, and Erythrai (see Tsetskhladze 2006 lxvii-lxxiii for a summary of names and dates for their colonies). Two thirds of the cities named in the Ionian *dodecopolis* were therefore apparently engaged in the colonization movement, and established colonies in areas as disparate as the Black Sea, the Propontis, the North Aegean, the western Mediterranean, and North Africa. Of these regions, the Black Sea in particular has seen a rapid increase in the number of excavations and publications in recent years and this has transformed our understanding of Ionian colonization. The recent publication of the 1999 Panionion conference (Cobet *et al.* 2007) saw the papers about recent developments in the archaeology of Ionia presented alongside those on the Ionian colonization of the Black Sea. This volume, and this approach in general, will do much to further our understanding and heighten the debate surrounding the nature of *metropolis*-colony relationships in Ionia. However, for the purposes of this paper my aim is not to address those relationships in detail, but to raise a number of broad themes and topics that might be taken into consideration when addressing it. The hypotheses sketched out here might also be usefully tested against other regions of Greece and the Greek colonial world.

There has been, in my opinion, a tendency to often conceive of the colonists involved in this movement as having been mono-culturally 'Greek'. This is perhaps a result of the shift in emphasis away from the *metropoleis* and towards the colonies, without having first appreciated the complex nature of the metropolitan communities themselves. It may also result from the fact that much of our understanding of 'Greek' identity has often been based on readings of the archaeology and literary traditions of the region that now constitutes the modern nation-state of Greece, rather than addressing the more complex issue of identity of the Greek communities that were positioned on the edge of the Anatolian landmass, *i.e.* the Ionians. This mono-cultural characterization is perhaps also a consequence of the application of reductionist models for examining the Greek-Native encounter that seek to simplify both cultures in order to analyze putative schemes for their interaction. For example, discussions of hybridity are made more complex if one, or indeed both, of the participant cultures were complex, mutable, and ill-defined to begin with. For example, it would be more accurate to describe the culture of sites such as Entremônt-en Provence as Phokaio-Celtic, rather than Graeco-Celtic as the culture of Phokaia was distinguishable from those of other Greek poleis in ways that can be identified in Entremônt (I am grateful to Vikki Jefferson of Oxford University for discussing her research with me on this topic and for our lively discussions of it).

There is also still a tendency for discussions of Greek colonization to be influenced by a desire to create segues with the literary accounts of later authors, which are often

Athenocentric and the products of later mythologizing or re-workings of some small kernel of fact. For example, if, as some scholars do, we were to accept as fact that the colonization of Ionia took place from 'mainland' Greece following the fall of the Mycenaean palaces, the so-called 'Ionian Migration', then we would expect that any traces of the pre-existing Karian/Lelegian population would have been assimilated or eradicated by the time of the archaic colonial movement, several centuries later. However, this is not the case. Not only do all scholars not accept the truth of these myths and their dating at face value (*e.g.* Lemos 2007), but also because there are enduring traces of Anatolian culture in cities such as Miletos and Phokaia throughout the archaic period.

Having very briefly outlined the pitfalls and potentials of a study of Ionian colonization, I would now like to highlight six themes that I consider worth of further research.

Six themes in Ionian colonisation

1. Given the diverse character of the Ionian *metropoleis*, alluded to above, the first theme that should be considered in relation to their role in the Greek colonization movement is that it should be recognized that the identity of the Ionian *metropoleis* differs not only from the 'standard' Greek identity of the 'mainland' *poleis*, but also from one another. This should hardly come as a surprise to us as this is the period in which Greek identity is still in what Jonathon Hall (1997) describes as its 'aggregrative' phase. That is, the period in the formation of the Hellenic identity at which it was normal for Greek communities to seek common ground with their peer groups and assimilate elements of difference as much as possible. In this context, it is important to note that Ionia is geographically and culturally part of Anatolia, and the Ionians of the Anatolian coast evidently sought to 'aggregate' some elements of neighbouring cultures onto their own.

It is increasingly clear that archaic Ionia displayed not only the cultural aspects considered to be quintessentially 'Greek', but also those of its neighbours in Anatolia – Karia, Phrygia, and Lydia. However, by the classical period a narrative about Ionia had been constructed in which the Ionians were generally shown to be in the ascendant over their Anatolian predecessors and peers (Nilsson 1986, esp. 59–65). This is epitomized by Herodotos' account of the foundation of Miletos (Hdt. 1.146) in which settlers of 'pure blood' from Athens murdered the Karians that they found living there and forced their wives into marriage. As a result of this, it is said, the women of Miletos refused to dine with their husbands or call them by name. This idea of the violent foundation of Miletos, once established, was to prove enduring and influential (Pausanias 7.2.5–6; Dion. Hal. 2.30.5; Greaves 1998), even in modern accounts of city's history (*e.g.* Kleiner 1968). However, the truth behind the construction of this classical-period façade may have been quite different, and in the age of colonization labels such as 'Greek' and 'Barbarian' did not yet have the currency that they would later come to develop. The precise definition of the local identities of the Ionian *metropoleis*, and the role of Anatolian influences on them, and mapping these onto their colonial foundations elsewhere, is therefore a potentially important line of future research.

2. Secondly, it seems reasonable to speculate that power-relations between the Greek and Anatolian elements within Ionian cities were perhaps more equitable than these later sources would lead us to believe. Evidence for the construction of elements of any hybrid Ionian Greek/Anatolian culture, if they could be securely identified, might then be cited as evidence of periods of equity between these groups (*cf.* Fitzjohn 2007 on the colonial encounter in Sicily). For example, the account of the foundation of Miletos given by Herodotos (1.146) could be read differently to infer that there had, in fact, been an assimilation of elements of Karian culture, such as family dining habits, into Milesian society, rather than their total eradication by the superior in-coming Greeks.

One means by which such a hybrid culture may have been constructed in order to create a uniquely Milesian, or other Ionian, 'third space' was by means of exogamous marriage. This is a proven way for an in-coming population to ingratiate itself with the host community. Such intermarriages between Greeks and Karians might account for why the women of Miletos apparently maintained some non-Greek customs as it would have been expedient for arriving Greeks to intermarry with the indigenous population when they arrived in Anatolia, whenever that was. Inter-marriage was also an approach that the Milesians appear to have used in their archaic period colonies in the Black Sea, such as Olbia-Borysthenes (Hdt. 4.77). Such openness to the possibility of exogamous marriage would allow the Milesian colonists to finagle their way into the upper echelons of the host community by means of judicious political marriages (Greaves 1999, 217–228; see also Dietler in this volume on traditions surrounding the foundation of Massalia). Such an attitude towards intermarriage may have been informed by the early experiences of the Milesians at home. The role of exogamous marriage in the Greek colonial movement is certainly a theme worthy of further serious consideration.

3. Another consequence of Ionia's geographical location in Anatolia is that the people of the region would almost certainly have been acquainted with interior of Anatolia and its harsh climate. During the winter, night-time temperatures in central Anatolia regularly drop to below freezing point for extended periods. To people familiar with such a climate, the winter conditions in the northern Black Sea colonies, such as Berezan, Olbia-Borysthenes, and Panticapaeum, would perhaps not have seemed so unusual. The cold winter temperatures experienced in the northern littoral of the Black Sea have been cited by some scholars as the reason why Ionian colonists adopted the semi-subterranean 'dugout' form of domestic architecture in some of their colonies there. It is possible that if the Ionians were already acquainted with the cold winter temperatures of Anatolia, then so too may this form of architecture, an example of which was discovered in the early Iron Age levels at Gordion, in central Anatolia. This was a rectangular pit house, 30–50 cm deep, and lined with mud plaster and dated to *c.* 1100–950 BC (Gordion Phase YHSS 7; Voigt and Henrickson 2000, 42).

Whereas some scholars have argued that the Berezan dugouts were a non-Greek innovation (*e.g.* Solovyov 2007, 532–537), others have argued that they are consistent with what we know of Ionian domestic at Miletos (*e.g.* Tsetskhladze 2006, xliv–xlv). The evidence from Gordion might appear to suggest that this form of architecture was more widespread in the regions bordering the Black Sea than has previously been thought. Perhaps instead of seeking to make strict local/Ionian/Anatolian cultural attributions for this form of architecture, it is perhaps best to recognize that as a house-form would have been familiar to both the Greek and non-Greek inhabitants of the Black Sea and its adoption may have been a pragmatic response to the particular conditions of climate, resources, and economy in which they found themselves. (If indeed they were houses. As Hans Lohmann has pointed out, there are parallels for such features from the Linearbandkeramik culture of prehistoric Europe, where they have been interpreted as being pits from which soil had been removed, and may therefore be unintended by-products of the construction process rather than actual houses (Treister 2007: 580, commenting on the dugout houses of Panticapaeum).)

4. As noted above, archaic Ionia, like the rest of Greece, was not a mono-cultural entity. Before the Greek world ever became polarized by the Peloponnesian War or unified under the rule of Alexander the Great (Hall 1997, 2002) a multiplicity of Greek cultures existed in Ionia. Consequently, the material culture of the Ionian *metropoleis* varied considerably from one to the next. Such variations in the culture of the individual Ionian *metropoleis* might reasonably be expected to have mapped themselves onto the colonies of those states. For example, Aphrodite has now been recognized as one of the most important deities in Miletos, where she was worshipped as a sea goddess (Senff 2003). This maritime aspect of her cult identity was similarly emphasized in Miletos' colonies in the Black Sea and elsewhere, where the epithets used were consistent with her identity as a sea goddess, as well as with purely local expressions of her cult identity (Ehrhardt 1988; Greaves 2004).

It has long been recognized that cult, and concomitant cultural phenomena such as calendars, is the most easily-recognizable and enduring element of *metropolis*-colony relationships across the Greek world. This seems to hold true in relation to the Ionian colonization movement as well, but the same cannot yet be said of burial practices. Burial traditions in the Ionian states varied greatly from one to the next, and over time. For example, Klazomenai is well-known for its distinctive painted terracotta sarcophagi, yet inhumation in these sarcophagi appears only to have come into use from the sixth century BC. Prior to this date, burial at Klazomenai appears to have been predominantly by cremation, and even in tumuli which were intended to imitate the Lydian élite of Anatolia (Ersoy 2007). We still know very little about burial practices in archaic Miletos, but from the handful of graves found so far, there is evidence for a range of different practices, including: inhumation in earth-cut graves, inhumation in stone sarcophagi, the use of stelae as grave markers, and even the use of a rock-cut burial chamber – the Lion Tomb (Müller-Wiener *et al.* 1988; von Graeve 1989; Forbeck and Heres 1997). Although it seems unlikely that we will ever recover as much information about burial practices in Miletos as we would like because the archaic necropolis appears to have been completely covered by the modern village of Yeni-Balat (Greaves 2002, 87–89), it is clear that practices here differed from those in Klazomenai, and other Ionian states. It therefore seems unlikely that a single 'typically Ionian' form of burial could ever be defined (this appears to have been the conclusion also of Olivier Mauriad (speaking in Oxford 15th October 2007)).

Given then that Ionian burial practices appear to be mutable geographically (*i.e.* from one Ionian city to another), locally (*i.e.* contemporary variations within the same state), chronologically (*i.e.* from one period to the next within the same place), and were conducted within a varying political context (*i.e.* the suggestion that tumuli at Klazomenai were a conscious imitation of Lydian burial mounds), how are we to make sense of unique burial practices in Ionian colonies such as those identified at Orgame (Vasilica. Lungu speaking at the Cambridge seminar 28th March 2007). In order for us to say definitively that such practices were entirely local, we must seek to understand them not only in relation to the practices of the indigenous population of the region, but also the varied and as yet not completely understood practices within Ionia itself, and even in relation to neighbouring regions of Ionia, such as Lydia. The picture that is emerging is that colonial burial practices did not follow the same pattern as other cult activity, which can often be related back to the *metropolis*, and appears to have been locally constructed and negotiated within a complex and changeable social and political environment.

5. In many of the historical traditions and academic writings about Greek colonization, the Delphic oracle holds a central position, yet the Ionian colonists appear to have answered to a different oracle: Apollo's oracle at Branchidai-Didyma. No contemporary historical sources exist to prove the direct involvement of Branchidai-Didyma in Ionian colonization, but there are some tantalizing pieces of evidence, such as the Berezan bone tablet (Burkert 1994), and some scholars have concluded that Branchidai-Didyma may have been involved in the colonization process (*e.g.* Malkin 1987).

If we accept that the oracle at Branchidai-Didyma did indeed sanction the founding of colonies at the same time that Delphi may have been similarly active, then this raises the possibility that, in order to fulfil their presumed functions as a 'clearing house' for information (Parke 1967, 45–46), these two oracles may have had developed distinct areas of regional responsibility (Greaves 2007). This may account for Miletos' prolific colonization, as the oracle was located wholly within the *chora* of Miletos and was dependent upon it. In the Berezan tablet it is referred to as Apollo of Didyma the Milesian (Gorman 2001, 193–194) and it is therefore possible that the many colonies attributed to Miletos were in fact those that had been sanctioned by the oracle at Branchidai-Didyma, regardless of the ethnic origins of its population. In one inscription, relating the city of Apollonia-on-the-Rhynadcus show us that in this case the colony chose the *metropolis*, not vice versa (Greaves 2007). Perspectives such as these should demonstrate that in the case of non-Delphic, Ionian colonization, the relationship with the oracle and its role in the colonization process can never be taken for granted. Even basic assumptions about Greek colonization (*e.g.* the primacy of Delphi as a sanctioning oracle, that 'milesian' colonies were peopled by Milesians, that the *metropolis* chose the colony, etc.) may all be usefully re-addressed when viewed from an Ionian perspective.

6. Finally, it is now becoming evident from our better understanding of the archaeological development of the Ionian colonies that many of them underwent significant changes in the character of their settlement at some point during their history. For example, at Berezan, Greek material initially appears in contexts with local pottery, when it is presumably a place for commercial exchange, but this is then followed by a phase in which more intensive Greek settlement takes place and begins to dominate the settlement (Solovyov 2007, 536–537). The same 'gear-change' in Greek engagement with colonial sites can also be identified elsewhere. The shift from primarily commercial involvement to full settlement can be related to events within the *metropolis*, where these can be identified. At Miletos, I have attempted to demonstrate that the control and agricultural exploitation of territory was central to the economy of that city and that trade was secondary to this central agrarian function. When Miletos lost territory to the Lydians and then the Persians, this prompted large sections of the population to migrate to places where the city had already established trading interests – thereby transforming trading posts into settlement colonies. There were therefore two stages to Miletos' activities as a colonizer: a commercial stage, followed by a settlement stage at the same site (Greaves 2002, 99–109; 2007). The same is almost certainly true of Phokaia, which had an initial phase of commercial engagement in the West, followed by mass re-settlement following the coming of the Persians, and may also be true of other Ionian colonizers.

So far, so uncontroversial – but what terms do we, or indeed the ancient Greeks, apply to these phases in the lifecycle of a colony? One of the most intractable issues in the study of Greek colonization has been the application by archaeologists of the Greek terms *emporion* (generally taking to mean a trading place) and *apoikia* (a settlement colony) to the archaeological remains of Greek colonial settlements.

Some scholars have made detailed surveys of how the term *emporion* was used and applied to different settlements in ancient Greek literature (*e.g.* Hind 1995/1996; Hansen 2006), others have surveyed the use of these terms by modern scholarship (*e.g.* Wilson 1997), and yet others have sought to identify their particular excavated sites with one, or indeed both, of these two terms (*e.g.* Ridgeway 1992 on Pithekoussai). However, what archaeologists have never collectively sought to do is to identify two distinct sets of archaeological phenomena within the archaeological record and apply these terms to them. Yet here we have two such phenomena: the commercial phase and the settlement phase of colonial sites across the ancient Greek world. Not only has there been a tendency to conceive of Greek colonization mono-culturally, as noted above, but also to view it achronologically. That is to say, we assume that these terms had a fixed and precise meaning in the Greek language (which may indeed have been true in the fifth century BC and subsequent centuries, but cannot be securely proven for the archaic period when fewer written sources exist) and therefore that any Greek settlement must have been categorizable to a Greek as either an *emporion* or an *apoikia*. If we extend our chronological scope we begin to appreciate that the use of these terms in Greek literature is specific to the writer and his time and cannot be easily generalized. We also begin to realize that in the *longue durée* it is quite conceivable that Greek colonial settlements might have been describable as both an *emporion* and an *apoikia* at different times in the life of that community. We have traditionally conceived of the *emporion/apoikia* distinction as an either/or situation in which an identified colonial site must fit one or other of these terms, but not both at the same, or different, times. (Although it should be noted, in David Ridgeway's assessment of Pithekoussai, that often neither is entirely applicable and elements of both, as commonly defined, can be applicable to sites such as this.) Perhaps the distinction is one that can only be expressed temporally – *i.e.* that there can be an 'emporion' phase and an 'apoikia' phase to the life of many colonies. (In applying the terms 'emporion phase' and 'apoikia phase' I am not implying that this is how the terms *emporion* and *apoikia* were applied by the ancient Greeks themselves, just that the categories of settlements that these terms have traditionally conjured up for archaeologists are useful analogies in this context.)

It could be argued that those sites that might reasonably be described as *emporia* in the post-archaic period (*e.g.* Naucratis and Massalia) did not pupate into self-sustaining *apoikia*, because they were unable to develop the necessary territorial possessions (*i.e.* a *chora*) due to the presence of dominant local populations. It has long been recognized that such inequitable power-relations were in place during the archaic Greek encounter in Egypt, where they came into contact with an older, literate culture, but it requires us to challenge old ideas about the inherent cultural superiority of the Greeks over the 'barbarians' that they encountered in Gaul to accept that this is also true of Masslaia (Dietler, this volume). (The same may also be true of the Phokaian colony at Gravisca (Morel 2006: 372).) Just as some settlements never developed beyond their 'emporion' phase, so too must some colonies have been founded from the outset as 'apoikia' style communities.

Although there will be no easy resolution to the question of how to relate the Greek terms *emporion* and *apoikia* to the archaeological remains of Greek colonies, I would like to suggest that both terms might be applied to the same locality at different times in the life of that community.

Conclusions

In this paper I have argued that we have now reached a state in our knowledge about the Greek colonies at which it is timely to pose new questions about Greek colonies' relationship with their *metropoleis*, in order to develop a more nuanced understanding of them. In particular, the sustained research by academics working in Ionia and the Ionian colonies in the Black Sea and elsewhere have reached a stage where new questions can be posed and new perspectives achieved. I have outlined six topics that I consider worthy of further consideration:

1. That the Greek *metropoleis* were not mono-cultural. In the case of Ionia they differed considerably from one another and had incorporated elements of their neighbouring non-Greek, Anatolian cultures.
2. That power-relations between these *metropoleis* and their Anatolian neighbours, and similarly between their colonists and the indigenous populations that they encountered, should not always be assumed to be unevenly in favour of the Greeks. Modes of interaction with the Anatolian cultures practiced at home (*e.g.* intermarriage) might also be usefully applied in colonial encounters.
3. That the experience of engaging with Anatolian cultures in Ionia may have informed Ionian colonists' dealings with the indigenous populations that they encountered elsewhere. For example, it is conceivable that the use of dugout architecture would have been familiar to the Ionian colonists from their encounters with Phrygian culture in Anatolia.
4. Although the cult practices of the *metropolis* can sometimes be mapped onto those of the colonies, burial practices appear to be a more complicated matter. More research is needed here before the context in which local burial practices of the colonies developed can be properly understood.
5. Ionia had its own oracle at Branchidai-Didyma and this probably played a role in colonization. Prior assumptions about the role of oracles in the colonial process, based on the classical tradition of Delphi, may be challenged, or even inverted, in the light of evidence from Didyma.
6. Finally, it has been argued that the terms 'emporion phase' and 'apoikia phase' may be applied to the commercial and settlement phases of various Ionian colonies.

Ionian colonization therefore gives us multiple entry points from which to question the traditional narratives that have been constructed about Greek colonization and gain new perspectives on. As our knowledge of the colonized areas increases, we are approaching a point at which it is becoming both possible, and necessary, to re-address the nature of the *metropolis*-colony relationship; to shift our attention briefly away from the colonies and return to the *metropolis*.

Acknowledgments

I am enormously indebted to the organizers of the symposium for the invitation to attend, to offer my summary comments and to present them in written from for this volume. This paper is based on notes taken during the conference, and subsequently, and the many productive conversations I shared with colleagues in Cambridge. The ideas expressed here are only preliminary thoughts and have not yet been fully worked through. I trust that colleagues will be patient with the inevitable oversights and shortcomings in such a piece of work-in-progress.

Bibliography

Burkert, W. (1994) Olbia and Apollo of Didyma: A New Oracle Text. In J. Solomon (ed.) *Apollo: Origins and Influences*, 49–60. Tucson, University of Arizona Press.

Cobet, J., von Graeve, V., Niemeier, W-D. and Zimmermann, K. (eds) (2007) *Frühes Ionien eine Bestandsaufnahme.* Mainz am Rhein, Philipp von Zabern.

Ehrhardt, N. (1988) *Milet und Seine Kolonien.* Frankfurt am Main, Peter Lang.

Ersoy, Y. (2007) Notes on the history and archaeology of early Clazomenae. In J. Cobet, V. von Graeve, W.-D. Niemeier and K. Zimmermann (eds) *Frühes Ionien eine Bestandsaufnahme*, 148–78. Mainz am Rhein, Philipp von Zabern.

Fitzjohn, M. (2007) Equality in the colonies: concepts of equality in Sicily during the eight to six centuries BC. *World Archaeology* 39 (2), 215–228.

Forbeck, E. and Heres, H. (1997) *Das Lowengrab Von Milet (Winckelmannsprogramm Der Archaeologischen Gesellschaft Zu Berlin).* Berlin, Walter de Gruyter.

Greaves, A. M. (1998) The foundation of Miletus: Herodotus 1.146 and Dionysius of Halikarnassos 2.30. *Classical Quarterly* 48, 20–22.

Greaves, A. M. (1999) *The History of Miletus to the end of the archaic period.* (Unpublished PhD thesis, School of Classics). University of Leeds.

Greaves, A. M. (2002) *Miletos: A history*. London, Routledge.

Greaves, A. M. (2004) The cult of Aphrodite in Miletos and its colonies. *Anatolian Studies* 54, 27–33.

Greaves, A. M. (2007) Milesians in the Black Sea: Trade, Settlement and Religion. In V. Gabrielsen and J. Lund (eds) *The Black Sea in antiquity: Regional and interregional economic exchanges*, 9–21.

Hall, J. M. (1997) *Ethnic identity in Greek antiquity*. Cambridge, Cambridge University Press.

Hall, J. M. (2002) *Hellenicity: between ethnicity and culture.* Chicago, University of Chicago Press.

Hansen, M. H. (2006) *Emporion*: A study of the use and meaning of the term in the archaic and classical periods. In G. R. Tsetskhladze (ed.) *Greek Colonisation: An account of Greek colonies and other settlements overseas*, 1–39. Leiden, Brill.

Hind, J. G. F. (1995/1996) Traders and ports-of-trade (*emporoi* and *emporia*) in the Black Sea in antiquity. *Il Mar Nero* 2, 113–126.

Kleiner, G. (1968) *Die Ruinen von Milet*. Berlin, Walter de Gruyter.

Lemos, I. (2007) The migrations to the west coast of Asia Minor: Tradition and archaeology. In J. Cobet, V. von Graeve, W.-D. Niemeier and K. Zimmermann (eds) *Frühes Ionien eine Bestandsaufnahme*, 713–727. Mainz am Rhein, Philipp von Zabern.

Malkin, I. (1987) *Religion and colonisation in ancient Greece*. Leiden, Brill.

Morel, J. P. (2006) 'Phocaean Colonisation'. In G. R. Tsetskhladze (ed.) *Greek Colonisation: An account of Greek colonies and other settlements overseas*, 358–428. Leiden, Brill.

Müller-Wiener, W., Göksel, D., von Graeve, V., Biering, R. and Heinz, M. (1988) Milet 1987. Notgrabung in der archaischen Nekropole von Milet. *Istanbuler Mitteilungen* 38, 279–290.

Nilsson, M. P. (1986) *Cults, Myths, Oracles and Politics in Ancient Greece.* Göteborg, Paul Åstroms.

Özyiğit, Ö. (2006) Phokaia. In W. Radt (ed.) *Stadtgrabungen und Stadtforschung in westlichen Kleinasien.* BYZAS 3, 303–314.

Parke, H. W. (1967) *Greek oracles.* London, Hutchinson University Library.

Ridgeway, D. (1992) *The First Western Greeks.* Cambridge, Cambridge University Press.

Senff, R. (2003) Das Aphroditeheiligtum von Milet. *Asia Minor Studien* 49, 11–25.

Solovyov, S. L. (2007) Archaic Berezan: results of recent archaeological investigations and its historical interpretation. In J. Cobet, V. von Graeve, W.-D. Niemeier and K. Zimmermann (eds) *Frühes Ionien eine Bestandsaufnahme*, 531–540. Mainz am Rhein, Philipp von Zabern.

Treister, M. Y. (2007) Archaic Panticapaeum. In J. Cobet, V. von Graeve, W.-D. Niemeier and K. Zimmermann (eds) *Frühes Ionien eine Bestandsaufnahme*, 567–80. Mainz am Rhein, Philipp von Zabern.

Tsetskhladze, G. R. (2004) On the earliest Greek colonial architecture in the Pontus. In C. J. Tuplin (ed.) *Pontus and the outside world. Studies in Black Sea history, historiography, and archaeology*, 225–278. Colloquia Pontica 9. Leiden-Boston, Brill.

Tsetskhladze, G. R. (2006) Revisiting ancient Greek colonisation. In G. R. Tsetskhladze (ed.) *Greek Colonisation: An account of Greek colonies and other settlements overseas*, xxiii–lxxxiii. Leiden, Brill.

Voigt, M. M. and Henrickson, R. C. (2000) Formation of the Phrygian state: the Early Iron Age at Gordion. *Anatolian Studies* 50, 37–54.

Von Graeve, V. (1989) Eine spätarchaische Anthemienstele aus Milet. *Istanbuler Mitteilungen* 36, 143–151.

Wilson, J. P. (1997) The Nature of Greeks Overseas Settlements in the Archaic Period: *Emporion* or *Apoikia?* In L. G. Mitchell and P. J. Rhodes (eds) *The Development of the Polis in archaic Greece*, 199–207. London, Routledge.